30 40 50 Feet

Elevation vers St. James's Park Maison de Monseigneur le Comte de Spencer.

M. Darly sc.

SPENCER HOUSE

Chronicle of a great London mansion

SPENCER HOUSE

Chronicle of a great London mansion

Joseph Friedman

Foreword by Lord Rothschild

Specially commissioned photographs by Mark Fiennes

Zwemmer

To the memory of my father

Endpapers

Spencer House, west front; engraving by M. Darly after James Gandon, from John Woolfe and James Gandon, *Vitruvius Britannicus*, IV (1767), pls 39–40

Spencer House, north front; engraving by M. Darly after James Gandon, from John Woolfe and James Gandon, *Vitruvius Britannicus*, IV, pl. 37

Frontispiece

Spencer House, Library, detail of the chimney-piece. The chimney-piece is a replica of the original, designed by John Vardy, which was removed to Althorp in 1941. The lion's head and drapery of Vardy's original have been reproduced with absolute fidelity.
Carved by the Dick Reid Workshop in York, 1992

First published in 1993 by Zwemmer
an imprint of Philip Wilson Publishers Ltd
26 Litchfield Street
London WC2H 9NJ

ISBN 0 302 00617 6
LC 92-063274

Designed by Gillian Greenwood
Colour origination by Reprocolor International, Milan, Italy
Typeset in Great Britain by Jolly & Barber Ltd, Rugby
Printed and bound by Snoeck, Ducaju & Zoon, Ghent, Belgium

CONTENTS

FOREWORD

ST JAMES'S PLACE had become like home: once a week for some twenty-five years my cousin, Mrs James de Rothschild, would invite my wife and I to have dinner at her house in St James's Place and more often than not my father, who lived on the top floor, would join us. In 1982, shortly after I left N. M. Rothschild and Sons Ltd. to start on my own, Collins, the publishers, decided to give up their premises in St James's Place. We moved our companies into their buildings, and from my offices at Number 14, I could look directly on to Spencer House.

It was not long before my friends at the Economist Intelligence Unit, who were occupying Spencer House at the time, invited me over. The beauty and distinction of the state rooms, even in an uncared-for and run down condition, were overwhelming. I knew that the EIU were thinking of rationalizing their activities and moving elsewhere and I have to admit that I soon began to think about the possibility of acquiring their lease, restoring the house and moving our companies in there. But was it really possible to carry out a fastidious restoration of the house and its great rooms? Could we afford the costs of renovation and at the same time make use of the house in a way which would be commercially justifiable to our shareholders? Gradually a plan emerged: if the Trustees of Spencer House would grant us a long lease and if Westminster Council would agree to give planning permission in perpetuity for office use, then the 'planning gain' could be invested in restoring the state rooms to their former glory.

We convinced ourselves that a reasonable commercial case could be made out. Negotiations progressed, terms were at last agreed, and work began, under the direction of a professional team whose talents embraced every aspect of the detailed restoration of a great house. The architects, Rolfe Judd, designed and managed the project, and brought to it their invaluable experience in the conservation of historic buildings. Our structural engineers, S. B. Tietz and Partners, stretched ingenuity to the limit in the application of modern technology to the consolidation of the historic fabric. Voce Case and Partners had the task of discreetly installing state-of-the-art mechanical and electrical services, to equip the building for the twenty-first century. On site, the demands of the professional team were carried out by the main contractors, Wates Special Works Ltd., and the quantity surveying was the responsibility of the Leonard Stace Partnership.

When it came to the interior design and decoration, we turned to David Mlinaric, for his imaginative skill in interpreting historical evidence and creating interiors with atmosphere, as well as authenticity. I had worked with Mlinaric for many years, and of course he is well-known for his success in this field with projects for the National Trust. The redecoration was entrusted to the specialist building and decorating firm, C. Tavener and Son Ltd. and their sub-contractors, Hare and Humphreys Ltd., who provided the marvellous expertise in colour mixing and gilding.

On reflection, I think there were two fairly unusual factors that contributed greatly to the success of the project. Firstly we spent a great deal of time on initial research – both in producing surveys, and in commissioning Joe Friedman to assess the building and its history. His two-volume report was presented as part of the planning application, and

Spencer House, Great Room, detail of replica chimney-piece (PLATE XXXVI, p. 306–307)

was a foundation stone for the restoration. Secondly, we opened up our own forum for consultation and discourse. A panel of experts – John Cornforth, John Harris, Gervase Jackson-Stops, Peter Thornton and in the chair, Colin Amery – was invited to advise on every aspect of the scheme, down to the minutest detail. We also had the advantage of Dan Cruickshank's encyclopaedic knowledge of Georgian architecture, as our special architectural adviser, and both Westminster City Council and English Heritage were party to the discussions throughout. John Martin Robinson, on behalf of English Heritage, helped the implementation of the scheme with his unique blend of pragmatism and prodigious knowledge.

Literally hundreds of people have contributed during the course of the project. I cannot mention everyone by name here, but it is only right that this book contains an appendix listing many of the companies and individuals who had a substantial role in the restoration. Our list is by no means definitive, but I hope that the house itself now stands as a testament to the collective efforts of all those who gave their skills and dedication to the project. Joe Friedman's chapter on the restoration illuminates the scale of the undertaking, and the fact that the team worked wonderfully well together, united throughout in their efforts by their admiration and affection for the building.

During the restoration, one of the most difficult decisions we had to make was whether to copy the chimney-pieces that had been removed to Althorp during the war, whether to try and find eighteenth-century examples to replace the originals, or to commission new pieces in a modern interpretation. It was not only a question of the chimney-pieces, but also of replacing door furniture, doorcases, the doors themselves, dado rails and skirting mouldings. Nothing is more depressing than a copy of an original, poorly executed and lacking in vitality. Having discussed the subject with Dick Reid and seen the quality of carving that his workshop was producing in York, we decided to copy all the missing architectural ornament. I think everyone would agree that his team of craftsmen, and indeed, all the craftsmen involved at Spencer House, responded to the challenge magnificently and we are sure the right decision was made. Of course, none of this work could have been executed so successfully without the support that we had at Althorp. It was the generosity of the late Lord Spencer and his wife in allowing access to the original fixtures that enabled us to go for the most demanding option, and to achieve the highest standards in modern replication. Encouraged by the results, we extended our aims to include the furnishing of certain rooms with top-quality copies of the Spencer House furniture designed by John Vardy and James Stuart – again with the support of the Spencer family who own many of the original pieces. There is no question that these replicas rival the best that the eighteenth-century craftsmen produced.

Such challenges inevitably involve risks. From the outset, it was my great hope that the technical expertise of English craftsmen – at least of craftsmen working here – would answer the demands of every aspect of the project and that we would not have to go to Italy for the restoration of special finishes, or the carving of the marble. The project to recarve all the chimney-pieces in Carrara marble is the first of its kind in this country for many, many decades – but it is encouraging to know that the lessons learnt, and the expertise developed, will have broader ramifications within the skilled craft industries in England.

Squaring the circle of commercial interests with a fastidious restoration was a difficult task and in turn produced other problems and challenges. How could we ever assemble contents worthy of the architecture of the house? By offering public access to the house, we have enjoyed two great advantages: firstly, the public have been able to appreciate the interior of the house for the first time in its history. Secondly, permitting public access allowed us to approach the Royal Collection, the Victoria and Albert Museum, the Tate Gallery, the National Trust (Waddesdon Manor) and a number of other public institutions for loans, and their response has been overwhelmingly generous. One of the most exciting prospects, as we set out to furnish the rooms, was that of reinstating some of the Spencer furniture in its original setting. Fortunately, our hopes coincided with a shift in opinion, inside many institutions, in favour of displaying works of art in the locations for which they were originally designed. For the first time since the late eighteenth century, John Vardy's magnificent giltwood sidetables, appropriately decorated for the Dining Room with garlands of grape-vines and masks of Bacchus, can be seen in their proper context. One was returned on loan by Temple Newsam House in Leeds, the other by the Victoria and Albert Museum.

More ambitious still was our desire to recreate the full splendour of James Stuart's Painted Room. In 1977, the Victoria and Albert Museum acquired the unique set of sofas and chairs which Stuart designed to complement his ravishing decorative scheme, inspired by the painted interiors of Herculaneum, Pompeii and ancient Rome. Until recently, they were displayed in the Library of Kenwood House. With the cooperation of English Heritage, and the visionary support of the Victoria and Albert Museum, the furniture has returned and the ingenuity and elegance of Stuart's interior can once again be fully appreciated. Peter Thornton and John Hardy, who had the foresight to secure the purchase of the furniture by the Victoria and Albert Museum in 1977, have helped us in many ways, but especially in encouraging us in this quest.

A number of private individuals kindly decided to place works of art from their collections on loan; some while their houses were undergoing building or restoration work, as in the case of Southill Park and Glyndebourne; others perhaps because they found in Spencer House a sympathetic temporary home to which they felt they could safely entrust their possessions. The Fine Art trade, too, has assisted us again and again with magnificent loans. All those who have helped are named at the end of the book, and both the range and the quality of the works of art to which the public now has access have been greatly enhanced by their generosity. Our own limited budget allowed us from time to time to acquire works of art of particular relevance to the house. In this, we have relied heavily on the expert judgment of Christopher Gibbs and John Harris, and the result is, I believe, a collection which answers magnificently the splendour of the architecture.

If our companies were able to occupy the private family apartments and the old servants' quarter as offices, what of the furnished State Rooms and their new function? In the eighteenth century, the house, as Joe Friedman describes in his excellent study of its history, was a centre for politics, the arts and entertainment. We decided to try to develop this side of the house's life again. Could we justify in commercial terms recruiting a staff so as to offer distinguished facilities to companies and individuals, and create a place where they could meet, dine or listen to music, rather as they had done in the eighteenth century? This aspect of the house has developed in a way in which surely the 1st Lord Spencer would have been delighted. The first major dinner was held by the Society of Dilettanti, whose influence on the creation of the house, and its social life, was so profound. Appropriately, Her Royal Highness The Princess of Wales was present as a freeholder and direct descendant of the 1st Lord Spencer, who was a key member of the Society.

Since then, this aspect of the life of the house has gone from strength to strength. The NATO summit lunch at Spencer House in July 1990 was attended by Prime Ministers and Presidents from around the world. President Bush and President Mitterand were again at Spencer House for the G7 summit lunch with John Major the following summer. International companies like Mobil, Boeing and Fuji Bank have chosen to celebrate important occasions in the house, and the New York Stock Exchange held a dinner to mark their bi-centenary last year. On Guy Fawkes night, 1992, Sainsbury's gave a farewell party for their distinguished retiring Chairman, Lord Sainsbury. Arts organizations, too, have found the house an appropriate focus for activities: the London City Ballet has entertained there, and the Royal Fine Art Commission hosted the presentation of the Building of the Year Award in 1990. More recently, Classic FM launched the new radio station with a concert and dinner.

Great balls have taken place, including one for ex-King Constantine of Greece, which began at Bridgewater House next door and moved to Spencer House later in the evening. Another splendid dance was given by Mr John Paul Getty Jnr. Most recently, all the living British Prime Ministers paid tribute to Her Majesty The Queen at a dinner held in her honour, to celebrate the fortieth anniversary of her accession, and Spencer House was considered the setting which was most appropriate for this historic event.

I am especially grateful to the Spencer family Trustees for their participation and support in the negotiations over the restoration and use of the house, and within our own companies, among the many people involved I would like to thank Moira Mullen, who co-ordinated the major phase of the restoration project. In addition, the help of Clive Gibson, Paddy Drummond, Henry Wrong, Celia de la Hey, Stephen Jones, Philippa Hart, John Johnston, Howard Meadows and Diane Faulkner has been invaluable. Over the last six years, the demanding task of restoring the building has involved the skill of a veritable army of individuals, and this book is dedicated to them. I would also like to dedicate it to the Princess of Wales, the present Earl Spencer, and their sisters Lady Sarah McCorquodale and Lady Jane Fellowes – all of whom have helped and encouraged us throughout in our efforts to restore to its full glory the house constructed in 1756 by their forebear, the 1st Lord Spencer, whose remarkable patronage, starting at the age of twenty-one, surely resulted in a mansion as beautiful and original as any that remains standing in London today.

Jacob Rothschild

February 1993

ACKNOWLEDGEMENTS

I AM GRATEFUL to Her Majesty The Queen for permission to quote from the royal archives.

I also wish to express my thanks to the J. Rothschild group of companies, who commissioned the present book, especially the chairman, Lord Rothschild, Clive Gibson, Paddy Drummond, Henry Wrong, Moira Mullen, Stephen Jones and Philippa Hart. I owe a particular debt of thanks to Celia de la Hey whose constant support and guidance have been invaluable, and I am likewise indebted to David Mlinaric, through whom I first became involved with Spencer House. I also wish to thank Lord Spencer, who offered valuable assistance in the final stages of my research.

In the preparation of this book I have consulted numerous scholars and experts in various fields whose assistance it is a pleasure to acknowledge: Colin Amery, Georgina Battiscombe, Geoffrey Beard, David Beasley, Hugh Belsey, Vincent Bouvet, Kerry Bristol, Ann Brown, Timothy Clifford, Frances Collard, Howard Colvin, Dan Cruickshank, Oliver Davies, Peter Day, Dudley Dodd, Jane Dormer, Jacqueline Dugas, Mireille Gallinou, Christopher Gibbs, Philippa Glanville, Peter Gordon, John Hardy, John Harris, Tom Helme, Captain David Horn, Sir Malcolm Innes, Peter Jackson, Gervase Jackson-Stops, Ian Jones, Mark Jones, John Kenworthy-Browne, Tim Knox, Susan Lambert, Alastair Laing, Todd Longstaffe-Gowan, Michael McCarthy, Vera Magyar, Jennifer Montagu, Arnold Nesselrath, Andrew Norris, Sylvia Ferino Pagden, David Pearce, Margaret Richardson, Jane Roberts, Hugh Roberts, Martin Robertson, John Martin Robinson, K. Robson, Ingrid Roscoe, Judy Rudoe, Francis Russell, Lord St John of Fawsley, Frank Salmon, Diana Scarisbrick, David Scrace, Brian Sewell, Kim Sloan, Letitia Stevens, James Stourton, Dorothy Stroud, Peter Thornton, Nicholas Turner, David Watkin, Roger White, Humphrey Whitfield, John Wilton-Ely, Giles Worsley, James Yorke. I am especially grateful to Lady Margaret Douglas-Home for sharing with me the results of her researches into the life of Georgiana, Countess Spencer. I am likewise grateful to Sir Brinsley Ford for permission to consult his papers on the Grand Tour at the Paul Mellon Centre for Studies in British Art.

I should also like to express my thanks for the cooperation I have received from the staff of the following archives, libraries, museums and organizations: Agnew's, Albany, Althorp House, the *Architects' Journal*, the Army Museum, the Army and Navy Club, the Ashmolean Museum (Department of Antiquities), the Berkshire County Record Office, Berry Brothers & Rudd, the Fondazione Marco Besso, the Bibliothèque d'Art et d'Archéologie (Fondation Jacques Doucet), the Biblioteca Hertziana, Blenheim Palace, the Bodleian Library, the Boston Museum of Fine Arts, the Boston Public Library, the Bowes Museum, Bowood House, the Bridgeman Library, the British Library (departments of Manuscripts, Printed Books, and Maps), the British Museum (departments of Prints and Drawings, Greek and Roman Antiquities, Medieval and Later Antiquities, Coins and Medals), Brooks's Club, the Business Archives Council, the local studies division of Cambridge Central Library, the Cambridgeshire County Record Office, the Capitoline Museum, the *Census of Antique Art and Architecture known to the Renaissance*, Chatsworth House, Christie's,

Clerical Medical and General, the College of Arms, the Conway Library, the Cooper-Hewitt Museum, *Country Life*, the Courtauld Institute, Coutts Bank, the Doria Pamphili Gallery, Dove Brothers, Drivers Jonas, the *Economist* magazine, English Heritage, the Fitzwilliam Museum, the library of the Foreign and Commonwealth Office, Fortnum & Mason, Frere Cholmeley, the Gabinetto Fotografico Nazionale (Rome), the J. Paul Getty Museum, the library of Goldsmiths Hall, the Greater London Record Office, the Guards Museum, the Guildhall Library, Hagley Hall, the Hertfordshire County Record Office, Hoare's Bank, the library of the House of Lords, the Hulton Picture Company, the Hunterian Museum and Art Gallery, the Henry E. Huntington Museum and Art Gallery, the Imperial War Museum, the library of the Inner Temple, the Kent County Record Office, the Kunsthistorisches Museum (Vienna), Lock's, the London Library, Longleat House, the library of the Middle Temple, the archives department of the Minet Library, the Museum of London, the National Arts Library, the National Gallery (London), the National Gallery of Scotland, the National Gallery of Art (Washington), the National Monuments Record, the National Portrait Gallery, the National Portrait Gallery of Scotland, the National Trust, the New York Public Library, the Norfolk County Record Office, the Northampton Library, the Northamptonshire County Record Office, the Nottinghamshire County Record Office, the archives of the Passionist Order, the Paul Mellon Centre for Studies in British Art, the Public Record Office, the Queen's House (Greenwich), the RIBA Drawings Collection, the library of the Royal Agricultural Society, the Royal Bank of Scotland, the Royal College of Music, the Royal Commission on Historical Manuscripts, the Royal Library and Archives (Windsor Castle), the library of the Royal Society of Arts, the John Rylands University Library of Manchester, S. J. Phillips, the Sir John Soane Museum, the library of the Society of Antiquaries, the Society of Dilettanti, Sotheby's, the library of the University of Southampton, Syborn Atkinson & Colborn Architects, the Tate Gallery, the Tower of London, the Vatican Museum, the Victoria and Albert Museum (departments of Furniture and Woodwork, Silver, Prints and Drawings), the Warburg Institute, the local studies division of the Westminster Public Library, White's Club, the Witt Library.

In particular I wish to thank Anna Maria Amadio, the Duke of Bedford, the Earl of Bessborough, Robin Bishop, Jacqueline Bower, Terence Charman, Pamela Clark, Viscount Cobham, Guido Cornini, D. Duffie, Margaret Evans, Roger Harvey, Eeyan Hartley, Adrian Henstock, Henry Hoare, Mr Hodkinson, Father Hubert, Ralph Hyde, Jean Kennedy, Victoria Hutchins, Ian Murray, Jonathan Newman, Barbara Peters, Viscount Petersham, Nigel Ratten, Jane Ridley, David Riley, Michael Roberts, Ralph Smith, Kathryn Thompson, Fiona Vallis, Samuel Whitbread, Lesley Whitelaw, the Marquess of Zetland.

I am likewise grateful for the assistance I have received from the team that worked on the recent restoration of Spencer House, particularly Ben Bacon, Kevin Casey, Roger Furness, Ernie Gowing, Don Hands, James Hardwick, Peter Hare, Bob Hayes, Paul Humphreys, Clare Kooy-Lister, Mike Love, Alan Mansell, Anthony Miloserdovs, Dick Reid, George Sumners, Paul Velluet, Stephen Westbrook, Clare Wilkins, Dennis Whittome.

I should like to express my thanks to my editors at Philip Wilson Publishers Limited, Joan Speers and Daniel Giles, and to Mark Fiennes for the excellent photographs he has produced. I also wish to thank Dolores Karney and Emma Bayntun-Coward, who assisted in the typing of the manuscript, and not least my friends, without whose support I could not have stayed the course.

Joseph Friedman

1 Northumberland House, Trafalgar Square, shortly before its demolition; illustration from The Graphic *(7 February 1874). Built in the early years of the seventeenth century, with Neo-Classical interiors by Robert Adam, Northumberland House was perhaps the greatest of all London mansions*

2 Northumberland House, demolition underway; engraving from The Illustrated London News *(30 January 1875). The house was replaced by a street running down to the Embankment*

INTRODUCTION

If we sought for one particular feature distinguishing London from the other capitals of Europe, apart from its immense proportions, it would probably be found in the number of its large houses.

Edwin Beresford Chancellor. 1908[1]

[1] Edwin Beresford Chancellor, *The Private Palaces of London, Past and Present* (1908), p.ix

In less than a century the heart of London has been radically transformed. The city described by Chancellor in 1908, characterized by magnificent mansions lining its principal streets, is today unrecognizable. Rome retains it *palazzi*, Paris its *hôtels particuliers*; but, with few exceptions, London's great houses have vanished. Spencer House, as one of only a tiny number of surviving examples, is vitally important, evoking a townscape which was once the envy of the world.

Some of the London mansions were destroyed by fire, others by enemy bombs, but most were simply torn down. The interwar years were particularly destructive, although the process continued right up until the 1960s. It is heart-breaking to look over photographs of the houses which have been lost: Northumberland House, destroyed to make way for a street running down to the Embankment (FIGS 1 and 2); Devonshire House and Chester-

1

2

3 Demolition of Devonshire House, 1925; etching by Job Dixon, from Edwin Beresford Chancellor, Disappearing London *(1927). Dixon's animated etching makes this dire event seem almost jolly*

4 Devonshire House, Piccadilly, the Saloon, c1900. Built to the designs of William Kent, Devonshire House was an outstanding example of the Palladian style and one of the grandest London mansions to survive from the eighteenth century

3
4

5 Chesterfield House, demolition in progress, 1937. On the site developers erected an apartment building of breathtaking banality

6 Chesterfield House, Mayfair, the Drawing Room, c1900. In the state apartments of this magnificent mid-eighteenth-century mansion, Rococo decoration reached its zenith

5

6

7 Dorchester House, wreckers set to work in the forecourt, 1929. The building was replaced by the famous Dorchester Hotel

field House, torn down and replaced by apartment blocks (FIGS 3–6); Dorchester House, razed and rebuilt as the Dorchester Hotel (FIGS 7 and 8).

The royal palaces survive, but of the mansions of the nobility and gentry, only the most meagre fragments remain: the water gate of York House, marooned in a municipal park on the Embankment; the Great Hall of Crosby Palace, dismantled and rebuilt on the river at Chelsea; the Music Room from Norfolk House, partly reassembled at the Victoria and Albert Museum. In some cases fragments have even gone abroad. The drawing room from Lansdowne House is now an exhibit in the Philadelphia Museum of Art, the dining room has been reassembled at the Metropolitan Museum in New York and the lodges of Devonshire House today flank the entrance to an estate on Long Island. Even where houses have not been demolished they have generally been gutted or otherwise mutilated.

Most of the great London mansions were built by the landed aristocracy during the seventeenth and eighteenth centuries. With the transition from an agrarian to an industrial economy in the nineteenth century, land lost its value and the aristocracy saw its income and influence dwindle. The importation of cheap grain in the 1870s led to a severe agricultural depression, forcing down the value of land still further, while death duties, first introduced in the 1880s, hastened the process of decline. The First World War was another devastating blow, compounded by the Second.

The continuing rise in the cost of living meant that by the late 1920s the expense of maintaining a grand London mansion was more than many owners could bear. Even among the new class of rich industrialists, there were few who could afford to live on this scale; nor did they have any great desire to do so. In an earlier age wealthy members of the middle-classes had sought to emulate the aristocracy. But the new generation had greater self-confidence and was forging its own, very different, way of life. Members of the aristocracy, in any case, were fast scaling down their own standard of living, moving to smaller houses and even flats.

In Paris, Rome and other European cities, comparable houses found new roles as embassies, ministries and apartment buildings. But London, at the turn of the century, was in a unique position as the hub of a vast territorial and commercial empire, a centre of business and tourism, with a fast-expanding population. This created specific demands. The capital needed modern purpose-built offices, hotels, mansion blocks and an efficient network of roads. Its great houses, located in the very heart of the city and sometimes occupying large tracts of land, were a natural target for developers and town-planners. A handful escaped. Home House became the head-quarters of the Courtauld Institute. Lancaster House was adapted as a setting for government receptions and conferences, and Apsley House was converted to house the Wellington Museum. But the vast majority perished. During the 1920s and 30s alone more than half a dozen of the capital's

8 Dorchester House, Park Lane, the Great Staircase. Inspired by the palaces of Renaissance Italy, Dorchester House achieved a synthesis of architecture and art matched by few other buildings of the Victorian age

finest mansions were bulldozed. Nothing could be done to halt the destruction. Legislation governing the protection of historic buildings was still in its infancy; indeed it was partly as a result of the demolition of the great London houses that legislation of this kind was eventually enacted, alas too late.

Even the memory of London's houses has faded. Few Londoners of the generation which has grown up since the Second World War are aware that the modern buildings on Piccadilly and Pall Mall occupy the sites of seventeenth- and eighteenth-century mansions. In recent years we have seen a surge of interest in the country house, fuelled by exhibitions, television documentaries, campaigning by amenity groups and a seemingly endless series of books and articles. Public awareness has never been greater and many fine buildings have been saved from destruction and dilapidation; but in all of this the London house has largely been overlooked, and the result is a widespread misconception affecting our understanding of the country house itself.

It is important to stress that in architectural terms the London house was no less significant than the country house. The construction of these buildings involved the greatest English architects, assisted by the country's leading artists and craftsmen, and they were quite as important in setting the pace of architectural change, possibly more so, since they received a far greater degree of exposure owing to their conspicuous metropolitan location. The great London houses generally contained the finest art treasures in their owners' collections. People often marvel at the contents of English country houses and make unflattering comparisons with those of their European equivalents, but it is important to remember that in many cases these very contents came originally from the family's London mansion.

Another misconception, again reinforced by the emphasis on the country house, is that the aristocracy and gentry are, and have always been, essentially rural in their orientation. Without denying their obvious historical and emotional ties to the land, it is essential to remember that during the eighteenth century, when their power was at its height, the aristocracy and gentry were very much a metropolitan class, decidedly urban in their habits and outlook. They generally spent as much time in the capital as in the country, and in this respect were closer than is generally supposed to their counterparts in France, whose lives were largely spent in Paris and at Court.

Against this background, the survival of Spencer House is nothing short of miraculous. Credit must go to the 7th Earl Spencer (1892–1975), who held on to the building during the critical period between the wars, although for financial reasons he and his family were forced to move elsewhere. That the house is now in such outstanding condition is due to its current occupants, the J. Rothschild group of companies, who, with the cooperation of the 7th Earl's descendants, have masterminded one of the most ambitious and successful restoration projects of recent years.

Spencer House was built in the middle years of the eighteenth century by John, 1st Earl Spencer (PLATE I, p. 49), an ancestor of the present Princess of Wales. It was immediately recognized as one of the most splendid buildings in the capital. Arthur Young, who visited the house when first unveiled, was in raptures. 'I do not apprehend', he wrote, 'there is a house in Europe of its size, better worth the view of the curious in architecture, and the fitting up and furnishing great houses, than Lord Spencer's in St James's Place'.[2]

In historical terms the importance of Spencer House is hard to exaggerate. Rarely can one say of any building that its construction marked a watershed in the development of taste. But at Spencer House one clearly sees this process at work; indeed the building marks not one revolution in taste but two. At the time the house was built English

[2] Arthur Young, *A Six Weeks Tour through the Southern Counties of England and Wales*, 2nd edn (1769), p.354

architecture was dominated by the Palladian style, which as its name suggests drew inspiration from the work of the sixteenth-century Venetian architect Andrea Palladio. The style had been established in England in the previous century by Inigo Jones and his pupil John Webb. After a lapse, in which the Baroque style took hold, the tradition was revived again in the early part of the eighteenth century, finding its most famous exponent in William Kent. At the same time other styles came into fashion, including variants of the Gothic, the Chinese and Continental Rococo. However, around the middle of the eighteenth century, in the wave of excitement that followed the discovery of Pompeii and Herculaneum, a new style developed, now known as Neo-Classicism, which aimed to revive the art and architecture of Classical Antiquity. The style was initially influenced by Rome, but in time the focus shifted to Greece.

The construction of Spencer House was a perfect microcosm of these developments. It was begun by a Palladian architect, John Vardy, a disciple of William Kent, but completed by James 'Athenian' Stuart (FIG 98, p. 125), an early exponent of Neo-Classicism and a pioneer of the Greek Revival. Vardy was responsible for the exterior of the building and the decoration of the ground-floor apartments, whose hybrid design reflects the transition from late Palladian to early, Roman-inspired Neo-Classical design. The first-floor interiors by Stuart were among the earliest fully-developed Neo-Classical interiors in Europe, combining decoration and furniture directly inspired by the Antique, and some of the first to feature elements specifically derived from the architectural remains of Greece, marking an important early step in the development of the Greek Revival. It is sometimes said that Spencer House was the first Neo-Classical town house to be built in London; certainly it did as much as any other to establish the Neo-Classical style, but the house's true importance lies in its stylistic complexity.

The house has much to teach us about the all-embracing role of the architect in the eighteenth century. Vardy and Stuart took responsibility for every detail, from fixtures to furniture, producing fully-integrated designs governed by a single unifying aesthetic. Their work has a resonant, musical quality, with diverse elements harmonized and orchestrated almost in the manner of notes and chords. Even works of art, such as paintings and statues, were selected and deployed to complement and enhance the proportions and the decoration. Many were purchased expressly for the house and even for specific interiors. Indeed we know that certain pictures were acquired for a particular position, dealers having been issued with precise measurements. In the Great Room the pictures were hung in specially-designed frames, carved to match the door and window architraves. In Lady Spencer's Dressing Room they were arranged on the wall according to a pre-established pattern which was integral to the overall design of the interior. In some cases one suspects that works of art may even have been the starting-point for particular schemes of decoration.

The intricacy and quality of the decoration are a reminder of the importance of craftsmanship in eighteenth-century architecture and the virtuosity of contemporary craftsmen. Many of the architectural fixtures at Spencer House can be admired as works of art in their own right; the original chimney-pieces were carved by some of the greatest sculptors of the period.

The house is likewise a reminder of the importance of symbolism, metaphor and allegory in eighteenth-century architecture, the use of essentially literary techniques of artistic expression. Vardy and Stuart invested their designs with coded meanings, often related to the function of the house and individual rooms or to past events from the Spencers' lives. The symbolism is sometimes elaborate, functioning on a number of different levels; often it is infused with humour. This combination of learning and wit provides an insight into the personalities of those who created the house, but it also speaks for the eighteenth century as a whole, evoking the intellectual atmosphere of a period equally drawn to study as to play.

At the same time Spencer House provides an insight into the procedures followed by eighteenth-century architects in developing their designs. Vardy and Stuart were temperamental opposites; their backgrounds were unalike and in stylistic terms their work was quite distinct. But the system they followed was essentially the same: both borrowed heavily from the past, sometimes producing exact or near-exact copies of elements derived from earlier buildings, which they found reproduced in illustrated books or which they themselves had sketched. Unique and original as it is, Spencer House is to a large extent a composite.

This highlights at once the reverential, almost devotional nature of eighteenth-century architecture. Through the medium of their borrowings, architects and patrons paid homage to their predecessors, aligning themselves with particular schools and individuals. Inevitably this gave architecture a strong polemical potential. Set against the background of the revolution in art and aesthetics in the mid-eighteenth century, Spencer House can be seen as a manifesto, in which the patron, John Spencer, expressed his growing commitment to the Neo-Classical aesthetic and his gradual disenchantment with the Palladian, the Rococo and other styles of the period.

One also sees that originality, in the modern sense at least, was scarcely recognized as a value; indeed it was regarded with some mistrust. Invention lay not so much in devising new forms as in finding new ways of manipulating existing ones. Architects and patrons saw nothing disreputable in this; on the contrary it was accepted that this was the process by which architecture naturally evolved. Nor was there any attempt at secrecy. Vardy and Stuart worked from recognized sources and clearly intended their references to be understood. It was precisely through the choice and adaptation of sources that an architect demonstrated his erudition and ingenuity. Precedent lent legitimacy and validity to a design, anchoring it within a received tradition, and one may be sure that the architects of Spencer House drew their client's attention to any borrowings they made. After all it must have been immensely flattering to John Spencer to know that his house was linked, through its architectural detailing, to some of the greatest buildings and monuments in the Western tradition. In some cases it was probably Spencer himself who called for a particular feature to be included. Surviving records reveal that several of the illustrated books from which the decoration of Spencer House was derived were in his library at Althorp.

An analysis of the sources at Spencer House provides valuable clues as to the scope of architectural knowledge in the eighteenth century. Spencer and his architects were evidently steeped in the architecture of the past, for the breadth of reference is extraordinary. There are borrowings from ancient Greece and Rome, ranging from the fifth century B.C. to the age of Augustus. There are borrowings also from the Renaissance, the Baroque and the early eighteenth century. There are echoes of Raphael, Giovanni da Udine and Giulio Romano; of Palladio and Borromini; of Inigo Jones, John Webb, Colen Campbell and William Kent. Nor are the borrowings solely confined to architectural sources. Vardy and Stuart also made use of elements derived from painting, sculpture and other branches of the fine and decorative arts; from statues and bas-reliefs; candelabra and altar stands; frescoes and easel paintings; coins, medals, gems and vases.

It was from illustrated books that most of these elements were quarried. Working backwards, it is sometimes possible to identify the publications from which Vardy and Stuart drew inspiration, which in turn reveals the remarkable extent of their personal libraries, comprising foreign and English books of every period. Not that Vardy and Stuart worked from books alone; as we shall see, they also made use of manuscript drawings, either in their own or in others' private collections.

A study of the sources at Spencer House sheds light on eighteenth-century attitudes to the art and architecture of the past. While guiding us to an understanding of contemporary taste, it also discloses how the Western artistic tradition was organized into canons and traditions in a way that was quite specific to the period. From a twentieth-century perspective the combination of diverse elements is sometimes quite bewildering.

It is illuminating also to observe the way that Vardy and Stuart made use of their sources. In some cases they produced faithful copies of the elements they borrowed; one of the most remarkable and novel features of Spencer House was the accuracy with which Antique details were reproduced, reflecting a new concern with archaeological authenticity characteristic of the burgeoning Neo-Classical movement. On the other hand they frequently took great liberties in altering and adapting elements to suit their own specific needs. The fact that they drew on such a wide typological range of sources shows that architecture was open to influences from all branches of the arts, enriched rather than diminished by cross-fertilization. Altogether Spencer House provides a striking illustration of the freedom and diversity of a period in architecture which is sometimes seen as hidebound by narrow conventions and purist notions of artistic propriety. It need hardly be added that the attitudes the house embodies differ considerably from those which obtain in architecture today, and that the breadth of reference bespeaks a knowledge of art and architecture at which we can only marvel.

But the influence of Spencer House extended far beyond architecture. During the all-important months of the Season, when the whole of fashionable society gathered in the capital, the mansions of the nobility and gentry provided the setting for many of the most important receptions in the social calendar. They were likewise at the centre of politics; for in the eighteenth century, and even in the nineteenth, social entertainment was as much a part of the political process as parliamentary debate. Under the guise of balls and assemblies introductions were made and alliances cemented that might lead to the formation or dissolution of governments. London's mansions were similarly a focus of cultural activity; a setting for concerts and recitals; a gathering-place for artists and writers; a forum for intellectual debate; a showcase for paintings, sculpture and other works of art; a testing-ground for new ideas in architecture and interior design; a parading ground for the latest fashions in dress and jewellery. Buildings of this kind also had enormous economic importance. The larger houses could be staffed by as many as forty or fifty servants; supplying their needs guaranteed employment for thousands more in supporting trades.

Spencer House naturally played a particularly important role. The 1st Earl Spencer was the head of one of England's most illustrious aristocratic families. He and his descendants were linked by ties of family and friendship to the royal and noble houses of England and much of Continental Europe. They were senior figures in politics both at Court and at Westminster. They were likewise great collectors and patrons of the arts. Among their protégés and friends they counted novelists, poets and playwrights; architects, painters and sculptors; actors, composers and musicians; scientists and scholars. Spencer House was clearly of enormous importance to the family. Quite apart from the huge sums they spent on building and maintaining the house, they generally spent the greater part of the year there and it evidently provided them with their principal base of operations.

Much of the present book is taken up with an analysis of the design and construction of Spencer House. There are chapters on the careers of its principal architects, and I have also tried to elucidate the role of Colonel George Gray (FIG 27, p. 71), an architectural adviser engaged by John Spencer to oversee the design of Spencer House. Wherever possible I have provided the names of craftsmen who worked at Spencer House, together with biographical profiles. Subsequent alterations have also been recorded, for although of relatively minor significance in themselves, they involved several leading architects, among them Sir Robert Taylor, Henry Holland (FIG 205, p. 219) and Philip Hardwick. At the same time I have endeavoured to decode the iconography of the house in order to reveal its hidden significance. Above all I have attempted to trace the sources of the building's design, an approach which I believe must be developed. The longer I worked on Spencer House the more convinced I became that virtually every feature was derived from some earlier building or artefact and that its meaning was largely to be found in the choice, adaptation and combination of these elements.

The life of any house is to a large extent the life of its occupants, and this is partly a history of the Spencers themselves, the private as well as the public side of a fascinating family saga. Although primarily built for parade and entertainment, Spencer House was a family home and served an important domestic function. I have focused on the life of John, 1st Earl Spencer, of whom there is as yet no published study nor even an entry in the *Dictionary of National Biography.* He played an important part in the cultural life of his period, not only through the construction of Spencer House but through his activities as a patron and collector in a wide variety of areas, including music, sculpture, painting, drama, literature, jewellery and gold and silver plate. All too often architecture is studied in isolation, but for John Spencer and others of his class the construction of houses was part of a much broader pattern of artistic patronage. I have also focused on the 1st Earl's wife, Georgiana Poyntz (PLATE II, p. 50), another neglected figure deserving of greater study.[3] In addition there are profiles of John and Georgiana's children, including the notorious Georgiana, Duchess of Devonshire, and her equally troublesome sister, Lady Bessborough, together with other prominent descendants up to and including the present generation. I have also tried to shed light on the functioning of the house and more particularly the size and composition of the domestic staff. Records are few and fragmentary, but wherever possible I offer names and biographical details for the large team of servants who kept the house running: housekeepers and housemaids; nurses, governesses and private tutors; butlers and valets; porters and footmen; cooks and scullions; coachmen and postillions. Also included is an account of the neglected and sometimes improbable characters and organizations to whom the house at various times has been let.

The book begins with the prior history of the site. The construction of Spencer House was not an isolated event but part of the development of St James's, which itself marked the beginning of the development of the whole of London's West End. In particular I have examined the life of the previous owner of the site, Lord Montfort (FIG 9, p. 26), and the circumstances of his strange and bloody suicide. But one of the principal aims of this book is to commemorate and celebrate the recent restoration of the house, widely hailed as one of the most important and successful projects of its kind ever undertaken. Through the efforts of the J. Rothschild group of companies and the team working under its direction, something has been achieved which in aesthetic terms, and in terms of its impact on contemporary thinking in architecture, at least in the sphere of conservation, is almost as important as the house's original construction. In the final chapter I set out to explore the ideas that lay behind the restoration and the sometimes novel techniques and procedures which guaranteed its success. If Spencer House has much to teach us about the past, it also sets an important agenda for the future.

[3] Georgiana, Countess Spencer is the subject of an unpublished biography by Lady Margaret Douglas-Home, *A Mere Miss Poyntz*, from which I have borrowed the title of my own account, together with much useful information. I wish to thank Lady Margaret for her kindness in allowing me unrestricted access to the manuscript

ABBREVIATIONS

The following abbreviations are used in all notes
For dates of publications, see Bibliography

AP	Althorp Papers, British Library, Manuscripts Department
BL	British Library
BMPD	British Museum, Department of Prints and Drawings
CH	Caroline Howe
DB	Drummonds Bank archives
GH	Gavin Hamilton
GJS	George John, 2nd Earl Spencer
GLRO	Greater London Record Office
GBV	George Bussy Villiers, 4th Earl of Jersey
GS	Georgiana, Countess Spencer
GSH	George Simon Harcourt, Viscount Nuneham, 2nd Earl Harcourt
HB	Hoare's Bank archives
HRO	Hertfordshire Record Office
JS	John, 1st Earl Spencer
PRO	Public Record Office
RIBA	Royal Institute of British Architects, Drawings Collection
SBFP	The Grand Tour Papers of Sir Brinsley Ford (Paul Mellon Centre for Studies in British Art)
SJSM	Sir John Soane Museum
TC	Thea Cowper
V&A	Victoria and Albert Museum
WC	William, 3rd Earl Cowper
WH	Sir William Hamilton
WPL	Westminster Public Library

PART I

PROLOGUE

1 AN END AND A BEGINNING

On NEW YEAR'S DAY 1755 Henry Bromley, 1st Baron Montfort, forty-nine years old and a former M.P. and Lord Lieutenant of Cambridgeshire, summoned his lawyer and two witnesses to his house in London, where he proceeded to draw up a will. Before putting his signature to the document, Montfort asked his lawyer whether the will would hold good if he, the testator, committed suicide. When the lawyer replied that it would, Montfort asked to be excused for a moment and passed into an adjoining room where he picked up a pistol, put it to his head, and fired. By the time the lawyer reached him, Montfort was already dead. It is at this point, with Montfort's bloody end, that the history of Spencer House really begins; for as we shall see, if Montfort had not committed suicide it is doubtful Spencer House would ever have been built, not in its present form at least, and not on the present site, nor even by the same architect.

Montfort's suicide caused widespread surprise; he had always been a pleasure-seeker, a jovial and popular member of White's Club where he was known as a good bottle and card man. Indeed he had dined at the club the previous evening, seeing in the new year with his usual circle of friends. Montfort was particularly famed for his appetite and in a lifetime spent at the dinner table had grown to an enormous size. Even the French were impressed. The King himself, Louis XV, stepped back in amazement when introduced to Montfort at Versailles, declaring aloud, '*En vérité ce milord anglais ne laisse pas d'être assez bien nourri*' (FIG 9).[1]

9 Caricature sketch of Henry Bromley, 1st Baron Montfort, c1750. When introduced to Montfort at Versailles, Louis XV stepped back in astonishment, declaring aloud, 'En vérité ce milord anglais ne laisse pas d'être assez bien nourri'

Montfort's ancestry was relatively obscure; it was rumoured that his grandfather, John Bromley, had been a simple pedlar. But heralds had concocted a pedigree four and a half yards long showing descent from Chancellor Bromley, and far from being a pedlar, Montfort's grandfather had been a gentleman of property, a member of the Supreme Council of Barbados and High Sheriff of Cambridgeshire. Montfort inherited an ample fortune, including large estates and a splendid manor house, Horseheath Hall, originally built by Sir Roger Pratt. There were extensive plantations in Barbados, manned by countless slaves, and Montfort was further enriched by his marriage to a wealthy heiress, Frances Wyndham, daughter of a Somerset landowner. In addition to money and property Frances bore her husband two healthy children, a son, Thomas, who succeeded, and a daughter, Frances, who later married the eldest son of the Earl of Cadogan.

Montfort was a respected politician, a staunch supporter of the Whig party, and a shrewd negotiator with a distinguished record of public service and a solid grounding in matters relating to the constitution. The Prime Minister, Sir Robert Walpole, credited Montfort with 'the most compendious understanding I ever knew',[2] and a childhood friend paid tribute to his personal qualities when he wrote that Montfort had 'the character of a man of as much strict Humour & Integrity as is to be met with amongst the greatest examples of it'.[3] Educated at Eton and Clare College, Cambridge, Montfort was elected to Parliament in 1727 as Whig M.P. for Cambridgeshire and in 1730 became Lord Lieutenant of the county. In 1741, at the age of thirty-six, he was raised to the peerage as 1st Baron Montfort of Horseheath.

DETAIL, PAGE 24
A view of St James's and the area to the east, from J. Kip, Veue et Perspective de la Ville de Londre, Westminster, Parc St Jacques *[sic] (c1710) (FIG 23, p. 47)*

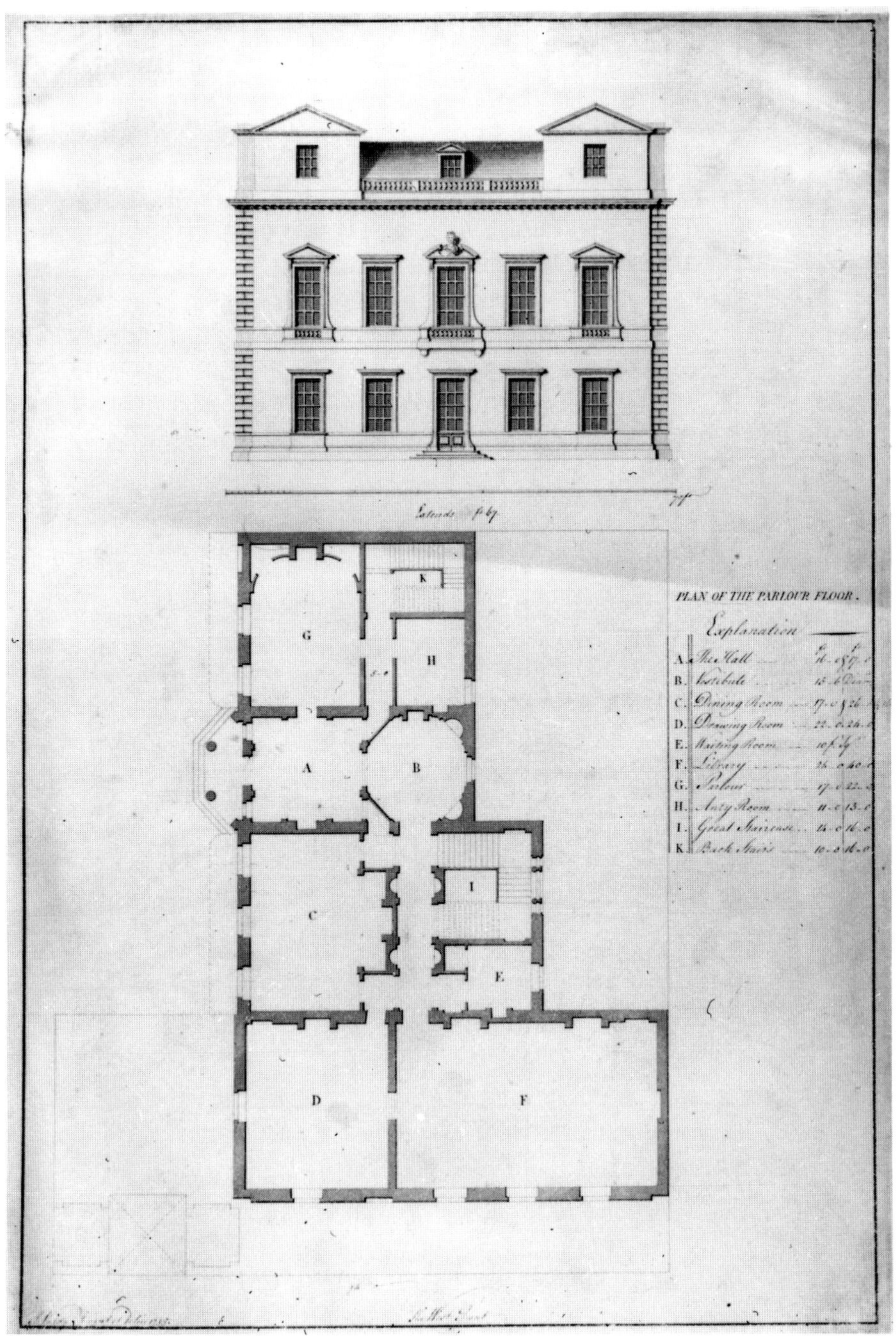

10 Plan and elevation of a house for Henry Bromley, 1st Baron Montfort, by John Vardy, 1755. The date and inscription would indicate that the design was drawn up after Montfort's death, possibly for publication or to attract another client

On the face of it Montfort had everything to live for; a contemporary declared that at one time the Baron 'would have betted any man against himself for self-murder'.[4] However, there were others in Montfort's circle who had detected a change in his behaviour and growing signs of strain. Companions grew suspicious when a few days before his suicide Montfort enquired as to the easiest means of self-destruction, and on New Year's Eve, at the stroke of midnight, when a fellow-member of White's raised his glass to him and drank his good health, Montfort was seen to pass his hand across his eyes, concealing an expression of pain. Some attributed the suicide to *tedium vitae*, others to the natural melancholy of the British and the sluggish circulation of their blood.[5] But the truth was far simpler, and money lay at the root of it.

[1] *Letters of Henry Fox, Lord Holland* (Roxburghe Club, 1945), p.45, quoted in George Edward Cokayne, *Complete Peerage*, 9, p.132

[2] Quoted in Algernon Bourke, *The History of White's*, 2 vols (1892), 2, pp.105–06

[3] William Cole in BL Add MS 5808, f.43

[4] Sir Robert Walpole, quoted in Bourke, op. cit., p.105

[5] John W. Croker (ed.), *Letters of Mary Lepel, Lady Hervey, with a Memoir, and Illustrative Notes* (1821), pp.206–07

After the most promising start, Montfort's career had lost impetus and his influence was waning fast. Despite repeated entreaties, he failed to persuade the Prime Minister, the Duke of Newcastle, to grant him the Governorship of Virginia, and his application for another position, that of Master of the Royal Hounds, was likewise rejected.[6] He had been forced to relinquish his seat as M.P. for Cambridgeshire following his elevation to the peerage and furthermore had been replaced as Lord Lieutenant. Nor could he count on the consolations of marriage, for his wife had died in childbirth while still in her twenties, and he had never found another. To make matters worse, he was running short of cash. He had recently suffered a losing streak at cards, gambling himself to the verge of financial extinction, while two of his most important creditors died on the very same day owing him a large sum of money which could not be recovered from their heirs. Montfort had spent a fortune on improvements to Horseheath Hall, engaging the services of the leading Palladian architect William Kent, and his peerage too had cost him dearly, the honour having been part of a financial trade-off involving the King's mistress, the Countess of Yarmouth, and a sum estimated at £30,000.

Montfort had also embarked on an extravagant building project in London. In 1752 he purchased the lease of a site in St James's Place, then belonging to the dowager Countess of Burlington.[7] The site was occupied by three old houses, which were let to various tenants, but Montfort planned to demolish these buildings and construct a single palatial house for his own occupation. By the terms of his lease he was required to make an immediate down-payment of £2,000, and to spend a further £8,000 on the projected works, while paying ground rent at an annual rate of £105. It was stipulated also that the works should be completed within a period of seven years, and Montfort lost no time in engaging an architect. William Kent, whom he had employed at Horseheath, was now dead, and he turned instead to Kent's former assistant and pupil John Vardy, whom he had met some ten years earlier and who may also have had a hand in the works at Horseheath.[8] Vardy drew up the necessary plans (FIG 10),[9] but on New Year's Day 1755, when Montfort put a gun to his head, the site had not yet been cleared and the houses there were still occupied.

In accordance with Montfort's will,[10] the property passed with the rest of his estate to his only son, Thomas, who succeeded as 2nd Baron Montfort. Thomas inherited some of his father's worst characteristics. A reckless spendthrift, he later sold the family seat at Horseheath and ran down the estate to such an extent that his own son, Henry, was forced to accept a state pension as a 'decayed member of the peerage'.[11] Unwilling, and no doubt unable, to fulfil the terms of the building lease in St James's Place, he allowed the property to revert to the freeholder, Lady Burlington. A few weeks later the site changed hands again when it was purchased by a young man of twenty. The young man in question was John Spencer.

[6] BL Add MS 32,688, f.466; 32,691, f.99; 32,704, f.252; 32,710, f.104; 32,725, f.325; 32,727, f.106; 32,730, ff.120, 345

[7] The lease is not among the documents in the Middlesex Deeds Register at the GLRO, but a copy of the agreement is preserved in PRO CRES 2 / 816.

[8] Vardy and Montfort would probably have met around 1744, when the architect published an engraving of a design by William Kent for a silver tureen commissioned by Montfort for Horseheath Hall [Vardy, *Some Designs of Mr Inigo Jones and Mr William Kent* (1744), p.26.]

[9] *A Design for a House for Lord Montford in St James's Place on part of the Ground where Mr Spencers House now stands*, signed and dated 'J. Vardy Invent et delin 1755' [GLRO, Maps and Prints, Westminster DD 5408]

[10] PRO PROB 11 / 815, ff.83–5

[11] Cokayne, op. cit., 9, p.133

2 FROM SHEEPFARMERS TO COURTIERS

La noblesse est un grand avantage qui, des dix-huit ans met un homme en passe, connu et respecté comme un autre pourrait avoir mérité à cinquante ans! C'est trente ans gagnés sans peine.

Blaise Pascal[1]

11 Charles Spencer, 3rd Earl of Sunderland (1675–1722), by Godfrey Kneller (Blenheim Palace). Sunderland was John Spencer's paternal grandfather. A great bibliophile and art collector, he was a trusted royal servant and senior statesman

IT IS NOT QUITE TRUE to say that in the eighteenth century England was governed by the aristocracy; but it is not very far from the truth, and John Spencer (1734–83) had the good fortune to be born into this privileged élite. At the age of twenty he was the perfect embodiment of Pascal's reflection on the advantages of nobility; he was the head of one of England's most illustrious families, with a colossal fortune and the most brilliant connections in every sphere.

The Spencers claimed descent from the medieval Despencer Earls of Gloucester and Winchester, and were entitled to use the Despencer arms. Although the claim was probably exaggerated, there was a legitimate line of descent dating back to the early fourteenth century and for upwards of one hundred years the Spencers had been accepted members of England's most senior nobility (see Appendix I).

The family first came to prominence in Tudor times during the lifetime of Sir John Spencer (d.1522), who built up a fortune through sheep-farming, obtaining a patent of arms from the College of Heralds and a knighthood from Henry VIII. In the years that followed the family continued to prosper. Profits from sheep-farming were ploughed into the purchase of land, which in turn brought political power, and through a succession of advantageous marriages, the family scaled the social ladder. Four generations on, Robert Spencer (1570–1625) was raised to the peerage as 1st Baron Spencer, while his grandson, Henry, 3rd Baron Spencer (1620–1643) was created 1st Earl of Sunderland. Robert Spencer, 2nd Earl of Sunderland (1641–1702), achieved fame as one of the most able, if unethical, statesmen of his day, changing his politics and even his religion in order to curry favour with three successive monarchs, Charles II, James II and William of Orange, all of whom he secretly betrayed. Charles Spencer, 3rd Earl of Sunderland (1675–1722), was Secretary of State under Queen Anne and George I, also serving as Lord Lieutenant of Ireland, Lord President of the Council and Groom of the Stole (FIG 11). By his wife, Lady Anne Churchill, a daughter of the great Duke of Marlborough, he had three sons, Robert, Charles and John (FIG 12). Robert succeeded as 4th Earl of Sunderland but died unmarried in 1729, with the result that the title passed to Charles. Five years later, by a complex process of inheritance, Charles also succeeded to the title and estate of his grandfather the Duke of Marlborough, and although he retained the Sunderland title, the bulk of the Sunderland estate passed to his younger brother John.

At the time he inherited the Hon. John Spencer (1708-46) was only twenty-six years old (FIG 13), but he had already made a promising start to a career in politics. In 1732 he was elected Whig M.P. for Woodstock in Oxfordshire, a borough controlled by his elder brother, and he held this seat through three successive parliaments until 1744, when he successfully contested Windsor. He had also made a highly advantageous marriage. His

[1] Quoted in François Bluche, *La Vie Quotidienne de la Noblesse Française au XVIIIe Siècle* (Paris, 1973), p.11

wife, Lady Georgina-Carolina Carteret (FIG 14), was the daughter of a senior statesman and courtier, John, 2nd Earl Granville, being descended on her mother's side from the old Dukes of Somerset and the Earls of Essex. A famous beauty, she brought her husband a dowry calculated at £30,000; her godfather, moreover, was King George II.

As a character Spencer was something of a rogue. His behaviour was often wild and unruly; he drank and smoked to excess, and on one occasion was arrested for brawling and very nearly jailed. He was also extravagant; indeed it was said of him that he never used any but gold coins, refusing to soil his hands with silver. Unable to deny himself the slightest luxury, Spencer spent wildly, buying up paintings, old master drawings, prints and fine porcelain, while indulging in gambling, hunting and other costly pursuits. He was famous also for his love of bathing, a habit he followed with unusual regularity. His attitude to life was carefree and frivolous. Even the choice of his wife was more or less an accident, her name being simply the first to appear on a list of eligible young ladies

12 The Duke and Duchess of Marlborough with their five children, by Johan Baptist Closterman, c1697 (Great Hall, Blenheim Palace). Lady Anne Churchill, wife of the 3rd Earl of Sunderland, is seated second from right. It was principally the fortune he inherited from the Duchess of Marlborough which enabled John Spencer to build Spencer House

13

14

13 The Hon. John Spencer (1708–46) with his son John, later 1st Earl Spencer, by George Knapton, 1745

14 Lady Georgina Carteret (1716–80), wife of the Hon. John Spencer, by John Vanderbank

handed to him by his elders. Spencer had a prankish sense of humour and frequently played practical jokes on family and friends, especially his grandmother, Sarah, Duchess of Marlborough. Once, after a typical show of insolence, the Duchess dismissed him from the room, declaring that he should never darken her doorstep again, whereupon he rapidly skirted the building and climbed back in through the window. On another occasion, when the Spencers were gathered together at dinner, the Duchess remarked on the pleasure it gave her to be surrounded by all the various branches of her family, to which John replied in an audible aside, 'The branches will flourish better when the old trunk is buried'.[2]

For all his teasing, John was always the Duchess's favourite grandson, and when she died in 1744 she left him the greater part of her personal estate. Not that he lived very long to enjoy it. In 1746, after two years of uninterrupted bingeing and at the age of only thirty-eight, he collapsed and died, a martyr, as Walpole remarked, to 'Brandy, Small Beer, and Tobacco'.[3]

[2] Quoted in Albert Edward John, 7th Earl Spencer 'Althorp, Northamptonshire, A Seat of the Earl Spencer', *Country Life* (25 June 1921) p.794

[3] W. S. Lewis (ed.), *The Yale Edition of Horace Walpole's Correspondence*, 48 vols (1895–1979), 19, p.272

3 A FABULOUS INHERITANCE

SPENCER HAD FATHERED two children, a son, John, born in 1734, and a daughter, Diana, who followed in 1735 (FIG 15). Diana died in 1743, but John survived and inherited virtually the whole of his father's estate. There were considerable debts, amounting in total to some £100,000,[1] but these were as nothing compared with the assets. Indeed, the young John Spencer's inheritance made him one of the richest young men in England.

The Sunderland estates, combined with those of the Duchess of Marlborough, made up a vast network covering tens of thousands of acres in a dozen different counties. During the young John Spencer's minority, moreover, the family trustees used their powers to direct over £120,000 towards the purchase of additional land, and by the time he came of age the estate was generating over £30,000 a year, while £240,000 had accumulated in cash.[2] More than money, the estate was a source of power. At a time when land-ownership was directly linked to political influence the possession of so much property naturally gave Spencer an important say in local and national affairs.

Spencer also inherited several fine houses. Chief among these was Althorp in Northamptonshire, for two hundred years the Spencers' principal seat (FIG 16). The house dated from Tudor times but had been repeatedly enlarged and remodelled, most recently during the lifetime of John Spencer's father. To John Evelyn it seemed a 'palace',[3] the

15 John Spencer as a child, dressed as Bacchus, with his younger sister Diana, dressed as Ceres, by George Knapton, c1742. In his youth Spencer was painted by several leading portrait painters, but this is the only known likeness of his sister, who died the following year

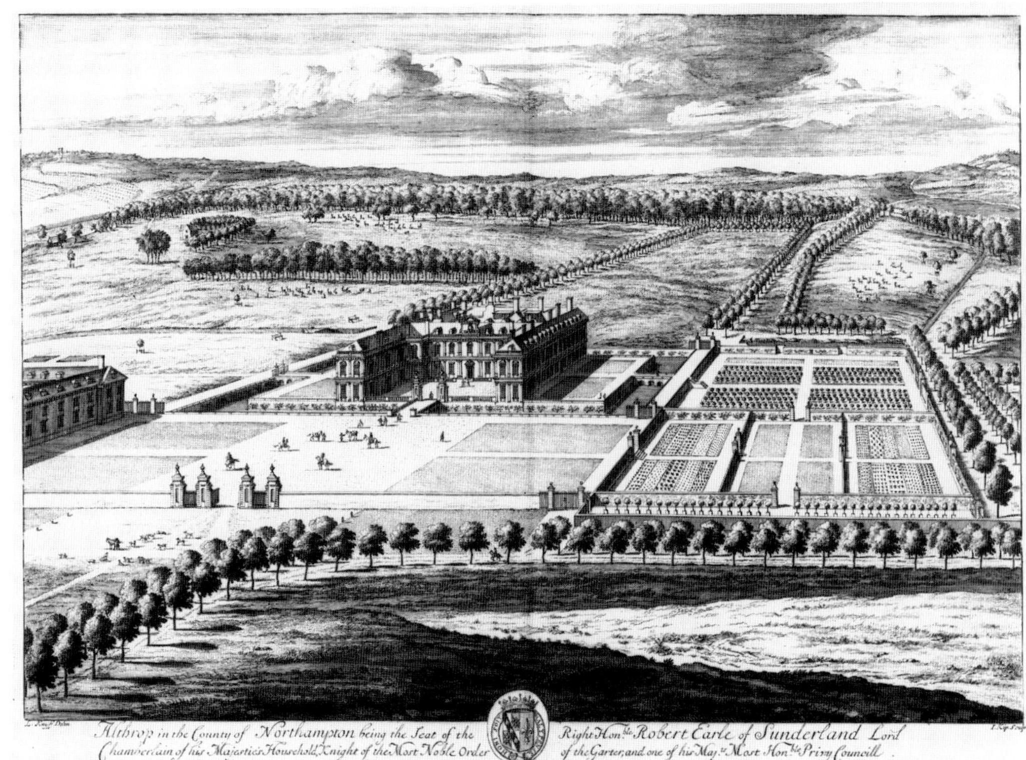

16

16 *Althorp, Northamptonshire; engraving by J. Kip after L. Knyff, from Kip,* Britannia Illustrata, *I (1720), pl.27. Begun in Tudor times, the house was the Spencers' principal seat, a 'palace' as John Evelyn described it, surrounded by formal gardens laid out to a plan by Le Nôtre*

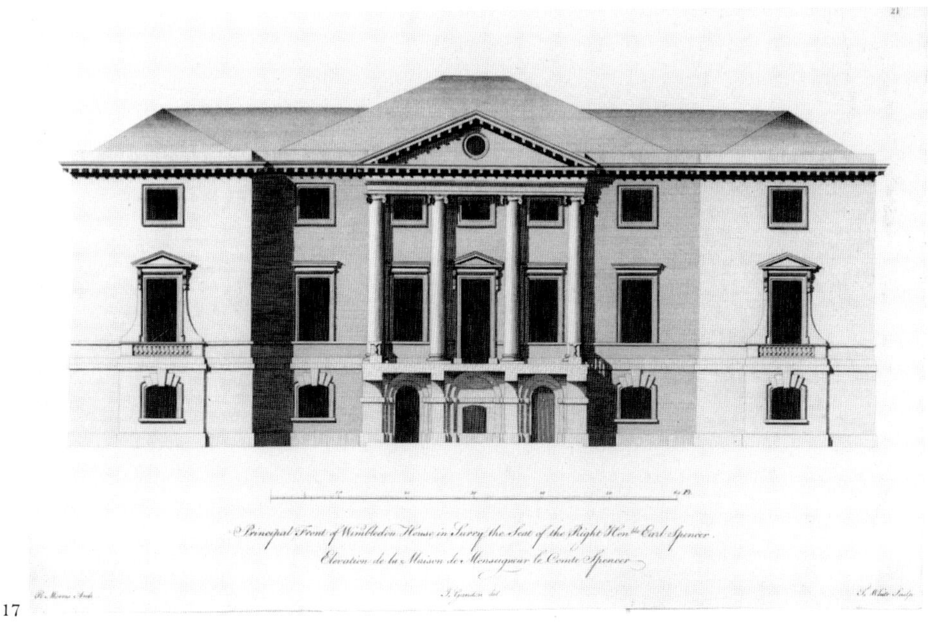

17

17 *Wimbledon Park House, Surrey, principal front; engraving by T. White after J. Gandon, from* Woolfe and Gandon Vitruvius Britannicus, *V (1771), pl.21. Situated at the heart of an 800-acre estate on the outskirts of London, the house at Wimbledon was built by the Duchess of Marlborough to designs by Roger Morris and the Earl of Pembroke*

exterior clad in mellow red brick with limestone dressings, the interior containing a celebrated staircase and gallery dating from the seventeenth century and a noble Palladian entrance hall with giant hunting scenes by Wootton. There were magnificent stables, designed by Roger Morris, and formal gardens laid out to a plan by Le Nôtre.[4]

Another important property was Wimbledon Park in Surrey, an estate of some 800 acres on the outskirts of London, which boasted a garden by Bridgeman and an imposing Palladian mansion built for the Duchess of Marlborough by Roger Morris and the Earl of Pembroke (FIG 17).[5] There was also a house at Holywell on the outskirts of St Albans,

[1] Edward William Harcourt (ed.), *The Harcourt Papers*, 14 vols (Oxford, 1880–1905), 8, p.71

[2] AP D31

[3] E. S. de Beer (ed.), *The Diary of John Evelyn* (O.U.P., 1959), p.886

[4] AP P1, P2

[5] AP P2, P13–P17; Minet Library, Archives, 30/1768/MF

conveniently situated on the road from London to Althorp (FIG 198, p. 206). The core was Tudor, but the building had been substantially remodelled and enlarged by the architect William Talman, and the grounds were extensive, covering some twenty acres, with orchards, meadows and the remains of a formal garden laid out by the 1st Duke of Marlborough.

Spencer likewise had the use of the Home Park at Windsor, having succeeded his father as Ranger, a position he held until around 1758 (FIG 18).[6] He thus enjoyed the benefits of another substantial property, comprising several acres of immaculately-planted gardens, a deer park and a handsome lodge built in the early part of the century.[7] A visitor, John Macky, described the gardens as 'very fine', the park 'finely shaded' and 'well stocked with Deer' and the Ranger's lodge 'a very Charming Habitation'.[8] In addition there was a shooting lodge at North Creake in Norfolk, while in London there was a large terrace house in Grosvenor Street and another in Upper Brook Street.[9]

18 The Lodge, Windsor Home Park; detail from W. Collier, Plan of the Town and Castle of Windsor and Little Park etc., *engraved by J. Pine and published in Eton, 1742. Having inherited the post of Ranger, John Spencer was entitled to the use of the Home Park at Windsor and thus disposed of a handsome lodge set in several acres of immaculately planted gardens*

Along with these houses Spencer inherited a magnificent art collection. At Althorp alone there were over 400 paintings, including works ascribed to some of the greatest European masters: Holbein and Rubens; Rembrandt and Teniers; Michelangelo and Leonardo da Vinci; Tintoretto and Veronese; Caravaggio, Poussin and Lebrun; Salvator Rosa, Carlo Dolci, Parmigianino, Ludovico Carracci, Carlo Maratta, Domenichino; Van Dyck and Kneller; Jervas and Lely.[10] There was also an outstanding collection of old master drawings, ranging in date from the fifteenth to the early eighteenth century, notable among which were a portfolio of 117 drawings by Stefano della Bella and a volume of thirty-three sketches ascribed to Leonardo da Vinci.[11] There were busts and Antique statues; fine Oriental and European porcelain;[12] and wondrous jewellery, including the fabled Marlborough diamonds, which alone were valued at £100,000.[13] Other treasures included a superb collection of gold and silver plate, centred around the famous service presented to the 1st Duke of Marlborough when Ambassador to the States General;[14] lacquer cabinets, giltwood chairs, coromandel screens and other fine furniture;[15] carpets and textiles; and a substantial library of books and manuscripts.[16]

Not the least of Spencer's assets were the members of his own family, many of whom held key positions at Westminster and at Court. The Prime Minister himself, the Duke of Newcastle, was a relation. Spencer's maternal grandfather, Lord Granville, was at one time Secretary of State and Lord President of the Council, Gentleman of the Bedchamber to George I and Ambassador to Sweden and the Hague. His uncle, the 3rd Duke of Marlborough, served as Lord of the Bedchamber, Lord Steward of the Household, Lord Privy Seal, Lord Justice Regent, Master General of the Ordnance and Lord Lieutenant of Oxfordshire and Buckinghamshire. Another uncle, the Duke of Bedford, was First Lord of the Admiralty, Lord Lieutenant of Ireland and Lord Lieutenant of Bedfordshire and Devon, also serving as British Ambassador to France, Lord Privy Seal and Lord President of the Council. A third uncle, the Earl of Shelburne, occupied the offices of Secretary of State and President of the Board of Trade and Foreign Plantations. The Marquess of Tweeddale, also an uncle, was at one time Secretary of State and Lord Justice General of Scotland. Among the members of Spencer's own generation, his first cousin, Lord Weymouth, was twice appointed Secretary of State, also serving as Lord Lieutenant of Ireland, Lord of the Bedchamber, Master of the Horse to Queen Charlotte and Groom of the Stable. Another first cousin, the 4th Duke of Marlborough, became Lord Privy Seal and Lord Chamberlain of the Household, while a third, Viscount Bateman, was appointed Lord of the Admiralty, Lord Lieutenant of Herefordshire and Treasurer of the Household.

Another dimension was added in 1750 when Spencer's mother remarried. Her second husband was William, 2nd Earl Cowper (FIG 19), whose father had been Lord High Chancellor and whose mother was at one time Lady of the Bedchamber to Caroline, Princess of Wales. Lord Cowper himself had served as Lord of the Bedchamber to George II, while his son, Viscount Fordwich, born of a previous marriage, was a godson of George III and Princess Amelia.

As far as one can tell, there was only one black sheep in John Spencer's family. This was his maternal uncle, Lord Robert Carteret, a delinquent and a drunkard whose habit it was to parade in St James's Park wearing a striped jockey's waistcoat, out-size breeches and a coachman's hat with the flaps turned down. He brought disgrace on himself when he married the superintendent of a notorious French bath house and is chiefly remembered for his ghoulish behaviour while staying with the Duke and Duchess of Bedford, when at five o'clock one morning he burst into their apartment, drenched in blood, having severed the ears of every horse in the stable and pinned them to his lapels.

19 William, 2nd Earl Cowper, by Bartholomew Dandridge. The son of a former Lord Chancellor, Earl Cowper was a noted connoisseur and an influential figure in John Spencer's education and his development as a collector and patron of the arts

[6] AP F180

[7] J. Rocque, *Plan of Windsor Park* (1738); W. Collier, *Plan of the Town and Castle of Windsor and Little Park, Town and College of Eton* (1742)

[8] John Macky, *A Journey Through England*, 2 vols (1714–22), 1, p.28

[9] *Survey of London*, XL (1980), pp.42, 217

[10] In addition to the printed catalogues listed in the bibliography I have referred to the following manuscripts: AP D15, *An Account of the Pictures at St Albans* [i.e. Holywell House] (*c*1690); Ibid., *Pictures at Marlbro House belonging to her Grace* [i.e. the Duchess of Marlborough] (n.d.); AP L15, *Catalogue of the Pictures at Althorpe and Wimbleton belonging to the late Honble Mr Spencer . . . by George Knapton, 25 Oct 1746*; BL Add MS Sloane Papers 5726 F, art.1, *A List of Painted Portraits (Althorp)*; AP F169, Georgiana, Countess Spencer, *Pictures in my Dressing Room in London* (*c*1770); BL – Add MS Sloane Papers 5726 E. art.1, *Summary catalogue of portraits at Spencer House* (*c*1790); AP L16, *Catalogue of the Pictures at Althorp made in November 1802*; AP L17, *Catalogue des Tableaux Suisses qui sont dans la Salle d'Eté à Holywell* (*c*1800); AP L19, *Catalogue of Paintings at Althorp 1821–31*, annotated by Lavinia, Countess Spencer; AP L27, *Notes by Frederick, 4th Earl Spencer, concerning the subjects of some of the portraits at Althorp* (*c*1850)

[11] AP D15, George Knapton, *The Inventory & Valuation of the Collection and Drawings belonging to the late Honourable Mr John Spencer* (1750)

[12] AP D15, L15

[13] AP D15; R. Forrer, *Catalogue of Intaglios, Cameos, Seals and Rings at Althorp, The Property of the Earl Spencer* (1939) [MSS; copy held by S. J. Phillips Ltd]

[14] AP D15, L15

[15] AP L18

[16] AP D15

4 A MAN WHOSE VALUE FEW PEOPLE KNOW

SPENCER HAD EVERY ADVANTAGE, and under normal circumstances would almost certainly have occupied high political office. But there was one significant catch. Towards the end of her life the Duchess of Marlborough had quarrelled with the Crown and in her will she forbade both her grandson and great-grandson from accepting any position, either civil or military, from the King, on pain of forfeiting the whole of her estate. She could not have made her wishes clearer when she stipulated that 'he [John Spencer] shall not accept or take from the King or Queen of these Realms any pension or any office of employment, Civil or Military. Then and in such case . . . all and every the powers and Authority to him . . . shall cease and be void to all intents and purposes as if the said John Spencer were actually dead.'[1]

Spencer was thus prevented from taking as full a part in public life as he would have wished and from occupying the position for which, by birth and fortune, he was so well fitted. Nonetheless he took a keen and active interest in politics. In accordance with family tradition he sided with the Whigs; indeed his personal politics were a typically Whiggish mixture of liberalism and high-handedness. He had a horror of religious intolerance, and was generous to his social inferiors, but he would never have questioned the primacy of the Anglican Church nor the right of the aristocracy to govern. His fortune allowed him a certain independence,[2] and he was sometimes critical of government policy, as in the case of the attempted suppression of the American uprising, which he bitterly opposed.[3] Yet he remained at heart a patriot and could always be expected to rally to the party in a time of crisis.[4]

In March 1756, three months after he came of age, Spencer stood as M.P. for Bristol, and although defeated on this occasion, the following December he was returned as M.P. for Warwick. In the years that followed he proved a staunch supporter of the government and in 1761 his loyalty was rewarded when his kinsman, the Duke of Newcastle, at that time Prime Minister, interceded on his behalf to secure him a peerage as Viscount and Baron Spencer of Althorp.[5] Although he was forced to relinquish his seat in the Commons, he quickly established himself as an active member of the Lords and his influence was considerably increased when in 1765 he was granted the title Earl Spencer.[6] Despite an acknowledged gift for speech-writing, he rarely addressed the House, preferring to work behind the scenes, but he served on at least one parliamentary committee and made a major contribution to the Whigs' political fortunes through the financing of elections.[7] He was particularly successful in St Albans, a borough formerly controlled by the Duchess of Marlborough, where through bribery, corruption and every form of political manipulation he invariably installed the candidate of his choice. His greatest triumph, however, was the election in Northampton in 1768 when he succeeded in breaking the long-standing political monopoly of the Earls of Halifax and Northampton. The 'contest of the three Earls', as it became known, was one of the most costly and corrupt in English political history. All three contestants spent wildly. According to one report, Spencer

[1] *A True Copy of the Last Will and Testament of Her Grace Sarah, late Duchess Dowager of Marlborough, with the Codicil thereto annexed* (1744), pp.34–5

[2] HRO, D/EP. F296, JS to WC, 24 May 1782

[3] AP F117, WH to GS, 20 Mar 1781

[4] Ibid., JS to WH, Dec 1769

[5] The peerage was granted in direct response to a letter sent by Spencer to Newcastle, which survives among the latter's papers in the manuscripts department of the British Library and which is well worth quoting for the light it sheds on the workings of the peerage at this time and the machinations which lay behind Spencer's promotion. The letter, dated 27 Nov 1760, was as follows: 'My Lord, As Yr Grace has done me ye honor to undertake to mention to ye King my humble request for a Peerage, I flatter myself your Grace will excuse my giving you this trouble, least I shou'd not have fully explained myself when I had ye honor of speaking to you this morning. As I am now ye representative of ye Sunderland Family & as my particular circumstances are such (from ye Duchess of

stationed footmen on either side of the front door at Althorp with trays of sandwiches for voters, each sandwich containing two gold sovereigns. Halifax was ruined; he was forced to sell his estate at Horton and abandoned all interest in politics. Northampton too, deep in debt even before the election began, was forced to sell the contents of Castle Ashby and retired to the Continent, where he promptly died of a broken heart. Even Spencer is said to have been 'seriously embarrassed financially'.[8] According to rumours circulating at the time, the election cost him upwards of £120,000.

To further his ambitions at a national level Spencer also took some part in local politics, serving at one time as High Steward and Mayor of St Albans. He was likewise active at Court, where he established a warm rapport with the royal family. George II stood as godfather to his son, while the dowager Princess of Wales, Princess Amelia and the Duke of York were all close friends. It was a matter of lasting regret to him that he never received the Garter,[9] an honour awarded to many of his closest relations, but it says something for his character and ability that despite the restrictions imposed by his great-grandmother's will, he managed to play a significant part in public life.

Although politics was always central to his activities, Spencer had many other interests. He took a serious view of his duties as head of the family and always remained on the closest terms with his mother and his stepfather, Lord Cowper. Following Lord Cowper's death he provided his mother with a handsome dower house in Richmond, which he furnished at his own expense. When she herself died in 1780 he was heartbroken, the news having been kept from him for fear of the pain it would cause.[10] Spencer also developed a strong bond of affection with his step-brother, Viscount Fordwich. The two grew up together as boys, and although Fordwich later moved to Florence, having succumbed to the charms of Italy during the Grand Tour, Spencer corresponded with him until his death and was constantly in his company when he visited Florence during his own Grand Tour in 1763–64.[11] At the same time Spencer maintained close connections with other members of the family, such as his cousin the 4th Duke of Marlborough, to whom he was godfather. To his wife Georgiana, whom he married in 1755, he was a devoted husband, and to his children an affectionate father, taking a close interest in their education.

Like his father before him Spencer was rather extravagant and spent beyond his means. Records reveal that from one account alone his expenses averaged over £31,000 a year and that between the time he inherited and his death in 1783 he managed to spend almost a million pounds;[12] in 1756 alone his outgoings totalled £200,000.[13] However, a large share of his expenditure was taken up with clearing his father's debts, an act which gained him considerable credit since he was under no legal obligation to do so, and he also invested wisely in property, greatly increasing the size of the family estate. During the first eight years of his minority he laid out some £72,000 on land in Northamptonshire, Dorset, Berkshire and Surrey,[14] while in 1763 he purchased the manors of Battersea and Wandsworth,[15] and in 1770 formed a consortium to build Battersea Bridge, with the obvious intention of attracting development.

Spencer also gave generously to charity. He was President of the British Lying-in Hospital and made regular donations to other hospitals such as St Bartholomew's, Lock's, St George's and the infirmary at Northampton. At the same time he helped provide for the orphans and widows of the clergy and he likewise supported the charity schools at Wimbledon and Althorp. The Spencer archive contains literally hundreds of letters from individuals who sought and received his financial assistance.[16]

As a senior member of the aristocracy Spencer naturally led an active social life. He was a generous host and kept an excellent table and cellar. He was a member of

Marlborough's will) that I cannot receive any Favour from ye King except a Title, I shou'd hope that if his Majesty thinks me worthy of a Peerage he will not confer on me a less dignity than that of a Viscount & it is for that honor I must beg yr Grace to lay me at his Majesty's feet. I am very cautious of not desiring to assume any of ye Titles which have been in ye Sunderland Family, some of which are now vested in ye Duke of Marlborough but confine myself to ye Title of Althorpe which has never been made use of & which place I am in possession of, ye Capital Seat of that Family. What I humbly desire is, that his Majesty will be graciously pleas'd to create me Viscount Spencer of Althorpe, & I shou'd be extremely obliged to his Majesty if at ye same time that he gives me ye Title of Viscount Spencer of Althorpe, he will confer on me likewise ye Title of Baron Spencer of Althorpe. I was determin'd not to make this application to his Majesty through anybody but Yr Grace, having ye honor to be allied to you so nearly by ye Marlborough Family & I hope Yr Grace has observ'd that ever since I sat in Parliament I have never fail'd in supporting ye King & his Ministers to ye best of my ability. I am, my Lord, with great Respect Yr Graces most obedient humble servt, J: Spencer.' [BL Add MS 32,915, f. 115]

[6] BL Add MS 36,133, f.101

[7] BL Add MS 34,375, ff.244–8, 252

[8] Lady Margaret Douglas-Home, *A Mere Miss Poyntz*

[9] HRO D/EP F296, JS to WC, 24 May 1782

[10] HRO D/EP F296, GS to WC, 22 Aug 1780; AP F117, GS to WH 3 Oct 1780

[11] Spencer's Grand Tour is documented in AP F41, F174–F175; also in SBFP [numerous refs]

[12] HB, Account of JS, 1755–83

[13] Ibid.; AP F180

[14] AP D31

[15] AP F181, P2, P13–P17; Minet Library, Archives, 4621, 5777, 5779, 5879–5886, 14761, 14823; *An Act to impower the Right Honourable John, Lord Viscount Spencer, to make Leases of the Manor of Battersea and Wandsworth, and of Lands and Grounds in Battersea and Wandsworth, in the County of Surrey, purchased in Pursuance of the Will of the Most Noble Sarah, late Duchess Dowager of Marlborough, in order for building upon and improving the same,* Acts of Parliament, House of Lords, 17 Feb 1764

[16] AP F132–F165; *Gentleman's Magazine,* LIII, p.980

numerous clubs, including Brooks's and White's, and generally attended the principal events in the social calendar. At various times, in the memoirs of the period, we find him dining at Holdernesse House and the residence of the French Ambassador; playing cards with the Duke of Bedford; gathering with other guests at an assembly at Pembroke House and a Masquerade in honour of the King of Denmark; visiting the pleasure gardens at Ranelagh; and travelling up the Thames by launch in company with the Countess of Pembroke, the Earl of Carlisle and a gathering of distinguished visitors from France, including the Prince de Salm, Mme de Castiglione and Monsieur Champcenet, Chamberlain to Louis XVI. In a rare surviving letter to his son of 1777 he described his life as one of 'Balls, Assemblys & Ranelagh Gardens'.[17] Spencer was handsome, with dark romantic looks; he was also something of a dandy, running up considerable bills with fashionable London outfitters and wig-makers.[18] The shoe-buckles he wore on his honeymoon were encrusted with diamonds valued at £30,000, and at a party in 1768 he cut a dashing figure in a costume described by one fellow guest as 'a pale blue lutestring domino, trimmed with a darker blue in chenille and gold . . . and white leather shoes with blue and gold roses'.[19]

Yet Spencer was in fact a rather private person, generally quite shy and withdrawn, especially in large gatherings. A relation, the Dean of Durham, expressed surprise when as a child he managed to put aside his usual 'reservedness'[20] and take part in an amateur play. Even in later life he was nervous of public appearances. After hearing him speak in the House of Lords, Lady Mary Coke reported, 'Lord Spencer moved the Address, & as much as cou'd be heard was very pretty, but he was extremely frighted & spoke very low'.[21] Spencer also had a tendency to melancholy. A companion complained of his 'unhappy disposition to look always on the worst side of things, and if he does not find a subject for fretting to make one'.[22] However, in the proper circumstances he could be extremely charming. According to his daughter-in-law, Lavinia Bingham, Spencer's 'manners, when he wished to please, were so fascinating that it was scarcely possible to resist his influence'.[23] The diarist Mrs Delaney was equally won over; for her there could be 'few such noble and generous spirits in the world'.[24] Spencer was at his best in the company of close relations and friends. One such friend, Viscount Palmerston, understood him perfectly. Spencer, he reflected, 'seems to be a man whose value few people know. The bright side of his character appears in private and the dark side in public; nobody would wish to change this for its opposite, to which, however, many owe their high reputation. It were only to be wished that the bright side were a little more visible; for of the many who see Lord Spencer, it is only the few who live in intimacy with him who know that he has an understanding and a heart that might do credit to any man.'[25]

Spencer's shyness and melancholy were partly due to ill health. All his life he suffered from bouts of sickness and in later years was subject to crippling chest and stomach complaints. He was frail as a child and many believed he would not survive into manhood. In 1754 a contemporary described him as 'in a wretched state of health',[26] while a travelling companion on the Grand Tour afterwards remarked that he was 'ill the whole time'.[27] Not a year went by when Spencer was not obliged to travel to Bath or Spa to drink the waters, or to Scarborough to bathe and take the sea air. More than once he went under the surgeon's knife, and there are copious bills from apothecaries among his personal papers. In the end, however, eighteenth-century medicine was powerless to help him and he died while still in his forties.

Periods of sickness must have been especially galling to Spencer for one of his greatest loves was sport. He was an excellent horseman, a crack shot and also had an enthusiasm for ice-skating and billiards. His greatest love was fox-hunting, of which he described himself as 'madly fond', a prey, as he expressed it, to the 'hunting rage'.[28] He headed his own personal hunt at Althorp and was for many years the Master of the Pytchley, where, assisted by the legendary huntsman Dick Knight, he brought to perfection the so-called 'flying' method. At the same time he bred perhaps the finest pack of fox-hounds in the country, receiving orders from as far afield as Naples, where the King himself was a customer. Spencer regarded the hounds more or less as family members; when sending bitches to outside studs he insisted they travel by carriage in the condition of ladies of rank. He was equally attached to the horses. There is a story that when a favourite hunter, 'Merry Tom', was killed in a riding accident, Spencer had it buried on the spot where it fell, complete with bridle and saddle, in a solemn ceremony approximating to a Viking funeral ritual. A stone was erected with the inscription, '*To the memory of Merry Tom*', but tradition has it that the tablet was later removed after local wags from a neighbouring hunt appended the rejoinder, '*Ridden to death by Foolish John*'.[29] Another great favourite was 'Mouton', a large Dutch Barge dog who, through a series of misadventures, became something of a celebrity. On one occasion 'Mouton' accompanied Spencer's wife to the house of a friend. Entering the hall, he immediately spied a portrait of another dog, recently painted by Stubbs, which was propped up on the floor waiting to be hung. Believing it to be the real thing, he ran at the canvas and tore it to pieces. On another occasion he was walking with his master down Piccadilly when, at the gates of Devonshire House, he growled at a passing stranger. Not without justification the stranger responded with a kick, but Spencer was so outraged he drew his sword and ran at the man, pursuing him all the way to Hyde Park Corner where he was forced to give up the chase.

Spencer also had a love of gambling, especially cards and horse-racing, which together absorbed a fair share of his income. Indeed it was said that during his lifetime Althorp 'became almost a gambling house'.[30] He likewise had a fondness for foreign travel and generally spent a part of each year abroad. Foreign travel could be an uncomfortable and even hazardous experience in the eighteenth century. The roads were rough and carriages poorly-sprung. The food was sometimes inedible, the accommodation primitive, and there was always the fear of bandits, disease and other perils. More than once the Earl and Countess were obliged to lodge like simple peasants in rude country inns.[31] There were endless carriage accidents, some of them serious, involving long delays as wheels and other parts were repaired or replaced. On one disastrous occasion a running footman in the Spencers' retinue fell into a marsh and drowned,[32] and in 1779 a ship in which they were sailing was pursued by French cutters, only narrowly escaping capture. But there were obvious incentives and rewards, and over the years Spencer and his wife covered most of the Continent, including France, Italy, Switzerland, Belgium and Germany.

There is no record of Spencer having been sent away to school or university; his early education was apparently entrusted to a minor clergyman, the Reverend Mr Holloway, afterwards rector of Middleton Stoney in Oxfordshire,[33] and his intellectual powers were slow to develop. However, under the influence of his step-father, Lord Cowper, a noted scholar and connoisseur, he began to explore the world of art and ideas, and eventually emerged as an active and influential figure on the cultural scene.

From the quantities of bills from booksellers which survive among his papers it is clear that Spencer was a voracious reader and that his interests were diverse, ranging from English and foreign literature to ancient and modern history, philosophy and science, Classical archaeology and mythology.[34] The great library formed by his grandfather, the 3rd Earl of Sunderland, had been removed to Blenheim by the 5th Earl, but over the years Spencer assembled a collection in its place described by one leading scholar as

[17] AP G2, JS to GJS, 6 May 1777

[18] AP F182

[19] Lady Llanover (ed.), *The Autobiography and Correspondence of Mary Granville, Mrs Delaney*, 6 vols (1861–62), 4, p.186

[20] *Letters of Spencer Cowper, Dean of Durham 1746–74* (1956), p.131

[21] J.A. Home (ed.), *The Letters and Journals of Lady Mary Coke*, 4 vols (Edinburgh 1889–96), 1, p.96

[22] Revd William Arden, quoted in Brian Connell, *Portrait of a Whig Peer, compiled from the papers of the second Viscount Palmerston 1739–1802* (1957), p.52

[23] Sir Denis Le Marchant, *Memoir of John Charles Viscount Althorp Third Earl Spencer* (1876), p.XIX

[24] *The Autobiography and Correspondence of Mary Granville, Mrs Delaney*, 4, p.55

[25] Connell, op. cit., pp.46–7

[26] *The Autobiography and Correspondence of Mary Granville, Mrs Delaney*, 3, p.305

[27] Revd William Arden, quoted in Connell, op. cit., p.52; AP F186

[28] AP F117, JS to WH, 25 Dec 1765

[29] Guy Paget, *The History of the Althorp and Pytchley Hunt 1634–1920* (1937), p.12

[30] Le Marchant, op. cit., p.2

[31] In a travel diary Georgiana noted that in one foreign inn she and the Earl were 'forced to go up a sort of ladder instead of staircase to our bedchambers & most of the Men Servants lay upon the ground in a kind of loft at our door.' [AP F175]

[32] PRO SPF 105/308, Changuion to Mann, 6 Nov 1763 [SBFP]

[33] AP F130, Holloway to JS, 16 Sept 1756

[34] AP F184

'excellent', containing 'intellectual treasures of the highest value'.[35] In 1756 he purchased the library of the late Dean of Lincoln, Dr William George, a former principal of Eton and Vice-Chancellor of Cambridge University, comprising some 5,000 volumes of rare tracts and miscellaneous writings dating back to Elizabethan times.[36] Spencer also gave support and encouragement to contemporary writers. He was a particularly close friend and patron of the novelist Laurence Sterne (FIG 195, p. 200), whom he showered with money and gifts; and Sterne responded by dedicating to him a part of *Tristram Shandy*, having previously submitted the manuscript for his approval.[37] Spencer was likewise a friend of the poet John Scott, greatly admired by contemporaries for his moral eclogues and political pamphlets, especially by Samuel Johnson, who also moved in Spencer's circle.[38] On visits to Paris Spencer dined with the celebrated writer and wit, the Chevalier de Boufflers and the literary *eminence*, Mme du Deffand. In Switzerland he stopped to visit Voltaire at Ferney.[39]

Theatre was another interest. When in London Spencer regularly attended performances at Drury Lane and was also in the habit of making twice-weekly visits to the Haymarket Theatre.[40] He was a devoted friend and supporter of the actor and impresario David Garrick (FIG 196, p. 200), whom he met on the Grand Tour, and was pall-bearer at Garrick's funeral.[41] At the same time he befriended the rising young playwright and politician, Richard Brinsley Sheridan, whose career he helped to promote. Even when travelling abroad he liked to attend the theatre; among his surviving papers are programmes and souvenirs from the *Comédie Française*, the *Comédie Italienne*, and the royal theatres at Versailles and Fontainebleau.[42]

Although in later life a bungled operation severely impaired his hearing, Spencer also had a deep love of music. He was a particular admirer of Handel and was frequently to be found at concerts, recitals and the opera. Indeed he may well have played an instrument himself, for his wife and children were all keen amateur musicians, and there are quantities of bills among the Spencer papers relating to the repair and maintenance of harpsichords, pianofortes and violoncellos, as well as sheet music, strings and other musical supplies.[43] Spencer patronized the Italian musician Giacobbe Cervetto, at one time head of Garrick's orchestra at Drury Lane, who acted as music master to the Spencers and regularly performed for their benefit at private concerts and other musical entertainments. He was also a patron of Cervetto's son James (FIG 194, p. 199), a virtuoso cellist who was performing all over Europe before he was ten, and who like his father was often called upon to play for the Spencers. Another protégé was the harpsichordist and composer Thomas Linley, joint musical director at Drury Lane, whom Spencer engaged as music master to his elder daughter Georgiana; yet another was the German pianist J. D. Benser, an associate of Johann Christian Bach, who acted as music master to Spencer's younger daughter Harriet and also gave occasional concerts. Spencer was an important customer of the Scottish music publisher Robert Bremner, and of another Scot, John Broadwood, founder of the famous firm of piano makers, as well as his partner Burkat Shudi, a leading harpsichord maker. At the same time the Earl made donations to the Society for the Support of Decayed Musicians and their Families.[44]

The fine and decorative arts were a particular passion. During the trips he made with his wife to the Continent, Spencer visited all the most notable buildings and art collections. In Paris he toured the Hotel de Biron and the Bibliothèque Royale; the Cabinet de Médailles and the Tuileries Palace; the picture gallery of the Palais du Luxembourg and numerous private collections. On excursions to Versailles he was shown the Petit Trianon and Louveciennes.[45] In the south of France he stopped to admire the Maison Carrée at Nimes.[46] In Brussels he inspected the celebrated collection of Count Varelst,

[35] Sir William Jones, quoted in John Shore [Lord Teignmouth], *Memoirs of the Life, Writings, and Correspondence of Sir William Jones* (1804), p.37

[36] AP F130, Revd William Arden to JS, 20 Nov 1756

[37] AP F176

[38] AP F114, GSH to GS, 18 May 1780

[39] AP F41, GS to CH, 18 Sept 1763

[40] AP F114, GSH to GS, 21 Dec 1776

[41] AP F116; R. Forrer, *Catalogue of Intaglios, Cameos, Seals and Rings at Althorp, The Property of the Earl Spencer*, No. 5 (1939)

and in Dusseldorf he viewed the picture gallery of the Elector Palatine.[47] But it was Italy which yielded the greatest treasures, confirming Spencer in what he described as his 'taste for Virtu',[48] and during his year-long tour of 1763–64 he amply fulfilled the objectives of all Grand Tourists, visiting Venice, Verona and Vicenza; Mantua, Milan and Pisa; Bologna and Florence; Rome and Naples; Paestum, Herculaneum and Portici.

Spencer was a friend to some of the foremost connoisseurs of the period, including Quentin Craufurd, the Duke of Roxburghe, Sir William Hamilton, the Marquess of Rockingham, Sir Thomas Robinson and the Dean of Ossory. He was a member of the Royal Society of Arts, which he joined in 1757,[49] as well as the famous Society of Dilettanti, to which he was elected on his return from the Grand Tour in 1765.[50]

Spencer was especially active as a collector and patron. Over the years he made significant additions to the family gallery of old master paintings. His tastes reflected the values of eighteenth-century connoisseurship, being characterized by a marked preference for the masters of the High Renaissance and the *seicento*, especially the painters of the Bolognese school, as well as the Classical landscapes of Poussin and Claude, and the works of Rubens, Wouwermans and other Dutch masters.

In 1758 Spencer was among the bidders at the sale in London of the Henry Furnese collection, where he acquired an allegory of *Liberality and Modesty* by Guido Reni and a portrait by Andrea Sacchi, *The Musician Marc'Antonio Pasqualini being crowned by Apollo*. In a letter to Sir Horace Mann, Horace Walpole noted that Spencer had paid 'no less than two thousand two hundred pounds' for the pictures, an exorbitant sum which reflected the value attached at that time to large-scale paintings by the Bolognese masters, which were then a great rarity in English collections.[51] Not long afterwards Spencer was bidding again at the Sir Luke Schaub sale where, despite heavy competition from the Duchess of Portland and the Earl of Egremont, he managed to acquire a number of old master paintings by various artists: a *St Sebastian* by Guercino; a *Landscape with Figures* by Poussin; a *Venus at her Toylet* by Annibale Carracci; and a *Landscape with Figures and Horses* by Wouvermans.[52] At the Sir William Hamilton sale in 1761 Spencer was again top-bidder for two important paintings, *Witches at their Several Hellish Ceremonies* by Salvator Rosa, and a portrait by Rubens, since identified as *The Daughter of Sir Balthasar Gerbier*.[53] Spencer's tour of Italy provided him with further opportunities to purchase paintings. In 1764 he acquired two large works by Salvator Rosa from the Accaiuoli family in Florence, *Cincinnatus called from the Farm* and *Alexander and Diogenes*.[54] In Rome he acquired a head of Psyche, believed to be by Raphael,[55] and a painting described by Garrick as 'a very good sketch of a picture by Baroche'.[56] Through Gavin Hamilton, a Scottish painter and dealer based in Rome (FIG 136, p. 154), he managed to acquire two magnificent paintings by Guercino, then in the Palazzo Locatelli in Cesena, a *King David* and *The Samian Sibyl*, which he purchased in 1768.[57] He made repeated attempts to purchase Guido Reni's famous *Magdalen* at the Palazzo Barberini,[58] and at various times was in treaty for other celebrated works by artists such as Pietro da Cortona, Leonardo da Vinci, Ludovico Carracci, Paolo Veronese, Parmigianino and Andrea del Sarto.[59] Spencer also recieved assistance from his friend, Sir William Hamilton, who, as British Envoy to Naples, was in a good position to seek out works of art on his behalf. In 1768 Hamilton informed him that for about £1500 'I could procure you . . . as fine a picture by Correggio as any in the world.' The painting was in a private collection, but as Hamilton explained, the owner had recently 'had a loss & might be tempted perhaps'. However, the negotiation came to nothing, apparently because Spencer was momentarily short of funds, having recently spent 'so much in elections'.[60] On another occasion Hamilton urged Spencer to acquire a *Glaucus and Scylla*, attributed at that time to Giulio Romano.

[42] AP F169

[43] AP F174, F184

[44] Ibid.

[45] AP F174

[46] AP F117, JS to WH, Dec 1769; AP F43, GS to CH, 4 Apr 1773; AP F169

[47] AP F41, GS to CH, 20 July 1764

[48] AP F117, JS to WH, 25 Dec 1765

[49] Royal Society of Arts archives. Spencer was proposed by the Dean of Ossory

[50] Library of the Society of Antiquaries, Minute Books of the Society of Dilettanti, Mar 1765. Spencer was proposed by Sir Thomas Robinson

[51] W. S. Lewis (ed.), *The Yale Edition of Horace Walpole's Correspondence*, 21, pp.172–3. Both paintings were sold by the 8th Earl Spencer to Wildenstein & Co. Both have since been sold abroad. The Sacchi is in the Metropolitan Museum in New York. The Reni is in a private collection, also in New York

[52] *A Catalogue of the Grand and Capital Collection of Italian, Flemish and Dutch Paintings of the Hon. Sir Luke Schaub, lately deceased etc.*, 26–28 Apr 1758, 1st day, Nos 49, 52; 2nd day, No. 50; 3rd day, No. 41 [marked copy in BL 7805.e.5 (6)]; Lewis, op. cit., 21, p.200. It is interesting to note that Spencer's stepfather bid on his behalf at this sale

[53] *A Catalogue of a well-known and approved Collection of Pictures* [i.e. that of WH] . . . *which will be sold by Auction by Messrs Prestage and Hobbs . . . on Friday and Saturday the 20th and 21st of February 1761*, 1st Day, Lot 78 ['Rubens . . . A Little Girl (one of the *Gerbier* Family) Leaning on a Tree']; 2nd Day, Lot 65 ['Witches at their several hellish Ceremonies']. The Salvator Rosa was sold by the 8th Earl Spencer to Wildenstein & Co in 1982 and is now in the National Gallery in London

[54] David Garrick to Duke of Devonshire, 25 June 1764 [SBFP]

[55] Ibid.

[56] Ibid.; James Martin, MS *Journal of his Grand Tour 1763/65*, 14 July 1764 [SBFP]

[57] AP F117, GH to GS, 4 May 1768

[58] Ibid., GH to JS, 29 Jan 1766; see n.54

[59] AP F117, GH to JS, 29 Jan 1766; GH to GS, 21 May, 26 June, 12 Oct 1766, 11 Apr, 20 May, 26 Dec 1767, 4, 21 May, 3 Dec 1768, 12 May 1770; GS to GH, 28 July 1766

[60] AP F117, WH to JS, 11 Oct 1768

The painting, he declared, was 'a most spirited one';[61] it formed part of the famous collection of Lady Betty Germain, but Spencer again held back.[62] In some cases, where a painting was not for sale, Spencer settled for a copy. From the young Italian artist Antonio Poggi he commissioned copies of Raphael's famous *Madonna della Sedia* in the Palazzo Pitti, Florence, and of Rubens' *Philosophers* in the Uffizi.[63] In addition he was sometimes obliged to commission copies of the paintings he did arrange to buy, not for himself, but for the owners of the originals, who frequently made this a condition of sale. In the case of the Salvator Rosas, in Florence, Spencer ordered copies from the resident English painter Thomas Patch.[64]

Spencer also took an interest in contemporary painting. He regularly attended exhibitions at the Royal Academy, to which he sometimes lent works, and patronized a number of the leading painters of his day. From Sir Joshua Reynolds he commissioned a celebrated series of family portraits which remain among the most beautiful and affecting the painter ever produced.[65] He also commissioned portraits from Thomas Gainsborough, sitting to the artist himself around 1763, as well as Pompeo Batoni, Angelica Kauffmann, Nathaniel Dance and lesser painters such as Robert Edge Pine and William Lane. At the same time he patronized the pastel painter Katherine Read and the miniaturist Jean Etienne Liotard (FIG 26, p. 57)[66] while commissioning animal paintings from George Stubbs (including a portrait of 'Mouton'),[67] Neapolitan views from Tolli[68] and Classical history paintings from Gavin Hamilton[69] and Francesco Zuccarelli.[70]

Spencer was particularly noted for his love of old master drawings, of which he formed an impressive collection, including a rare volume of studies ascribed to Pieter Brueghel. To these were added drawings by contemporary artists such as Gainsborough, Boucher and Bouchardon.[71] Spencer was himself an amateur draughtsman and engraver[72] and perhaps took lessons from the artist John Alexander Gresse, whom he engaged as drawing master to his children.[73] In addition to drawings Spencer also collected old prints, a selection of which he acquired through the painter and dealer George Knapton in 1756.[74]

During his visit to Italy Spencer conceived a particular passion for Antique statuary, of which he soon became a discerning judge. However, he quickly discovered that genuine examples were extremely scarce and subject to heavy trade and export controls, placing them almost beyond reach, even for a collector of his financial resources. As he expressed it himself in a letter to England from Rome, 'Ye sculptures I now grow to admire as much as any paintings, & cou'd I think take more pleasure in them; but this is a taste not so easily indulged as ye other for no money will purchase a capital statue of ye ancients, & a moderate one I think a very bad thing'.[75] Through Sir William Hamilton, he was in treaty at one time for a head of Mercury, then in a private collection in Capua;[76] he also came close to acquiring a statue of Bacchus, and another representing a faun, both offered for sale by Gavin Hamilton in Rome.[77] However, his only recorded acquisition was a relief of the nymph Egeria, formerly in the Palazzo Barberini in Rome, which he had particularly admired on his visit in 1763–64, and which was acquired on his behalf by Gavin Hamilton from another well-known dealer, Colin Morison. The relief is no longer in the Spencer collection, and all attempts to trace it have failed, but from documents in the Spencer archive it can be ascertained that it represented the scene from Ovid's *Metamorphoses* in which Egeria, heart-broken at the death of her husband Numa, and weeping copious tears, was turned into a fountain by the goddess Diana.[78]

Alongside the trade in genuine and not-so-genuine antiquities was another in miniature copies, generally of marble or bronze, which were used as ornaments on tables and

[61] Ibid., 23 Jan 1770

[62] *A Catalogue of the Noble Collection of Pictures, Miniatures, Bronzes, Gems, magnificent Embossed Plate, Ornaments in Gold and Silver, Coins and Medals, China, Japan, &c. of the Right Honourable Lady Elizabeth Germain, Lately Deceas'd; Being the Collection of the Old Earls of Peterborough; and also the Arundelian Collection*, Mr Langford & Son, Covent Garden, London, 7–10 Mar 1770. The *Glaucus and Scylla* was sold for £55:13:0, but not to the Spencers [2nd day, Lot 75]

[63] AP F117, GH to GS, 12 May 1770. Poggi had earlier tried, but failed, to secure permission to copy a Correggio in Parma

[64] James Martin, MS *Journal of his Grand Tour 1763/65*, 17 Nov 1764 [SBFP]

[65] AP F114, GSH to GS, Dec 1756; AP F122, GS to TC, 9 June 1772

[66] AP F122, GS to TC, May 1754

[67] AP F101, GSH to GS, 10 Apr 1766

[68] AP F117, WH to JS, 22 Jan 1765; BL Add MS 41200, ff.121–6 [SBFP]

[69] HB, Account of JS, Ledger D, f.372, 18 Apr 1768; Ledger E, f.266, 10 July 1772. The painting by Hamilton, *Agrippina with the Ashes of Germanicus*, was sold by the 8th Earl Spencer and is now in the collection

chimney-pieces. Spencer did not think such copies beneath him and acquired a set in marble representing three of the famous statues from the Tribuna at the Uffizi in Florence which he had particularly admired on the Grand Tour. The statues he chose were the *Arrotino*, the *Medici Venus* and the *Apollino*, and the copies, supplied once again by Gavin Hamilton, he pronounced 'very clever'.[79]

Spencer also took an interest in contemporary sculpture and during his visit to Rome was introduced to the resident English sculptor Joseph Nollekens, from whom he commissioned a version of his famous *Boy on a Dolphin* (FIG 139, p. 156). From the silversmith Thomas Gilpin he ordered a splendid dinner service (FIG 69, p. 108),[80] and he also made significant additions to the family collection of jewellery. In 1764, while travelling through Italy, he was introduced to the Venetian antiquary, Antonio Maria Zanetti, from whom he purchased a celebrated ring, formerly belonging to Prince Eugene of Savoy, mounted with a cameo in the form of a crouching leopard, believed to date from the Renaissance. In 1766 he was in treaty for an Antique cameo in Rome, then in the possession of the English dealer Thomas Jenkins,[81] and he later purchased several Antique-style cameos and intaglios from the celebrated Austrian gem-engraver Johan Anton Pichler and his son Giovanni.[82] During his courtship and honeymoon, moreover, he presented his fiancée Georgiana with numerous tokens of love in the form of seals, brooches and rings with sentimental inscriptions.[83] By contrast he seems to have had little interest in porcelain and pottery. His father had been a great collector,[84] but he frankly confessed that he had 'an aversion to China & Japan'[85] and is not thought to have made any significant acquisitions in this area,[86] although it is likely that at least some of the fine eighteenth-century porcelain at Althorp today entered the collection during his lifetime. The one exception he made was Antique vases. Although he is not known to have acquired any examples for himself, he followed with interest the publication of Sir William Hamilton's books on the subject. After perusing the first volume he praised Sir William; among the contents, he declared, were 'some pretty things'.[87]

Spencer was especially drawn to architecture, and it was here that he made his greatest contribution to the artistic life of the period. His interests were broad; an etching in his hand at the British Museum shows a building of Elizabethan or Jacobean date.[88] But his tastes were predominantly for the Classical tradition. He subscribed to some of the key architectural publications of the period, while on a more practical level he undertook extensive building works and gave employment to some of the foremost architects and craftsmen of the day. The house at Althorp was twice overhauled, first in 1755 and again in 1772–73,[89] the latter project involving Sir Robert Taylor, architect of the Bank of England. The grounds at Althorp were similarly remodelled, the old formal gardens being largely replaced by a landscape park designed by the leading exponent in this field, Capability Brown.[90] At Wimbledon, too, Brown laid out a magnificent landscape park,[91] while the house, as we shall see, was substantially redecorated. Spencer also made improvements to the house he owned at North Creake, as well as Pytchley Hall and a property he rented nearby at Farming Woods.[92] But his most important building project, indeed his most important single act of artistic patronage, was unquestionably the construction of Spencer House.

For all the land and possessions he inherited in 1755, the year he came of age, John Spencer lacked an adequate London residence. Sunderland House, the old family mansion on Piccadilly, had been sold in 1745, and the houses he inherited in Grosvenor Street and Upper Brook Street were no substitute. Spencer required a proper base from which to launch himself; a house that would provide a suitably splendid setting for the lavish

of the Tate Gallery, whose Trustees have recently placed it on loan at Spencer House

70 AP F117, WH to JS, 23 Jan 1770

71 *Catalogue of a Superb Cabinet of Drawings: The Entire Collection of a Nobleman [i.e. George John, 2nd Earl Spencer] Formed with Refined Taste and Judgement, About the Middle of the Last Century [i.e. by John, 1st Earl Spencer] ... which will be sold by Auction under the Direction of Mr T[homas] Philipe,* 10–18 June 1811

72 An etching by Spencer is preserved in BMPD, C.6*

73 Gresse was art tutor to George III

74 AP F169. A payment to Knapton, possibly related to this transaction, is recorded in HB, Account of JS, Ledger Y, f.251, 13 Apr 1757

75 JS to GSH, 13 Apr 1764, in Edward William Harcourt (ed.), *The Harcourt Papers*, 8, p.76

76 AP F117, WH to JS, 22 Jan 1765, JS to WH 25 Dec 1765

77 Ibid., GH to JS, 26 June 1766, GS to GH, 28 July 1768

78 Ibid., GH to JS 29 Jan 1766, GH to GS, 26 June 1766, GS to GH, 28 July 1766

79 AP F117, JS to WH, 25 Dec 1765

80 HB, Account of JS, Ledger Y, f.248, 25 Mar 1756

81 AP F117, GH to GS, 12 Oct 1766

82 Ibid., GH to GS, 12 Oct 1766, 11 Apr, 20 May 1767, 12 May 1770; Forrer, op. cit.

83 AP F122

84 AP L15

85 AP F117, JS to WH, 25 Dec 1765

86 AP F191 [minor orders from Wedgwood]

87 AP F117, JS to WH, Dec 1769

88 See n.72

89 AP F195

90 Brown had earlier been employed by Spencer's stepfather, Lord Cowper [HRO, Cowper Papers A8]

91 AP F41, CH to GS, Mar 1764; AP F100, GBV to GS, 13 May 1763; AP F101, GBV to GS, 15 May 1764; AP F197–F198; HB, Account of JS, payments to Brown spanning period July 1759 to Nov 1766 and totalling £8628, in Ledgers A, ff.266–7; B, ff.77–8; C, ff.129–30, 231–2, 468; D, f.133

92 AP F195

entertainments he planned and the magnificent collection of art treasures he would form; which would provide a home for his family and servants and an impressive establishment in which to conduct political and financial business; which, through its size and opulence and the quality of its design, would reflect his wealth, status and taste, consolidating and advancing his position in society and winning the respect and envy of his contemporaries.

Lord Montfort's suicide gave Spencer the opportunity he was looking for. It was not the most auspicious beginning, but the site in St James's Place was irresistible. The freeholder, Lady Burlington, was an old family friend and relation, and by the autumn of 1755 Spencer had acquired a lease, which was later extended and ultimately converted to freehold ownership.[93] He also persuaded Lady Burlington to grant him an additional piece of land adjacent to the site, enabling him to build on an even larger scale.[94]

[93] The original lease granted by the dowager Countess Burlington was extended by her heir the Duke of Devonshire on 24 June 1760 for a period of 99 years and at some time before 1766 the lease was converted to freehold [AP D31]

[94] The site originally granted to Montfort was considerably smaller, measuring approximately 100 feet from east to west and 68 feet from north to south [PRO CRES 2 / 816]

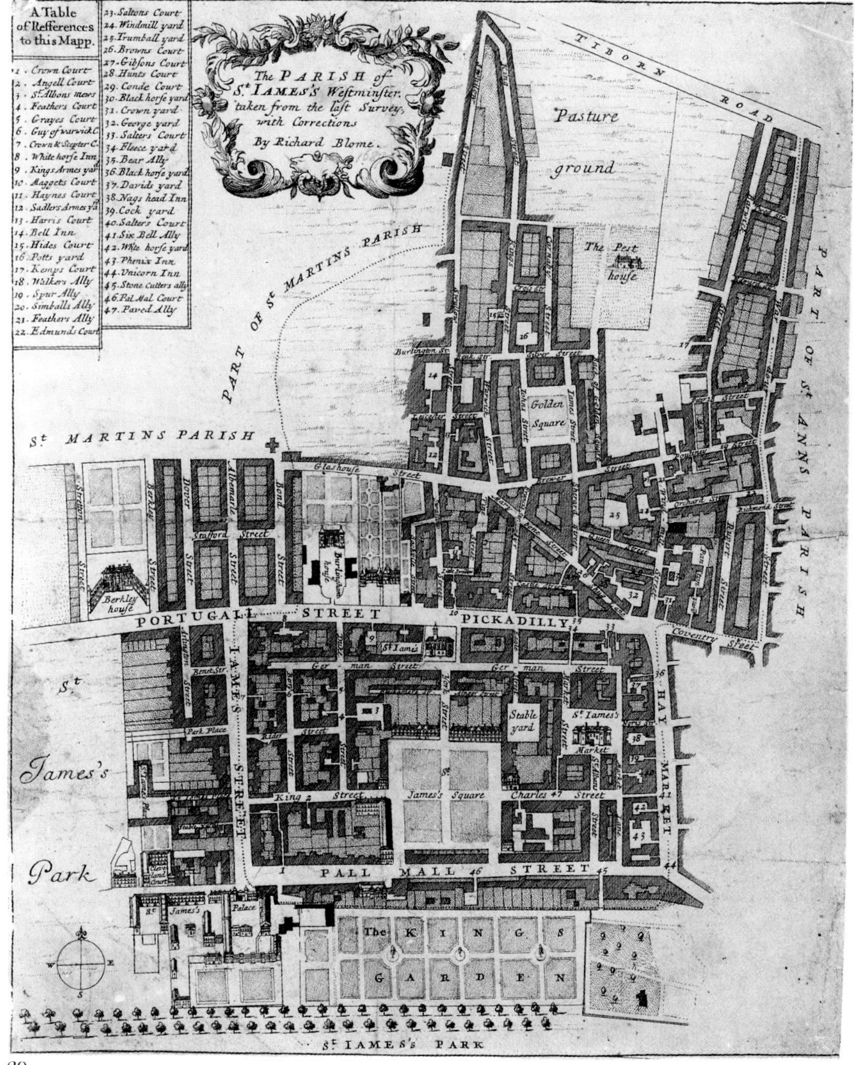

20

20 Plan of the Parish of St. James's, Westminster, *by Richard Blome (1689). The development of the area continued apace. St James's Place had been opened up to its full extent, the garden of Cleveland House having been shortened to make room for it*

21 *A bird's eye view of St James's, from William Faithmore,* An Exact Deliveration of the Cities of London and Westminster and the Suburbs *(1658). At the time this plan was made the development of St James's had barely begun. St James's Square had not yet been laid out, and the site of Spencer House was occupied by the garden of an earlier mansion, Berkshire House*

22 *Plan of St James's, from William Morgan,* London &c Actually Survey'd and A Prospect of London and Westminster *(1682). The development of St James's was now underway, with a network of streets having grown up on both sides of St James's Street. Berkshire House had been demolished, but another mansion, Cleveland House, stood in its place, the rest of the site being taken up with smaller buildings and yards. The opening up of St James's Place had begun [see key, 163], but had not yet reached the boundary with Green Park*

5 HEALTH, CONVENIENCE AND BEAUTY

IT IS NOT HARD TO SEE why Spencer should have chosen to build in St James's. Since its development in the late seventeenth century the area had been considered among the smartest in the capital.[1] In a guide to London published in 1720 St James's was described as 'well replenished with fine open streets, which are graced with good buildings, and generally well inhabited'.[2] In 1753 it was calculated that in St James's Square alone four Dukes and eight Earls had their London residence,[3] while in Arlington Street there were so many senior politicians that, according to Horace Walpole, an address here was almost *de rigueur* for anyone with ambitions of becoming a cabinet minister.[4]

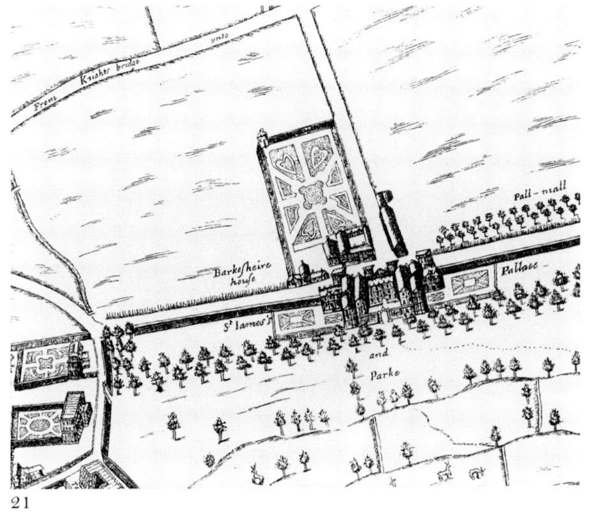

21

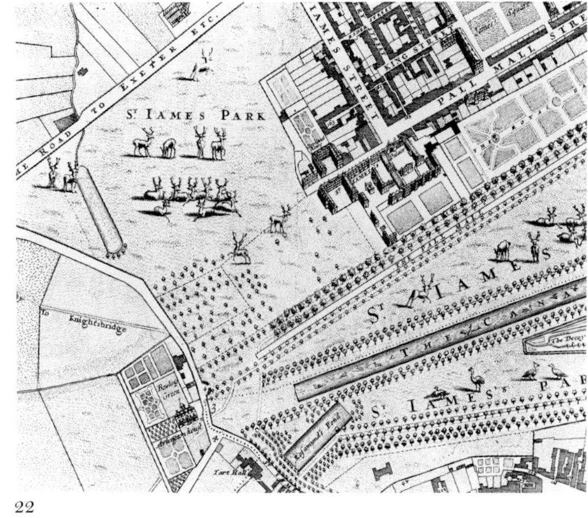

22

St James's Place itself was laid out in two stages, which accounts for its unusual L-shaped formation. Work on the first stage began some time before the mid-1660s (FIGS 20–22). The earliest buildings were relatively modest, but from the turn of the eighteenth century grander houses were erected, particularly at the western end along the perimeter of Green Park (FIG 23). As one early eighteenth-century commentator expressed it, St James's Place was 'a good street . . . The Houses are well built, and inhabited by Gentry'.[5] In 1734 the occupants of St James's Place included five peers, among them the Duke of St Albans and the Earls of Anglesey and Bradford, seven titled ladies (one of them a senior member of the aristocracy), an assortment of Baronets and Knights, a Bishop, and various members of the armed services and the professions.[6] By 1755, when Spencer purchased the site of Spencer House, they had been joined by the famous diarist and hostess Lady Hervey, and in later years other notable figures would settle here, including Mrs Delaney, Edward Gibbon and the poet laureate William Whitehead.

[1] The development of St James's prior to the construction of Spencer House can be traced through maps, plans and topographical views of the period, many of which are listed in James Howgego, *Printed Maps of London, circa 1553–1850*, 2nd edn (Folkestone, 1978), and in Bernard Adams, *London Illustrated 1604–1851: A Survey and Index of Topographical Books and their Plates* (1983). Among the printed sources the most noteworthy are William Faithmore, *An Exact Deliveration of the Cities of London and Westminster and the Suburbs* (1658); William Morgan, *London &c Actually Survey'd and A Prospect of London and Westminster* (1682); Richard Blome, *Plan of the Parish of St. James's, Westminster* (1689); John Kip, *Veue et Perspective de la Ville de Londre, Westminster Parc St Jacques* (*c*1710), and *Her Majesties Royal Palace and Park of St James's* (1715); John Rocque, *A Plan of the Cities of London and Westminster and Borough of Southwark* (1746). In addition there are several maps in manuscript form, which help to fill out the picture, notably *Land to North-West of St James's Park, now Green Park* (*c*1650) [PRO MPE 497]; *Lands in the Bailiwick of St James, between Piccadilly, St. James's Park, and Hyde Park* (1664) [PRO MR 325]; *St James's Street [reign of Charles II] (c1664)* [PRO MPE 506]; J. P. Desmaretz, *Survey of Westminster, Chelsea, and Kensington* (1717) [PRO MPH 258]; William Gough, *A Plan of His Majesty's Bayliwick of St James in the County of Middlesex* (1746) [BL (Maps), Crace Coll. Portfolio XII, No. 1]

[2] John Strype, *A Survey of the Cities of London and Westminster*, 2 vols (1720), 2, pp.80–81

[3] John Stow, *The History and Survey of the Cities of London and Westminster*, 2 vols (1753), I, p.663

[4] At one time or another Arlington Street was home to two Prime Ministers, Sir Robert Walpole and Henry Pelham, as well as several members of the Cabinet. Half in jest, half seriously, Horace Walpole remarked in 1743 'This is absolutely the ministerial street: Carteret has a house here too, and Lord Bath seems to have lost his chance by quitting this street' [Walpole to Sir Horace Mann, 25 May 1743, quoted in Nicholas Thompson *et al.*, *A House in Town: 22 Arlington Street, Its Owners and Builders* (1984), p.108]

[5] Strype, op. cit., p.78

[6] Beginning in 1716, the occupants of St James's Place can be identified from rate books in the local studies division of the WPL; also from documents at the PRO, notably CRES 2 / 1663; CRES 2 / 816; MR 271; MR 272

It was said at the time that there was no better location in London 'for Health, Convenience, or Beauty',[7] and the site acquired by Spencer was especially well-placed, since it adjoined the park and so had the benefit of good, clean air, a rare commodity in Georgian London and something of an obsession in the eighteenth century.[8] Constitution Hill, at the top of Green Park, was widely considered to be the most sanitary spot in the capital, a 'Health-restoring Eminence' as one writer described it,[9] renowned for 'the salubrity of the air'.[10] For John Spencer, who suffered all his life from bouts of ill health, this would have been an important consideration.

Moreover, since St James's Place was closed at one end with no through traffic, the Spencers would be spared the noise and pollution which characterized the busier thoroughfares of the city, choked with traffic of every description; horses and cattle; littered with rubbish and manure; dusty in warm weather, awash with mud when it rained; and rowdy with the cries of hawkers, barrow boys and others screaming to make themselves heard above the general din. By comparison St James's Place was a perfect oasis and the only time there was likely to be any disturbance was when Spencer himself, or one of his distinguished neighbours, entertained.

As to convenience, the site was only a few hundred yards from the Court at St James's Palace, while the Houses of Parliament could be reached by carriage in a matter of minutes. Many of Spencer's closest relations and friends lived in and around St James's. His grandfather, Lord Granville, had a house in Arlington Street, as did his cousin Lord Weymouth and his friend Sir William Hamilton. In 1758, moreover, work began on Pomfret Castle, a Gothic-style mansion in Arlington Street, for another relation, the Countess of Pomfret. The Dowager Viscountess Bateman, Spencer's maternal aunt, who later stood as godmother to his son, lived in Cleveland Row, as did Spencer's great-uncle, Frances, 2nd Earl of Godolphin, and the Duke of Bridgwater, who was related to Spencer by virtue of his marriage to Elizabeth Churchill, daughter of the great Duke of Marlborough. Spencer's uncle, the 3rd Duke of Marlborough, lived at Marlborough House off the Mall, while his mother and step-father were only a short distance away in Upper Brook Street.

At the same time there was easy access to shops and other local amenities. Household provisions, such as meat, vegetables and fruit, would largely have been supplied from Althorp, but if ever there was any shortage servants could be despatched to local victuallers, such as the grocer Charles Fortnum, who started his famous business in Piccadilly around this time and whose name appears in a trade directory kept by Spencer's wife.[11] There was also an open-air market, conveniently situated on the far side of St James's Square. Although the Spencers generally ordered their wine through friends on the Continent, there were plentiful supplies at Berry Brothers & Rudd in St James's Street, where there are records of orders from the family. Attracted by a rich and cultivated clientele, art dealers had also begun to settle in the area, as had their colleagues in the book trade, thus beginning an association which has lasted to this day. In 1767 the auction house, Christie's, opened in Pall Mall, and one imagines that Spencer, an avid collector, often ventured out in search of rare books and works of art, pausing also perhaps to inspect the latest wares of local outfitters such as Lock's, the hatters, which had started up in business in St James's Street in 1726.

There were several theatres, most notably the King's Theatre in Haymarket, of which Spencer was a regular patron, as well as numerous coffee houses and taverns, including the famous Star and Garter in Pall Mall, a favourite watering-hole for the members of the Society of Dilettanti. There was also a growing number of gentleman's clubs, of which Spencer is known to have joined at least two, Brooks's and White's.

23 A view of St James's and the area to the east, from J. Kip, Veue et Perspective de la Ville de Londre, Westminster, Parc St Jacques *[sic] (c1710). The site of Spencer House is just out of sight (left), but the wall of Green Park is clearly visible in the foreground*

[7] C. Corbett, *London in Miniature: Being a Concise and Comprehensive Description of the Cities of London and Westminster* (1755), p.195

[8] John Strype remarked, 'St. James's Place . . . openeth wide, and receiveth a fresh Air out of the Park' [op. cit., p.78]

[9] W. Nicoll, *The London and Westminster Guide* (1768). The identical description is given in Sir John Fielding, *A Brief Description of the Cities of London and Westminster* (1776), pp.17–18

[10] Scatcherd & Whitaker (publ.), *Ambulator: or, A Pocket Companion in a Tour Round London* (1793), p.7

[11] AP F200

[12] *New Review of London* (1728), quoted in Nicholas Thompson, op. cit., p.103

[13] John Woolfe and James Gandon, *Vitruvius Britannicus*, IV (1767), p.6

23

Another advantage was the uninterrupted view of Green Park. With deer and cattle roaming freely in the foreground, and the hills of Surrey rising above the tree tops on the horizon, it was like a landscape by Cuyp come to life. Those who lived on the fringes must sometimes have wondered if, by some magic, they had not been transported to the countryside. Writing of Arlington Street, which likewise backed on to the park, a contemporary remarked, 'The front of the street is in the midst of the hurry of the town; and the back is in the quiet simplicity of the country'.[12] The same point was made in relation to Spencer House itself by the authors of *Vitruvius Britannicus*, who wrote, 'The situation . . . is admirably fine, enjoying at once the advantage of town and country'.[13]

The park was also a place to stroll and take exercise, the perfect location for horse-riding. No less important, it was a place where society wandered. Like St James's Park, it was a parading ground for the nobility and gentry, the 'focus', it was said, 'of beauty, rank and fashion', thronged by 'numberless pedestrians who in gay, cheerful and well-dressed groups, give an animation to the scene, of which only those who have witnessed it can form an adequate conception'.[14] In building his house on the edge of the park Spencer was sure to attract attention; indeed he could hardly have chosen a more conspicuous location.

The only disadvantage was a wall running along the western perimeter of the site, dividing the street from the park, and a public footpath on the near side of this wall which provided a link between St James's Place and Catherine Wheel Yard. Lord Montfort had tried to have this footpath closed or covered over, but the Crown, who as owners of the park and freeboard had jurisdiction in this matter, refused.[15] Owing perhaps to his greater influence, and the scale and quality of his plans, Spencer was more successful. Directly he acquired the site, he applied for consent to take down the park wall and build in its place a broad stone terrace surmounted by a balustrade running the full length of the property and projecting about two feet into the park. This was to provide a platform for the magnificent west front, the chief elevation, greatly enhancing its apparent size and grandeur, while offering a delightful spot from which to view the park and take the air. The construction of the terrace involved the relocation of a public sewer running directly beneath the footpath,[16] but similar encroachments had been made by Spencer's neighbours,[17] and on 3 March 1756, after consulting with the Ranger of St James's Park, the King gave consent for the terrace to be built, authorizing the closure of the public footpath and surrendering the narrow strip of ground in Green Park free of charge.[18] The way was now clear for Spencer to proceed with the construction of his house.

[14] John B. Papworth, *Select Views of London* (1816), pp.16–17. Papworth's remarks are echoed in an earlier guide to London for French visitors, where the author comments, '*Il y a dans Green-Parc une promenade appellée Constitution Hill, fort fréquentée*' [Lerouge (publ.), *Curiosités de Londres et de l'Angleterre*, 2nd edn (Bordeaux, 1766), p.17]

[15] PRO CRES 2 / 816

[16] AP P2.1063E, *A General Outline of the Ground in St James's Place where Mr Spencer's House stands and the adjacent Buildings*

[17] PRO CRES 2 / 816

[18] Following the passing of the Nullum Tempus Act Spencer had to apply for a renewal of the warrant [AP F43, CH to GS, 23 Apr 1773]

1 John, 1st Earl Spencer (1734–83), by Thomas Gainsborough, c1763. The portrait is believed to have been painted at Bath during one of Spencer's frequent visits. In later years the painter worked from a studio in Pall Mall a short distance from Spencer House

6 A MERE MISS POYNTZ

THE CONSTRUCTION OF SPENCER HOUSE was not a task which Spencer faced alone. In this, as in so many other undertakings, he was assisted by his wife Georgiana (PLATE II). Indeed to a large extent the house was built for Georgiana, and for the life which Spencer hoped to share with her. Spencer purchased the site a short time after their engagement and construction began in the period immediately following their marriage. The project dominated their first years of life together and was an early opportunity for them to work as a couple, planning, discussing and sharing ideas. The house provided them with their first real home in London, one of their very own making, and a conspicuous feature of its design are the many symbolic references to love, harmony and matrimony. It is clear Georgiana took an active part in the project, especially the furnishing and decoration of the interior and the choice of paintings and objects; she also made a vital contribution to the life of the house in the years following its completion. Before proceeding any further, therefore, it is important to provide some account of Georgiana and of the remarkable events of her courtship and marriage to John Spencer.

There was considerable surprise when it was announced in society that John Spencer, scion of one of England's most illustrious families, and heir to one of the greatest fortunes in the kingdom, was to marry Georgiana Poyntz. The girl had little money and her family was relatively obscure; nor was she any great beauty. And yet to anyone in full possession of the facts it would have seemed that Georgiana was the ideal partner.

The Poyntz family had been established in England since the Conquest and many of Georgiana's early ancestors had been powerful landowners and trusted royal servants. However, in the aftermath of the Civil War, the family lost influence and by the seventeenth century had declined to such an extent that Georgiana's grandfather was forced into trade, working as an upholsterer and tapestry weaver in the City of London. It was only in the lifetime of her father, Stephen Poyntz (1685–1750) (FIG 24), that the family began the hard climb back to prominence, and it was entirely due to his exceptional merits and industry that Georgiana was able to make so advantageous a marriage.

Stephen Poyntz was educated at Eton College, afterwards winning a scholarship to King's College, Cambridge, where he graduated as an M.A., with a fellowship, in 1711. After a brief period as private tutor to the children of Viscount Townshend and various travels on the Continent, apparently in company with the Duke of Devonshire, he found employment as Joint Treasurer of the Excise and afterwards Envoy Extraordinary and Minister Plenipotentiary to the King of Sweden. A few years later he was appointed one of Britain's representatives at the Congress of Cambrai and on his return was chosen to serve as Governor to the young Duke of Cumberland, the second son of George II. This gave him an entrée to the royal circle and direct access to the King, with whom his influence was said at one time to be as great as that of the Prime Minister. In 1735

II Georgiana, Countess Spencer, by Pompeo Batoni, Rome, 1764. The portrait was painted during the Spencers' Grand Tour and shows Georgiana in the characteristic attitude of a lady of culture. The early guitar and book of compositions attest to her love of music, while the ruins in the background recall her fascination with Classical art and architecture. 'Rome & Rome only', she declared, 'is the place to see and admire the perfection to which painting, sculpture and architecture have been carried'

24 The Rt. Hon. Stephen Poyntz, by Jean Baptiste Van Loo. Although of noble ancestry, Stephen Poyntz was the son of a tapestry weaver and upholsterer yet rose to wealth and social prominence. It was largely due to his success that his daughter, Georgiana, was able to marry so distinguished an aristocrat as John Spencer

Poyntz was sworn of the Privy Council and when the Duke of Cumberland came to form his own household, Poyntz was appointed Steward, remaining a close adviser until his death in 1750.

In 1733 Stephen Poyntz married Anna Maria Mordaunt (FIG 25), daughter and co-heiress of a senior Army officer, Brigadier General Lewis Mordaunt. Anna was wealthy and well-connected, being a niece of the Earl of Peterborough. She was also a famous beauty and a great royal favourite, constantly in attendance at Court, where she served as Maid of Honour to Queen Caroline. In Court circles she was known as '*La Bavardé*' because of her endless chatter, and several of her contemporaries, including Gibbon, found her an insufferable bore. However, she also had charm and an uncanny ability to diagnose and cure all manner of physical complaints, earning the undying gratitude of the French royal family when, on a visit to Versailles, she cured Madame Victoire, a daughter of Louis XV, of a painful illness which had baffled the best medical brains of France.

Three years after his marriage Stephen Poyntz purchased Midgham Park, a large estate near Newbury in Berkshire, thereby cementing his ties with the landed gentry.

25 Anna Maria Poyntz, by Jeremiah Davison, 1735. Known in Court circles as 'La Bavarde', *Georgiana's mother was garrulous to a point that some found intolerable, but she was also a great royal favourite*

Under the direction of the well-known architect Henry Flitcroft the house at Midgham was remodelled. In due course five children were born, four of whom survived. A son, William, was born in 1734 and ultimately inherited. It was a mark of the family's standing at Court that the Queen consented to be his godmother while the Duke of Cumberland readily agreed to stand as godfather. After studying at Christ Church, Oxford, William married Isabella Courtenay, a descendant of Ralph, Duke of Montagu, and sister-in-law of the Earl of Cork, and gladly settled down to the life of a country squire at Midgham. A second son, Charles, was born in 1735. Princess Amelia, daughter of George II, was his godmother, and he followed his brother to Christ Church, where he took Holy Orders. Through the Spencer influence he later became Rector of North Creake in Norfolk, Prebend of Llandaff Cathedral and Dean of Durham. A daughter, Louisa, died unmarried at an early age but was briefly engaged to the Duke of Devonshire.

Georgiana was born at St James's Palace on 8 May 1737 and was named in honour of the King, George II, who stood as godfather at her christening. She was striking rather than beautiful, although some saw a resemblance to the captivating Duchess of Grafton. The artist James Martin, who saw her at a reception in Florence, thought her the most attractive woman present, 'much handsomer', he wrote, 'than any of the Italian Ladys'.[1] Her poise was impeccable, her figure admirable, and she dressed and danced to perfection. In contrast to Spencer, her health was excellent. Although she twice miscarried, she bore her husband three healthy children, including an heir, and survived into her late seventies, remaining fit and active to the end.

Georgiana's physical constitution was matched by a robust moral sense. She was deeply religious, an active figure in the Sunday School movement; her papers are full of hand-written prayers, and she kept a close eye on her servants' attendance at church. On one occasion she scolded the Bishop of Derry for irreligion after he dared to expound on the commercial advantages of Sunday trading, and in Italy she was scandalized by the *cicisbeo* system, whereby a married woman of rank and fashion was expected, if not required, to carry on at least one extra-marital affair. Like Spencer, she involved herself in a wide range of charitable works, being especially active in the field of education and the welfare of the sick and elderly. It is true she had a weakness for cards, but in all other respects her conduct was exemplary, although she was powerless, as we shall see, to prevent her daughters from straying dangerously from the path of righteous or even semi-respectable behaviour.

Georgiana was also exceptionally intelligent and well-educated. Among her many accomplishments she could write and converse in faultless French and Italian. At the same time she shared many of Spencer's interests. She was evidently musical, for she mastered a variety of instruments, including the viol da gamba, the harpsichord, the piano and the guitar.[2] She kept a box at the opera and frequently attended concerts and recitals. She subscribed to music by the French philosopher Jean Jacques Rousseau[3] and also gave support and encouragement to Vincenzo Orgitano, musical tutor to the daughters of the King of Naples,[4] as well as the violinist and composer Felice Giardini, who dedicated to her six trios for the guitar, violin and piano forte.

Georgiana also had a love of theatre; she was a great admirer of the Shakespearean actress Hannah Pritchard[5] and formed a particularly close attachment to David Garrick, with whom she corresponded for more than fifteen years.[6] Her reading was extensive,[7] and in her preferred subjects, history and literature, she could hold her own with any young man from the Universities. Horace Walpole once referred to her jokingly as 'the Goddess of Wisdom',[8] and indeed she was something of a blue-stocking, being an amateur poetess,[9] the founder of a conversational club for ladies[10] and a regular at Mrs Montagu's literary gatherings.

Georgiana had a particular love of the fine and decorative arts; she was herself a keen needleworker[11] and amateur artist, taking drawing lessons from a professional master in London.[12] Her enthusiasm was matched by considerable knowledge and tastes which accorded well with Spencer's. In a list she made of the paintings in her Dressing Room at Spencer House she carefully noted the subjects and artists, but also the schools to which these artists belonged and the masters under whom they had studied (see Appendix III). Like Spencer she particularly admired the art of the High Renaissance and the *seicento*, and her visit to Italy was spent in a state of rapture. She was spellbound in Parma by the 'glorious Correggios',[13] while in Bologna she noted 'many fine pictures . . . the famous St Cecilia by Raphael, the martyrdom of St Agnes by Domenichino, many good Carraccis . . . and a fine crucifiction by Guido & his Capital Picture of the St. Peter and St. Paul'.[14] In Florence she stood entranced before Raphael's famous *Madonna della Sedia*, while in the Tribuna of the Uffizi she succumbed, like Spencer, to the beauty of the Antique statues. As she expressed it in a letter to England, 'The very capital ones are the four famous statues of the Venus of Medici, the dancing Faun, the two Wrestlers, & the Arrotino, or

[1] James Martin, MS *Journal of his Grand Tour 1763/65*, 9 vols, entry for 28 Oct 1763 [SBFP]

[2] AP F201; AP F122, GS to TC, 17 Apr 1761

[3] AP F174

[4] AP F117, WH to GS, 26 Mar 1782

[5] AP F114, GSH to GS, 1768

[6] AP F116

[7] AP F45, GS to CH

[8] W. S. Lewis, *The Yale Edition of Horace Walpole's Correspondence*, 35, p.357

[9] AP F170

[10] AP F174

[11] AP F199. In June 1772 the cabinet-makers Gordon & Taitt supplied

slave, which are all in a room belonging to the Gallery, where there is likewise a great Collection of fine Busts, Bronzes, Pictures &c, but these statues are the chief & are indeed amazingly fine & expressive'.[15] But for Georgiana, as for Spencer, the high-point of the Italian trip was Rome. After touring the Classical remains of the Forum and the Palatine, the Papal and Princely collections of Antique and modern statuary and paintings Georgiana declared, 'Rome, & Rome only, is the place to see and admire the perfection to which painting, sculpture, and architecture have been carried'.[16] While in Rome Georgiana sat to Batoni (PLATE II, p. 50); at other times she sat to Reynolds, Gainsborough and Angelica Kauffmann. Several of these portraits were engraved. Georgiana clearly played an important auxiliary role in Spencer's activities as a patron and collector; indeed she became an active patron and collector in her own right. From the artist John Flaxman she commissioned a series of illustrations from Aeschylus which were afterwards engraved and published.[17] She likewise commissioned portraits from Reynolds and at one stage used her influence to smooth the path for Zoffany when he travelled to Florence to paint his famous picture of the Tribuna.[18] After Spencer's death she undertook the remodelling of the house and grounds at Holywell.[19]

Another shared interest was sport. Georgiana was a keen horsewoman and naturally joined the Althorp and Pytchley Hunts. Even in London she would sometimes venture out on horseback rather than travel by carriage or chair. Although she claimed to have little understanding of politics, her correspondence is full of political reflections and gossip, and she evidently played her part in Spencer's career as an M.P. and a member of the House of Lords.

Georgiana had none of Spencer's shyness and was perfectly at ease in society, where her qualities won her many friends and admirers. Lord Bristol described her as 'my model of a woman . . . She has so decided a character that nothing can warp it, and then such simplicity of manners one would think she had never lived out of the country, with such elegance 'tis as if she had never lived in it'.[20] Cardinal Albani, the great antiquarian, whom she met in Rome in 1764, described Georgiana as the most accomplished woman he had ever met,[21] while for the politician Richard Rigby she was, and would always be, 'the first woman in the world'.[22] Madame du Deffand, doyenne of the Parisian literary establishment, was another great admirer and reported in letters that on a visit to Paris in 1772 Georgiana had taken the city by storm.[23] Laurence Sterne dedicated a section of *Tristram Shandy* to Georgiana;[24] Sheridan did likewise with his monody on the actor David Garrick, reasoning that her 'approval and esteem were justly considered by Mr. Garrick as the Highest Panegyrick his Talents or Conduct could acquire'.[25] The poet Sir William Jones declared that without her inspiration he would never have composed his *Solima*.[26] Georgiana's correspondents included Edmund Burke, the Prince of Hesse, the Princess of Orange, the Electress Palatine, the duchesse de Bourbon and the wife of Prince Ferdinand of Prussia.[27] Princess Esterhazy made Georgiana a present of her portrait. The Prince of Wales expressed his devotion by sending her a barrel of his favourite Dutch pickled herrings.

Little wonder then that the young John Spencer was immediately captivated. It was true, Georgiana had little money; 'A mere Miss Poyntz' was Walpole's acid verdict.[28] But with a vast fortune of his own to look forward to, Spencer had no real need of a dowry and lost no time in proposing. Nor did he ever have cause to regret his decision. His marriage to Georgiana was one of the great love-matches of the day. Even the Duke of Queensberry, a notorious cynic, was forced to concede that the Spencers were 'really the happiest people I ever saw in the marriage system. *Enfin c'est le meilleur ménage possible*'.[29]

the Spencers with 'a neat inlaid firescreen, one side cover'd with her Ladyships Needlework'

[12] The name of John Wood, a drawing master in Beaumont Street, London, appears in a trade directory kept by Georgiana [AP F200]

[13] AP F41, GS to CH, 29 Oct 1763

[14] Ibid.

[15] Ibid., 2 Nov 1763

[16] Ibid, Jan 1764

[17] *Compositions from the Tragedies of Aeschylus, Designed by John Flaxman, engraved by Thomas Piroli, The Original Drawings in the Possession of the Countess Dowager Spencer* (1795). Georgiana's own copy of this publication is preserved in the John Rylands Library, Manchester, having formed part of sale of the 2nd Earl Spencer's library in 1892

[18] HRO, D/EP F296, GS to WC, 23 June 1772

[19] AP F130

[20] Lady Margaret Douglas-Home, *A Mere Miss Poyntz*

[21] PRO SPF 105/314, Cardinal Albani to Sir Horace Mann, 12 Nov 1763 [SBFP]

[22] George Winchester Stone Jr, and George M. Kahrl, *David Garrick, A Critical Biography* (1979), p.623

[23] In a letter to Horace Walpole Mme du Deffand wrote, '*Milady Spencer a eu le plus grand succès: on n'a jamais eu pour aucune étrangère autant d'empressement et rendu autant d'honneurs; elle les a mérités; on ne peut en effet être plus aimable*' [*Lettres de Madame du Deffand à Horace Walpole 1766–1780*, Mrs Paget Toynbee (ed.), 3 vols (1912), 2, p.506, letter of 13 June 1773]

[24] Laurence Sterne, *The Life and Opinions of Tristram Shandy, Gentleman*, VI (1762)

[25] Richard Brinsley Sheridan, *Verses to the Memory of Garrick. Spoken as a Monody at the Theatre Royal in Drury Lane* (1779); AP F177–F178. The music on this occasion was composed by Thomas Linley, Sheridan's father-in-law, whom the Spencers employed as music master

[26] John Shore, *Memoirs of the Life, Writings, and Correspondence of Sir William Jones*, p.131

[27] AP F130

[28] Douglas-Home, op. cit.

[29] *Letters of David Garrick and Georgiana, Countess Spencer 1759–1779*, Earl Spencer and Christopher Dobson (eds) (Cambridge, 1960), p.xv

7 NEVER WAS SUCH A LOVER

THE COUPLE MET IN LONDON in 1754, possibly through Spencer's grandfather, Lord Granville, who had worked alongside Georgiana's father as joint representative to the Congress of Cambrai many years earlier, or alternatively through Lord Cowper, who was distantly related to the Poyntzes and whose son, Lord Fordwich, had himself been rumoured to be engaged to Georgiana at one time. By all accounts it was love at first sight. Spencer was relentless in his pursuit of Georgiana and received every encouragement from his family, especially his mother, who was said to have been 'in despair' over his former attachment to a ravishing but empty-headed débutante, Miss Bishop.[1] 'Never', wrote Mrs Delaney, 'was such a lover'.[2] In February 1755 the couple were seen together at a performance of Handel's *Allegro Penseroso and Moderato*, utterly absorbed as if in a state of enchantment.

Through a series of frank and often touching letters, Georgiana poured out her feelings to her cousin and confidante, Thea Cowper. The correspondence, in which Georgiana refers to Spencer by the sweet but transparent code-name of 'Recneps', shows the depth of the young girl's attachment, and her growing excitement as the courtship developed.[3]

In the spring of 1755 Georgiana was invited to Wimbledon Park, the Spencers' estate on the outskirts of London, and on her return to the capital immediately penned a full account of the excursion. 'Now my dear Thea,' she announced, 'I will own it & never deny it that I do love Spencer above all men upon Earth.' The party had set off from Lord and Lady Cowper's house in Upper Brook Street. There, Georgiana wrote, 'I saw mon cher Recneps looking handsomer than an angel.' While Spencer and Georgiana's brother made their own way to Wimbledon on horseback, she and Lady Cowper followed by carriage. Over the course of the next few days John and Georgiana were hardly apart, rising before the rest of the party so as to share the first moments of the day together. When the time came for the couple to separate, Georgiana confessed she was 'ready to dye ten times with stifling sighs & tears which were ready to burst.' Spencer too, she wrote, was similarly affected '& by some intelligible signs had me believe he was much in the same condition.' Before parting Spencer gave Georgiana a diamond and ruby ring, the reverse engraved with the inscription, '*Mon Coeur est tout à toi. Garde le bien pour moi*'. As he sped off on horseback, Georgiana could not help admiring the spectacle of her handsome beau 'riding vastly well . . . in his utmost perfection . . . on a very fine prancing grey horse with a long tail & mane his saddle of Green & Gold . . . he did look charmingly. Indeed every body was struck with his figure.'

Separation made Georgiana miserable, and how could it be otherwise, she asked, 'while my dear dear Recneps is away.' 'I wished to God,' she continued, 'he lov'd me half as well as I love him. Oh then I could write of him for ever & not be tir'd.' The couple were soon reunited, however, and to mark the occasion Spencer presented Georgiana with a brooch for her riding habit, composed, as she explained to Thea, of 'two doves a cooing & the Motto on the back part "*Imitons les en Amitié*".'

On one occasion a letter arrived from Spencer while Georgiana was seated at the

[1] John W. Croker (ed.), *Letters of Mary Lepel, Lady Hervey*, p.197

[2] Lady Llanover (ed.), *The Autobiography and Correspondence of Mary Granville, Mrs Delaney*, 3, pp.305, 319

[3] The correspondence is preserved among the Althorp Papers under reference F122. Unless otherwise stated all quotations in this and the chapter which follows are from this source

dinner table with her family. 'Oh Thea,' she wrote, 'I immediately began stuttering stammering & blundering & colour'd so violently that I thought I must have gone from the table.' As winter gave way to spring there were outings to the pleasure gardens at Ranelagh, and other entertainments, and when, that summer, Spencer arrived back in London from the country, handsomer than ever after several days' sport in the sun and open air, Georgiana nearly fainted away. 'Since I was born,' she declared, 'I never saw anything so charming as he is . . . Oh Thea you would adore him if you saw him he is vastly tann'd but ev'ry thing adds to his beauty. If you had seen me when he came in you would have laugh'd at me for I colour'd so much & felt & look'd so silly I did not know whether I was most inclin'd to laugh or cry.'

There was concern in the autumn when Georgiana came down with measles. Lady Cowper feared it was small pox, and Spencer, sharing her concern, gallantly declared that whether or not it was small pox, and whether or not Georgiana's complexion was spoilt, nothing could alter his feelings. From the Home Park at Windsor he sent her 'a large bason full of the very finest roses . . . [and] a nose gay . . . of an immense size, that is past describing there is almost all sorts of sweet flowers among others a good many yellow roses.'

Finally it was announced that the couple were to be married (FIG 26). The wedding was scheduled to take place at Althorp on Saturday, 27 December 1755, a week to the day after Spencer's coming of age. Secretly, however, the couple were planning to marry in private a few days earlier, on 23 December, although no one, not even their immediate family, was aware of this and they themselves would be surprised by the eventual turn of events.

26 John Spencer and Georgiana Poyntz around the time of their engagement; twin miniatures by Jean Etienne Liotard, c1754. From the moment they met John and Georgiana were inseparable; their marriage was one of the great love-matches of the day

8 A CLANDESTINE WEDDING

JOHN SPENCER'S coming-of-age and marriage were events of major importance, especially for the people of Althorp and Northamptonshire, and lavish celebrations were planned. Preparations were already underway when a party consisting of the bride and groom, Lord and Lady Cowper and Georgiana's mother and elder brother set off from London for Althorp on 12 December.

The first night was spent at Holywell House, St Albans, and the following morning the party travelled on to Newport Pagnell, where rooms had been booked in a local inn. A crowd of admirers had gathered in the forecourt there, and Georgiana and her companions had to force their way through to the door. The next day they continued on to Althorp, but twelve miles from the house they were met by the Mayor and Aldermen of Northampton, together with over 100 of the town's tradespeople who had gathered on horseback to escort them on their way. The cavalcade moved on to the gates of Northampton. First to enter the town were the horsemen, riding in pairs, followed by John Spencer's carriage, the carriage of Lord Cowper, three post-chaises for maids and a retinue of servants, all of which, Georgiana wrote, 'made a greater shew than you can imagine.'

The crowds were such that Georgiana feared they would never find a way through, but by late afternoon the party reached Althorp and for two days there was relative calm as the travellers recovered from their exertions. On the Wednesday they inspected a giant enclosure in a nearby field, where a timber structure had been erected for the coming celebrations, together with two other buildings housing a larder and a cellar, and a towering chimney with an oven in which an ox was to be roasted. The following day they visited the kitchens, where an army of cooks and confectioners, many of them French, were busy preparing cakes and other delicacies.

On the afternoon of 19 December, being the eve of Spencer's coming-of-age, guests began to arrive and that evening the celebrations got underway with dancing, music and cards. Leading Georgiana away from the crowd, Spencer presented her with the Marlborough diamonds, a moment of considerable emotion for them both. At midnight, when Spencer officially came of age, bells began to ring for seven miles around. The following morning Georgiana was up at seven selecting from her wardrobe a 'New pink & silver negligée', and at eight o'clock she was joined by Spencer, who led her down to breakfast, where the couple received the best wishes of everyone present, including the servants. A band played in the hall all day and at the entrance to the house there were fanfares and drum-rolls. After breakfast Spencer rode out to the enclosure to show himself to the crowd, which was threatening to descend on Althorp if he failed to do so. One thousand local people had been expected but in the event over five thousand attended and by the time the party broke up at four o'clock that afternoon they had consumed twenty-seven hogsheads of beer and at least four oxen. The same number arrived the following day when the celebrations resumed and again consumed a vast amount of food and ale, although contrary to expectations there was neither bloodshed nor rioting.

While Spencer mingled with his tenants, Georgiana returned to her room and changed into a pretty new outfit comprising a 'Blue Silver Gown & pretty coat the Diamond Cup pompon necklace earrings Roses for my shoulder & Sleeve knots & Nosegay.' By this time another wave of guests had arrived, including all the local gentry. The company gathered in three rooms on the ground floor where they remained until dinner, conversing together and at the same time casting inquisitive and critical looks at the bride. Georgiana was mortified. 'The thoughts of so many peoples staring at me', she confided to Thea, '& the flurry & fright that put me into made me so ill & gave me so violent an head ache that I had like to have fainted away which drew ev'ry bodys eyes still more upon me.'

At last Spencer returned and dinner was served. Tables had been laid in the gallery and guests formed a procession, parading through the principal apartments and mounting the great stairs, observed by a crowd of on-lookers who had come to witness the spectacle. The meal was exquisite, 'Three courses & an Excessive fine Desert', as Georgiana described it, with places set for 400. At the head of the main table sat Spencer's mother, Lady Cowper, while Spencer himself and Georgiana sat at the lower end. Soon the drinking of healths began and Georgiana blushed again as her own was toasted to riotous applause.

Dinner was followed by dancing, and Spencer and Georgiana opened the proceedings with a minuet followed by a country dance. However, Georgiana complained that her dress was too heavy for dancing, and she and Spencer joined the less energetic guests for tea, cards and lemonade. Supper was served at midnight and climaxed once more in a magnificent 'Desert . . . very fine & vastly pretty.' The party broke up at three in the morning and guests retired to their rooms, every available corner of the house having been given over to accommodation.

When Georgiana awoke the following morning she let it be known that she would not be joining the party for breakfast, claiming she had a headache. In reality she was simply embarrassed; for, as everyone in the house now knew, a bevy of 'Doctors and Proctors' had arrived that morning with a licence from the Archbishop of Canterbury authorizing her forthcoming marriage. Conquering her fears, Georgiana descended for lunch but she was immediately covered in confusion when Spencer approached with the licence and asked her half-jokingly if she would marry him that very day. The exchange took place within earshot of Lady Cowper and before the couple knew it the countess had seized on her son's suggestion, pronouncing it 'the best scheme in the world'. Within minutes she had laid an elaborate plan.

That evening there was to be another ball at Althorp. Spencer and Georgiana would start the dancing as usual and then discreetly retire to Lord Cowper's Bedchamber. There they would be joined by the members of their immediate family and by Spencer's former tutor, the Reverend Mr Holloway, who agreed to conduct the ceremony. In the event, there were one or two hitches. Holloway lost his way and when he finally found it again he insisted on reading the service at a snail's pace. Georgiana was so overcome by emotion she trembled and could hardly stand. Her brother William wept. But the ceremony was duly performed, and the Spencers' guests, dancing in the rooms below, were none the wiser.

Ever '*La Bavardé*', Georgiana's mother could not resist the temptation to write at once to a friend with an account of the evening's proceedings:

> Mr. Spencer and 'Don' [a family name for Georgiana] began the ball in the hall with all the servants. Lord Cowper went into Lady Cowper's dressing room, so did I the backway and Mr. Spencer and William after us, but poor Holloway blundered about and we could not get him in half an hour. When he came he would read every word of the special licence. Then we went into Lord Cowper's bedchamber, took off the tops of two stools, and a pillow off the bed for Holloway and the young couple to kneel upon. Holloway read so slowly and prayed

> with such devotion that the ceremony lasted three quarters of an hour. Mr. Spencer and 'Don' behaved as well as possible with the greatest seriousness and spoke distinct though low. As soon as it was done he kissed her, and they both knelt quite down to Lady Cowper and almost to my Lord. William cried a little, we all hugged and kissed and dispersed as soon as possible. They are all dancing. I must go and see them. Eleven o'clock. Not a creature mistrusts our wedding. I never saw anything equal to Mr. Spencer's behaviour this whole evening. 'Don' looks haggard, but very happy. Both he and she are just asleep now, I hope, in their several rooms.[1]

Mrs Poyntz was wrong to suppose that Spencer and Georgiana were asleep or would keep to their 'several rooms'. According to one report, there was pandemonium the following morning when an old French chambermaid entered Georgiana's room and was 'so – not unreasonably – horrified when Mr. Spencer put his head out of the bed-curtains and asked what o'clock it was, that she ran roaring and crying to Mrs. Poyntz's chamber with the shocking Intelligence!'[2]

Somehow the secret held, but there were awkward and sometimes comical moments. Before their guests Spencer and Lord Cowper continued to refer to Georgiana as Miss Poyntz, toasting the coming wedding and drinking the health of the future bride. The celebrations continued, with dancing every night, and on the morning of 27 December, the day fixed for the wedding, guests began to arrive in their hundreds, with those who had travelled great distances priding themselves on their punctuality and all feeling privileged to have been invited to so grand and momentous an event.

One can imagine the reaction when it was announced that Spencer and Georgiana were already man and wife, and had been so, moreover, under everybody's nose, for almost a week. The news was broken by Lady Cowper, who led the couple into the Breakfast Room and told the whole story, much to the embarrassment of Georgiana, whose only comfort, she wrote, was that 'ev'ry body looked as silly at their disappointment as I did at all them wishing me joy.' When the guests had recovered from the shock they sat down to breakfast, after which Georgiana acceded to requests from the servants to appear before them in an outer room. Inevitably the hope was expressed that there might soon be an heir and Georgiana confessed to 'great confusion' when 'the old Housekeeper went down of her knees to pray that she might see Lady Cowper a Grandmother within this twelvemonth.'

After prayers the company retired to change. Georgiana had dressed in a modest way for breakfast, appearing in 'a little white satin night gown without a hoop very fine Valenciennes handkerchief Ruffles tucked ruff & cap a clean apron & white ribbands not shoes gloves.' Now, as the acknowledged wife of John Spencer, she appeared in a resplendent 'Silver Tissue Negligée' set off by the complete Marlborough diamond parure. Spencer was equally splendid, in a 'white & silver robe'. Georgiana thought they both looked 'vastly fine' and that Spencer in particular 'look'd like an angel'. There followed a sumptuous lunch at which Georgiana took her place at the head of the table. The cooks and confectioners had excelled themselves and any lingering doubts about the joke the Spencers had played were soon washed away. Course followed course, as the company consumed a remarkable array of 'Tarts & Pyes' encrusted with the arms and mottoes of the Spencer and Poyntz families. The climax once again was the 'Desert', more a work of art or architecture than simple confectionery, glazed in sugar with the bride and bridegroom's coat of arms and topped in the centre by 'the Temple of Hymen in which there was a little altar with incense running on it . . . Most of the Deities were assisting about the Altar & they were all surround by Numbers of Little Cupids there was besides this two Maypoles with people dancing round & at the top of each Maypole was a flag with a motto, Hymen held a scroll too.'

[1] Lady Margaret Douglas-Home, *A Mere Miss Poyntz*

[2] Ibid.

Nor were the servants denied a share of the celebrations. After lunch a large silver cistern was filled with punch and they were left to consume almost forty gallons. In the meantime the hall at Althorp had filled with 'Millions of People', and in a time-honoured ceremony Georgiana raised her glass to them all and drank their health, so initiating an endless round of bumpers accompanied by 'loud huzza's' and a fanfare of French horns. By the end of it the company was quite 'stunn'd' and Georgiana was relieved when the following day most of the guests departed. On the Thursday after the wedding a large waggon left Althorp for London, packed to overflowing with the Spencers' possessions and on the following Sunday the Spencers themselves headed south.

9 AN IMPRESSIVE DEBUT

THE JOURNEY TO LONDON took two full days, but reports of the Spencers' progress travelled ahead of them; and little wonder, since they were accompanied by a cavalcade of over 200 horsemen whose arrival in towns and villages along the way caused a wave of panic. Inhabitants barricaded their doors and took up arms, believing that a foreign invasion was underway, bent on destruction and led by the Pretender and the King of France combined. As Lady Hervey reported:

> One has heard nothing for some time past but the magnificence, or rather the silly, vain profusion on account of Mr Spencer's wedding; and, what is the most extraordinary is, that it was quite disagreeable to both young people, and entirely the effect of the vanity and folly of a daughter of Lord Granville's; I mean Lady Cowper, Mr. Spencer's mother. They came to town from Althorp, where they were married, with three coaches and six horses, and two hundred horsemen: the villages through which they passed were put into the greatest consternation: some of the poor people shut themselves up in their houses and cottages, barricarding themselves up as best they could. Those who were more resolute, or more desperate, armed themselves with pitchforks, spits, and spades; and, to be sure, by the coaches and six horses, both the Pretender and the King of France were come too. In short, great was the alarm, and hapy [sic] they were when this formidable cavalcade passed by without setting fire to the habitations, or murdering the inhabitants.[1]

Even in London, where people were used to ostentatious display, the size of the Spencers' retinue and the magnificence of their equipage inspired amazement. Directly they arrived, John and Georgiana called at Leicester House to pay their respects to the Dowager Princess of Wales, and afterwards visited St James's Palace where they were received by the King. A witness to the spectacle later recalled, 'The procession consisted of two carriages and a chair. In the first carriage were the bridegroom and Lord Cowper with three footmen, behind in the second the mother and sister of the bride, also with three footmen, behind the bride followed in a new sedan chair lined with white satin, a black page walking before and three footmen behind, all in the most superb liveries. The diamonds worn by the newly-married pair were presented to Mr Spencer by Sarah Duchess of Marlborough, and were worth £100,000. The shoe-buckles of the bridegroom were alone worth £30,000'.[2]

Stepping out of her chair, Georgiana revealed the full loveliness of a new presentation gown coloured 'White and silver as fine as brocade and silver could make it'.[3] She was equally splendid in the outfits she wore on subsequent visits to Court, the second 'blue and silver', the third 'pink', the fourth 'white and gold colour in a fabric costing £6 a yard'.[4] With a sharp eye for detail a fellow courtier assessed the value of Georgiana's jewellery:

> Her diamonds worth £12,000, her ear-rings three drops, all diamonds, no paltry scrolls of silver; her necklace, most perfect brilliants, the middle stone worth £1000 set at the edge with small brilliants, made in the fashion of a small butterfly skeleton, has a very good effect with a pompon and behind where you may suppose the bottom of the caul a knot of diamonds, with little puffs of diamonds where the lappets are fastened and two shaking springs, brilliants for her hair, six roses, all brilliants for stays set in the form of a star, and a seal of Mercury cut in very fine turquoise stone; set as a standing for a Spaniel dog the body

[1] John W. Croker (ed.), *Letters of Mary Lepel, Lady Hervey*, pp.214–15

[2] Lady Llanover (ed.), *The Autobiography and Correspondence of Mary Granville, Mrs Delaney*, 3, p.402

[3] Sir Denis Le Marchant, *Memoir of John Charles Viscount Althorp, Third Earl Spencer*, p.4

[4] Ibid.

[5] Ibid.

[6] W. S. Lewis, *The Yale Edition of Horace Walpole's Correspondence*, 9, p.387

[7] Paget Toynbee and Leonard Whibley (eds.), *Correspondence of Thomas Gray*, 3 vols (O.U.P., 1935), 2, p.754

[8] *Survey of London*, XL, p.42

[9] AP F122, GS to TC, 17 Apr 1761

> of a pearl of the size of the Duchess of Portland's dolphin, the head and neck made out with finely wrought two little brilliants for eyes and a brilliant collar. It cost seventy guineas.[5]

Georgiana's reputation as one of the best dressed women of her day continued to grow, and was confirmed again at a royal masquerade where, in a blue and silver dress, overlaid with white lustring spotted with silver, a diamond-encrusted stomacher and other jewels, she turned the head of every guest. Even Horace Walpole, no ladies' man, was forced to concede that Georgiana cut 'a very pretty figure',[6] and in a description of the Coronation of George III the poet Thomas Gray singled her out as one of 'the noblest and most graceful figures among the ladies'.[7] The Spencers were hailed as one of the most beautiful and fascinating couples in London, courted and fêted by all of society. In the first two weeks alone Georgiana received over 600 visits. The Spencers' only complaint was that they did not yet possess an adequate residence in which to receive. On their arrival in London they had moved into the house Spencer owned in Grosvenor Street. This was to be their base for the next four years or so.[8] The house was spacious and well-located, but Spencer, as we know, was dreaming of greater things. Indeed he had already acquired the site in St James's Place and even now work was underway on the design of a palatial mansion which would answer his and Georgiana's every need.

For the next ten years the construction of this building dominated their lives to the point where it threatened to displace all other activities. There were times ahead when even their closest friends had to make do with a few moments snatched from the absorbing business of examining and approving designs and workmanship. Thea Cowper must have shrugged her shoulders when in the spring of 1761 she received a hurried note from Georgiana at Althorp informing her that she would shortly be arriving in London but that a meeting between them was unlikely as her primary objective was 'to give directions for . . . the furnishing the house in town', although she gave her word that she would 'try all I can to escape from workmen &c one half hour just to see how you do'.[9] But no great building was ever erected that did not involve the close participation of an enlightened and enthusiastic patron, and with expert guidance from John and Georgiana Spencer, the house in St James's Place was destined to become one of the finest private residences ever built in the capital.

PART II

CONSTRUCTION

10 THE CHOICE OF AN ARCHITECT

ALONG WITH THE SITE Spencer had retained the services of Lord Montfort's architect, John Vardy. As the man on the spot Vardy was an obvious choice; he may even have had some stake in the building lease.[1] But there was more to recommend him. Although relatively young, only thirty-seven years old, Vardy had already worked on a wide variety of commissions, public as well as private, and had earned a reputation as an able builder and administrator. He was also a talented draughtsman and a versatile designer, able to turn his hand to interior decoration and furniture as well as architecture. His pedigree was impeccable, having trained under the great English architect, William Kent. He had been schooled in the tradition of Palladio and his followers, but was able to work in a variety of styles, and although he had no first-hand experience of Classical Roman architecture, never having travelled outside England, he was familiar with Classical buildings and monuments through books and engravings. In addition he was well-connected, with contacts in Spencer's immediate circle.

Vardy was born in Durham in 1718, the son of an unskilled labourer. He showed an early talent for drawing, and by the age of eighteen had travelled south to London where he found employment in the Office of Works, the Government department responsible for the construction and maintenance of royal and state-owned buildings and parks. The Office of Works was the heart of the architectural establishment and had been a training ground for many of England's most eminent architects and craftsmen. Vardy's appointment was remarkable in view of the obscurity of his origins, and one suspects the involvement of an influential patron, possibly Lord Burlington, the famous amateur architect who, while occupying no official position within the Office of Works, was an all-powerful figure behind the scenes, lobbying on behalf of protégés and securing them positions within the administration.

Vardy's first official appointment was as Clerk of the Works at the Queen's House, Greenwich, and he later served in the same capacity at Hampton Court, Chelsea Hospital and the Palaces of Whitehall, Westminster, St James's and Kensington, having responsibility for maintenance and some new building work. Together with William Kent, whose assistant he became, Vardy worked on the design of the Horse Guards building in Whitehall, begun in 1733, and after Kent's death in 1748 took charge of its completion. Vardy was likewise entrusted with the design of a new building housing the King's Bench Records and the Exchequer Bill Office opposite Westminster Abbey, built in 1755–58, and he may also have been responsible for the Parliament Office in Old Palace Yard, erected in 1754–56.

A job in the Office of Works was no obstacle to a career in private practice; on the contrary it was a useful stepping-stone, conferring prestige and opening up a world of valuable contacts. Over the years Vardy undertook a broad range of private commissions, including churches, funerary monuments, town and country houses, garden pavilions, banking premises and museum buildings. In the process he built up a network of

III Spencer House, Dining Room; design by John Vardy for the decoration of the window shutters, 1758. It is not known whether the present design was ever executed, but the smoking censer was probably intended as an allusion to the Antique practice of burning incense at meals to clear the atmosphere between courses

IV Spencer House, Palm Room; design by John Vardy for the coffering and other mouldings, c1758. During the recent restoration the drawing helped to establish the original colours used in the decoration of the alcove

V Spencer House, Dining Room; preliminary design by John Vardy, 1755. This attractive watercolour drawing is an example of a presentation technique commonly employed by English architects around the middle of the eighteenth century, showing the intended decoration of all four walls on a single page, with alternative suggestions for the detailed finishing of individual elements and the inclusion of furniture such as pier glasses and sconces. The design was substantially altered in execution

[1] According to the *Survey of London*, John Vardy himself acquired the building lease from Lady Burlington following the death of his client. I can find no trace of the agreement in the Althorp Papers. Nor does it appear to be among the deeds in the Middlesex Land Register at the Greater London Record Office. However, the large sums paid to Vardy from John Spencer's account at Hoare's Bank (see Appendix II) would indicate an involvement which extended beyond design work and the supervision of craftsmen and labourers

PAGE 64
Spencer House, ground floor passageway (FIG 58, p. 100)

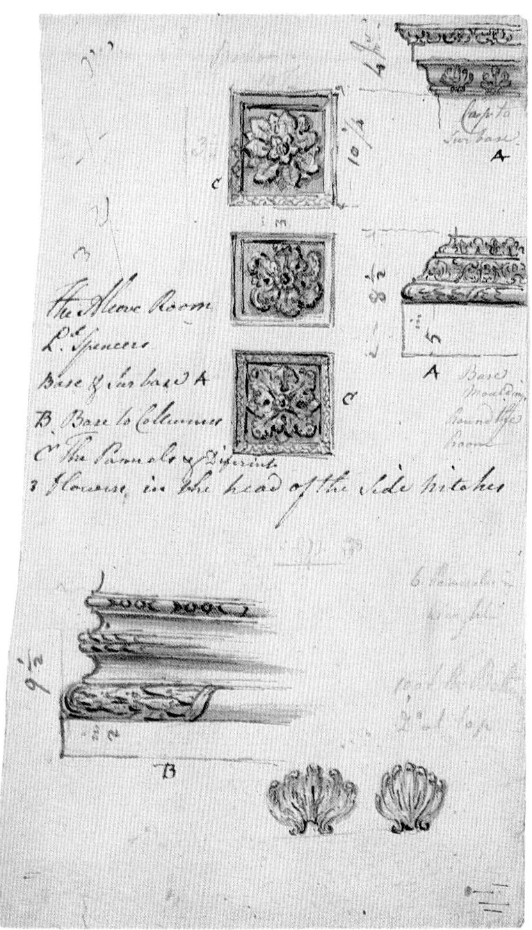
The Alcove Room
Ld. Spencers
Base & Surbase A
B. Base to Collumns
C The Pannels
3 Flowers in the head of the Side nitches
A
B
C

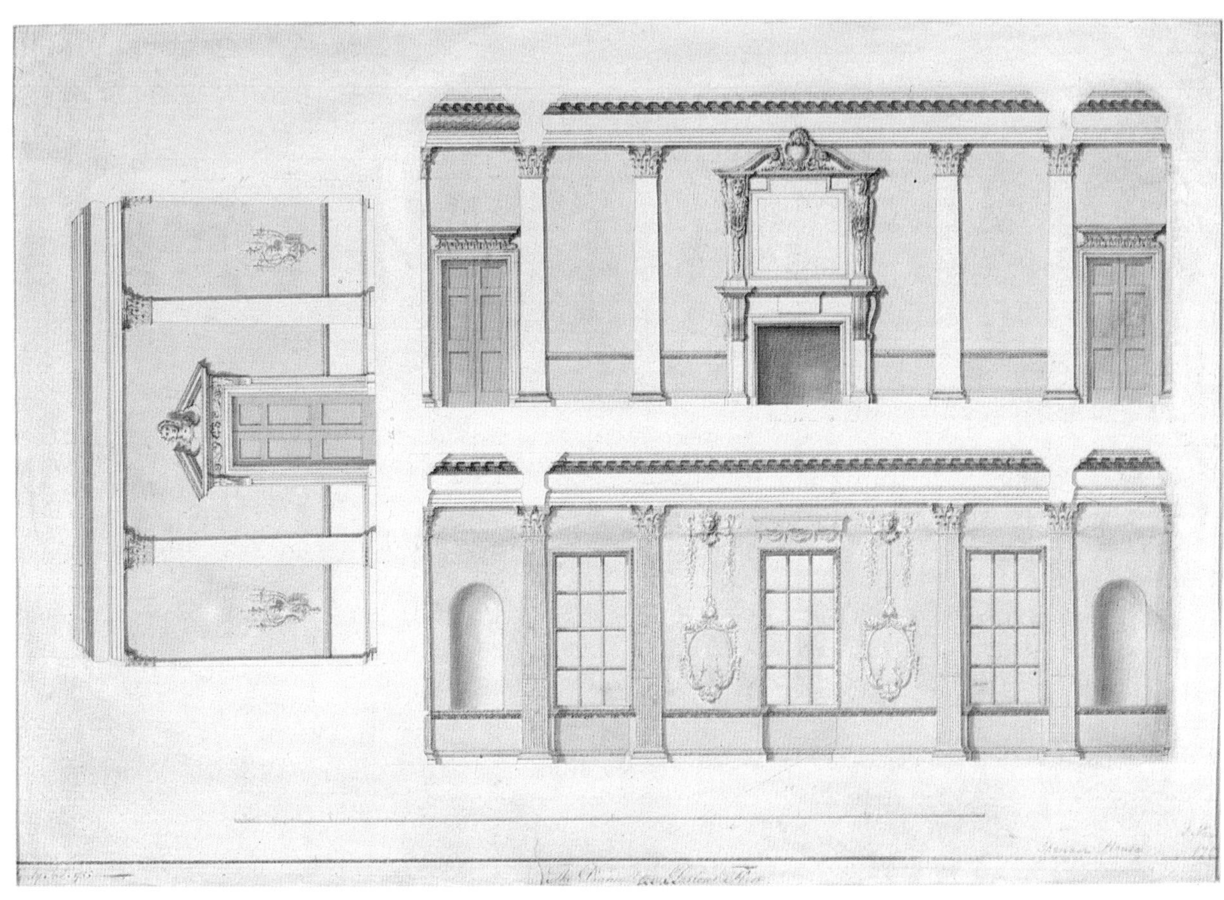

MDCCLVIII

[2] AP F122, GS to TC, 5 Apr 1759

influential clients, including senior members of the aristocracy, high-ranking military officers, financiers and government officials, as well as commercial and charitable institutions.

Vardy may well have had the benefit of a personal recommendation from someone within Spencer's immediate circle of relations and friends. He would certainly have been known to the freehold owner of the site, Lady Burlington, whose husband, as we have seen, was closely connected to the Office of Works and a particular friend and patron of Vardy's master, William Kent. He would likewise have been known to Spencer's stepfather, Lord Cowper, since in 1751 he had been commissioned to design a headquarters for the Society of Dilettanti, of which Cowper was a prominent member and which Spencer himself would join in 1765. Vardy might also have been recommended by Spencer's first cousin, Viscount Bateman, for whom he is thought to have built Shobdon Church in Herefordshire. Another possible link was Colonel Wade, a friend of Spencer's wife Georgiana,[2] for whom Vardy had built a town house in Whitehall. It is possible also that Vardy was recommended by Georgiana's cousin, Thea Cowper, whose father, as Clerk of the Parliament, occupied the office the architect reputedly designed in Old Palace Yard. But there was another, more important link.

VI Spencer House, Palm Room; design by John Vardy for the south wall and alcove, 1757. This beautiful watercolour section is one of the most enchanting surviving designs for Spencer House. Particularly striking are the figures in the niches, which represent actual statues in the Spencer collection

VII Spencer House, Painted Room; design by James Stuart for the north wall, 1759. This exquisite watercolour drawing is proof of Stuart's abilities as an artist and shows the north wall more or less as executed (PLATES XIV and XV pp. 162 and 163). The date of the drawing appears in Roman numerals above the door

11 AN ARCHITECTURAL EMINENCE

AT THE TIME CONSTRUCTION BEGAN John Spencer was only twenty-one years old. He had a passion for architecture and considerable knowledge, but his tastes were not yet fully formed; nor did he have any experience of building works. His step-father, Lord Cowper, could offer guidance; Georgiana, too, was a help, and there were others from whom he might have sought advice. But this was to be a long and demanding project and Spencer felt the need of a stronger presence, a person of experience and authority who would help him develop his ideas and mediate between himself and his architect. He decided, therefore, to engage the services of an architectural adviser and turned to the man best suited to the job, Colonel George Gray (FIG 27), who joined the team at Spencer House some time before the autumn of 1755.[1]

Gray is a shadowy figure; his life is poorly documented and he has never been the subject of any serious study. And yet in the history of Spencer House, and of English architecture generally, he was clearly a figure of importance. Gray was born around 1710, the younger son of an obscure Scottish Baronet, Sir James Gray 1st Bt, who according to Horace Walpole was 'first a box-keeper and then footman to James the Second'.[2] Sir James had been raised to the Baronetage by Queen Anne in 1707 and married one Hester Dodd, of whom little is known except that she lived to a great age and bore her husband three other children besides George: a son and two daughters. One of the daughters, Elizabeth, married a man by the name of Nicholl; the other, Carolina, remained a spinster. The son, James, succeeded to the Baronetcy in 1722 and became a prominent diplomat, serving successively as British Resident in Venice, Envoy Extraordinary to the King of Naples and the Two Sicilies and Minister Plenipotentiary to the King of Spain. In the course of his travels he fathered two illegitimate children, but he never married and on his death in 1773 his title passed to George, who also inherited the bulk of his estate. George, however, lived for only a few weeks longer, dying at Bath after a long and painful illness.[3] Gray had married; his wife Charlotte, with whom he lived in Bolton Row near Hanover Square, was the daughter of Major-General Robert Hunter and the sister of a member of Parliament, Thomas Orby Hunter. But the couple had no children and the title thus became extinct.

Early in life George Gray entered the army. In 1730 he purchased a commission and four years later joined the 1st Foot Guards as ensign. In 1741 he was promoted to Captain and transferred to the 47th Foot, transferring again to the 18th Foot in 1743. Promoted to Major in 1745, he was appointed Lieutenant-Colonel of the 1st Troop Horse Guards in 1749 and ten years later became a full Colonel, transferring to the 61st Foot. In 1768 he joined the 37th Foot and in 1770 was promoted Lieutenant-General. During his career Gray saw action in Minorca and Flanders and took part in the suppression of the Jacobite Rising in Scotland in 1745. He was active in politics, siding with the Whigs, and was a strong supporter of the Duke of Newcastle, under whom he served as M.P. for Winchelsea from 1759 to 1760.[4]

27 George Gray, by George Knapton, 1744. By profession a soldier, Gray pursued a parallel career as an amateur architect. As Secretary and Treasurer of the Society of Dilettanti he made a significant contribution to the development of Neo-Classicism and, in his role as architectural adviser to John Spencer, he was responsible for many of the most innovative aspects of the design of Spencer House

But Gray's chief interest in life was architecture, particularly Classical architecture, a subject on which he was considered an authority. He was a friend to some of the foremost antiquarians and architects of the period and formed an impressive collection of architectural books and related artefacts, including paintings of the ruins at Paestum, which he placed at the disposal of artists and scholars.[5] He was himself an amateur architect, and while there are no known buildings by him, and only two surviving drawings, neither of which shows any great talent or technical ability,[6] he was clearly an active and influential figure on the architectural scene, widely consulted in matters relating to architectural design.

Gray's main contribution to architecture was made through the Society of Dilettanti, of which he was a founding member and Secretary and Treasurer for over thirty years. The Society had been formed around 1732 as a dining club for English Grand Tourists.

[1] SJSM 69/1/1

[2] W. S. Lewis, *The Yale Edition of Horace Walpole's Correspondence*, 20, p.409

[3] AP F42, CH to GS, 10 Nov 1772; AP F43, CH to GS, 12 Jan 1773

[4] BL Add MS 32,892, f.322

[5] Michael McCarthy, 'New Light on Thomas Major's *Paestum* and Later English Drawings of Paestum', in *Paestum and the Doric Revival 1750–1830* (New York, 1986), pp.47–50; Eileen Harris, *British Architectural Books and Writers 1556–1785* (C.U.P., 1990) [Entry for Major]

[6] BL, Maps, King's Topographical Drawings, XXIV.23–r (drawing of portico of Grand Storehouse at Tower of London); RIBA (design for gateway, Caversham Park, Oxfordshire) [Colvin, *Biographical Dictionary*, pp.360–61]

The members, most of them gentlemen of leisure, generally met at one or other of the smarter London taverns, where in a bibulous and sometimes riotous atmosphere they indulged in quasi-masonic rituals involving bizarre clothing and accessories. The wine-god Bacchus was adopted as the society mascot and Horace Walpole once quipped that the fact of having made the Grand Tour was merely a pretext, drunkenness being the only true qualification for membership. However, as time progressed the Society took on an increasingly serious and purposeful role. Scholars, artists and designers were encouraged to join, and although drinking remained high on the agenda, there gradually emerged a more sober programme based on the idea of regeneration in English art and design through the promotion of Classical values and the spread of knowledge about the Classical world.

To this end the Society sponsored archaeological expeditions to ancient sites and the publication of antiquarian research, including some of the earliest measured drawings of Greek and Roman remains. Simultaneously, at an individual level, the members offered encouragement and employment to artists and designers of the burgeoning Neo-Classical movement. In this way the Society of Dilettanti became a major driving force behind the revolution in taste in the middle years of the eighteenth century, and is rightly considered to have done more than any other body to reform public taste. No less a figure than William Wilkins, architect of the National Gallery, later remarked that the Society had, in his own words, 'done more towards the acquisition of architectural knowledge . . . than all the governments and societies of England united'.[7]

As a senior member of the Society, George Gray deserves a large share of the credit for this achievement. At a practical level he was directly involved in the admission of new members and the organization of all the Society's projects, raising funds, drawing up subscription lists, drafting publishing proposals, attending personally to every detail. At a theoretical level also he made a significant contribution, taking a leading part in the debate which laid the way for the Classical revival. He was among the first to argue for archaeological accuracy in the reproduction of Classical elements. Indeed as early as 1753 he was calling for a building to be erected in London that would be an exact replica of the Temple of Augustus at Pola, reasoning that the further an architect strayed from the practices of the Ancients the more he erred, and that only by faithfully reproducing the forms and details of Classical architecture would his designs escape censure.[8]

The temple was never built, but the construction of Spencer House offered an opportunity to experiment with similar ideas and Gray must have leapt at it. He was probably introduced to Spencer by Lord Cowper, a fellow member of the Society of Dilettanti and a long-standing friend. Indeed in 1738 Cowper had himself sought Gray's advice in connection with building works on his estate at Cole Green Park.[9] Gray and Spencer immediately saw eye to eye; they shared the same aesthetic, the same deep love of Classical Antiquity, and soon became firm friends, a tie cemented in 1765 when Spencer was welcomed into the Society of Dilettanti on his return from the Grand Tour. Gray was likewise acquainted with Vardy, having dealt with him over the proposed construction of the headquarters of the Society of Dilettanti, and presumably he endorsed his appointment as architect of Spencer House. However, as the project developed tensions arose between the two men which led, as we shall see, to rupture and a dramatic change of direction which was to have far-reaching consequences, not only for Spencer House, but for the whole future course of English architecture.

[7] Edwin Beresford Chancellor, *The Private Palaces of London, Past and Present*, p.338

[8] *Historical Notices of the Society of Dilettanti* (1855), p.47

[9] HRO D/EP.F249, George Gray to William, 2nd Earl Cowper, 5 July 1738

12 ARTIFICERS AND ARTISTS

A PROJECT OF THE SIZE and sophistication of Spencer House called for the best available craftsmen and artists, and Vardy gathered together a team that was second to none (see Appendix II). For some it was the climax to a long and distinguished career, for others an auspicious debut. Several had worked with Vardy on previous projects or went on to work with him on subsequent commissions. For all concerned it was an opportunity to practice their craft at the highest level and to further their talents and skills; to collaborate with leading figures from other fields and to exchange ideas and techniques; to lend their name and make their own distinctive contribution to a building of unique importance.

The shell of the building was erected by two leading bricklayers, Edward Gray and James Eaves. Gray was an active figure on the architectural scene and his interests clearly extended beyond mere bricks and mortar, for he subscribed to both Isaac Ware's *Palladio* of 1738 and the fourth volume of *Vitruvius Britannicus*, published in 1767. He frequently worked with Sir Robert Taylor, architect of the Bank of England, and also collaborated with Robert Adam on the construction of Number 20 St James's Square. Although he had no known connection with Vardy, he was later employed by the Office of Works, working on the construction of Somerset House and the King's Bench Prison.[1] Sir William Chambers, with whom he worked on Melbourne House in Piccadilly, berated Gray for the 'infamous' quality of his workmanship and materials,[2] but at Spencer House he could not be faulted, for the brickwork was exceptionally sound in composition and construction. The other bricklayer, James Eaves, also subscribed to *Vitruvius Britannicus*, and had an existing connection with Vardy, having worked with him on at least one previous commission.[3] In addition, he had been employed on the construction of a mansion in Grosvenor Square.[4]

Another key figure was the mason, whose primary task was to clad the shell of the building in stone. Vardy chose perhaps the greatest practitioner of the day, John Devall (1701–1774).[5] Devall, who in 1760 became Master of the Masons' Company, was a colleague in the Office of Works, where since 1742 he had held the post of Sergeant Plumber. At Spencer House, as on other projects, he may have been assisted by his son, also John, another well-known mason. He had worked with Vardy on the construction of the Horse Guards in Whitehall and collaborated with him on at least one other private commission.[6] At the same time he would probably have been known to George Gray, and perhaps Lord Cowper, since in 1753 he had been commissioned by the Society of Dilettanti to prepare a consignment of stone intended for the headquarters they planned to build in Cavendish Square. Certainly he was known to the bricklayer James Eaves, with whom he had worked on a project in Grosvenor Square, while his son later collaborated with the other bricklayer, Gray, on Somerset House and the King's Bench Prison.[7] Although primarily a stone mason, Devall also operated as a speculative builder and at various times was involved in the development of several important sites in London. In addition to the more basic work of cutting and dressing stone, Devall was capable of finer work such as the carving of chimney-pieces and other features, and in the

1 *Survey of London*, XXIX, p.164; XXXII, p.369; H. Colvin (ed.), *History of the King's Works*, V (1976), pp.357, 465

2 *Survey of London*, XXXII, p.369

3 DB, Account of John Vardy, 1755

4 *Survey of London*, XL, p.146n

5 Rupert Gunnis, *Dictionary of British Sculptors 1660–1851* (1951), pp.128–9; Geoffrey Beard, *Craftsmen and Interior Decoration in England 1660–1820*, 2nd edn (1986); Colvin, *King's Works*, V, p.349; *Survey of London*, XXIV, part IV, p.13; XXIX, pp.89n, 164; XXXI, p.286; XXXIII, pp.254–5; XXXVI, p.40n; XL, pp.118, 120n, 146n; Howard Colvin, *Biographical Dictionary of British Architects 1600–1840*, 2nd edn (1978) p.831

6 DB, Account of John Vardy, 1755

7 Gunnis, op. cit., p.129; Colvin, *King's Works*, V, p.466; *Survey of London*, XXIX, p.148

course of a career spanning half a century took a leading part in many important building projects, including Westminster Bridge, the Mansion House, Guy's Hospital, Holkham Hall and Woburn Abbey.

Another mason who worked at Spencer House, although his contribution was relatively minor, was Joseph Carr, who had experience of working with both Vardy and Devall, having collaborated with them on the construction of the Horse Guards. His only other known commission was a small-scale building project in Soho Square.[8]

The ironwork at Spencer House, including railings, balustrades, lamps, locks and other details, was entrusted to a team that included and was probably headed by the well-known ironsmith, John Palmer. Palmer was a member of a dynasty of smiths that dominated the trade in the middle years of the eighteenth century. Another member of this dynasty, William Palmer, carried out extensive repairs and alterations at Spencer House in the 1770s.[9] A third, James Palmer, was employed by John Spencer's step-father, Lord Cowper, on works at a house in Great George Street in the early 1760s.[10] John Palmer himself, who may also have worked on a house in Grosvenor Square around 1755,[11] was evidently a skilled craftsman with a developed interest in architecture, for in addition to the magnificent ironwork he produced at Spencer House, he is known to have subscribed to *Vitruvius Britannicus.*

The statues and urns on the west front were carved by Michael Henry Spang (d.1762), a Danish-born sculptor who had settled in England around 1756. Spang's earliest recorded commission was a seal for the Society of Arts, which he modelled to the designs of the Italian painter, Cipriani. In 1759 he was engaged by Robert Adam to carve the chimney-pieces in the principal reception rooms at Kedleston Hall in Derbyshire, and the following year he worked for Adam again, sculpting the dolphins and ship-prows on the Admiralty Screen in Whitehall. As a sculptor of the human figure, Spang showed his worth in a monument to the poet James Thomson, erected in Westminster Abbey, and he also produced a terracotta figure of the painter William Hogarth, as well as an anatomical model used in classes at the Royal Academy Schools. He exhibited at the Society of Artists and was a protégé of Sir William Chambers, being among the subscribers to Chambers' *Treatise on Civil Architecture* of 1759.[12]

Another well-known sculptor who also had a hand in Spencer House was Joseph Wilton (1722–1803), who went on to become one of the leading English artists of the second half of the eighteenth century. Wilton was born in London but trained abroad, studying successively under Laurent Delvaux in Flanders and Jean-Baptiste Pigalle in Paris. He later travelled to Rome, where his work attracted considerable notice, and where in 1755 he was awarded the Jubilee Gold Medal by Pope Benedict XIV. That same year Wilton returned to England, and by the latter part of 1758, when he joined the workforce at Spencer House, he had established himself as one of the most promising sculptors of his generation, winning commissions on a wide variety of projects, including monuments, busts and statues, as well as chimney-pieces and other architectural features. Although he does not appear to have worked on any previous commission with Vardy, his father, an ornamental plasterer, was an associate of the mason John Devall Senior, and in later years he was employed by the Office of Works, notably on the construction of Somerset House, where he collaborated with both John Devall Junior and the bricklayer Edward Gray.[13]

The carved decoration in wood, including ornamental joinery and possibly furniture, was produced by Vardy's own brother, Thomas, who had followed him to London around 1740, finding work as an apprentice to the King's Master Carver, James Richards.[14] In 1750 he was admitted a freeman of the Joiners' Company of London and in time trained up a number of apprentices himself, one of whom, John Davis, may also have worked at Spencer House. In 1753 he was admitted to the Livery of the Joiners' Company and in 1788 was elected Master. Thomas and his brother were close associates and had worked together on various projects in the years leading up to the Spencer House commission.[15] Although primarily a craftsman, Thomas appears to have shared his brother's interest in the broader subject of architecture and design; he subscribed to William Chambers' *Treatise on Civil Architecture* of 1759, and one of his sons later became an architect, inheriting all his uncle's architectural papers and books. As a carver Thomas had few equals and was much in demand. Although he failed to win the contract for the Mansion House in London, for which he tendered in 1755, he later worked on several important commissions involving distinguished patrons and architects, and was responsible in particular for much of the carved decoration at Cobham Hall, Kent, as well as tablets for chimney-pieces at Hill Park and Valence in the same county.

The plasterwork at Spencer House was entrusted to two established masters. The first, Thomas Clark (d.1787), was a long-time associate of Vardy.[16] In 1752 he had been appointed Master Plasterer in the Office of Works, a position he held until his death, and he is also known to have worked with Vardy on at least one other private commission in 1754–55.[17] Perhaps his greatest achievement was the plaster decoration at Norfolk House, St James's Square, dating from 1748 to 1752, a virtuoso riot of Rococo ornamentation which, while radically different from anything required from him at Spencer House, and stylistically repugnant to both John Spencer and George Gray, demonstrated in the most conspicuous way his great technical mastery and flair. From Spencer House Clark went on to found a firm of plasterers in his own name, and worked on many other high-profile commissions, public as well as private, including the remodelling of Carlisle House in Soho for the infamous adventuress Theresa Cornelys, and the decoration of Somerset House, where he would have encountered other artist-craftsmen from the Spencer House team.

The other plasterer engaged by Vardy was Joseph Rose (*c*1723–80), described by Sir Thomas Robinson, a friend of John Spencer and a well-known amateur architect and patron, as 'the first man in the kingdom as a plasterer'.[18] Born into a family of plasterers from Norton near Sheffield, Rose had been apprenticed in 1738 to Thomas Perritt of York, acting as his assistant on the decoration of Temple Newsam House near Leeds. He later moved to Doncaster, where he established an independent firm, and in 1745 was engaged by the architect James Paine to carry out plaster decoration at the Mansion House, Doncaster. In the years which followed Rose collaborated with Paine on many other building projects, including Cusworth Hall, Ormesby Hall and Sandbeck Park in Yorkshire, Felbrigg Hall in Norfolk and Glentworth House in Lincolnshire. In 1760 Rose was joined by his brother and two nephews, one of whom, Joseph Rose Junior (1745–99), succeeded to the business on his death. The company had a virtual monopoly on high-quality plaster decoration in the second half of the eighteenth century, winning commissions from all the most prominent architects of the period and producing work of unrivalled beauty and refinement.[19]

There would have been others who made up the team at Spencer House: carpenters, joiners, roofers, painters, upholsterers and, lower down the scale, glaziers, scaffolders, carters and labourers, as well as colourmen, drapers and other suppliers. Unfortunately their names have not been recorded, but it may be assumed that they all had the requisite experience and motivation for, despite the laborious building methods of the day, the house rose remarkably fast.

[8] *Survey of London*, XXXIII, p.52n; Colvin, *King's Works*, V, p.438n

[9] AP F199

[10] HRO D/EP.T4228

[11] *Survey of London*, XL, p.159

[12] Gunnis, op. cit., p.361; Beard, op. cit.; Sir William Chambers, *Treatise on Civil Architecture* (1759), pp.16–17; Horace Walpole, *Anecdotes of Painting*, F. W. Hilles and P. B. Daghlian, (eds), 5th edn (1939), pp.153–4

[13] Gunnis, op. cit., pp.434–7; Colvin, *King's Works*, V, pp.372–3

[14] Roger White, 'John Vardy 1718–1765: Palladian into Rococo', in *The Architectural Outsiders* (1985), pp.63–81, 212–13; Gunnis, op. cit., p.408; Geoffrey Beard & Christopher Gilbert, *Dictionary of English Furniture Makers 1660–1840* (1986), p.919

[15] DB, Account of John Vardy, 1754–55

[16] Colvin, *King's Works*, V, p.466; *Survey of London*, XXIX, p.192; XXXIII, p.75; XL, p.118n

[17] DB, Account of John Vardy, 1754–55

[18] Beard, op.cit, p.279

[19] Geoffrey Beard, *Decorative Plasterwork in Great Britain* (1975)

13 A REVOLUTION IN TASTE

CONSTRUCTION PROBABLY BEGAN in the spring of 1756, directly Spencer received consent to breach the wall dividing St James's Place from Green Park, and by the following autumn half the shell was standing.[1] Although the house was not ready to be occupied until 1760,[2] and was not finally completed until 1766,[3] by 1759 the exterior was finished and work was well advanced on the decoration of the interior.

The principal facade was that overlooking Green Park (opposite). The facade is shown in a north-west perspective by Vardy, engraved in 1763 (FIG 192, p. 189),[4] and in an elevation drawn by the architect, and engraved about the same date (FIG 28).[5] However, the earliest surviving record is another drawing by Vardy dated 1759 (FIG 29, p. 81).[6]

The facade was clad in Portland stone, brilliant white against the London sky. At ground-floor level there were plain rectangular windows framed by rusticated arches and a broad balustraded terrace, supported below by a wall with vermiculated (literally worm-eaten) rustication, lunette windows and a central door. There was no garden as yet and the terrace projected directly into the park. At first-floor level the facade was of plain ashlar, with aedicule-style windows, screened by balustrades and surmounted by an alternating pattern of triangular and segmental pediments. In the centre was a row of six Doric columns, flanked on either side by single columns of the same Order and matching

[1] Lady Llanover (ed.), *The Autobiography and Correspondence of Mary Granville, Mrs Delaney*, 3, p.445

[2] In Nov 1760 Lady Spencer noted in her diary that she had 'slept three nights in the new House in Town'. This was apparently the first time she or anyone else from the Spencer family had done so [AP F167]

[3] AP F117, JS to WH, 25 Dec 1765

[4] North-west perspective of Spencer House, engraving by T. Miller after John Vardy, inscribed *To The Rt Honble Ld Visct Spencer this North West View of his House in St. James's Place is Humbly Inscribed by his most Obedient and most Humble Servant John Vardy... 1763* [GLRO, Maps and Prints, Westminster DD, 15430]

[5] *The West Front of Ld Spencers House to the Green Park*, drawn and engraved by John Vardy, *c*1763 [GLRO, Maps and Prints, Westminster DD, 5387]

[6] *The West Front of the Honble John Spencer Esqrs House in Saint James's Place as Designed and Executed by J. Vardy, Architect, in 1759* [V&A, Prints and Drawings, Q1a.3322]

28 Spencer House, west front; drawn and engraved by John Vardy, c1763. Seen from a distance, the pedimented Portland stone facade gave the house the appearance of a Classical temple

VIII Spencer House, north-west view; watercolour drawing, c1780. Before the construction of the garden, cattle and deer wandered freely beneath the terrace

IX Spencer House, Morning Room. Adjoining the Entrance Hall, with direct access to the rear staircase, this sober Palladian interior might originally have served as a waiting room or an office in which Lord Spencer conducted business

x *A view of Green Park, English School, c1760. The view shows Spencer House when newly built. Before the present garden was added in the last years of the eighteenth century, the terrace projected directly into Green Park*

*XI Spencer House, Dining Room, detail of original sideboard (*FIG *77, p. 112)*

end pilasters. The columns and pilasters were surmounted by a full entablature, the frieze composed of an alternating pattern of triglyphs, paterae and bucrania (sacrificial ox skulls) (FIG 30). The entablature broke forward above the central colonnade and again above the individual columns on either side, creating a lively interplay of light and shadow, projection and recession. Miniature circular windows in the frieze brought light into second-floor rooms at the north and south end. At roof-top level the facade was crowned by a parapet with inset balustrades supporting a pair of richly carved vases. In the centre was a broad triangular pediment, surmounted by a conforming arrangement of statues and pierced in the centre with a large circular window framed by crossed palm branches.

The west front is interesting for its use of symbolism. The statues above the pediment were particularly appropriate in view of the function and situation of the building. At the apex was Ceres, goddess of corn, represented in traditional form as a hooded female figure carrying a sheaf of grain. According to legend, Ceres taught mankind the cultivation of the earth and was thus associated with food and plenty. On the left was Bacchus, god of wine, crowned with ivy and vine leaves and carrying a staff composed of a thyrsus branch, his shoulder draped with the leopard skin worn on his legendary expedition to the East. Like Ceres, Bacchus taught mankind the cultivation of the earth, especially the vine, and was thus a symbol of hospitality and conviviality. In addition he was the mascot of the Society of Dilettanti. On the right was Flora, goddess of gardens and flowers, bearing the horn of plenty, her traditional attribute. Since the west front was in essence the garden front, facing the park, Flora had an obvious place here, especially in view of her marriage to the west wind, Zephyrus, who by the sweetness of his breath brought forth flowers and fruits. It is possible also that the crossed palm branches in the pediment were intended as symbols of Harmony. The terrace wall, with its rough, fortress-like

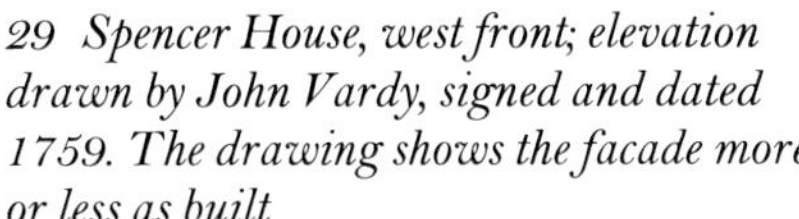

29 Spencer House, west front; elevation drawn by John Vardy, signed and dated 1759. The drawing shows the facade more or less as built

30

31

30 Spencer House, west front, detail of frieze. In keeping with the order of the columns below, the frieze was Doric, with an alternating pattern of triglyphs, paterae and bucrania

31 Palazzo Chiericato, Vicenza, by Palladio, as illustrated in Isaac Ware, The Four Books of Andrea Palladio's Architecture, *Book II (1738), pl.III. In this, as in other buildings, Palladio used the frieze which Vardy later reproduced at Spencer House*

appearance, was clearly designed to ward off trespassers, and in the transition from vermiculated rustication to plain rustication, and from the latter to smooth ashlar columns, architectural ornament and finally the Gods of Olympus, it is tempting to see a metaphor, often used by architects of the Renaissance, for the rise of civilization through the divine medium of architecture. Another point concerns the use of Portland stone, a costly material principally associated with public buildings and monuments rather than private houses. Even the grandest London mansions were generally of brick, with stone used only for the dressings. By adopting Portland stone for the principal facade of his London house, Lord Spencer drew attention to his enormous wealth and also ensured that the building stood out from its neighbours; but at the same time he elevated the structure above the domestic level, almost to the status of public architecture, establishing an obvious visual association with such famous landmarks as the Banqueting House and the Horse Guards. People could then judge whether the Spencers were not as permanent a feature of the life of the country as some of England's other national institutions.

The design of the facade was essentially Palladian; indeed it is possible that Vardy drew inspiration from William Kent's unexecuted designs for Whitehall Palace. The frieze, with its alternating pattern of bucrania, triglyphs and paterae (FIG 30) was identical to that used by Palladio on the principal facade of the Palazzo Chiericato in Vicenza, illustrated in the *Quattro Libri* (FIG 31),[7] and in an unpublished design for a town house (FIG 32). The latter had been acquired by Lord Burlington in Italy in 1719 and served as the basis of his own design for the garden front of General Wade's house in London built in 1723 (FIG 33).[8] Wade's house, standing north of Piccadilly and not far

[7] Vardy subscribed to Isaac Ware's edition of Palladio in 1738 [*The Four Books of Andrea Palladio's Architecture*], as did George Gray and John Spencer's stepfather the 2nd Earl Cowper

[8] For the influence of Palladio's design see Dan Cruickshank, 'Tracing a Palladio Elevation', *The Architectural Review*, CLXXV, No.1045 (March 1984), pp.44–7. The north front of Spencer House also has affinities with another building by Vardy of about the same date, the Stone Building in St Margaret's Lane, erected in 1755–70

32

32 Design for a town house, by Palladio. Acquired by Lord Burlington in Italy in 1719, the present drawing served as the basis of his own designs for General Wade's house in London, built in 1723. The frieze was used by Vardy on both the west and north fronts of Spencer House and the general composition clearly relates to the north front pavilions

33

33 Drawing by Henry Flitcroft of the garden front of General Wade's house, built to a design by Lord Burlington in 1723. Inspired by a drawing by Palladio (FIG 32). Wade's house was one of the most admired buildings of its kind in London and an obvious point of reference for Vardy in his design of the north front pavilions at Spencer House

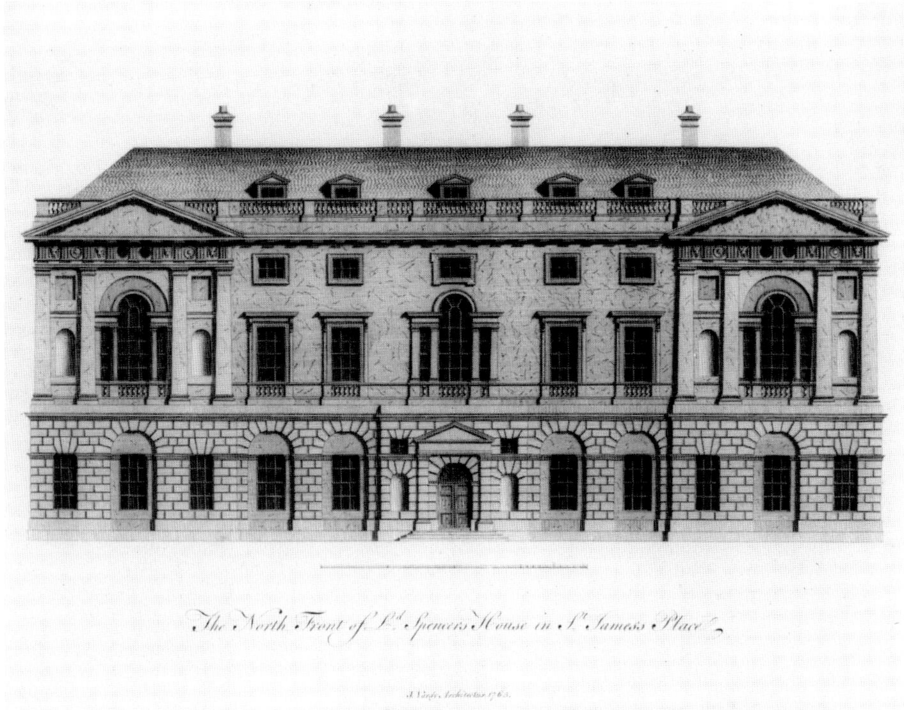

34

35

from the site of Spencer House, was greatly admired in the eighteenth century and would certainly have been a point of reference for Vardy. At the same time there were elements of Baroque inspiration, such as the individual columns with projecting entablatures and the crossed palm branches in the pediment. The latter feature was prefigured in the designs of James Gibbs for St Martin-in-the-Fields,[9] and those by John James for St George's, Hanover Square, but would appear to originate in the architecture of Borromini, who used this device repeatedly, notably above the entrance to the Palazzo Propaganda in Rome (FIG 36).[10] However, the most striking feature of the west front was the emphatic use of Classical architectural elements. Indeed the whole facade was clearly conceived as a Classical temple front, a point underscored by the use of Portland stone, which naturally evoked the bleached marble remains of ancient Greece and Rome. The lynch-pin of the design was the giant hexastyle Doric portico. The portico did not quite span the full width of the building, but its size and prominence marked an important step towards the adoption of the full temple front in buildings of the Neo-Classical period.[11] The statues, moreover, were correctly disposed in accordance with early reconstructions of Antique temples, while the frieze, though previously used by Palladio and his followers, ultimately derived from the Temple of Apollo Sosiano in Rome (FIG 37). Even the circular window in the pediment was of Classical derivation, inspired perhaps by the Temple of Augustus at Pola, a building particularly admired by George Gray.

It was usual in the eighteenth century for a distinction to be observed in the design of garden fronts and street fronts. The latter were generally less elaborate and so it was at

36

34 Spencer House, north front; drawn and engraved by John Vardy, 1763. The pavilion to the left was never built since the site was not available for sale, and the resulting asymmetry naturally attracted some criticism. The design was less elaborate than that of the park front and also more conventional, with clear borrowings from the work of Vardy's Palladian forerunners (FIGS 32 and 33)

35 Elevation of His Majesty's Lodge in Richmond Park; *engraving from Woolfe and Gandon,* Vitruvius Britannicus, *IV (1767), pls 1–2. The architects Roger Morris and the Earl of Pembroke used the identical frieze to that later reproduced by Vardy at Spencer House and the general arrangement of architectural elements is strikingly similar to that of the pavilions on the north front*

36 Palazzo Propaganda, Rome, detail of window over entrance, by Borromini, as illustrated in Domenico de' Rossi, Studio di Architettura Civile, *3 vols (Rome, 1702–21),* I *(1702), pl.74. The motif of a circular window framed by crossed palm branches, which Vardy used in the pediment at Spencer House, ultimately derives from this source*

37 Temple of Apollo Sosiano, Rome, as illustrated in Isaac Ware, The Four Books of Andrea Palladio's Architecture, *Book I (1738), pl.XV. The frieze at Spencer House ultimately looks back to this source*

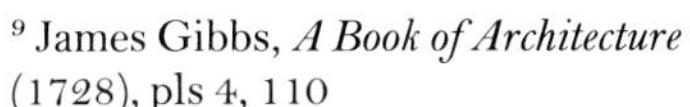

37

[9] James Gibbs, *A Book of Architecture* (1728), pls 4, 110

[10] In the years following the construction of Spencer House the feature was widely copied, notably in the design of the twin pavilions in Cavendish Square built by George Tufnel in 1769–70 and on the main front of the Excise Office, Old Broad Street, built in 1769–75 to the design of William Robinson, a colleague of Vardy's at the Office of Works. It has since become a standard motif and is found in English Classical buildings of every period

[11] Sir John Summerson, 'The Society's House: An Architectural Study', *Journal of the Royal Society of Arts* (15 Oct 1954), pp.920–33

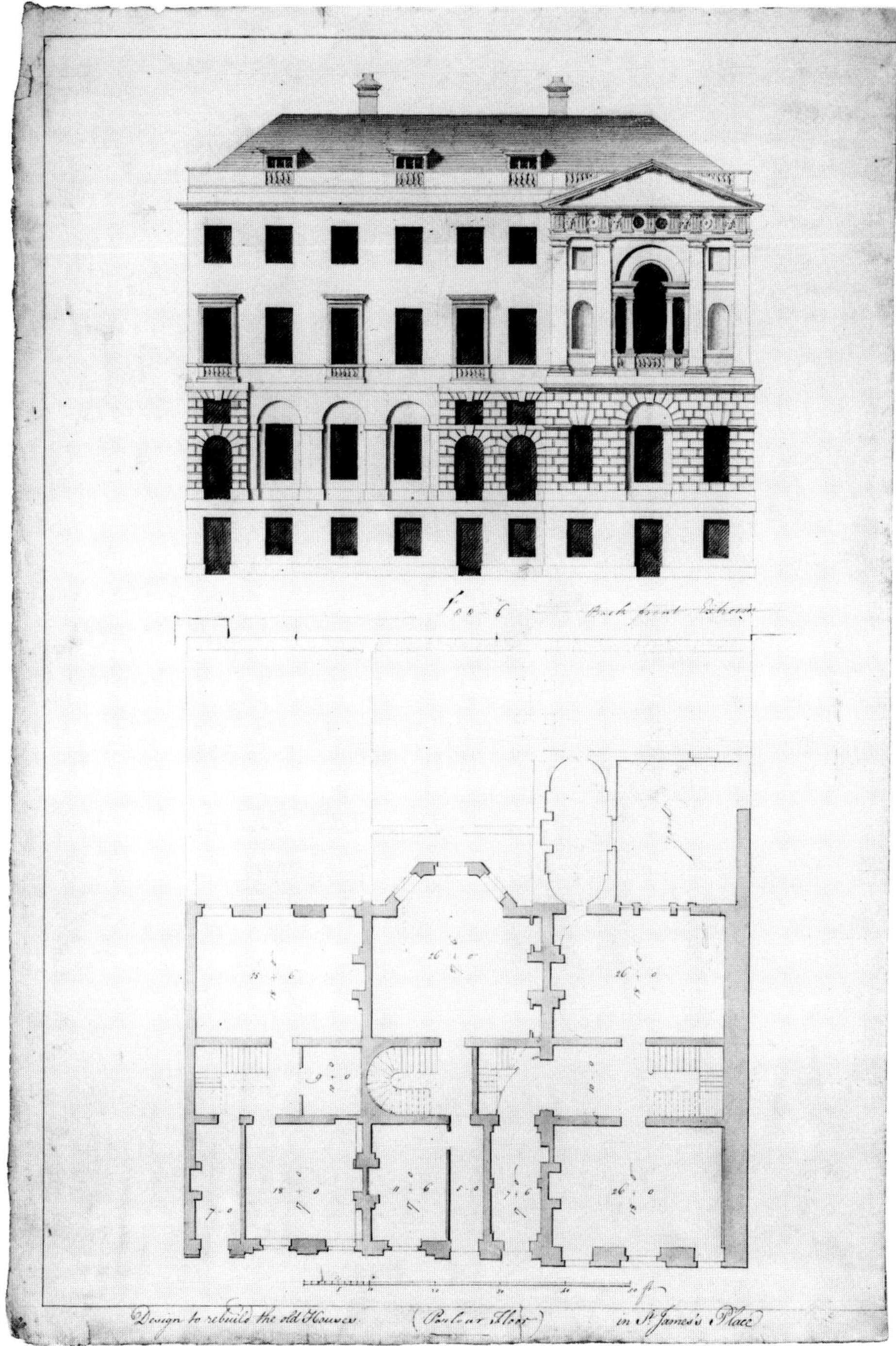

38 Plan and elevation showing the proposed reconstruction of three houses adjoining Spencer House to the east, c1755. The design reveals that the Spencers at one time intended to extend the house beyond the east pavilion, perhaps as part of some speculative development

Spencer House, where the north front, facing St James's Place, presented a relatively austere appearance. Vardy's original designs show a broad, symmetrical facade with matching pavilions at either end (FIG 34, p. 84).[12] A separate design for the east pavilion, also ascribed to Vardy, reveals that at one stage Lord Spencer planned to extend the house still further in this direction (FIG 38).[13] However, the east pavilion could not be built, since the Earl was unable to acquire the site, at that time occupied by the house of a neighbour who refused to sell. Although the Spencers did eventually manage to acquire the property, together with two adjoining houses, the missing pavilion was never erected

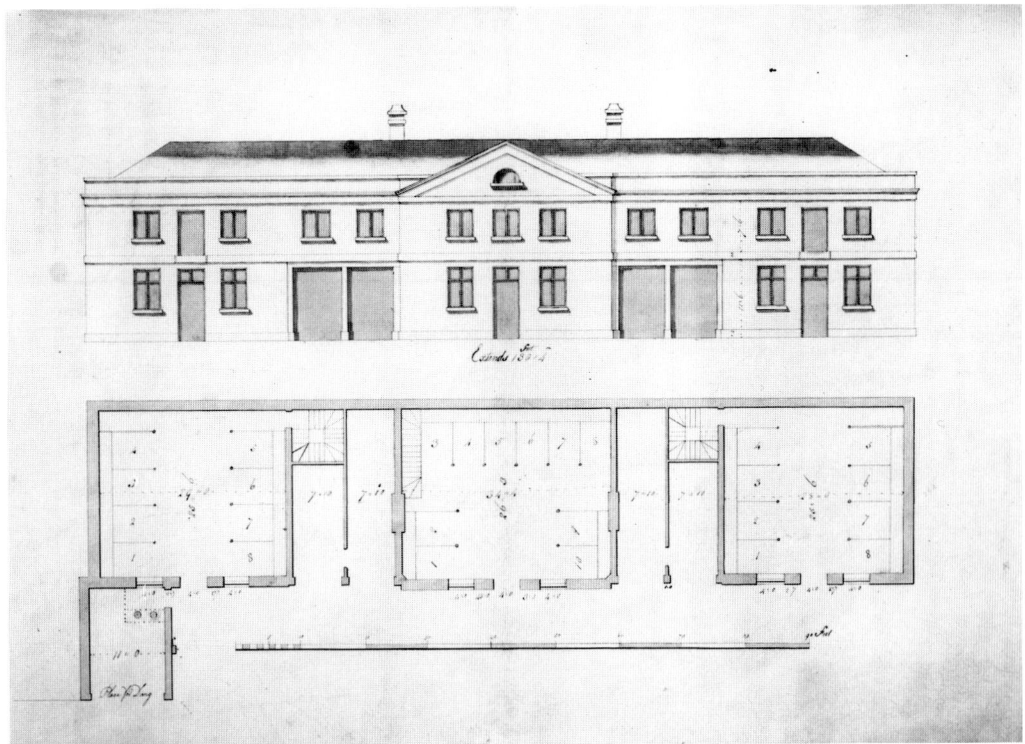

39 Plan and elevation of Spencer House stables in Catherine Wheel Yard, c1765. The stables survived, in altered form, until the Second World War, but suffered serious bomb damage and were ultimately demolished

and to this extent the house remained unfinished. An interesting feature of the facade was the entrance which, with its central doorway flanked by pilasters and niches, consciously recalled a triumphal arch. The pavilion, too, deserves attention, having apparently been inspired by the King's Lodge at Richmond, a building cared for by Vardy and his colleagues at the Office of Works (FIG 35, p. 84), and the garden front of General Wade's house, both of which derived from the unpublished design by Palladio in Lord Burlington's collection (FIG 32, p. 83), referred to earlier.

To the south the house backed on to Catherine Wheel Yard, a thoroughfare for servants and tradesmen, and the facade here was correspondingly plain, two storeys high and clad in brick and stone. The only architectural features of note were the entrance, framed by a pedimented doorcase with Ionic columns, and a Venetian window. A photograph of 1926 shows a stone mounting block on one side of the entrance. The block no longer exists but may perhaps have been built at the same time as the house, for on the opposite side of Catherine Wheel Yard were the original Spencer House stables. The stables have since been demolished, but they are glimpsed in early photographs, and there is a surviving design in the Spencer archive, traditionally ascribed to Vardy (FIG 39).[14] The design shows a building two storeys high with a pitched roof and a central pavilion surmounted by a pediment framing a Diocletian window. The facade extended for over 130 feet, and at ground-floor level there was space for a minimum of six carriages, together with stalls for as many as twenty-six horses. The first floor would have provided accommodation for coachmen and other servants connected with the stables, while the attic probably served as a loft for the storage of horse-feed and straw.

Several of the great London mansions had been built on the French model, *entre cour et jardin*, set back from the street behind a forecourt with either railings or solid brick walls flanking a central carriage gate, and a garden extending to the rear. A conspicuous example was Burlington House in Piccadilly. However, the site of Spencer House would

[12] *The North Front of Ld Spencers House in St James's Place* [GLRO, Maps and Prints, Westminster DD, 5389]

[13] *Design to rebuild the old Houses in St. James's Place* [AP P2]. Two further designs for this project (floor plans) are preserved under the same reference, and there is also a plan of St James's Place of about the same date inscribed *Ground wanted to Complete Mr Spencer's North Front* [AP P2.1063E]

[14] Ground plan and elevation of Spencer House stables, attributed to John Vardy, *c*1765 [AP P19]. Prior to the construction of the stable block in Catherine Wheel Yard Lord Spencer rented a six-horse stable in the same location [AP P2.1063E]. He also rented an eight-horse stable and two coach houses in Cleveland Yard, although on 13 July 1763 he disposed of his lease to a local stablekeeper, Ralph Beckford [AP F181]

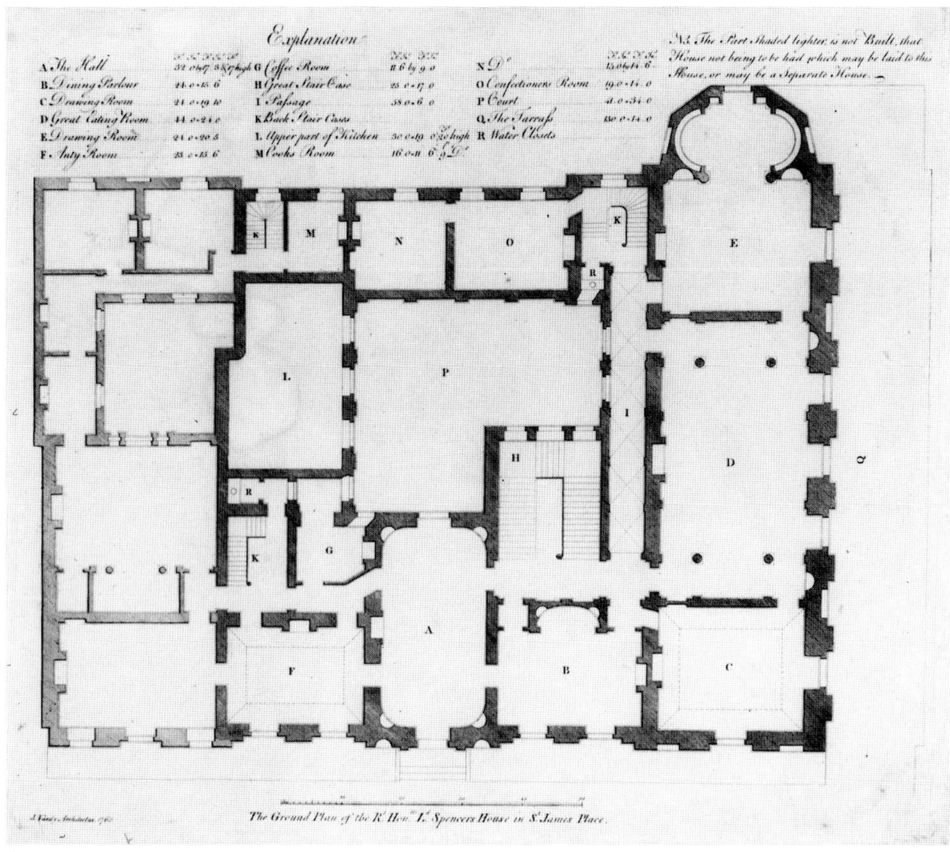

40

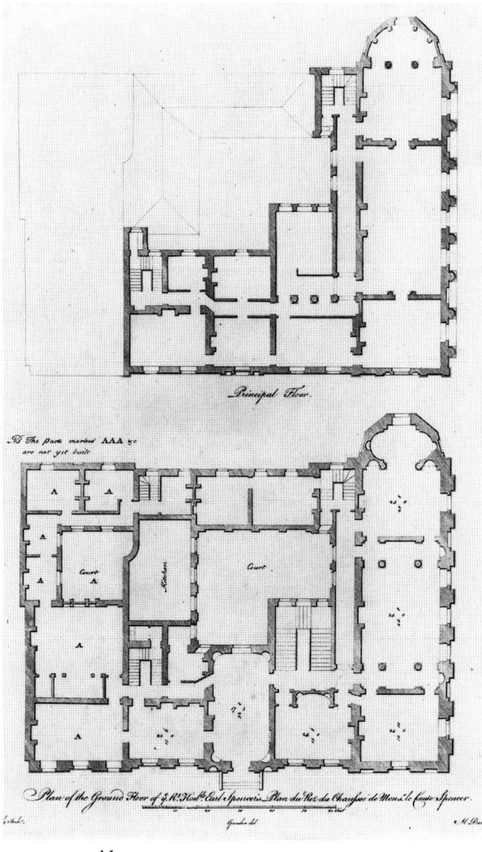

41

not allow for this arrangement and Vardy decided instead to organize the building around an internal L-shaped courtyard. A ground plan by Vardy, marked with the names of individual rooms, was engraved in 1763 (FIG 40),[15] and the same plan was published in modified form in *Vitruvius Britannicus* in 1767 after the architect's death, together with a plan of the first floor (FIG 41). In addition there is a splendid section, signed by Vardy and believed to date from about 1758, which shows the relative size and ceiling height of the rooms running east-west through the centre of the house, as well as decorative details such as joinery and plasterwork (FIG 42).[16] Fortunately also there are numerous surviving designs by Vardy for specific interiors and individual features, all of which will be illustrated and discussed in the course of the present chapter.

Internally the composition of the house followed the pattern of most London mansions. The state apartments or public reception rooms were located on the ground and first floors, with the private apartments on the second floor and the basement and upper storeys given over to the use of servants.

It is best to begin with the basement, since this in a sense was the generator or engine, containing the equipment and manpower which kept the house running. The rooms at this level, some of which are shown in Vardy's section (FIG 42), were of simple design but solid construction, generously-proportioned, with stone floors and vaulted ceilings supported by powerful brick and stone piers; several had panelling and handsome marble chimney-pieces. Light and air fed in from an external area or walkway skirting the building, which also gave access to cellars where coal, wood and other indispensable materials and tools were stored. The largest of the basement rooms was the kitchen, a cavernous two-storey interior located in the east wing, as indicated on Vardy's plan of 1763 (FIG 40). The kitchen received light and ventilation from three large windows

40 Spencer House, ground plan; drawn and engraved by John Vardy, 1763. The lightly-shaded area to the left shows the plan of the projected east wing, which was never built. A key provides the names of rooms

41 Spencer House, plan of ground and first floors; engraving by M. Darly from a drawing by James Gandon after an original design by John Vardy, published in Woolfe and Gandon, Vitruvius Britannicus, *IV (1767), pl.37. Slight variations reveal that Vardy's original ground plan of 1763 had been modified*

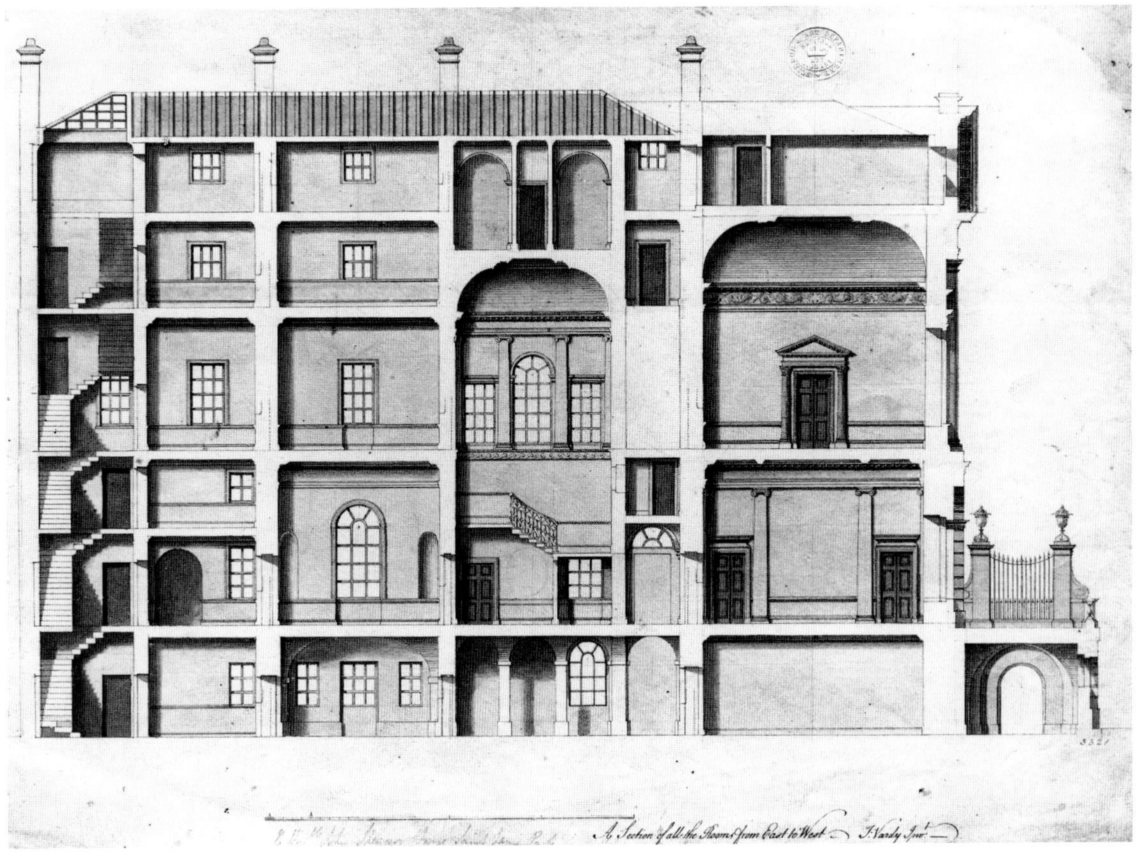

42 Spencer House, east-west section; drawing by John Vardy, c1758. The section shows the relative size and ceiling height of rooms on every level, together with decorative details such as plasterwork and joinery. Visible at ground-floor level are the Coffee Room, Entrance Hall, Staircase Hall and Dining Room. The Great Room is shown at first-floor level, with two other interiors, possibly a bed chamber and closet. One sees at once that the family quarters on the second floor were relatively modest, not much larger than those occupied by servants in the attic and basement

giving on to the internal courtyard, but since these were located at ceiling height, far above the heads of the staff, the preparation of food and other activities would have remained invisible from outside. Also indicated on Vardy's plan is a 'Confectioners Room' and two adjoining apartments, each described as a 'Cooks Room'. Other documents reveal that the basement also contained a coal cellar, a butler's pantry, a housekeeper's room, an office for the steward, a maids' room, a scullery, a still room, a wine cellar, a pastry room and at least one larder, as well as a servants' hall where the staff came together for meals and other gatherings. Another important room was the ice house, containing a circular brick pit where ice taken from lakes and ponds in winter was stored for use in summer. In addition there would have been a strong room where the family's gold and silver plate was kept secure. The attic rooms, seen again in Vardy's section (FIG 42), were comfortable, if modest, having the benefit of individual chimney-pieces and good-sized windows. Accommodation at this level included a room for Lord Spencer's valet and a store room where the servants' clothes were kept.[17]

The mansions of the nobility were primarily built for parade, and the living quarters, to which guests were rarely if ever admitted, were generally quite spartan. Spencer House was typical in this respect, for as Vardy's section shows, the second-floor rooms, containing the Spencers' private apartments, were modestly-proportioned, not much larger in fact than those occupied by their servants on the floor above, while the decoration was apparently quite simple and unpretentious. Indeed the Countess of Warwick was moved to remark, 'at Spencer House . . . entertainment had been considered first and comfort afterwards'.[18]

The largest and most impressive rooms were the state apartments on the ground and first floors, which provided the setting for formal family gatherings and public receptions.

[15] *The Ground Plan of the Rt Honble Ld Spencer's House in St James Place*, drawn and engraved by John Vardy, 1763 [GLRO, Maps and Prints, Westminster DD, 5392]

[16] *A Section of All the Rooms from East to West*, signed 'J: Vardy Invt' [V&A, Prints and Drawings, Q1a.3321]

[17] Information relative to arrangements in the basement and attics is derived from AP F199, AP L20 541B

[18] Frances, Countess of Warwick, *Afterthoughts* (1931), p.250

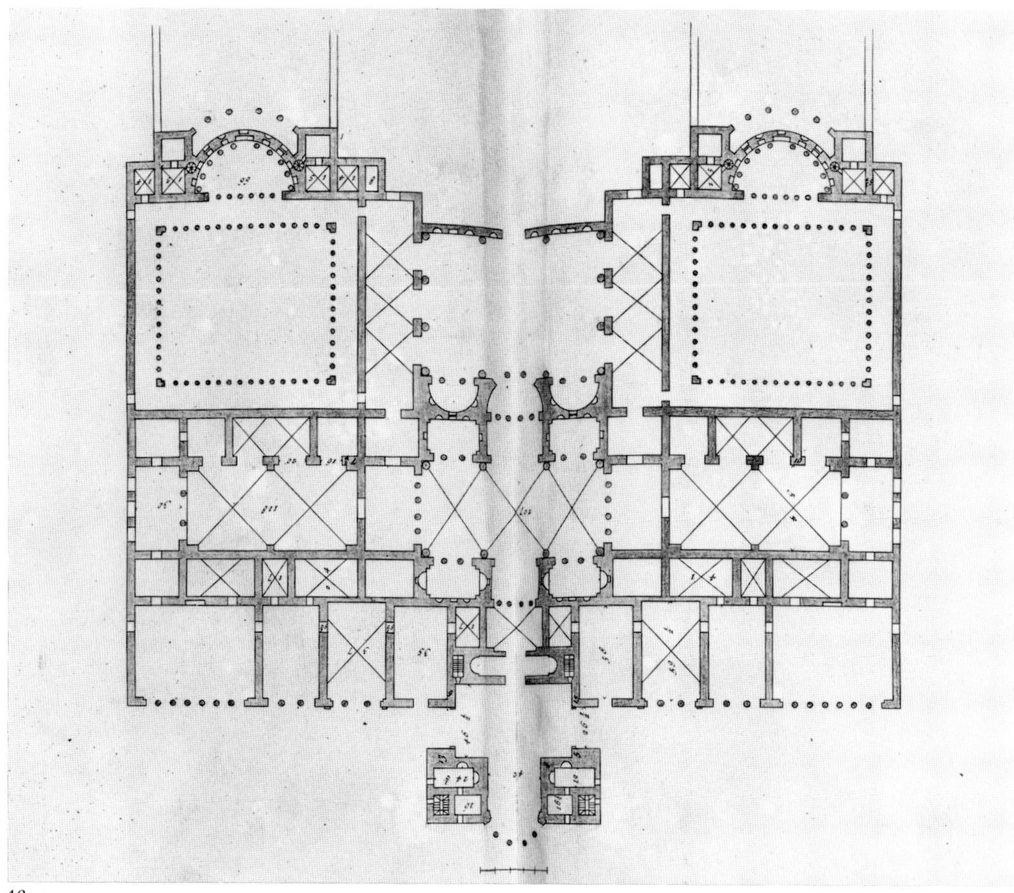

43

43 Plan of the Baths of Nero, Rome; engraving by Fourdrinier from Lord Burlington, Fabbriche Antiche Disegnate da Andrea Palladio Vicentino *(1730), pl.3. The use at Spencer House of interlocking spaces of different shapes, with columnar screens and apses, clearly looks back to the planning of the Roman baths*

44 Spencer House, Entrance Hall, detail of frieze and soffit. The order of the frieze was Doric in keeping with the severe masculine character of the room. The bucrania and instruments of sacrifice conjured up visions of the ancient world and were derived from the Temple of Jupiter Thunderer, Rome (FIG 46). The soffit was taken from that of the Theatre of Marcellus, illustrated alongside the frieze of the Temple of Apollo Sosiano in Palladio's Quattro Libri *(FIG 37, p. 85)*

45 Spencer House, Entrance Hall; photograph by Bedford Lemere, 1895. In grand Classical houses of the eighteenth century entrance halls were considered to be not so much part of the interior as an extension of the exterior, and the Entrance Hall at Spencer House was designed accordingly in an austere, architectural manner, the floor laid with stone, the plasterwork and joinery painted in complementary tones of grey and off-white

The rooms were planned around a central staircase and made up a flexible circuit that could be extended or contracted according to the number of guests and the range of entertainments. Through the use of *enfilades*, or rooms arranged on an axis, Vardy made the most of a restricted site, opening up dramatic perspectives which gave an impression of space and grandeur far beyond the house's true size. At the same time he varied the shape and dimensions of adjoining rooms, creating a lively sequence of contrasting spaces, with sudden shifts in scale and geometry. The effect was partly achieved through the introduction of architectural features such as apses, alcoves and columnar screens, a planning device earlier used by Burlington and Kent but ultimately derived from the Roman Baths (FIG 43). On a more practical level, a network of passageways and staircases guaranteed the easy circulation vital to the smooth running of the household.

The first of the principal apartments was the Entrance Hall (FIG 45). In grand Classical houses of the period rooms of this kind were considered to be not so much a part of the interior as an extension of the exterior, and the Entrance Hall at Spencer House was designed accordingly in a sober, architectural manner. The room was built on a rectangular plan with bowed corners containing niches and an arched window in the centre of the south wall overlooking the internal courtyard. The floor was flagged in stone with the walls and ceiling painted in complementary tones of grey and off-white. The chimney-piece was also of stone, the jambs forming powerful consoles ornamented with acanthus, the frieze carved with sacrificial rams and volutes. Above the chimney-piece was an inset plaster relief of the charioteer Antinous, favourite of the Emperor Hadrian (FIG 48, p. 94). The frieze was decorated with a pattern of skulls of rams and oxen, interspersed with instruments of sacrifice and war such as knives, hatchets and the

4

5

head-dresses of pagan priests, as well as paterae and festoons (FIG 44). The Order was Doric, as expressed by the guttae below the frieze, in keeping with the simplicity and bold masculine character of the room, also establishing a link with the exterior of the building where the columns, pilasters and frieze were likewise of the Doric Order. The ceiling was composed of circular and other geometric compartments enriched with foliage and ribboned bands of asparagus. In the centre was a floral boss, modelled in high relief. The doorcases were decorated with pulvino friezes, while the dado rail followed a pattern of serried fish scales. The furniture in the Entrance Hall included a remarkable suite of mahogany chairs of severe appearance, the seat rails carved with bucrania, festoons and guttae, echoing the decoration of the frieze. The back rests took the form of lugged panels, each painted in the centre with a griffin, the Spencer crest, surmounted by an Earl's coronet (FIG 51, p. 96). Suspended from the ceiling was a gilded lantern, possibly that which hung here in later years, which was decorated with miniature palm trees. In addition there was a traditional hooded porter's chair with button-down leather upholstery.[19] The niches might have contained lamps, statuary or ornaments, possibly the Neo-Classical urns and ewers which appear here in early photographs.

The design of the Entrance Hall was partly of Palladian inspiration. The pulvino friezes above the doors were of a type commonly used by Vardy's master, William Kent. The compartmental ceiling was another characteristic Palladian feature. Although specifically designed for the room, the hall chairs conformed to an established pattern and are closely related to a design by Thomas Chippendale of 1759, published in the third edition of the *Gentleman and Cabinet-Maker's Director* (FIG 52, p. 96).[20] However, as with the west front, the most striking feature was the use of specifically Classical elements. The frieze was clearly derived from the Temple of Vespasian in Rome (FIGS 46 and 47), while the soffit above was copied from the Temple of Apollo Sosiano (FIG 37, p. 85). Most interesting of all was the relief of Antinous, a cast after a celebrated Roman marble original excavated at Hadrian's Villa near Tivoli in 1735 (FIG 48). The latter belonged to the famous antiquarian, Cardinal Albani, and was housed at his villa on the outskirts of Rome. During their visit to Rome in 1763 the Spencers were introduced to Albani and toured the villa, where the Cardinal frequently entertained. They were clearly impressed for, in a letter to the Cardinal, Georgiana wrote of the villa and its contents in the most laudatory terms.[21] There can be little doubt that she and the Earl were shown the relief, which was among the Cardinal's most prized possessions; it is likely also that they themselves conceived the idea of obtaining a cast and using it as they did in the Entrance Hall at Spencer House, for they followed exactly the arrangement at the Villa Albani where the original relief had similarly been installed above a chimney-piece, as illustrated in a design by Albani's architect Carlo Marchionni of 1756 (FIG 50).[22] The cast itself is thought to have been supplied through the agency of Matthew Brettingham, a well-known English dealer in Rome, and may have been a gift from Albani himself, who on a separate occasion presented Georgiana with a copy of an Antique alabaster vase which she had particularly admired on her tour of the villa.[23] It is interesting to note that the cast was taken from the relief prior to its restoration, which involved the addition of chariot reins and other details; it was thus more authentically Classical, providing a near-accurate record of the relief in its original state, recorded also in an engraving after Pompeo Batoni published in 1736 (FIG 49).

The Entrance Hall was adjoined to the east by a room referred to on Vardy's plan as the 'Anty Room' but known today as the Morning Room (PLATE IX, p. 77). This may have served as a waiting room or office in which Lord Spencer conducted business. It had

46 Temple of Jupiter Thunderer, Rome, the frieze, as illustrated in Desgodetz, Les Édifices Antiques de Rome *(1682), p.135. The frieze in the Entrance Hall at Spencer House was clearly inspired by this celebrated Classical building in the Forum*

47 Temple of Jupiter Thunderer, Rome, as illustrated in Giovanni Battista Piranesi, Vedute di Roma *(1753–54). Piranesi's view shows the temple prior to its excavation, with the columns buried in earth up to their capitals. The Spencers would have seen the temple in this state when they visited Rome in 1763–64*

[19] The chair is mentioned in a journal of 1772–73 kept by the 1st Earl's younger daughter, published in Earl of Bessborough and A. Aspinall (eds), *Lady Bessborough and her Family Circle* (1940)

[20] The similarity is noted in Peter Thornton and John Hardy, 'The Spencer Furniture at Althorp', section I, *Apollo* (Mar 1968)

[21] AP F130, GS to Cardinal Albani (Draft), 1765. Georgiana praised the Cardinal for what she described as the '*goût distingué qui brille si singulièrement dans le recueil d'antiquités dont votre maison est remplie*'

[22] Cooper Hewitt Museum, New York, 1901–39–1327. The cast of Antinous and its use at the Villa Albani are discussed in Francis Haskell and Nicholas Penny, *Taste and the Antique* (Yale University Press, 1982), pp.65, 144–6; also in Peter C. Bol (ed.), *Forschungen zur Villa Albani, Katalog der Antiken Bildwerke 1*, 3 vols (Berlin, 1989–92), 1, Cat. No. 108, pls 188–90

[23] AP F130, Cardinal Albani to GS, 29 Dec 1764; Ibid., GS to Cardinal Albani 1765 (draft)

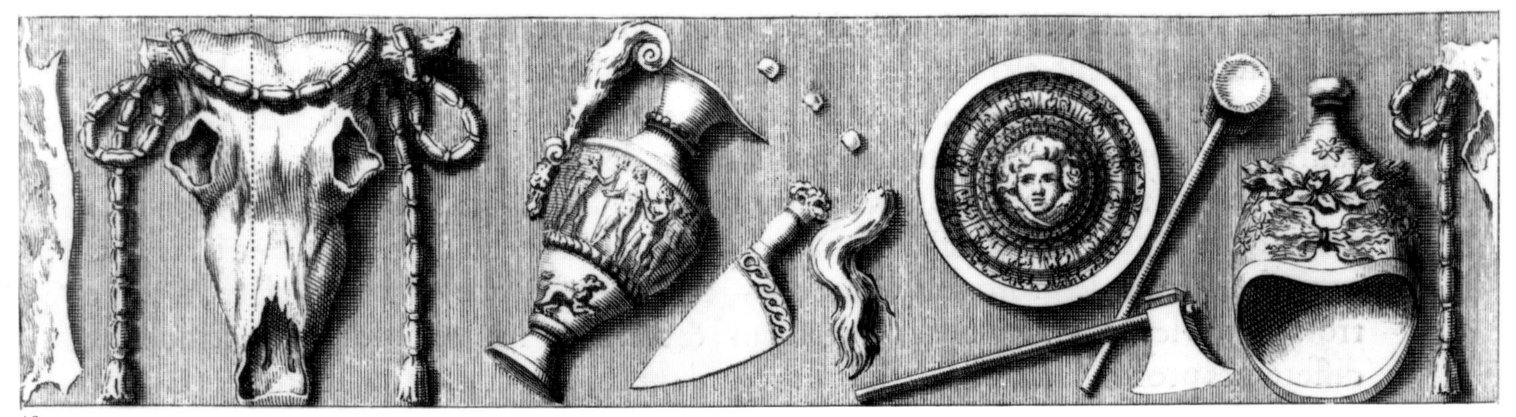

46

47

49 Villa Albani, Rome, relief of Antinous; engraving by Michele Soreglio after Pompeo Batoni, from Rodolfo Venuti, Collectanea Antiquitatum Romanarum *(Rome, 1736), pl.IX. The engraving shows the relief prior to restoration, and it was still in this state when the cast at Spencer House was made*

50 Villa Albani, Rome; design by Carlo Marchionni for the installation of the relief of Antinous above a chimney-piece, c1756. The design shows the relief after restoration, with trailing ribbons and other additions

LEFT
48 Spencer House, Entrance Hall, relief of Antinous over chimney-piece. The relief was a cast of a famous Roman original in marble excavated at Hadrian's Villa in 1735. The latter belonged to the antiquarian Cardinal Albani and was displayed at his house on the outskirts of Rome, which the Spencers visited during their Grand Tour

51

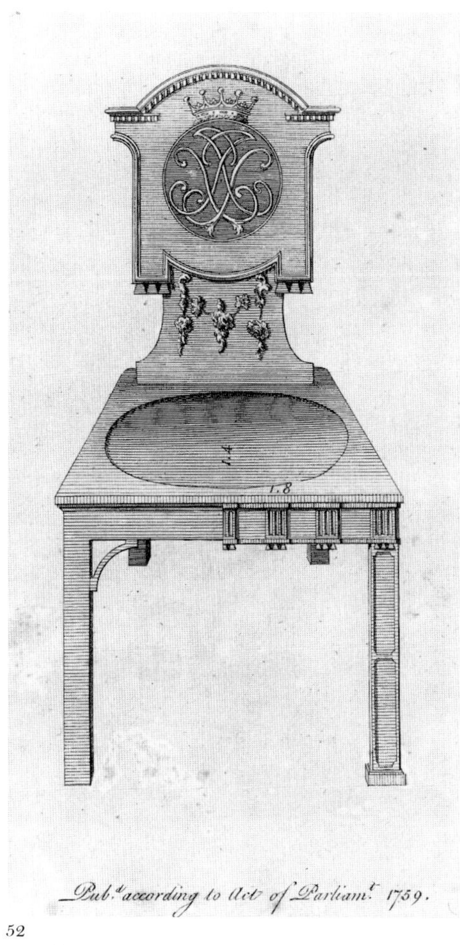

52

51 Spencer House, hall chair. The chair was clearly designed to complement and enhance the decoration of the Entrance Hall. The seat rail was carved with a similar pattern of bucrania and festoons to that of the frieze. The central panel on the back rest was painted with a griffin, the Spencer crest, surmounted by an Earl's coronet, which was added sometime after Spencer's elevation to this rank in 1765

52 Chair design by Thomas Chippendale, 1759; engraving by J. Taylor from Chippendale, The Gentleman and Cabinet-Maker's Director, *3rd edn (1762), pl.XVII. The design is roughly contemporary with the hall chairs at Spencer House, and seems to be closely related*

53 Spencer House, Staircase Hall; photograph of 1926. Much of Vardy's original decoration was later effaced, but the balustrade was retained, as was the soffit of the first-floor landing, albeit in altered form

the advantage of being situated at the foot of the secondary staircase so that Spencer could enter and exit without passing through the Entrance Hall, where there might have been callers he wished to avoid. Little is known of the room's original decoration. The only surviving features are the window surrounds, carved with stylized foliage, and the handsome coved ceiling, decorated with acanthus leaves and a bold Greek fret. The neighbouring 'Coffee Room', indicated on Vardy's plan (FIG 40, p. 88) has likewise been remodelled and there is no proper record of its original decoration. The secondary staircase, in Portland stone, rose through the full height of the house. According to documents of the 1770s the walls were decorated at this time with green baize, while the steps were decorated with Wilton carpet.[24]

The principal staircase, or 'Great Staircase' as it is described on Vardy's plan, was situated to the west of the Entrance Hall (FIG 53). The interior has since been altered, but Vardy's section (FIG 42, p. 89) reveals that the architect intended the walls to be decorated at first-floor level with Roman Ionic pilasters rising to a dentilled cornice and a coved ceiling with a central compartment. The section also shows a wave-scroll frieze running below the pilasters and a surviving Venetian window on the south wall, mirrored on the landing opposite by a conforming screen, as indicated in the plan of the first floor illustrated in *Vitruvius Britannicus* (FIG 41, p. 88). The staircase itself was a feat of engineering as much as architecture, three flights of cantilevered Portland stone steps rising from the ground to the first floor. The balustrade was of fretted metal fashioned in imitation of festooned drapery (FIG 53), possibly inspired by the famous 'tulip' staircase

[24] AP F199

53

54

54 Spencer House, Staircase Hall, soffit of first-floor landing. The flattened consoles with Greek-fret mouldings are a later addition, but the panels conform to Vardy's original design (FIG 55)

55 Spencer House, Staircase Hall; design by Vardy for the soffit of the first-floor landing, 1758. Alongside the design for the soffit is a drawing of the frieze which Vardy used in the alcove of the Palm Room (FIG 80, p. 114)

56 Palmyra, soffit, as illustrated in Robert Wood, The Ruins of Palmyra *(1753), pl.XXIX. Vardy made use of this feature when designing the soffit in the Staircase Hall at Spencer House*

57 Palmyra, door bracket, as illustrated in Wood, The Ruins of Palmyra *(1753), pl.XLVII. The bracket was adapted by Vardy to provide a horizontal support for the first-floor landing in the Staircase Hall at Spencer House*

55

56

by Inigo Jones at the Queen's House, Greenwich, where Vardy had earlier been employed as Clerk of the Works. Equally remarkable was the soffit of the first-floor landing (FIG 54), for which there is a separate design by Vardy dated 1758 (FIG 55).[25] The design shows Vardy making use of the most recent discoveries in the field of archaeology, for the hexagonal and rhomboid decoration of the panels between the brackets was clearly derived from the Great Temple at Palmyra, drawings of which had only recently been published in Robert Wood's *The Ruins of Palmyra* of 1753 (FIG 56).[26] The brackets, too, were derived from Wood's *Palmyra*, having been adapted from illustrations of vertical doorcase consoles (FIG 57). The frieze below the landing followed a pattern of lion and wolf masks, linked by festoons, which may also have been copied from an Antique source.

[25] *The Sketch of the Sophite of the Great Stair Case between the Consoles*, signed and dated 'J: Vardy 1758' [V&A, Prints and Drawings, A149 3436–198]

[26] A copy of Wood's *Palmyra* is listed among Lord Spencer's books at Althorp in a document of 1763 [AP F169]

58 Spencer House, ground-floor passageway. Primarily intended for the use of servants, the passageway connected with a staircase leading down to the basement, also giving access to the Dining Room and Palm Room. Its design was suitably plain, the floor flagged in stone, the walls painted a matching tone of grey and the groin-vaulted ceiling supported by Tuscan corbels corresponding to the lowest of the Classical Orders

59 Spencer House, Ante Room; photograph of c1890. This handsome Palladian interior was originally known as the Little Eating Parlour and is thought to have served for family meals and intimate dinner parties

The Staircase Hall was adjoined by a passageway running north-south, primarily intended for the use of servants, which communicated with a back staircase leading down to the basement (FIG 58). The design was suitably austere, the floor flagged in stone, the walls painted a matching shade of grey and the groin-vaulted ceiling supported by Tuscan corbels corresponding to the lowest of the Orders.[27] At either end were arches, coffered after the fashion of the Basilica of Maxentius in Rome. The passageway had two large windows overlooking the internal courtyard, and also contained a collection of lanterns, of which there is sadly no visual record.[28]

To the north the Staircase Hall led through to a room overlooking St James's Place, described on Vardy's plan as the 'Dining Parlour' and in another design as the 'Little Dining Room', but known today as the Ante Room (FIG 59). This was probably the setting for family meals and small dinner parties. The focus of the interior was a semi-circular alcove in the centre of the south wall with coffering and inset niches, which provided shelf-space for cisterns and other elements of gold and silver plate. The alcove was flanked on either side by doors which were themselves surmounted by oval niches, possibly containing busts, and the whole arrangement thus produced the effect of a triumphal arch. The frieze was decorated with serried oak leaves bound by ribbons, and the ceiling followed a bold geometric design, with circular and semi-circular compartments divided by ribs enriched with guilloche mouldings. Fabric hangings were rarely used in dining rooms, since they retained the smell of food, and the walls of the Ante Room were apparently painted a dark shade of green, contrasting with the decorative plasterwork and joinery, which were white. The fashion for draw curtains had not yet developed at this time and here as elsewhere in the house festoon curtains would have been used, probably of figured silk damask. There is no record of the original chimney-piece, which

[27] According to Sir William Chambers, the Tuscan Order was especially suitable 'to adorn the lower Apartments, Offices, Stables, and other places that require strength and simplicity, where richer Orders would be improper' [*Treatise on Civil Architecture* (1759), pp.16–17]

[28] AP F199

59

60

61

60 Spencer House, Ante Room; design by Vardy for a console table and matching pier glass, 1758

61 Double-bodied sphinx; etching by Wenceslaus Hollar, 1652. Based on a drawing ascribed to Giulio Romano, this remarkable etching was clearly the source for Vardy's console design (FIG 60)

62 Holkham Hall, Statue Gallery. Designed by Vardy's master, William Kent, the apse is of the same type used in the Ante Room at Spencer House

63 Temple of Venus and Rome, the apse. Illustrated in Palladio's Quattro Libri, *the apse was among the most admired remains of Classical Roman architecture. It had been adapted by William Kent in his designs for Chiswick House and Holkham Hall and was used again by Vardy as the basis of the alcove in the Ante Room at Spencer House*

was later removed; nor is anything known of the original furniture, which can no longer be identified among the surviving pieces in the Spencer collection. However, there would almost certainly have been one or more dining tables, as well as a set of matching dining chairs, probably of mahogany with leather covers. The alcove would have contained a sideboard, and there would also have been a table and pier glass between the windows opposite. A design for a table and pier glass was submitted by Vardy in 1758, but apparently remained unexecuted (FIG 60).[29]

The sources of Vardy's designs were remarkably diverse. The alcove was of a type used by Kent at Holkham Hall (FIG 62) and by Burlington at Chiswick Villa. The frieze

[29] *Table & Glass as Designed for the Little Dining Room*, signed and dated 'John Vardy Invt 1758' [BMPD 1962–7–14–60]

[30] A copy of Hollar's etching is preserved in the British Museum [BMPD P.258]. There is an entry for the etching in Richard

62

63

Pennington, *A Descriptive Catalogue of the Etched Work of Wenceslaus Hollar* (C.U.P., 1982), pp.xxiv, 38. However, the entry does not provide the name of the publication from which the etching was taken, which remains unknown. I have been unable to locate the drawing on which the etching was based, which may perhaps have been reattributed

[31] Rodolfo Falb (ed.), *Il Taccuino Senese di Giuliano da Sangallo* (Siena, 1902), pl.43

and ceiling were also of Palladian inspiration. The pier table, however, was copied from an etching by the seventeenth-century German artist, Wenceslaus Hollar (FIG 61), which was based in turn on a drawing ascribed to the sixteenth-century Italian artist, Giulio Romano.[30] To look back still further, the drawing by Giulio Romano, now sadly lost, was almost certainly based on a Roman relief or some other Classical fragment, as yet unidentified, for a remarkably similar drawing appears in a book of sketches after the Antique by the fifteenth-century Italian artist, Giulio da Sangallo.[31] The alcove, too, was of Classical extraction, looking back ultimately to the apse of the Temple of Venus and Rome (FIG 63).

64

65

64 Spencer House, Library; photograph by Bedford Lemere, 1895

65 Witches at their Several Hellish Ceremonies, *by Salvator Rosa. Now in the National Gallery in London, this disturbing painting hung at one time above the chimney-piece in the Library at Spencer House, having been acquired by the 1st Earl Spencer at the Sir William Hamilton sale in 1761*

From the Ante Room a door on the right hand side of the alcove led through to a tiny lobby communicating in turn with an adjoining room described on Vardy's plan as the 'Drawing Room' but referred to in other documents of the period as the 'Library' (FIG 64). The ceiling was coved and may originally have been decorated with the present wave-scroll border. The doorcases were carved with serried acanthus leaves, while the chimney-piece was of white marble, the frieze mounted with a tablet of Siena marble flanked by scrolling acanthus, the jambs in the form of volutes carved with lion masks, drapery and foliage. The walls were probably papered, and although there is no record of the original furniture, it is reasonable to suppose that the room contained one or more bookcases, as well as work tables and seating furniture, probably upholstered en suite with the window curtains. The only painting known to have hung here was a scene of witches by Salvator Rosa, which Lord Spencer purchased at the Sir William Hamilton sale in 1761 (FIG 65).

The Library led through to the principal dining room, described on Vardy's plan as the 'Great Eating Room' (FIG 66). Measuring over forty feet in length, this was the largest of the ground-floor interiors, providing a suitably splendid setting for large family dinners and public banquets. The design of the room evolved from a watercolour drawing by Vardy dated 1755 (PLATE V, p. 67),[32] but was substantially altered in execution, as can be seen from Vardy's later section (FIG 42, p. 89) and the ground plan published in *Vitruvius Britannicus* (FIG 41, p. 88).

The ceiling was divided into oval and rectangular compartments, with ribs enriched with guilloche bands (FIG 71, p. 109). In an earlier age the flat of the ceiling might have been painted with historical or mythological scenes, but decoration of this kind was no

66 Spencer House, Dining Room; photograph by Bedford Lemere, 1895. Although substantially altered in the late eighteenth century, much of the original decoration of the Dining Room was retained. The present photograph shows the walls hung with damask, which was added in the 1870s. Fabric hangings would not have been used originally, since they retained the smell of food

67 Spencer House, Dining Room; design by John Vardy for the window soffits, 1758. Like the design for the window shutters (PLATE III, p. 67), it is not known whether this was ever executed. The central motif is closely related to that in the cupola of the alcove in the Palm Room

68 Spencer House, Dining Room; preliminary design by John Vardy for the chimney-piece, 1755. The iconography of Vardy's design was closely related to the function of the room. The overmantel was flanked by figures of Bacchus and Ceres, symbolic of wine and food. The lintel of the chimney-piece was decorated with a relief representing two drunken putti. Only the chimney-piece itself was executed, the overmantel having been rejected

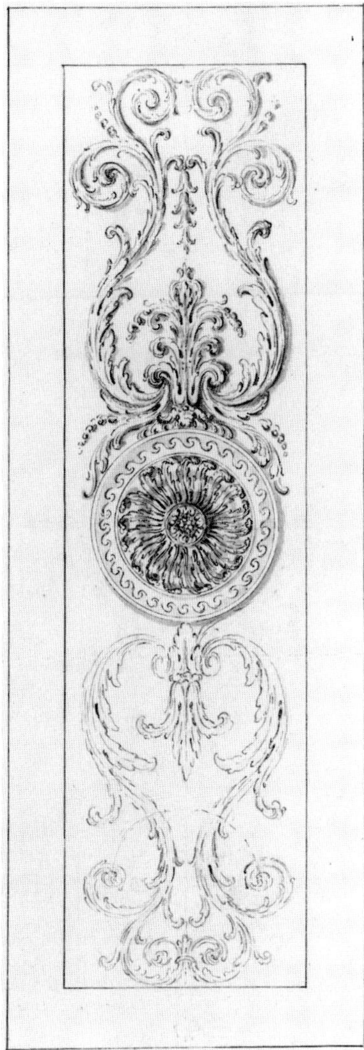

67

68

longer the fashion and the ceiling was simply painted white. The frieze was decorated with bucrania, putti and candelabra, the ground painted green, the ornaments white and gilt (FIG 73, p. 110). The walls and joinery were painted to match. The room was crossed at either end by columnar screens, with matching pilasters lining the walls. Vardy experimented at first with the Corinthian Order but eventually opted for Roman Ionic. The columns and pilasters have since been replaced, but it is possible that the shafts were originally painted in imitation of Siena marble, as the architect apparently intended (PLATE V, p. 67). A separate design by Vardy indicates that he also intended the window shutters to be painted with smoking censers (PLATE III, p. 67),[33] while another shows the window soffits decorated with scrolling acanthus and rosettes with wave-scroll borders (FIG 67).[34] It is not known whether these designs were ever executed, since the windows were later altered and the original shutters and soffits destroyed. The chimney-piece was of Carrara marble, the jambs and lintel richly carved with figures and ornaments. In Vardy's original section the chimney-piece was accompanied by an overmantel (PLATE V, p. 67), which also appears in another, more detailed design by the architect (FIG 68),[35] but the overmantel was never executed.

[32] *The Dining Room Parlour Floor*, signed and dated 'J Vardy Invt 1755' [GLRO, Westminster DD, 5393]

[33] *A Piece of Ornament for the Pannells in the Window Shutters*, initialled 'J:V', the reverse inscribed *1758* [RIBA G4/3(2)]

[34] *The Sophites of the Dining Room Windows at Mr Spencers*, initialled and dated 'J:V. 1758' [RIBA G4/3(1)]

[35] *Dining Room Parlour Floor Chimney Piece, with the frame over it*, signed and dated 'John Vardy Invt 1755' [SJSM 69/1/1]

69

70

69 Silver tureen, by Thomas Gilpin, from a dinner service commissioned by John Spencer, c1756. The tureen is engraved with the Spencer arms impaling those of Poyntz and would certainly have been used during dinner parties at Spencer House, complementing the famous Marlborough plate

70 Dining chair, c1750–60; one of a suite of twenty-three in the Spencer collection at Althorp, possibly intended for the Dining Room at Spencer House

71 Spencer House, Dining Room, detail of ceiling. In an earlier age the ground of the ceiling might have been painted with allegorical or mythological scenes, but the fashion for such decoration had passed and Vardy used a simple off-white scheme

72 Banqueting House, Whitehall, ceiling, by Inigo Jones, as illustrated in William Kent, The Designs of Inigo Jones, *I (1727), pl.52. As the most famous dining room in England, and the work of the great English architect Inigo Jones, the Banqueting House was an obvious source for the ceiling of the Dining Room at Spencer House (FIG 71)*

At either end of the room were magnificent giltwood sideboards with Siena marble tops (PLATE XI, p. 80 and FIG 77, p. 112), on which the Spencers would have displayed their finest gold and silver plate, elements of which might also have been placed in the niches on the west wall (FIG 69). One of the sideboards is illustrated in another design by Vardy, which also shows a matching pier glass, apparently unexecuted (FIG 78, p. 113).[36] The room would also have contained a suite of dining chairs, probably in mahogany with leather seats, as in the 'Little Eating Parlour'. A suite of this kind survives at Althorp and might well be that originally used here, being consistent in terms of quality, style and date, and having the additional feature of miniature Ionic capitals to the front legs, which would have matched the Order of the columns and pilasters in the Dining Room (FIG 70).[37] When the Dining Room was in use the chairs would have been placed in the centre, grouped around one or more occasional tables; at all other times they would have been backed up against the walls. The window curtains were almost certainly of figured damask, depending from giltwood pelmets of the sort illustrated in Vardy's original section. Among the paintings displayed here were two mythological landscapes, the first representing the slaying of a dragon, possibly Perseus and Andromeda, the other representing the abduction of a woman by a centaur, probably Nessus and Dejanira.

Once again the interior clearly showed the influence of the Palladian tradition. The ceiling (FIG 71) was derived from the Banqueting House in Whitehall by Inigo Jones, where Vardy had earlier been employed as Clerk of the Works (FIG 72), while the frieze

[36] *Two Tables & Two Glass's at each End of Great Dining Room, Parlour Floor,* the reverse inscribed *For the Honble John Spencer Esqrs Great Dining Room in St James's place at Each End of the Room* [BMPD 1962–7–14–61]. Identical pier glasses appear in another design by Vardy for an unidentified reception room [RIBA G4/1]. The sideboards were removed from the room during the lifetime of the 2nd Earl Spencer and subsequently sold. One was acquired by the V & A, the other by Temple Newsam House in Yorkshire. Both have since been placed on loan at Spencer House

[37] The chairs were first linked to the Dining Room at Spencer House in Thornton and Hardy, op. cit., p.187. The authors' attribution of the chairs to Ince and Mayhew was vigorously contested by the 7th Earl Spencer [V&A, Department of Furniture and Woodwork, Spencer House file]

71

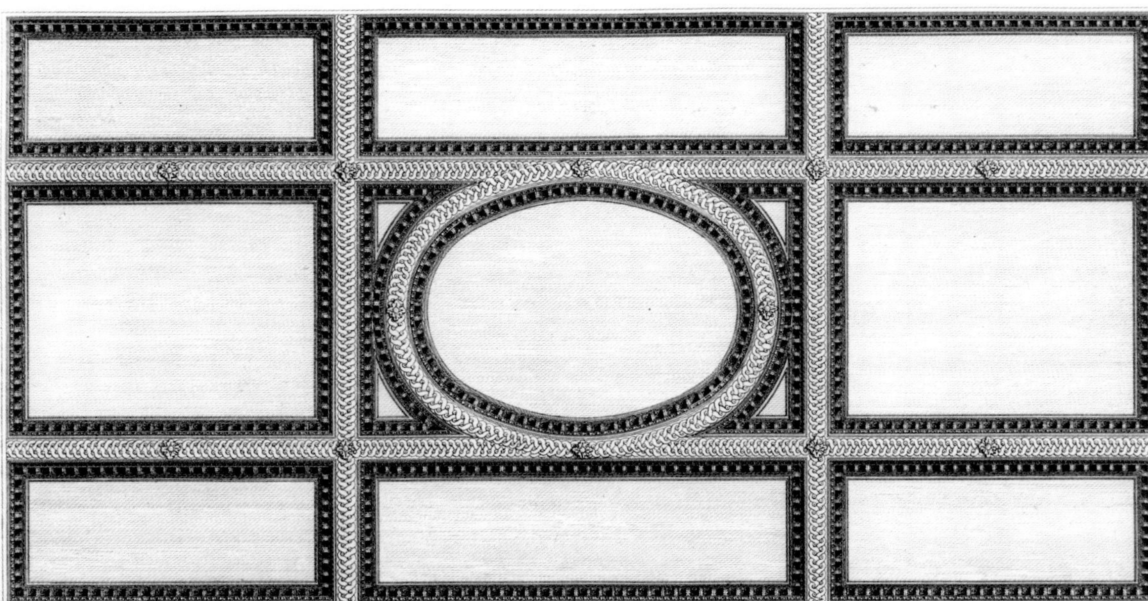

72

73

74

(FIG 73) was prefigured in the Entrance Hall at Holkham by Kent (FIG 74). The sideboards (PLATE XI, p.80, and FIGS 77 and 78) followed a pattern familiar since the Renaissance (FIG 76).[38] The influence of Antiquity was also strong. The frieze, though earlier used by Kent, was ultimately derived from the Temple of Fortuna Virilis in Rome (FIG 75). Moreover, it was reproduced with far greater fidelity than at Holkham, indicating a significant shift towards a stricter adherence to Classical precedent. The sideboards, too, ultimately looked back to Classical prototypes (FIG 79). It is noteworthy also that most of the overtly Palladian elements in Vardy's preliminary design, such as the overmantel and the doorcases with broken pediments, were finally eliminated.

The decoration of the Dining Room was likewise remarkable for the multi-layered use of symbol and metaphor. It was surely no accident that Vardy chose to reproduce the ceiling of the Banqueting House, then as now the most famous dining room in England; nor was it merely fortuitous that he borrowed the frieze of the Temple of Fortuna, a goddess associated with abundance. The smoking censers in his designs for the window shutters provided a discreet allusion to the Classical custom of burning incense at meals to clear the atmosphere between courses. The chimney-piece was decorated with miniature bands of fruit, repeated in the carved decoration of the window surrounds, and with a relief representing drunken putti in a vineyard (FIGS 66 and 68, pp.106 and 107). The overmantel, though rejected, was decorated with figures of Bacchus and Ceres, divinities associated with food, wine and hospitality. Masks of Bacchus appeared on the sideboards (FIG 77), flanked by festooned vines and bunches of grapes. Even the columnar screens may have been intended as a play on the theme of plenty, for according to Thomas

73 Spencer House, Dining Room, detail of frieze and capitals to columns. Vardy's original frieze has survived, but the capitals are a later addition, having been installed by Henry Holland in the late eighteenth century. Originally the capitals were of a Roman Ionic Order. Those introduced by Holland are Greek and were derived from the Temple on the Ilyssus (FIG 206, p. 220)

74 Holkham Hall, Entrance Hall. The frieze is virtually identical to that used by Vardy in the Dining Room at Spencer House (FIG 73)

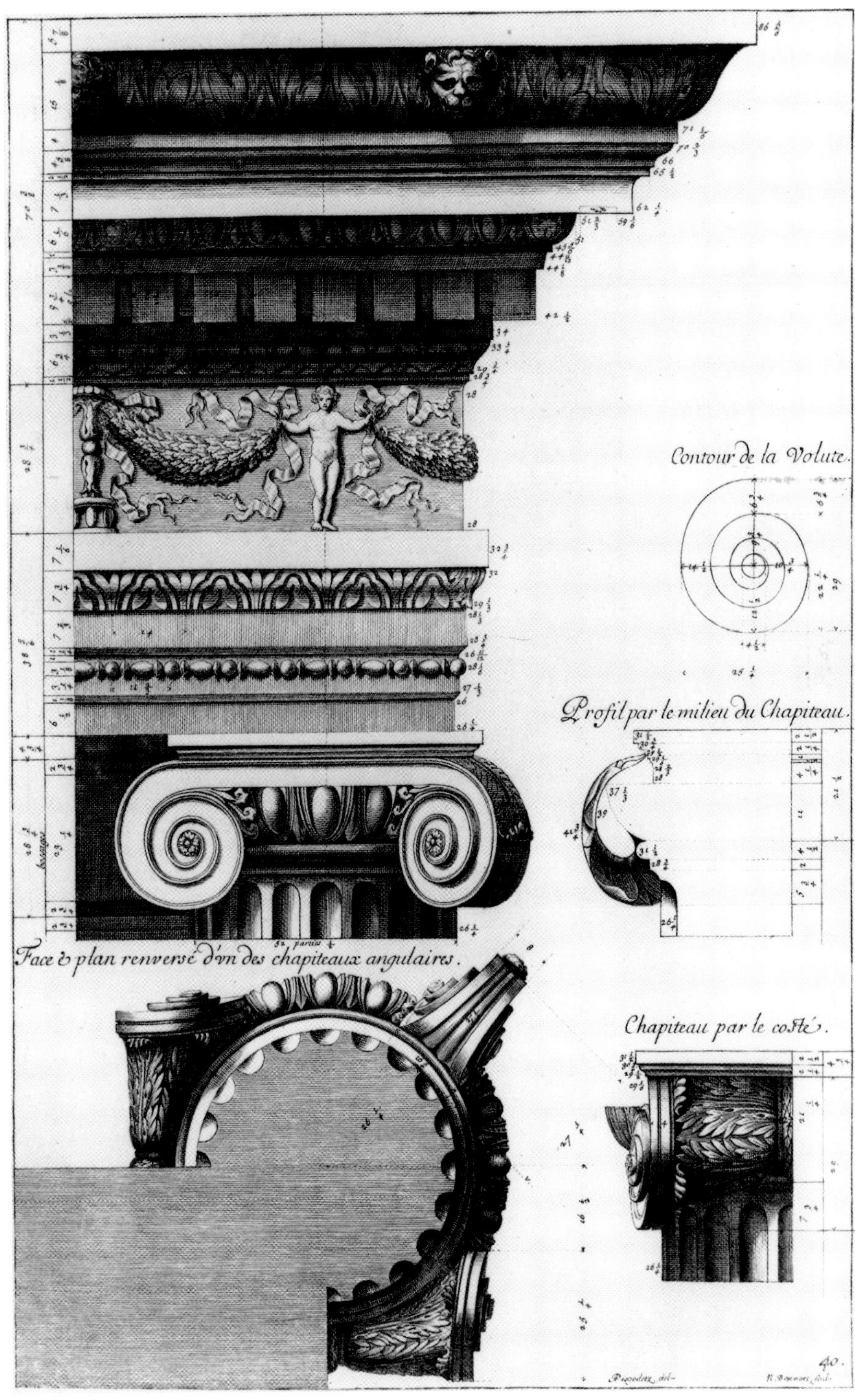

75 Temple of Fortuna Virilis, Rome, the frieze, as illustrated in Desgodetz, Les Édifices Antiques de Rome *(1682), p.43. The frieze in the Dining Room at Spencer House was copied exactly from this source (*FIG *73). The choice was especially appropriate since Fortuna was a goddess associated with abundance*

Sheraton columns were symbolic of sustenance and thus especially appropriate to the decoration of dining rooms.[39]

The last of the ground-floor apartments was that adjoining the Dining Room to the south. Identified on Vardy's plan as a 'Drawing Room' (FIG 40, p. 88), it was later converted into a study, becoming known as 'Lord Spencer's Room', but it might best be described as the 'Palm Room', for the most conspicuous feature of its design was a screen of Corinthian columns in the form of luxuriant palm trees.

[38] The Spencer House sideboards should also be compared with those designed by Kent for the Saloon at Houghton Hall, Norfolk, illustrated in Michael I. Wilson, *William Kent, Architect, Designer, Painter, Gardener, 1685–1748* (1984), pl.36

[39] Thomas Sheraton, *The Cabinet-Maker and Upholsterer's Drawing Book*, 2 vols (1793–94), 2, p.440

76

76 Design for a basin, School of Andrea Mantegna. There are striking parallels between the present drawing and Vardy's design for the sideboards in the Dining Room at Spencer House (FIGS 77 and 78). Both, however, ultimately look back to Antiquity (FIG 79)

77 Spencer House, Dining Room, original sideboard. Designed by John Vardy and probably carved by his brother Thomas, the sideboard looks back by way of the Renaissance to the furniture of Classical Antiquity. The mask of Bacchus and trailing vines are obviously intended as references to wine and hospitality

77

78 Spencer House, Dining Room; design by John Vardy for a sideboard and matching pier glass, 1758. Only the sideboards appear to have been executed

79 Marble table (cartibulum) from the House of Meleager, Pompeii. The use of animals, real and imaginary, was a characteristic feature of Greek and Roman furniture, and Vardy's Dining Room sideboards ultimately look back to tables of the kind illustrated here (PLATE XI, p. 80, and FIG 77)

78

79

80 Spencer House, Palm Room; photograph of 1926. Corinthian in Order, the Palm Room provided the logical conclusion to a carefully managed architectural circuit which led the visitor from the Doric simplicity of the Entrance Hall (FIG 45, p. 91) to the Ionic elegance of the Staircase Hall (FIG 53, p. 97) and Dining Room (FIG 66, p. 106), climaxing here in an explosion of colour and ornament

The eighteenth century produced some exotic interiors; at her house in Hill Street Mrs Montagu created an Oriental Room which was said to be 'like the temple of some Indian God'.[40] But there was surely no more exotic interior in the whole of Georgian London than the Palm Room at Spencer House (FIG 80). Corinthian in Order, the room provided the logical solution to a carefully-managed architectural circuit which led the visitor from the Doric simplicity of the Entrance Hall to the Ionic elegance of the Staircase Hall and Dining Room, climaxing here in an explosive display of colour and ornament.

The interior was conceived around 1757, the date which appears on a surviving watercolour section by Vardy which shows the screen and alcove more or less as executed (PLATE VI, p. 68).[41] The colour scheme was similar to that in the Dining Room. The walls were painted pea-green, with the decorative plasterwork and joinery in white and gilt, the coffering in the alcove being partly picked out in pink, in accordance with a separate design by Vardy showing details of the mouldings tinted in watercolour (PLATE IV, p. 67).[42] The ceiling was of striking design, with pronounced Greek fret mouldings, while the frieze followed an alternating pattern of griffins and candelabra (FIG 81). The alcove rose to a coffered dome divided by foliated ribs, with a circular medallion in the

[40] Christopher Simon Sykes, *Private Palaces: Life in the Great London Houses* (1985), p.139

[41] *Alcove Bow Room Ground Floor*, by John Vardy (1757) [SJSM 69/1/2]

[42] *The Alcove Room Ld Spencers . . . The Pannells of Diference 3 flowers in the head of the Side Nitches* [RIBA G4/3(3)]

81

82

81 Spencer House, Palm Room, detail of frieze. The frieze incorporates the griffin, the Spencer crest, representing an obvious play on the heraldry of Vardy's patron

82 Temple of Antoninus and Faustina, Rome, the frieze, as illustrated in Desgodetz, Les Édifices Antiques de Rome *(1682), pl.III. The frieze in the Palm Room was reproduced with scrupulous accuracy from this source (FIG 81)*

centre composed of a rosette within a Vitruvian scroll border, virtually identical to that designed by Vardy for the soffit of the Dining Room windows (FIG 67, p. 107). Around the base of the dome ran a distinctive foliated frieze, illustrated in the architect's design for the soffit of the first-floor landing (FIG 55, p. 99). The chimney-piece was of Siena and white marble, the jambs forming herms of the poets Homer and Hesiod, the lintel carved with an elegant frieze composed of paterae, festoons, an urn and a pair of crossed palm branches echoing the decoration of the columns (FIG 86). Among the contents of the room was a remarkable suite of seating furniture, likewise decorated with palm-leaf ornaments, the frames white and gilt to match the joinery, the covers of green silk

83 Spencer House, Palm Room, north-east view; photograph of 1926. Visible in the photograph is the original chimney-piece, flanked by terms of Hesiod and Homer, and an original pier glass, specifically designed for the room, with palm leaf decoration echoing that of the columns opposite (FIG 80)

83

84

85

84 Capitoline Museum, Rome, bust of Hesiod; engraving by Giovanni Rossi from Bottari, Musei Capitolini *(1750), pl.44*

85 Capitoline Museum, Rome, bust of Homer; engraving by Giovanni Rossi from Giovanni Gaetano Bottari, Musei Capitolini, *I (Rome, 1750), pl.54. This famous bust, a Roman copy of a lost Greek original, was among the most admired exhibits in the Capitoline Museum. Casts had been made from it, and one of these was probably used as the basis of the version in the Palm Room*

86 Spencer House, Palm Room, original chimney-piece, flanked by terms of Hesiod and Homer

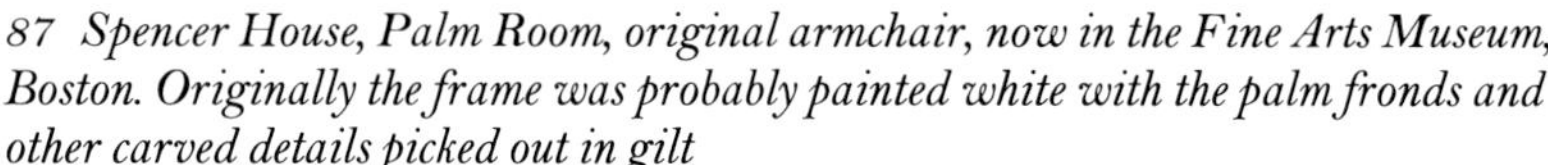

87 Spencer House, Palm Room, original armchair, now in the Fine Arts Museum, Boston. Originally the frame was probably painted white with the palm fronds and other carved details picked out in gilt

88 Design for a pier glass by John Vardy, c1755, possibly a preliminary study for the pier glass from the Palm Room, Spencer House

damask complementing the colour of the walls (FIG 87).[43] The seating furniture was accompanied by a matching pier glass, which hung in the centre of the north wall and which relates quite closely to another surviving design by Vardy, possibly a preliminary study (FIG 88).[44] The room would also have contained a chandelier or lantern, possibly that which later hung in the Entrance Hall, decorated alike with miniature palm trees (FIG 45, p. 91).

In Vardy's section the niches between the columns contain statues of blackamoor archers in pink togas, firing arrows from out of their jungle-like setting. The statues were not imaginary; they were genuine Roman marble figures in the Spencer collection formerly belonging to the Duke of Marlborough (FIG 89). Although too large in reality to fit the niches, an oversight perhaps on the part of the architect, the inclusion of the statues in Vardy's design is a striking instance of the fusion of the fine and decorative arts. The place of the blackamoors was ultimately taken by a pair of white marble urns, and the room is also known to have contained a painting of two moneylenders, which hung above the chimney-piece.

[43] The suite comprised at least one sofa, eight armchairs, two large stools, and two smaller stools. The suite was removed from the Palm Room during the lifetime of the 2nd Earl Spencer and while the two large stools were retained and are still at Althorp, the remaining pieces left the Spencer collection. A sofa and one of the armchairs are now in a private collection in England. Two further armchairs are in the Boston Museum of Fine Arts, two more in a private collection in the United States, and another pair was recently acquired by the London dealers Jonathan Harris and Christopher Gibbs. The two small stools are believed to be in a private collection in the United States. One of the armchairs and one of the small stools are shown in Margaret Jourdain, *English Furniture: The Georgian Period 1750–1830* (1953), pls 36, 52. The

armchairs in Boston were formerly in the collection of the Earl of Harrington, from which they were sold through Sotheby's in 1963 [Sotheby & Co, *Important English Furniture*, London, 8 Nov 1963, Lot 180]

[44] RIBA, G4/12. The connection between the glass and Vardy's design was first made in Thornton and Hardy, op. cit., p.188. It should be added that the design relates closely to another by Kent, reproduced in Margaret Jourdain, *The Work of William Kent* (1948), pl.136

[45] Benedictus Arias Montanus, in *Biblia Sacra Hebraice Chaldaice Graece et Latine*, 8 vols (Antwerp, 1569–72) 8, pl.9

[46] RIBA, Jones-Webb [130]

[47] Chatsworth collection O&S 128

[48] Isaac Ware, *A Complete Body of Architecture* (1756), p.433

89 One of a pair of blackamoor statues in the Spencer collection at Althorp. The statues had formerly belonged to Lord Spencer's great-grandfather, the 1st Duke of Marlborough, and are said to have been dredged from the Tiber. Although too large to fit the niches in the Palm Room, their inclusion in Vardy's design is a striking instance of the fusion of art and architecture

Remarkable as it was, Vardy's design was not unprecedented. As a motif used in the decoration of interiors the palm can be traced to the very origins of architecture. Indeed palm trees were believed to have decorated the Temple of Solomon and were a conspicuous feature of early reconstructions.[45] However, the immediate source for the Palm Room was an unexecuted design by John Webb for the King's Bedchamber at Greenwich (FIG 90).[46] Vardy had already shown his liking for this design when, believing it to be the work of Webb's master Inigo Jones, he published an engraving of it in *Some Designs of Mr Inigo Jones and Mr William Kent* in 1744 (FIG 92). The attribution to Jones was not that wide of the mark, for Webb's design was almost certainly based on another by Jones for a stage set used in a royal masque (FIG 91);[47] but then it is hardly surprising to discover a theatrical source for so theatrical an interior as the Palm Room.

The frieze of griffins had earlier been used by William Kent in the Drawing Room at Holkham Hall, and the frieze beneath the dome in the alcove (FIG 55, p. 99) was also of Palladian extraction, having been copied from that by Colen Campbell in the Stone Hall at Houghton. Once again, however, there were elements derived from the art and architecture of Classical Antiquity. The busts on either side of the chimney-piece were copied from Roman originals in the Capitoline Museum in Rome (FIGS 84 and 85), while the frieze of griffins ultimately looked back to the Temple of Antoninus and Faustina in Rome (FIG 82, p.115). This was especially appropriate since the griffin was the Spencer crest, its use representing an obvious play on the family heraldry. It is possible also that the palms had some symbolic purpose. The palm was a recognized symbol of victory and harmony, but also of marital love and more particularly fertility. For this reason it was often used in the decoration of bedrooms, as for instance in that designed by Webb for the King at Greenwich. If, therefore, one were to seek for hidden meanings, the use of the palm might conceivably have been intended as a reference to the bond between the Spencers, recently married and looking forward to a life blessed by love, harmony and the birth of many children.

While work went ahead on the ground-floor apartments, Vardy turned his attention to the design of the first-floor apartments. Among his surviving drawings is the plan he prepared for publication in *Vitruvius Britannicus* (FIG 41, p. 88), which shows an *enfilade* of three grand reception rooms along the west front, mirroring the arrangement on the floor below. In the centre, as indicated in Vardy's section (FIG 42, p. 89), was a lofty interior rising through two storeys to a coved, compartmental ceiling with a frieze of Classical design, ornamented with foliated scrolls, and bold architectural doorcases composed of Corinthian columns surmounted by pediments. Rooms of this height and size were a relative novelty. Up until this time it was rare for the owners of London mansions to receive more than a few dozen guests at a time and reception rooms were proportioned accordingly. However, around the middle of the eighteenth century fashions in entertaining began to change. It now became quite common for people to receive far larger numbers of guests, sometimes as many as six or seven hundred at a time, and this created the need for grander reception rooms, generally known as Great Rooms. Most of the mansions built in London around the middle of the eighteenth century were provided with rooms of this kind, while earlier houses which lacked them were frequently remodelled or extended in order to accommodate this vital feature, sometimes to their architectural detriment.[48]

The *enfilade* running north-south connected with another running east-west. There were three rooms in all, including a bedchamber and closet for the use of Lady Spencer, while two further rooms situated on the opposite side of an intermediate passageway were probably intended to provide similar accommodation for the Earl. The closet

90

91

90 Design by John Webb for the Bedchamber of Charles II at Greenwich Palace, 1662. Webb's design was never executed but survived among the papers of the Office of Works, or possibly those of Lord Burlington. It was the starting-point for Vardy's design for the Palm Room at Spencer House (FIG 80, p. 114)

91 Set design for the royal masque The Fortunate Isles and their Union, *by Inigo Jones, c1624. The present drawing was probably the source for Webb's design (FIG 92) and thus for the Palm Room at Spencer House (FIG 80, p. 114) [Chatsworth Collection, O&S 128]*

92

92 Design for the Bedchamber of Charles II *at Greenwich Palace, as illustrated in John Vardy,* Some Designs of Mr Inigo Jones and Mr William Kent *(1744), p.4. More than ten years before the construction of Spencer House, Vardy published the present engraving of Webb's original design, attributed at the time to Webb's master Inigo Jones. Lord Spencer would certainly have been familiar with the engraving and might himself have suggested that Vardy use it in his designs for the Palm Room*

93

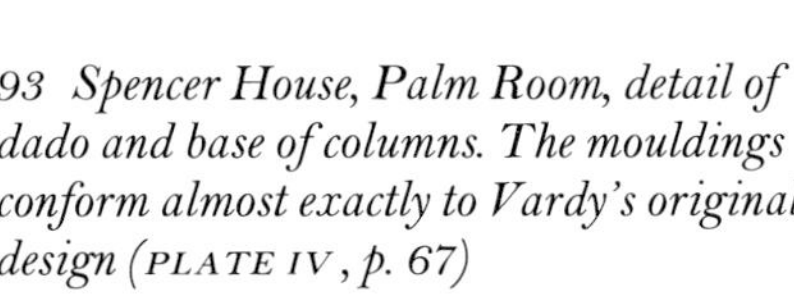

*93 Spencer House, Palm Room, detail of dado and base of columns. The mouldings conform almost exactly to Vardy's original design (*PLATE IV*, p. 67)*

94 Spencer House, Lady Spencer's Closet; design by John Vardy, 1757. The design shows the architect's plans for the decoration of the east wall and ceiling. The Spencer griffin appears above the door

occupied by Lady Spencer, or Mrs Spencer as she then was, is illustrated in a design by Vardy of 1757 (FIG 94).[49] An interesting feature are the miniature griffins above the door on the right, another visual pun on the Spencer heraldry, but the ceiling, illustrated in a separate design (FIG 95),[50] deserves particular attention as an example of the so-called 'grotesque' style, a type of decoration dating back to Roman times. The term 'grotesque' originated in the fact that the earliest examples had been discovered in ancient chambers buried deep in the earth, so resembling grottoes. The style had been revived in Italy during the Renaissance but had later crossed to England, and the immediate source for Vardy's design would appear to have been the ceiling of the Audience Chamber at Kensington Palace, designed by his master, William Kent (FIG 96). Indeed Vardy was Clerk of the Works at Kensington Palace at exactly the time he worked at Spencer House and would thus have had ample opportunity to study Kent's ceiling in detail.

An inscription makes clear that the closet was adjoined by a bedchamber, as was customary, and while the evidence is inconclusive, there is a possible connection here with an unidentified design by Vardy for the chimney-piece of a first-floor bedroom, with

[49] *A Sketch for Mrs Spencers Closet Joyning to the Bed Chamber 1 Pair of Stairs, Chimney side, Cove & Cieling*, signed 'J. Vardy Invt', the reverse inscribed *For Mrs Spencers Closet Next the Bed Chamber one Pair of Stairs, a sketch by J: Vardy 1757* [SJSM 69/1/3]

[50] Design by John Vardy for ceiling of Lady Spencer's Closet, Spencer House, *c*1758 [V&A, Prints and Drawings, Q1a.3319]

95 Spencer House, Lady Spencer's Closet; design by John Vardy for the ceiling, c1757. The design is an interesting example of the so-called 'grotesque' style of decoration, which ultimately derives from the painted interiors of ancient Rome

96 Kensington Palace, Audience Chamber, the ceiling. During the period he worked at Spencer House, Vardy was employed as Clerk of Works at Kensington Palace and his design for the ceiling of Lady Spencer's Closet (FIG 95) was clearly influenced by the ceiling of the Audience Chamber, devised by his master William Kent

95

96

*97 Design by John Vardy for a bedroom chimney-piece, possibly intended for Lady Spencer's Bedchamber at Spencer House. The amorini, as agents of love, were ideally suited to use in a bedchamber and were encased in similar style to the columns in the Palm Room (*FIGS *80, p. 114 and 93, p. 121)*

jambs in the form of winged angels emerging from tree trunks similar to those in the Palm Room (FIG 97).[51]

It is not known how far Vardy had progressed with the execution of these various designs but in 1758, some time before the early autumn, he was notified by the Spencers that the completion of the first-floor apartments was to be entrusted to another architect and their decoration radically revised.[52] It must have been a bitter blow, especially humiliating for someone of Vardy's professional standing. But events at Spencer House were symptomatic of a greater change. Architecture was now in a state of flux. A new generation of designers was emerging, and the old Palladian style was fast giving way to a radically different aesthetic directly inspired by the art and architecture of Classical Antiquity. Vardy had tried hard to keep pace with these changes; some of his designs for Spencer House are remarkable for their use of specifically Classical elements and the scrupulous accuracy with which these elements were reproduced. But he had been raised in the Palladian tradition and it is noticeable how much of his work looked back to Palladian sources.

There is also George Gray to consider. Gray was involved from the outset and clearly took a serious and professional view of his duties; he charged for his services, and the sum he received, two hundred guineas, suggests a significant contribution.[53] His initials are found on several of Vardy's designs, indicating that the architect was required to seek his prior approval before putting such designs into execution. There is proof, furthermore, that Gray had the authority to amend designs and occasionally did so. A signed inscription indicates that he ordered Vardy to eliminate the overmantel in his design for the Dining Room chimney-piece, which was indeed eliminated in execution.[54] Horace Walpole, who knew Gray personally,[55] claimed that it was he rather than Vardy who designed the remarkable west front,[56] and the same assertion was made by Thomas Frognall Dibdin, librarian and archivist to the 2nd Earl Spencer.[57] Such claims may be exaggerated, but when one compares the principal facade of Spencer House with that designed by Vardy for Lord Montfort's house (FIG 10, p. 27), it is hard to escape the conclusion that if Gray was not in fact the architect, he was very much the guiding spirit. Given his knowledge and love of Classical architecture, his involvement in archaeology and his explicit insistence on the utmost accuracy in the reproduction of Classical elements, Gray must surely take the credit for the more advanced aspects of Vardy's work at Spencer House. One may be certain also that he had a hand in Vardy's dismissal for he was a close friend and champion of the man brought in to replace him, James 'Athenian' Stuart.

[51] *Bed Chamber Chimney One Pair of Stairs* [V&A, Prints and Drawings, A.149.3436–200]

[52] The exact date of Vardy's dismissal is unknown, but from a document in the Penicuik Manuscripts, a letter from Robert Adam dated Sept 1758, it is clear that by this time Vardy's successor was already at work [Penicuik MS No.4852 quoted in Thornton and Hardy, op. cit., p.451, n.21]

[53] HB, Account of JS, Ledger Y, f.251, 9 Mar 1757, payment of 200 guineas to George Gray

[54] The reverse side of Vardy's design for the south wall of the Palm Room is inscribed *Geo: Gray . . . approved Decr 28th 1757*. The architect's design for the Dining Room window shutters carries the inscription *1758 approved Geo: Gray*, and the reverse side of his preliminary drawing for the Dining Room chimney is inscribed *Geo: Gray the lower part approved all statuary*

[55] There is a record of Walpole and Gray dining together in W. S. Lewis, *The Yale Edition of Horace Walpole's Correspondence*, 21, p.166

[56] *Anecdotes of Painting*, 5, p.161

[57] Thomas Frognall Dibdin, *Aedes Althorpianae* (1822), pl.lx n

14 'ATHENIAN' STUART

IT IS HARD TO DEFINE James Stuart (FIG 98); he was, in Reynolds' phrase, so 'various'. A gifted and successful painter, with an equal talent for landscapes, still lifes and portraits, he was a regular exhibitor at the Free Society of Artists and succeeded Hogarth as Sergeant Painter in the Office of Works. He was likewise an engraver and book illustrator; an art dealer and speculative builder; Surveyor of the Royal Hospital Chapel at Greenwich; a leading architect and designer who, in the course of a career spanning half a century, turned his hand to town and country houses, garden

98 James 'Athenian' Stuart; miniature by Philip Jean, c1765. The architect is pictured here around the time he completed work at Spencer House

buildings, churches, furniture, stage sets, funerary monuments, coins, medals, stained glass windows, even picture frames. He was at the same time a noted archaeologist and author; a member of several learned societies; a fellow of the Royal Society and the Society of Antiquaries; a friend to some of the leading scholars and thinkers of the period; a student of Latin and Greek, geometry and anatomy; a traveller conversant in Italian, French and modern Greek; an authority on the Venetian masters and the science of colour; a pioneer in the field of aesthetics; a figure of international repute whose work was known and discussed in every major city in Europe. Stuart's achievements are all the more remarkable when one considers that he was born into poverty, received little formal education, and spent a large part of his adult life in a state of dire inebriation.

James Stuart was born in a narrow lane off Ludgate Street in the City of London in 1713. His father, an impoverished Scottish mariner, died while he was still a boy and he was forced to take employment as an apprentice in the studio of a fashionable French fan-painter, Louis Goupy. Here he learned the elements of painting and engraving and at the same time developed an interest in Classical architecture, teaching himself Latin and ancient Greek. A few years earlier Goupy had accompanied Lord Burlington on his Grand Tour. In 1742, having scraped together sufficient savings, Stuart himself set off for Rome, travelling most of the distance on foot. By the end of the year he had reached his destination and soon established himself as a respected member of the artistic community, earning a reputation as a good judge of paintings and as an authority on the history and civilization of ancient Rome. He was much in demand as a *cicerone* or guide among the growing number of English tourists, and like many of his fellow artists, he augmented his income through dealing in antiquities and other works of art.

Stuart also became increasingly interested in archaeology, and in the spring of 1748 travelled south to Naples to inspect the excavations at Herculaneum and Pompeii. He was accompanied on this journey by Gavin Hamilton, Matthew Brettingham and Nicholas Revett. Hamilton we have encountered already as the artist and dealer who acted as Lord Spencer's agent and was commissioned by Spencer to paint *Agrippina with the Ashes of Germanicus*. Brettingham is the man believed to have supplied the cast of Antinous in the Entrance Hall at Spencer House. Revett is new to this account but no less important, a young Englishman of good family who had come to Italy to study painting.

More than sixty years had passed since the French archaeologist, Antoine Desgodetz, had published the first accurate measured drawings of the architectural remains of Rome in his famous study *Les Édifices Antiques de Rome* of 1682. The book had since become a standard work of reference for architects all over Europe, and much of the decoration of the ground-floor apartments at Spencer House was probably derived from this source. The archaeological investigation of Roman ruins was proceeding apace. Work was already underway on a voluminous survey of the excavations at Herculaneum and Pompeii, while the English archaeologist Robert Wood was preparing to travel to modern Syria and Lebanon to record the Roman remains at Palmyra and Balbec. In 1764 Robert Adam would bring forth his survey of the ruins of the Emperor Diocletian at Split.

By contrast the archaeological investigation of Greece had hardly begun. There were few detailed descriptions of the architectural remains and only the tiniest number of illustrations, most of them distorted and unreliable. And yet it was generally held that Greece, and more particularly Athens, was the cradle of civilization, the source from which Rome had derived not only her art and architecture, but philosophy, poetry, history and politics. During their expedition to Naples, Stuart and his companions must have reflected on this conundrum, for by the time they returned to Rome they had resolved to travel together to Greece to carry out a thorough survey of the principal architectural remains and to publish an accurate reference work similar in style to Desgodetz's *Les Édifices Antique de Rome*. It took time to organize the expedition; Hamilton and Brettingham eventually withdrew. But in January 1751 Stuart finally set sail from Venice with Revett, and by the end of March they were already at work amid the ruins of ancient Athens.

But why had no such expedition been mounted in the past? Why had Greece been neglected? The reasons were partly practical. For hundreds of years Greece had been under the control of the Ottoman Empire. Except for a brief period when it was held by the Venetians, Athens was governed by the Turks. Trade had kept the channels of communication open, and religious pilgrims continued to journey through Greece on their way to the Holy Land. However, it was generally recognized that to travel in the Ottoman Empire was fraught with danger, a point brought home in the most dramatic way by the cautionary tale of Francis Vernon, an English diplomat and scientist who, having embarked on a journey to the Levant in the late seventeenth century, was first taken prisoner by Tunisian Corsairs, later forced into slavery, and ultimately murdered in a quarrel over a penknife on the road from Trebizond to Persia. In time conditions improved; by the end of the eighteenth century it was not only safe but fashionable to tour the Greek islands, and during the Regency period Napoleon's blockade of Continental Europe made Greece an obvious destination for English travellers. In 1811 Chateaubriand noted the existence at Mistra of an English-style tavern selling port and roast beef, and the involvement of Lord Byron in Greece's gallant battle for independence merely added to the country's romantic appeal. However, in the late 1740s when Stuart and his companions first conceived the idea of an expedition to Athens, travel to this destination was still considered a difficult and hazardous undertaking.

But practical considerations were not the only obstacle. The reasons were also aesthetic. On the island of Sicily and at Paestum near Naples, there were several outstanding examples of ancient Greek temples in an excellent state of preservation which had been known to travellers for centuries. It would have been an easy matter to make measured drawings of these remains, but as yet no one had done so. The simple fact is that up until this point scholars and architects had not much admired this kind of architecture or considered it worthy of attention. On the whole they thought it heavy, ungainly and primitive, interesting perhaps from the historical point of view but in aesthetic terms grossly inferior to the later productions of the Romans and in no sense a model for modern architects to follow.

This view persisted for many years. Writing in 1767, the architect James Paine declared that there was nothing to be learned from what he considered 'the most despicable ruins of ancient Greece', adding that 'the particular forms of the best examples among them, are scarcely one removed from the rude essays of the Egyptians from which the Greeks borrowed them'.[1] In a lecture to the Royal Academy in 1768, the text of which was later published, Sir William Chambers, doyen of the English architectural establishment, inveighed against those who dared to suggest that English architects might base their designs on Greek rather than Roman models. 'They might with equal success', he thundered, 'oppose a Hottentot and a Baboon to the Apollo and the Gladiator as set up Grecian architecture against the Roman'.[2] In Italy the celebrated architect and artist Giovanni Battista Piranesi devised a whole new theory of cultural evolution whereby the Romans had derived their art and architecture not from the Greeks at all but from the Etruscans.[3]

However, there were others in Europe who took a different view. Around the middle of the eighteenth century, at precisely the time Stuart conceived his plan to record the ruins in Greece, one sees the emergence of a new aesthetic, related to contemporary developments in philosophy, posited on ideas of simplicity, purity and vigour rather than elaboration, sophistication and refinement. With it came a growing appreciation of early Greek architecture, which was seen to embody these values.

A leading figure in the pro-Hellenic movement was the German antiquarian and theorist, Johann Joachim Winckelmann, who could not have stated his ideas more clearly when he declared, 'the only way for us to become great . . . lies in the imitation of the Greeks'.[4] In fact Winckelmann never visited Greece; the most important years of his life were spent in Rome, and the art he most admired was generally either Hellenistic or Greco-Roman. But this is beside the point. Through the vigour and passion of his writing style he attracted a wide readership; his books sold in the hundreds and thousands and were translated into all the major European languages. They generated enormous interest in Greek art and civilization. Most important of all, Winckelmann challenged the assumption, central to Western aesthetics since the Renaissance, that the Greeks had

[1] James Paine, *Plans, Elevations and Sections*, I (1767), p.ii, quoted in David Watkin, *Athenian Stuart, Pioneer of the Greek Revival* (1982), p.22

[2] Sir William Chambers, *Treatise on Civil Architecture*, 3rd edn (1791), quoted in Watkin, op. cit., p.22

[3] Giovanni Battista Piranesi, *Della Magnificenza ed Architettura de' Romani* (Rome, 1761)

[4] J. J. Winckelmann, *Reflections on the Painting and Sculpture of the Greeks* (1755), quoted in J. Mordaunt Crook, *The Greek Revival* (1972), p.25

been surpassed by the Romans and thus, at a theoretical level, he helped to lay the foundations of the future revival of the forms and values of Greek art and architecture.

At the same time others besides Stuart were beginning to turn their attention to the hitherto neglected remains of ancient Greek buildings and monuments. In 1752, Richard Dalton published his *Antiquities and Views in Greece and Egypt*. In 1758, a Frenchman, Julien-David Le Roy, brought out *Les Ruines des Plus Beaux Monuments de la Grèce* and in 1759, Robert Sayer published his own *Ruins of Athens and Other Valuable Antiquities in Greece*. In 1750, the French architect Soufflot made measured drawings of the temples at Paestum, which were published in three separate editions in the 1760s. John Berkenhout produced another survey in 1767, *The Ruins of Paestum or Posidonia*, and in the following year, Thomas Major brought forth his own painstaking study, *The Ruins At Paestum*. At the same time the Greek remains in Sicily were minutely recorded by Pancrazi in the two volume *Antichità Siciliane*, published in 1751.

Throughout this period the influence of Greece began to be felt in art and design. In some quarters, as we have seen, resistance remained strong. Quite apart from their aesthetic preferences, architects who specialized in work of Roman inspiration had an obvious commercial interest in blocking the advancing fashion for the Greek style. Practice lagged behind theory. Although the elements of later Greek architecture were quickly accepted, being little different from the Roman, it took far longer for the forms and values of early Greek architecture to be absorbed into the mainstream. However, in the 1750s, for the first time since Antiquity, the baseless Greek Doric column made its appearance, and in the years ahead the influence of ancient Greece was felt in virtually every sphere of architecture and design.

In all of this James Stuart played a critical role. In the first volume of his *Antiquities of Athens*, published in 1762, he called, as Winckelmann had, for a re-evaluation of the relative merits of Greek and Roman art. Rome might be the equal of Greece 'in Magnificence', he wrote, but Athens was 'the Mother of Elegance and Politeness' and 'for the beauties of a correct style must be allowed to surpass her [Rome] as much as an original excels a copy'. The ancient remains of Athens were 'the Most perfect model of what is excellent in Sculpture and Architecture'. Architects were therefore advised to turn to Greece, for as Stuart argued, 'those Artists who aim at perfection must be infinitely more pleased and better instructed the nearer they can draw their examples from the fountain head'.[5] Stuart's arguments were clearly influenced by contemporary theories relating to the nature of cultural development, and more particularly the writings of Jean Jacques Rousseau, but he was among the first to apply these ideas to architecture and his remarks reached a wide audience and made an immediate and lasting impression.

The second volume of *Antiquities of Athens* did not appear until 1789, a year after Stuart's death; and it was left to others to complete the series, the last volume being issued in 1816. It is also true that whereas Stuart had argued for architects to draw nearer the 'fountain head', the buildings he featured in the first volume of the *Antiquities of Athens* were all of the Hellenistic period, and that it was only in the second volume that the ancient monuments of the Acropolis were finally illustrated. However, in terms of its quality and accuracy the *Antiquities of Athens* was unrivalled and immediately became the standard work of reference in this area.

In his architecture, also, Stuart made a vital contribution to the development of the Greek Revival. His work was eclectic, blending elements derived from a wide variety of sources, but he made extensive use of specifically Greek features. These were generally of a decorative rather than a structural order, and were more usually derived from later

99 The Erechtheion, Athens, as illustrated in James Stuart and Nicholas Revett, Antiquities of Athens, *II (1789), chap II, pl.II. The architect has included a portrait of himself, seated bottom right, sketching*

[5] James Stuart, *Antiquities of Athens*, I (1762), p.v

[6] Quoted in Watkin, op. cit., p.48

[7] In Feb 1782 Horace Walpole dined at Montagu house, recently completed to Stuart's designs. Afterwards he wrote, 'I dined on Monday with the Harcourts at Mrs. Montagu's new palace, and was much surprised. Instead of vagaries it is a noble simple edifice . . . though I had thought it so magnificent a house there was not a morsel of gilding, it is grand not tawdry, nor larded and embroidered and pompomed with shreds and remnants and *clinquant* like all the harlequinades of Adam, which never let the eye repose a moment.' [Horace Walpole to William Mason, 14 Feb 1781, quoted in Watkin, op. cit., p.48.]

rather than earlier Greek buildings. However, on a number of occasions Stuart produced complete reconstructions, one of which, a replica of the Theseion in Athens, was the earliest recorded building in Europe since Antiquity to make use of the baseless Greek Doric column. Contemporaries, who dubbed him 'Athenian', were convinced that he had come closer than any previous architect to reviving the forms and spirit of Greek architecture. After visiting the house he designed for Mrs Montagu in Portman Square, the philosopher James 'Hermes' Harris declared, 'I have seen an Edifice which for the time made me imagine I was in Athens, in a house of Pericles, built by Phidias'.[6] Others, including Horace Walpole, noted a contrast between the sobriety and robustness of Stuart's work and the shallow relief and refined, attenuated forms of Robert Adam.[7] Even to modern eyes Stuart's work has a weighty, plastic quality that seems to derive more from Greek sources than from Roman and which in an oblique if not a direct way pays homage to the architecture of the age of Pericles.

Stuart's expedition to Greece was scheduled to last a year, but he and Revett encountered considerable difficulties. In 1753 they were forced to flee from Athens during the disturbances that followed the death of Osman, Chief of the Black Eunuchs. Revett was pursued by a Maltese Corsair on the voyage from Athens to Salonika. Stuart became involved in a violent quarrel in which he knocked down a Greek official and in a separate incident was very nearly murdered by a gang of Turkish cut-throats. Everywhere they went the pair aroused suspicion. Poring over the ruins with scientific instruments, scrutinizing and sketching the landscape and the local population (FIG 99), they were

100 Sir James Gray, by George Knapton, 1741. It was Sir James, George Gray's elder brother, who proposed James Stuart for membership of the Society of Dilettanti, setting him on the path which eventually led to Spencer House

routinely mistaken for spies and hauled in for questioning. However, there were moments when obstacles fell away as if by enchantment. On one occasion a resident of Athens pulled down a house he owned in order to afford them a better view of the Tower of the Winds.

Stuart and Revett finally left Greece in 1755. They had cut their ties with Italy and returned directly to England, where they arrived in late October. Stuart's return marked the beginning of what promised to be a brilliant career. After eight years in Rome and four years in Greece he could be considered perhaps the greatest living authority in England on Classical art and architecture, and was soon overwhelmed with honours and commissions.

As an architect, Stuart's first major commission was the remodelling of Wentworth Woodhouse in Yorkshire, for which he submitted designs in 1755. In 1757 he was approached in connection with proposed alterations to Kedleston Hall in Derbyshire, and in the following year received a commission to carry out structural and decorative work in the house and grounds at Hagley Hall in Worcestershire. But it marked a new stage in his career when, around the autumn of 1758, he was called in by the young John Spencer to complete the decoration of Spencer House.

101 Wimbledon Park, Surrey; design by James Stuart for the interior, c1758/9. The house at Wimbledon was destroyed by fire in 1785 and the present drawing is virtually the only surviving record of Stuart's work there

Stuart had already given proof of his abilities as a designer; he had worked for some of the greatest connoisseurs in England. But there can be little doubt that he owed his appointment at Spencer House to Spencer's architectural adviser, George Gray. Like Gray, Stuart was a member of the Society of Dilettanti; indeed he had been proposed for membership by Gray's elder brother, Sir James, who was British Resident in Venice at the time he passed through that city on the way to Greece (FIG 100). Most of his early patrons were Dilettanti, and in 1763 he was appointed official painter to the Society. On hearing of Stuart's expedition to Greece, George Gray had personally arranged for the publication of the architect's proposals for the *Antiquities of Athens*, also organizing a subscription list. Among those he persuaded to subscribe were John and Georgiana Spencer. Persuading the couple to employ Stuart as their architect was a logical step; indeed the Spencers were so impressed by Stuart that they also commissioned him to remodel the interior of the old Palladian house at Wimbledon Park. The house at Wimbledon was destroyed by fire in 1785, and the only record of Stuart's work there is a description by Horace Walpole[8] and a handful of drawings (FIG 101).[9] However, the interiors at Spencer House suffered no such fate and remain among the finest Stuart ever produced.

[8] Paget Toynbee (ed.), 'Horace Walpole's Journals of Visits to Country Seats & c', *Walpole Society*, XVI (1927–28), p.15

[9] RIBA, CC4/38(1), CC4/38(2), CC4/39(1), CC4/39(2)

15 THE WAVING LINE

STUART SET TO WORK with energy and in 1759 produced his one surviving design for Spencer House, a magnificent watercolour section of the Painted Room showing the north wall more or less as executed (PLATE VII, p. 68).[1] The Spencers were initially delighted with Stuart's progress. In the autumn of 1760 Georgiana noted in her diary, 'Mr. Stuart does very well'.[2] However, by the following year it was apparent the schedule was slipping. Colonel George Gray, previously one of Stuart's most enthusiastic supporters, began to complain quite openly about his inefficiency, so much so in fact that Robert Adam got wind of the matter and began to imagine that he might be called in to take over, a prospect he relished.[3] The Spencers were able to entertain but only on a modest scale, restricting receptions to the apartments on the ground floor.[4] By 1763 the slow progress of work and soaring estimates had become a topic of open discussion in London drawing rooms.[5] The Spencers were travelling at this time on the Continent, and in their absence their steward, Andrew Solinus, did his best to maintain discipline. In the end, however, the Spencers found it necessary to enlist the support of their friend, Lord Jersey, who took on the role of project manager (FIG 102).

The problem was partly that Stuart was busy with other commissions. During the period he worked at Spencer House he was engaged on the construction of two other London mansions, Holdernesse House on Park Lane and Lichfield House in St James's Square. At the same time he carried out alterations to Nuneham Park in Oxfordshire, and also designed a range of garden buildings for the grounds of Shugborough in Staffordshire. But the root of the problem lay elsewhere. After the most promising and industrious start to his career, Stuart had begun a steady slide into alcoholism and dissipation, gradually forsaking the rewards of a busy architectural practice for the easy life of an idle drunkard. The Spencers were not the only ones to suffer at his hands. In 1768 Stuart was dismissed as portrait painter to the Society of Dilettanti when it was discovered that during the five years he had held the appointment he had not completed a single portrait. At Greenwich, the architect's duties as surveyor were increasingly performed by a disgruntled deputy. One of Stuart's clients, Sir Sampson Gideon, was forced to adopt the most stringent methods of verification in order, it was said, 'to prevent being imposed on by the workmen whose bills he [Stuart] assented to'.[6] Another client, Mrs Montagu, declared that 'in dealing with Mr. Stuart great caution is necessary . . . I speak it not on suspicion but certain information, that since he began my house he has been for a fortnight together in the most drunken condition . . . About a year and a half ago Stuart had by a long uninterrupted state of drunkenness brought himself into such a condition of mind and body as I feard [sic] irrecoverable, to this I attribute the many falsehoods of which I gave him proof by shewing to him his own letters. Tho he does not mean (I believe) to tell fibs, it is impossible to rely on anything he says. It wd be tedious to tell you how often I have been obliged to confront him with the workmen whom he blamed for not having executed his orders, and he was then obliged to confess he had forgotten to deliver the designs . . . In business the strait line is the line of beauty, but Stuart is apt to choose the waving line'.[7]

102 George Villiers, 4th Earl of Jersey, by Nathaniel Dance. During the Spencers' absence in Italy in 1763–64, Lord Jersey acted as unofficial project manager at Spencer House but, as he confessed himself, he found it hard to keep Stuart to his work

At Spencer House it was 1763 before Stuart submitted estimates for the plasterwork in the Great Room.[8] Poor weather caused delays in the drying process and the ceiling here was not finally ready to be gilded until February 1764.[9] Severe attacks of gout brought on by excessive drinking prevented Stuart from attending to business, and work did not begin on the ceiling of Lady Spencer's Dressing Room until the following March.[10] In November 1765, Stuart was still putting the final touches to the decoration of the Painted Room.[11] He assured Lord Jersey that he was constantly on site and would not rest until the house was completed, but when the Earl made enquiries at St James's Place he discovered from the porter that not a word of this was true. 'I called upon Steuard [sic] the other morning', he wrote to Georgiana, 'he said that he was going to St James's Place immediately & he hoped the Bow Window would be finished this week but I fancy sometimes he says the thing which is not for I understood him that he had been several times there lately but & upon enquiry I learnt of Ben that he had never seen him since your Ladyship was in town'.[12] It was only in December 1765, more than six years after Stuart began work and almost ten years from the start of construction, that Lord Spencer was able to inform his friend Sir William Hamilton that the end was at last in sight. 'My house in town', he wrote with relief, 'is at last near being finished, and I believe it will be fit to open next Spring'.[13]

[1] BMPD 1955–4–16–13

[2] AP F167, diary entry for 6 Nov 1760

[3] In Jan 1761 Robert Adam's brother wrote to him from Florence, 'If C[olone]l G[ra]y has really changed his opinion of the A[thenia]n you may yet have to finish some of the apartments in Mr. Spencer's House. That would be drol [sic] enough' [Penicuik MSS No. 4881, quoted in Thornton and Hardy, 'The Spencer Furniture at Althorp', section II: 'James Stuart's Neo-Classical Furniture for Spencer House and the work of John Gordon the chairmaker', *Apollo* (October 1968), p.451, n.22]

[4] AP F122, GS to TC, 1763

[5] AP F101, GBV to GS, 1763

[6] Howard Colvin, *Biographical Dictionary of British Architects 1600–1840*, p.795

[7] David Watkin, *Athenian Stuart, Pioneer of the Greek Revival*, p.50

[8] AP F100, GBV to GS, 1763. The Earl informed Georgiana 'The Estimate of the plaistering work alone of the Cieling, intended for your Great Room, amounts to 480£'

[9] AP F101, GBV to GS, 1 Feb 1764. In this letter Lord Jersey informed Georgiana 'I called the other day in St. James's Place & had the pleasure to find the Cieling in the great Room quite finished, & ready for the Gilders . . . They have been very unlucky in their weather for the drying of the Cieling which will have delayed the Gilding a little, but that will be only a few days . . . The rest of the works go on with as much Expedition as possible & Solinus seems to take true pains not to let them be a moment idle & to keep Stewart [sic] close to his business'

[10] AP F41, CH to GS, 20 Mar 1764. Mrs Howe informed Georgiana that together with her husband and Lord Huntingdon she had visited the house a few days earlier and that whereas 'the ceilings go on very well, none of the compartments in yr dressing room are yet begun'

[11] AP F101, GBV to GS, 15 Nov 1765

[12] Ibid.

[13] AP F117, JS to WH, 25 Dec 1765

16 NEARER THE FOUNTAINHEAD

STUART'S WORK was largely confined to the first-floor apartments, but in an effort to update the work of his predecessor, and to smooth the transition from one storey to the next, he also made changes in areas of the building designed by Vardy. It was Stuart surely who supervised the installation of the cast of Antinous in the Entrance Hall (FIG 48, p. 94), believed to have been acquired by the Spencers during their visit to Italy in 1763-64; and there is a strong possibility that Stuart was also responsible for the chimney-piece in the Palm Room (FIG 86, p. 117), which has strong stylistic affinities with others he designed, and which, according to a family tradition already established in the lifetime of the 2nd Earl Spencer, was carved by Scheemakers, a sculptor with whom Stuart was closely associated.[1]

In the Staircase Hall, the Roman Ionic pilasters indicated in Vardy's section (FIG 42, p. 89) were replaced by Greek Ionic pilasters, hung with festoons as on a Classical feast day and surmounted by a frieze of anthemion ornaments derived from the Temple on the Ilyssus, illustrated in the *Antiquities of Athens* (FIGS 103–105).[2] The ceiling was remodelled to form a barrel vault, closely resembling the soffit of a triumphal arch, with coffered compartments enriched with rosettes and divided by bands of guilloches. The Roman brackets designed by Vardy for the soffit of the first-floor landing were replaced with

103

104

[1] Thomas Frognall Dibdin, *Bibliotheca Spenceriana*, 4 vols (1814–15), 3, p.509

[2] Stuart used the identical frieze in the Boudoir at Holdernesse House and the Morning Room at Montagu House

103 Temple on the Ilyssus, the painted frieze from the architrave, as illustrated in Stuart and Revett, Antiquities of Athens, *I (1762), chap II, pl. VIII. The identical pattern of serried anthemion ornaments was reproduced in stucco in the frieze of the Staircase Hall at Spencer House (FIG 105)*

104 Arch of Constantine, Rome, bas-relief, as illustrated in François Perrier, Icones et Segmenta illustrium e marmore tabularum que Romae adhuc exstant *(Rome and Paris, 1645), pl. 31. The relief illustrates the ancient custom of draping festoons between the columns of temples and other public buildings, as evoked by the decoration of the pilasters in the Staircase Hall at Spencer House (FIG 105)*

105 Spencer House, Staircase Hall, detail of pilasters, frieze and ceiling. Roman Ionic pilasters are indicated on Vardy's section (FIG 42, p. 89), but those introduced by Stuart are of a Greek Ionic Order. The frieze is derived from the Temple on the Ilyssus (FIG 103), while the coffered, barrel-vaulted ceiling recalls the soffits of the great triumphal arches of ancient Rome. Swags hang between the capitals like those which were used in Antiquity to decorate temples and other public buildings on feast days (FIG 104)

106

107

flattened supports ornamented with Greek fret mouldings (FIG 106), while in the frieze below Stuart inserted Grecian lyres and ewers encircled by garlands, clearly inspired by those which he had discovered embedded in a wall near the Theatre of Bacchus during his visit to Athens, illustrated in the *Antiquities of Athens* (FIG 107).[3] Stuart also made alterations to the Venetian window on the south wall, embellishing the imposts with miniature rosettes derived from a marble altar he had found on the Island of Paros.[4] On the landing opposite, the screen indicated on Vardy's plan (FIG 40, p. 88) was replaced by a blank arch, flanked by doors, while the passageway behind was eliminated and the room to the rear enlarged. At ground-floor level, the walls were painted a stone colour, with

[3] The motif of a ewer encircled by a garland, commonly found on Roman altars, had been used by Stuart in the Entrance Hall at Wentworth Woodhouse, and a Grecian lyre, also encircled by a garland, appears in his designs for the Dining Room at Kedleston Hall

[4] James Stuart, *Antiquities of Athens*, IV, chap.VI, pl.IV

*106 Spencer House, Staircase Hall, detail of frieze below first-floor landing. In place of the Roman brackets designed by Vardy (*FIG *55, p. 99), Stuart introduced flattened consoles with Greek-fret mouldings and reliefs derived from Athenian prototypes.*

107 Reliefs representing a lyre and vase, as illustrated in Stuart and Revett, Antiquities of Athens, *II (1789), p.23. Stuart discovered these reliefs embedded in a wall near the Theatre of Bacchus. The motif of the vase appears again in the Painted Room (*FIGS *140 and 147, pp. 157 and 168)*

*108 Spencer House, Staircase Hall, gilt-bronze lantern with giltwood finial, c1760. The uprights of the lantern followed a similar pattern to the giltwood fillets used to mask the tacks holding the hangings in place in the Great Room. The finial derived from the Corinthian-style capital surmounting the Choragic Monument of Lysicrates in Athens (*FIG *109). In ancient times the latter supported a flaming torch; its use by Stuart represents an obvious play on the idea of fire and light*

109 The Choragic Monument of Lysicrates, as illustrated in Stuart and Revett, Antiquities of Athens, *I (1762), chap IV, pl.III. The capital surmounting the building was adapted by Stuart to provide a suitable finial for the lantern in the Staircase Hall at Spencer House (*FIG *108)*

108

109

the pilasters above picked out in white against a background of green, as if the whole interior were in fact the shell of a Classical temple, with a raised colonnade open to an arcadian landscape.

Suspended from the ceiling was a gilded lantern surmounted by a finial in the form of a Corinthian-style capital (FIG 108), the latter derived from the Choragic Monument of Lysicrates, illustrated in the *Antiquities of Athens* (FIG 109). The choice of this feature was particularly appropriate, since in ancient times the capital had supported a flaming torch, its use by Stuart representing an obvious play on the idea of fire and light. Although sparsely furnished, the Staircase Hall is also thought to have contained a pair of giltwood

110

111

110 Giltwood tripod, c1760. The tripod is one of a pair believed to have stood originally on the intermediate landings of the Staircase Hall at Spencer House. The design derives from a celebrated Roman original in marble (FIG 111)

111 Roman marble tripod, as illustrated in Piranesi, Antichità d'Albano e di Castel Gandolfo *(Rome, 1764), pl.VIII. Now in the Vatican Museum, the tripod was displayed during the eighteenth century in the church of Santa Maria della Stella at Albano. It was clearly the starting-point for the tripods designed by Stuart (FIG 110)*

112 Spencer House, Music Room; photograph of 1926. It was here that a tour of the first-floor apartments generally began, and the Spencers entertained their guests to concerts and recitals in this room

113 Spencer House, first-floor apartments, door furniture; photograph of 1926. The escutcheon takes the form of an elaborate letter 'S', a clear allusion to the Spencers

112

113

tripods, which served as pedestals for candelabra and which probably stood on the intermediate landings, where they appear in an early photograph (FIGS 53 (p. 97) and 110).[5] The overall design of the tripods was based on a famous Roman altar stand in the Church of Santa Maria della Stella in Albano, illustrated by Piranesi in the *Antichità d'Albano e di Castel Gandolfo* of 1764 (FIG 111).[6]

A circuit of the first-floor apartments generally began in the Music Room at the head of the stairs, which originally provided the setting for concerts, recitals and other musical entertainments (FIG 112). A particularly striking feature was the door furniture, with handles in the form of human masks, each escutcheon representing an elaborate letter 'S' made up of foliated scrolls, the whole executed in chased and gilded brass (FIG 113). The 'S' of course stood for Spencer, another of Stuart's visual puns, and must have given the family enormous pleasure, for it was repeated throughout the first-floor apartments. The frieze in the Music Room followed an alternating pattern of paterae, urns and ewers, partly derived from Classical prototypes which Stuart discovered in Greece (FIG 114),[7]

114

while the dado rail was decorated with a continuous wave-scroll band. The chimney-piece, in Siena and white marble, was carved with floral sprays, and the walls were probably hung with figured damask. The furniture included a magnificent giltwood pier table, with pilasters similar to those on the tripods in the Staircase Hall and a wave-scroll frieze which repeated the pattern of the dado rail. The table was accompanied by a matching pier glass, the frame laden with luxuriant scrolling acanthus and a heavy swag festooned across the surface of the mirror (FIG 112). The glass was crowned by a bulbous anthemion ornament framed by addorsed cornucopia, inspired perhaps by a celebrated fragment of an Antique Roman frieze preserved at the Palazzo Mattei in Rome (FIG 115).

[5] It should be noted that in a photograph of 1895 one of the tripods appears in Lady Spencer's Dressing Room

[6] W. Amelung, *Die Sculpturen des Vaticanischen Museum* (Berlin, 1908), cat.III, No. 236, p.46, pl.26

[7] Stuart used the identical frieze at both Lichfield House and Holdernesse House. The double-handled urns are derived from Antique prototypes illustrated in *Antiquities of Athens*, I, chap. I, p.1

115

114 Spencer House, Music Room, detail of frieze

115 Fragment of a Roman architrave with addorsed cornucopia, as illustrated in Piranesi, Della Magnificenza ed Architettura de'Romani *(1761), pl.XVII. Stuart used the same motif in his design for the pier glass in the Music Room at Spencer House*

117 Spencer House, Lady Spencer's Dressing Room, the ceiling. The circular compartments may originally have contained inset panels of the sort used in the Painted Room (FIGS 137 and 140, pp. 155 and 157)

118 Baths of Augustus, Rome, a ceiling, as illustrated in Bernard de Montfaucon, L'Antiquité Expliquée *(Paris, 1719), III (Supplément), pl.LVIII. Montfaucon's voluminous survey was a standard work of reference for architects of Stuart's generation and the present engraving was clearly the source for the ceiling in Lady Spencer's Dressing Room (FIG 117)*

LEFT
116 Spencer House, Lady Spencer's Dressing Room; photograph of c1890. This was not a dressing room in the modern sense but a salon in which Lady Spencer might have held her levée or morning reception

The Music Room was adjoined to the west by an interior known as Lady Spencer's Dressing Room (FIG 116). This was not a dressing room in the modern sense, but a room for entertaining, a private salon where Georgiana might have held her *levée*, or morning reception. During large assemblies the room would also have been used as an extension to the adjoining Great Room, while at the same time providing a link between the north and west wings. The decoration of the room was typical of Stuart's approach to design, archaeological yet synthetic; for while the ceiling was derived from the Baths of Augustus in Rome (FIGS 117 and 118),[8] the frieze was inspired by the Erechtheion in Athens (FIGS 119 and 120). Stuart also showed considerable ingenuity in adapting a square-shaped ceiling to the rectangular plan of the room, masking the difference through the introduction of moulded bands at either end. It is possible that Stuart intended the roundels in the ceiling to contain inset painted panels representing Classical scenes, as was now becoming the fashion. However, an analysis of the paintwork suggests that the roundels were originally the present pale blue, with the rest of the ceiling painted white, pink and buff, the mouldings being picked out in gilt; and it is interesting to note that Stuart used a

[8] Stuart designed similar ceilings for Holdernesse House and Rathfarnham Castle, Dublin

119

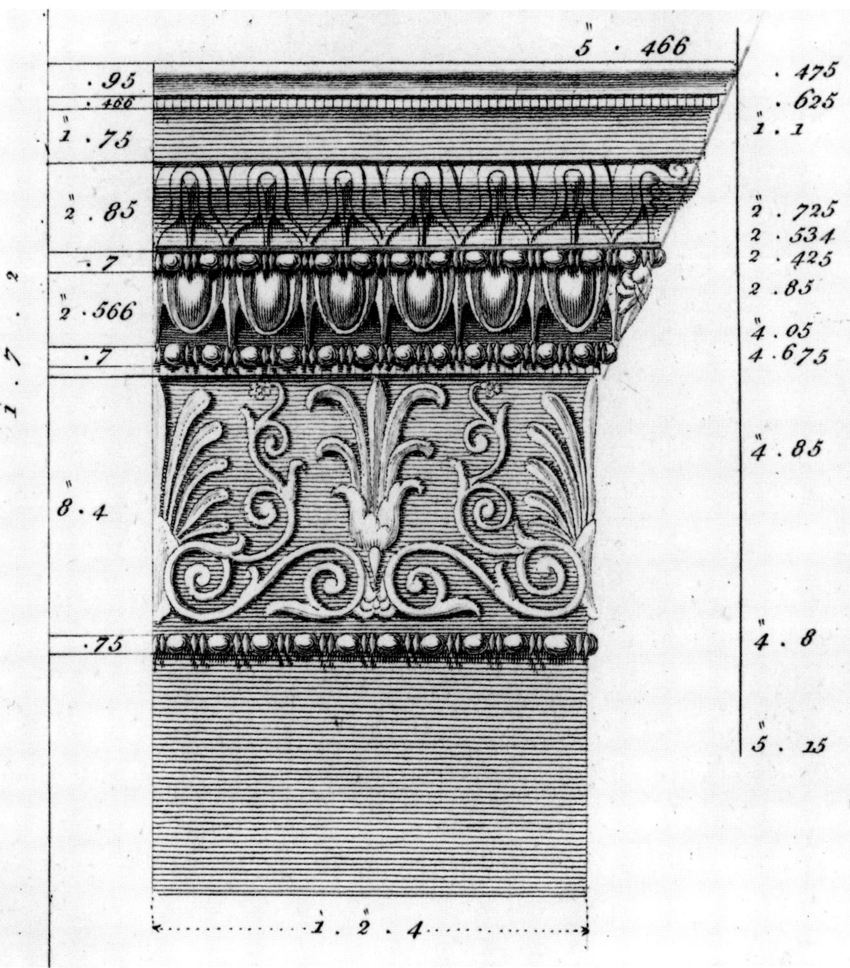

120

similar colour scheme in the decoration of the Royal Chapel at Greenwich. The chimney-piece was of Carrara marble, the frieze carved with the bust of a classical maiden in profile, possibly an idealized portrait of Lady Spencer herself, flanked by eagles terminating in foliated scrolls, the jambs ornamented with trailing fruit and foliage. The doorcases were carved with floral garlands and the walls were hung with figured silk damask, edged with giltwood fillets, neatly concealing the tacks which held the fabric in place.

The room also contained a fine collection of old master paintings, generally small in scale and religious or mythological in their subject matter. Some of these had been brought down from Althorp, but others were acquired while the house was under construction and were probably purchased expressly for the room (see Appendix III). All the pictures were hung according to a system devised by Stuart, each being suspended from a chain in the form of a giltwood ribbon. Stuart often advised his clients on the most suitable choice and arrangement of pictures; indeed on one occasion he suggested that a client's pictures be cut down to fit a particular scheme he had designed, and it is likely that in consultation with the Spencers he established a layout that would complement and enhance the proportions and decoration of the room.

To the south the Dressing Room led through to the Great Room (FIG 121), which served for grand assemblies and balls and may also have been used occasionally for large

119 Spencer House, Lady Spencer's Dressing Room, detail of frieze. The pattern was clearly derived from the Erechtheion in Athens (FIG 120)

120 Erechtheion, the frieze, as illustrated in Stuart and Revett, Antiquities of Athens, *II (1789), chap. II, pl. VIII. This was evidently the source for the frieze in Lady Spencer's Dressing Room (FIG 119) and shows Stuart making use of specifically Greek architectural features derived from buildings of the fifth century B.C.*

121 Spencer House, Great Room, looking north; photograph by Bedford Lemere, 1895. The interior was conceived as a temple to the pleasures of the Georgian rout

122 Spencer House, Great Room, relief of Apollo. Flanked by griffins guarding vases of flowers, the relief would seem to symbolize the flowering of the arts under the Spencers' protection

public banquets.[9] Lavish in its decoration and twice the height of any other room in the house, it was clearly intended to impress. The ceiling was coved, with coffered compartments in green, white and gold. Set into the cove were four circular reliefs, one on each side, representing figures from Classical mythology, painted in imitation of bronze (FIGS 122 and 123), while the angles of the ceiling were occupied by Classical vases and sacrificial rams (FIG 121). The frieze was decorated with a continuous band of foliated

[9] The room was described as 'the great dining room, one pair of stairs' in a design for the chimney-piece here which Vardy exhibited at the Free Society of Artists [Algernon Graves, *The Society of Artists of Great Britain 1760–1791. The Free Society of Artists 1761–1783. A Complete Dictionary of Contributors and their Work* (1907), p.267, No.197]

123 Spencer House, Great Room, relief of Venus. Inspired perhaps by Raphael's Galatea *at the Villa Farnesina, Rome, the relief represents a marine Venus in a chariot drawn by dolphins, with Cupid releasing imaginary arrows of love as if to pierce the heart of the onlooker*

scrolls. The walls were covered with figured silk damask, *en suite* with that in Lady Spencer's Dressing Room and held in place with identical giltwood fillets. The window curtains were of the same material, as were the covers on the seating furniture, which comprised a large suite of sofas, armchairs and side chairs, the frames of which were painted white and gilt to match the dado and other elements of architectural joinery (FIG 121).[10] At either end of the room were columnar doorcases. The chimney-piece, in the

[10] The suite survived intact at Althorp until the death of the 7th Earl Spencer. At least four of the armchairs were sold by the 8th Earl through Partridge Fine Arts in London. Two of these were acquired by the V & A

124 Spencer House, Great Room, pier glass. The frame is surmounted by putti driving chariots drawn by griffins, clearly inspired by Classical protoypes (FIG 125)

centre of the east wall, was of Carrara marble, with jambs in the form of pilasters supporting a full entablature. Between the windows were gilt-framed pier glasses and matching tables (FIGS 124 and 126), the latter fitted with slabs of *verd antique* marble, purposely supplied from Rome by Stuart's former associate Gavin Hamilton, who purchased them on the Spencers' behalf from the shop of Domenico de' Angelis in the Piazza di Spagna.[11] A magnificent glass chandelier hung from the centre of the ceiling, supplemented no doubt by candelabra which would have been placed on the pier tables and strategically positioned stands.

The iconography of the room was closely related to its function. Indeed the interior was clearly conceived as a temple consecrated to the chief pleasures of the Georgian rout. The decoration began not in the room itself but above the entrance in the adjoining passageway, where Stuart placed a relief representing two bacchantes, the first playing a trumpet, the other proffering a wine cup, a clear indication to the visitor that music and wine lay ahead (FIG 132, p. 151).[12] The theme of music and wine was continued within. The relief above the north wall represented Bacchus receiving wine from a cup-bearer, and was framed by Bacchic staffs entwined with vine leaves and bunches of grapes, as

[11] AP F117, GH to GS, 26 June 1766; Ibid., GS to GH, 28 July 1766; Ibid., GH to GS, 12 Oct 1766; Ibid., GH to GS, 11 Apr, 26 Dec 1767. The Irish dealer Matthew Nulty was likewise involved in this transaction

[12] Stuart used the identical relief at Rathfarnham Castle and on an organ case at Newby Hall, Yorkshire

125 Roman relief representing putti driving chariots, detail of a sarcophagus formerly in the Palazzo Giustiniani, Rome, illustrated in the Dal Pozzo-Albani collection of drawings after the Antique, Royal Library, Windsor Castle, Vol.8 [A47/162]. Figures of this kind are commonly found in Roman carvings and wall paintings and were evidently the inspiration for the putti charioteers above the pier glasses in the Great Room at Spencer House (FIG 124)

126 Spencer House, Great Room, pier table. The design represents a fusion of Antiquity and the Baroque

125

126

127

128

127 Spencer House, Great Room, detail of putto, coffering and frieze. The putto shows the influence of the Baroque, but the coffering and the frieze are derived from Antiquity

128 Temple of Rome and Augustus at Pola, the frieze, as illustrated in Stuart and Revett, Antiquities of Athens, IV *(1816), a likely source for the frieze in the Great Room at Spencer House (FIG 127)*

well as Bacchic leopards guarding wine flasks.[13] Figures of Bacchus and his followers also appeared in the frieze of the chimney-piece (FIG 130). The relief above the south wall represented Apollo, god of music and the arts, playing the lyre and receiving a crown of laurel from a figure of Victory (FIG 122, p. 144).[14] The relief was framed by laurel branches and by griffins guarding vases filled with flowers. The griffin was sacred to Apollo, but it was also the Spencer crest, and its use in this context may well have been intended to symbolize the flowering of the arts under the Spencers' protection. Masks of Apollo appeared in the carved decoration of the pier tables (FIG 126) and were echoed opposite in the capitals of the chimney-piece (FIG 130).

Love and romance were a vital part of any grand reception; indeed it was one of the functions of such entertainments to provide an opportunity for the sons and daughters of the nobility to seek out partners in marriage. Above the west wall was a relief representing

[13] The identical relief appears on the ceiling of the Library at Claydon House, Bucks, executed by Patroli around 1765 and illustrated in Margaret Jourdain, *English Decorative Plasterwork of the Renaissance* (1927), pl.172. It is also interesting to note that in 1766 Stuart exhibited a painting at the Society of Artists entitled *A Nymph supplying Bacchus with Wine* [Algernon Graves, op. cit., p.247, No. 171]

[14] The identical relief appears on the ceiling of the Library at Claydon House, Bucks. See previous note

[15] The identical relief was used by Robert Adam above a chimney-piece at No. 21 Portland Place, illustrated in Jourdain, *English Decorative Plasterwork*, pl.177

a figure of Venus, or possibly Galatea, driving a marine chariot drawn by dolphins (FIG 123, p. 145).[15] On one side was Hymen, god of marriage, identifiable by the lighted torch he carried, while on the other was Cupid, drawing back his bow and releasing imaginary arrows as if to pierce the heart of the onlooker. Roses, the flowers of Venus, formed a garland that encircled the relief, supported also by amorini, the agents of love. Another reference to love was found in the decoration of the pier glasses, each of which was surmounted by a pair of amorini driving chariots drawn by griffins (FIG 124). In fact the putti were not quite a pair, for while one was laughing as his griffin raced ahead, the other was in tears, his own griffin having stopped in its tracks. Again one suspects that the griffin had been used for its heraldic connection with the Spencers; and with the knowledge we have of the deep romantic bond between the 1st Earl and Countess, it is tempting to see a coded message to the effect that, whether yielding or resisting, the Spencers were always driven by love. The baskets in the centre, overflowing with fruit, were probably intended as symbols of love's abundant rewards, as perhaps were the swags between the legs of the pier tables, composed of roses, berries and pine cones. The last of the reliefs, located opposite, represented the Three Graces, attendants of Venus and symbols of feminine beauty, flanked by amorini clutching roses and draped with laurel, denoting triumph (FIG 127).

129 The Basilica of Maxentius, Rome, as illustrated in Piranesi, Vedute di Roma *(1774). Stuart used the identical coffering in the cove of the Great Room ceiling (FIG 127)*

130

130 Spencer House, Great Room, chimney-piece; photograph of 1926. Carved in Carrara marble, the frieze represented a bacchanal with figures derived from the Choragic Monument of Lysicrates in Athens (FIGS 133–35). Miniature masks of Apollo appeared in the capitals of the pilasters, and the architrave was modelled on that of the Incantada at Salonika (FIG 153, p. 171)

131 Incantada at Salonika, the bacchante, as illustrated in Stuart and Revett, Antiquities of Athens, *III, pl.XIII. The bacchante was reproduced by Stuart in the relief above the entrance to the Great Room at Spencer House (FIG 132)*

132 Spencer House, first-floor passageway, relief above entrance to Great Room. Two bacchantes, one playing the trumpet, the other carrying a wine cup, indicate to the visitor that the pleasures of music and wine lie ahead

131

132

The sources of the decoration of the Great Room were predominantly Classical. The coffering in the cove was derived from the Basilica of Maxentius in Rome (FIG 129). The reliefs above the cornice were clearly inspired by Antique gems and medals, and it is interesting to note that in the reliefs of Bacchus and Apollo, Stuart introduced faithful copies of a klismos chair and a bathron stool (FIG 122, p. 144), important elements of Greek and Roman furniture. The frieze followed a pattern common to many Classical buildings and monuments, but was probably inspired by the Temple of Augustus at Pola (FIG 128).[16] The amorini charioteers above the pier glasses were likewise derived from Classical prototypes (FIG 125, p. 147).[17] The architrave of the chimney-piece was adapted from the Incantada at Salonika, illustrated in the *Antiquities of Athens* (FIG 153, p. 171), which was also the source for the trumpet-playing bacchante in the relief above the entrance off the passageway (FIGS 131 and 132). The figures in the frieze of the

[16] A similar frieze is indicated in Vardy's original section

[17] Examples from Classical art of chariots drawn by griffins can be found in Giovanni Gaetano Bottari, *Musei Capitolini*, 4 vols (Rome, 1750–82), 4, p.77; *Antichità di Ercolano Esposte*, I, p.207

133

chimney-piece were principally copied from the Choragic Monument of Lysicrates, illustrated again in the *Antiquities of Athens* (FIGS 133–135). One of the figures, a bacchante playing a tambourine, was of a type commonly found in Antique sculpture and painting (FIG 167, p. 179). The jambs too were of Antique inspiration, as were the legs of the pier tables.

At the same time other influences were evident. The use of fully-rounded amorini above the cornice was a feature derived from the architecture of the Renaissance and the Baroque. The pier tables might have been inspired by similar examples in the so-called *Goût Grec* style, produced in France a few years earlier. The relief of Venus, while Classical in its subject matter, was closer in stylistic terms to the art of the sixteenth and seventeenth centuries and was probably inspired by Raphael's famous fresco of Galatea at the Villa Farnesina in Rome. The relief of the Three Graces was similarly post-Classical in style and composition. The seating furniture was squarely in the English tradition, similar to examples illustrated in contemporary pattern books such as those by Chippendale or Ince and Mayhew. It is noticeable that the sofas and chairs had none of the archaeological detailing one associates with Stuart and it is open to question whether they were not in fact commissioned before his arrival while Vardy was still in charge.

133 Choragic Monument of Lysicrates, Athens, detail of the frieze, as illustrated in Stuart and Revett, Antiquities of Athens, *I (1762), pl.XI*

134 Choragic Monument of Lysicrates, Athens, detail of the frieze, as illustrated in Stuart and Revett, Antiquities of Athens, *I (1762), pl.X*

135 Choragic Monument of Lysicrates, Athens, detail of the frieze, as illustrated in Stuart and Revett, Antiquities of Athens, *I (1762), pl.XXVI*

134

135

The Great Room was intended not only as a setting for receptions but also for pictures. It fulfilled the function of a private art gallery and contained some of the finest paintings in the Spencer collection. If Lord Spencer wished to be known as a generous and gracious host, he was no less eager to impress on his guests that he was a connoisseur and collector, a man of education and taste. In an age without public museums there can have been few rooms in London where art lovers could admire a comparable range of old master paintings. Two of the paintings were portraits by Rubens, representing respectively the Infanta of Spain and Archduke Albert of Austria, which Lord Spencer had brought down from Althorp.[18] However, as in Lady Spencer's Dressing Room, there were other paintings which had been purchased expressly for their setting. These included a magnificent pair of historical landscapes by Salvator Rosa, which hung on either side of the chimney-piece and which Spencer acquired in Florence from the Palazzo Accaiuoli during the Grand Tour: *Cincinnatus Called from the Farm* and *Alexander and Diogenes.* On either side of the door on the south wall were two further paintings acquired for the room, *King David* and *The Samian Sibyl* by Guercino, which Spencer purchased through Gavin Hamilton (FIG 136) from the Palazzo Locatelli in Cesena in 1768. There is a tradition also that two paintings acquired by Lord Spencer at auction in 1758, an allegory of Liberality and Modesty by Guido Reni and a portrait of a musician with Apollo by Andrea Sacchi, were likewise intended for the Great Room but were found to be too large and were therefore transferred to Wimbledon.[19] The choice and positioning of the paintings was integral to the room's design. From surviving letters between the Spencers and Gavin Hamilton we know that the paintings by Guercino were purchased to hang on the south wall, Hamilton having been issued with precise measurements corresponding to those of the space on either side of the central doorcase. Moreover, the Spencers ordered special frames for all the paintings, carved to match the mouldings on the doorcases and window-surrounds. In addition to paintings, the Great Room is also thought to have contained one or more of the miniature marble copies of Antique statues supplied by Hamilton in 1765. These were probably displayed on the chimney-piece, in accordance with prevailing fashion, appearing in this position in early photographs. The *Apollino* and the *Medici Venus* would have been especially appropriate, tying in perfectly with the room's iconography.

It must have been a dazzling spectacle when the Spencers entertained and the room filled with guests; the men in ruffles and powdered wigs; the women in silk and velvet gowns, set off by resplendent jewellery; a fire blazing in the hearth, with dozens of lighted candles burning brightly from the chandelier and candelabra; an orchestra playing and footmen circulating or standing to attention by the doors; all the seating furniture backed up against the walls and a space cleared in the centre for dancing and general conversation.

To the south the Great Room led through to the famous Painted Room, arguably the most important of the interiors at Spencer House (FIG 137). The room takes its name from the murals and inset painted panels which cover the walls and ceiling. Begun around 1759, the date which appears on Stuart's design for the north wall (PLATE VII, p. 68), it was the first English interior of any significance since the days of Thornhill and Kent to feature an overall scheme of painted decoration, and paved the way for a widespread revival of this tradition.[20] The interior was divided by a screen of Corinthian columns, with matching pilasters lining the walls and an alcove to the south. Two doors on the east wall communicated with the first-floor passageway, while a window opposite was flanked by matching gilt-framed pier glasses. Two further windows in the alcove were

136

[18] This can be deduced from the fact that the paintings, now at Althorp, are framed in identical fashion to the others which hung in the Great Room, the frames being carved to match the door- and window-surrounds

[19] The paintings were framed in identical fashion to the others which hung originally in the Great Room, suggesting that they, too, were intended to hang there. However, according to the researches of the 7th Earl Spencer the paintings were found, when framed, to be too large for the Great Room and were therefore transferred to Wimbledon. The Reni is indeed recorded at Wimbledon in John Woolfe and James Gandon, *Vitruvius Britannicus*, V (1771), p.4. During the lifetime of the 2nd Earl Spencer the original columnar doorcases on the north and south walls of the Great Room were removed and smaller doorcases installed in their place. This made it possible for the Reni and Sacchi, which survived the fire at Wimbledon in 1785, to be hung on the north wall, in which position they appear in photographs of the 1890s

[20] By 1759, the date of Stuart's design, the fashion for ceiling paintings and murals had all but died out in England. In the same year William Chambers published his *Treatise on Civil Architecture* in which he claimed 'painted ceilings . . . are not in use among us . . . the prejudices of our connoisseurs hath excluded all modern performance in painting from our houses' [p.84]

136 Gavin Hamilton, self portrait. Hamilton played a key role in the creation of the Great Room, supplying marble slabs for the pier tables and a magnificent pair of paintings by Guercino which originally hung on the south wall, as well as miniature marble copies of Antique statues which are believed to have stood on the chimney-piece

137 Spencer House, Painted Room, looking north-east; photograph of c1890. The Painted Room is generally acknowledged to have been the first fully-integrated Neo-Classical interior in England, and possibly Europe

137

138

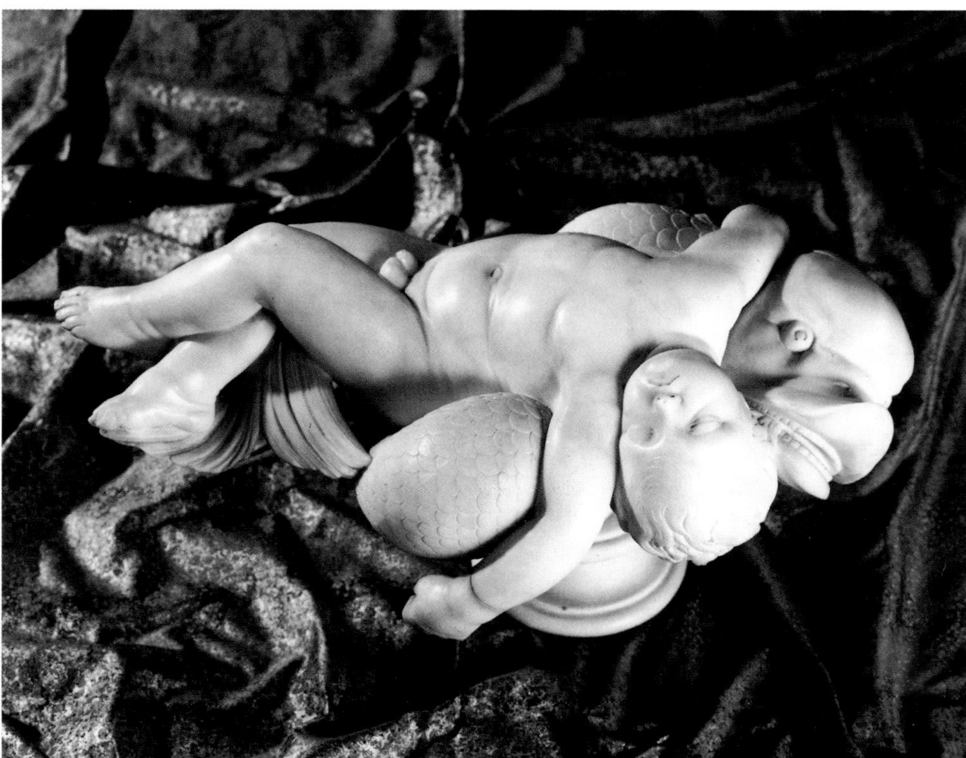
139

matched by a third in *trompe-l'oeil*, the glazing bars fitted with mirrors in place of transparent glass. The interior served as a drawing room and was furnished accordingly with sofas and armchairs (PLATE XVII, p. 164).[21] No doubt it was used for 'sitting out' during balls in the adjoining Great Room. Other articles of furniture included a pair of gilt-bronze candelabra mounted on painted wooden stands (FIG 170, p. 179) and a second pair of candelabra, which probably stood on the chimney-piece (FIG 172, p.179). From an early description we know that the room also contained two or more tables,[22] since lost but possibly of the kind illustrated in Stuart's section and in a related design by the architect which would seem to be a preparatory study for the same piece of furniture (FIG 138).[23] In addition the room may also have contained a remarkable giltwood candle-stand, now at Althorp, which has likewise been attributed to Stuart (FIG 177, p. 181).[24] It has also been claimed that the room contained the marble sculpture *Boy on a Dolphin*, commissioned by Lord Spencer from Joseph Nollekens in Rome (FIG 139),[25] and it is possible that one or more of the miniature marble copies of Antique statues acquired by Lord Spencer were shown here, as they were in later years. The interior would similarly have provided the perfect setting for the Classical relief of Egeria supplied by Gavin Hamilton, who suggested at the time that Stuart design a suitable pedestal for the carving.[26]

The murals and inset painted panels covered a wide range of subjects, but the dominant theme was marriage. Indeed the whole room was surely intended as a celebration of the union of John and Georgiana Spencer. The most striking reference was found in the frieze of the chimney-piece (PLATE XXI, p.174), which represented a Roman wedding; no ordinary wedding, moreover, but a clandestine wedding, a fact pointed out to early visitors,[27] providing the clearest possible allusion to the Spencers' own marriage at Althorp. Another wedding scene was represented in a circular grisaille panel in the apse (FIG 140), Greek this time, rather than Roman, as was clear from the fact that the

138 Design for a pier table, by James Stuart, c1760. The table is clearly related to that in Plate VII and was perhaps intended for the Painted Room. The use of the lion as a supporting element looks back to the furniture of Classical Antiquity

139 Boy on a Dolphin, *by Joseph Nollekens, c1764. Commissioned by the 1st Earl Spencer in Rome, the sculpture is believed to have stood in the Painted Room*

[21] The sofas and armchairs were sold by the 8th Earl Spencer and are now in the collection of the V&A. Recently they were placed on loan at Spencer House

[22] In his description of *c*1769 Arthur Young specifically mentions 'tables' [Arthur Young, *A Six Weeks Tour through the Southern Counties of England and Wales*, p.361]

[23] RIBA [CC4/35]

[24] Albert Edward John, 7th Earl Spencer, 'Furniture at Spencer House' *Country Life* (13 Nov 1926)

[25] Seymour Howard, 'Boy on a Dolphin: Nollekens and Cavaceppi', *The Art Bulletin* (June 1964), pp.177–89

[26] AP F117, GH to JS, 29 Jan 1766

[27] Arthur Young was specific on this point. 'The frieze contains a most exquisite painting representing a clandestine marriage' [Young, op. cit., p.360]

140 Spencer House, Painted Room, grisaille panel representing an ancient Greek wedding. The groom takes the bride by the wrist in accordance with ancient Greek custom

141

141 Spencer House, Painted Room, panel representing a sacrifice to Cupid. The panel proclaims the power of love

142 Spencer House, Painted Room, ceiling of apse; photograph of 1926. From bottom to top: Judgement of Paris; Sacrifice to Cupid; Apollo and Marsyas; Sacrifice to Minerva; Choice of Hercules

bridegroom took the bride by the wrist rather than the hand, according to ancient Greek custom. Above the door leading through to the Great Room was an oval panel representing a reclining female figure unveiled by a cherub (PLATE XII, p.161). The cherub carried a torch and a purple cloak, traditional attributes of Hymen, god of marriage, while the female figure was evidently intended to represent a bride on her wedding day, the unveiling symbolizing the transition from virginity to matrimony. Beneath the panel were flaming torches, symbols once more of Hymen, while the wall above was painted with roses and palm branches representing the union of love and peace. Another tribute to love was found in a panel in the ceiling of the apse representing a sacrifice to Cupid (FIG 141); yet another in an adjoining panel illustrated the story of the golden apple (FIG 142). According to legend, the goddesses Minerva, Juno and Venus competed for the prize of a golden apple awarded by Paris, son of Priam, King of Troy. Minerva offered

143

143 Spencer House, Painted Room, panel representing a musical centaur with Cupid and amorino. The centaur marches to the tune of love

XII Spencer House, Painted Room, panel representing a bride unveiled by Hymen. The purple robe and flaming torch are traditional attributes of Hymen, god of marriage. The bride carries a garland of roses, flowers symbolic of love

XIII Spencer House, Painted Room, panel representing an allegory of Water. Putti fish shells and pearls from a stream, which they fashion into necklaces

ON PAGES 162–3
XIV Spencer House, Painted Room, detail of north wall. The distinction between the iconography here and that on the other side of the wall (PLATE XV) recalls the division in the ancient world between the rival cults of Apollo and Dionysus

XV Spencer House, Painted Room, detail of north wall. The murals and inset panels on this side of the wall were given over to scenes of wildness and disorder, in contrast to those on the other side, which were governed by the theme of harmony

military glory, Juno promised a kingdom, but Venus offered marriage to the fairest woman in the world and so received the apple, the panel thus symbolizing the triumph of love and the sentiment that nothing in this world compares with marriage to a beautiful woman. On the north wall was another panel on the theme of love representing a pair of turtle doves nestling in a bed of roses (PLATE XIV, p. 162). Directly below this was a painting in which a centaur carrying a lyre marched to a tune played by Cupid on the pipes, while a second cherub crowned them both with garlands of roses (FIG 143). A related panel represented a wicked centaur being led on a chain of roses by Cupid with an amorino whipping him from behind (FIG 144, p. 165), and below this the wall was painted with evil-looking harpies whipped into service by amorini, signalling another triumph for love.

Grouped together on the west wall were four oval panels representing female figures in Classical drapery, evidently intended as allegories of the womanly or wifely virtues. The first carried a palm branch, a traditional symbol of peace and conciliation. The

XVI Spencer House, Painted Room, panel representing an allegory of hospitality and service. The panel was one of four representing feminine or wifely virtues

XVII Spencer House, Painted Room, detail of sofa. The winged lions were clearly inspired by Classical thrones such as those in Figures 168 and 169, p. 178

144 Spencer House, Painted Room, panel representing a centaur tamed by Cupid. Love triumphs over wickedness

second held a bunch of lilies, flowers associated with virginity, and at the same time caressed a lamb, symbolizing innocence. The third figure placed a garland of roses on a classical altar stand, suggesting love, devotion and sacrifice, while the fourth carried a wine cup and ewer, representing obedience, service and hospitality (PLATE XVI).

Wherever there is love and marriage, wine, music and dancing are bound to follow, and scenes of celebration were everywhere in evidence. Three of the panels on the ceiling represented female figures in Classical drapery dancing and playing musical instruments (PLATES XVIII and XX, p. 173). A fourth showed an innocent shepherd led astray by attendants of the wine god Bacchus (PLATE XIX, p. 173). On the north wall an idyllic Classical landscape provided the setting for music and dancing (PLATE XIV, p. 162), and

145

the festivities continued above the chimney-piece in a series of terracotta panels representing frolicking putti (PLATE XXI, p. 174 and FIGS 145 and 146). In the first a group of putti were engaged in tormenting a goat (FIG 145), an animal which in Antiquity was often sacrificed to Bacchus on account of the damage it caused to vines. Two putti appeared in the second panel, one playing the trumpet, the other brandishing a bunch of grapes (FIG 146). The third panel showed a similar scene with two putti partaking of wine, and a painted panel above represented another group of putti dancing and playing musical instruments. Also on the north wall was a pair of magpies, birds which in Antiquity were

145 Spencer House, Painted Room, terracotta panel representing putti tormenting a goat. In Antiquity the goat was sacrificed to Bacchus on account of the damage it caused to vineyards

146 Spencer House, Painted Room, terracotta panel representing frollicking putti. One putto plays the trumpet, while the other brandishes a bunch of grapes

146

sacred to Bacchus, perched on a festoon of grapes and vine leaves (PLATE XV, p. 163). Trailing ivy, thyrsus branches and wine pitchers provided further references to Bacchus and drinking. On the ceiling of the apse was another panel on a musical theme representing the story of Apollo and Marsyas (FIG 142, p. 159). According to legend, Marsyas, a Phrygian piper, challenged Apollo to a musical contest in order to win the heart of the goddess Cybele, but was defeated and suffered the punishment of being flayed alive. The panel in the apse showed the contest in progress with a crowned figure, possibly King Midas, sitting in judgement, surrounded by female figures perhaps representing the Muses.

147 Spencer House, Painted Room, grisaille panel representing an allegory of Honour and Virtue. The composition was based on a Roman coin (FIG 161, p. 176)

The mood of the Painted Room was festive and carefree, but duty was not forgotten. Alongside the panels devoted to love and music was another representing a scene from the legend of Hercules, in which the hero, caught between the rival attractions of pleasure and honour, proved his mettle by opting for the latter. Allegorical figures of Honour and Virtue were represented in a circular grisaille panel below (FIG 147), and duty to the arts was apparently the subject of another panel on the ceiling of the apse which represented a sacrifice to Minerva, the goddess of the arts (FIG 148).

The Four Elements were represented in a series of painted panels on the east and west walls. Fire was symbolized by a gathering of putti grouped around a furnace, forging gold necklaces and other items of jewellery, with examples of their handiwork painted in festoons below. Air was represented by another group of putti, one waving a fan composed of peacock feathers, symbol of Juno, goddess of the heavens, with further peacock feathers reproduced on the wall below (FIG 149). Water was symbolized by putti fishing pearls and shells from a stream, represented again in festoons on the wall (PLATE XIII, p. 161). The fourth panel, symbolic of Earth, showed a group of putti in a sylvan setting composing chains of roses, likewise festooned beneath the frame. Floral garlands appeared in four separate panels on the ceiling, adding to the impression of natural wealth and abundance, while the heavens were symbolized by a ring of miniature roundels representing the signs of the Zodiac.

148 Spencer House, Painted Room, ceiling panel representing a sacrifice to Minerva. The female figure was derived from an Antique gem (FIG 162, p. 176), while the altar and child were taken from Raphael's Sacrifice at Lystra *(FIG 179, p. 182)*

149 Spencer House, Painted Room, panel representing an allegory of Air. A putto in the centre waves a fan of peacock feathers, attributes of Juno, goddess of the heavens

148

149

But there was a further dimension to the iconography. Aside from their connection with love, music and honour, the panels in the apse representing Hercules, Paris and the contest of Apollo and Marsyas were clearly linked by the concept of choice. More interesting still, a close examination of the north wall reveals a division between the left- and right-hand side, the first given over to scenes of wildness and disorder, the other to scenes of peace and harmony, corresponding perhaps to that division in the ancient world between the rival cults of Dionysus and Apollo.

As in the Great Room, the sources of the decoration were predominantly Classical. The overall conception was clearly inspired by Roman painted interiors such as those which Stuart would have seen on his visit to Pompeii and Herculaneum in 1748, as well as the Domus Aurea and other examples of Antique painted decoration in Rome itself (FIG 150). The detailing, too, was markedly Classical, including features derived from Greek as well as Roman sources. The frieze was taken from the Erechtheion in Athens (FIGS 120 (p. 142) and 152); the doorcases on the east wall (FIG 151) were derived from the Incantada at Salonika (FIG 153); and the columnar screen has been traced to the

150

150 Colombario degli Arrunzi, Rome, interior view; detail of engraving by Giovanni Battista Piranesi published in Le Antichità Romane, *II (Rome, 1756), pl.x. The design of the Painted Room was clearly inspired by ancient Roman interiors of the sort illustrated in this engraving, which were decorated alike with murals, ceiling paintings and ornamental stucco*

151 Spencer House, Painted Room, detail of doorcase on east wall. The architrave was based on that of the Incantada at Salonika (FIG 153)

152 Spencer House, Painted Room, detail of capital and frieze. The frieze was adapted from that of the Erechtheion, Athens (FIG 120, p. 142)

153 The Incantada, Salonika, the architrave, as illustrated in Stuart and Revett, Antiquities of Athens, *3, chap.IX, pl.III. This was the source for the architraves of both the Great Room chimney-piece (FIG 130, p. 150) and the doorcases on the east wall of the Painted Room (FIG 151)*

151

152

153

154

154 Temple of Castor and Pollux, Rome, soffit, as illustrated in Desgodetz, Les Édifices Antiques de Rome *(1682), p.131, fig.63. The ceiling compartments in the Painted Room were clearly inspired by Classical decoration of this kind (FIG 137, p. 155)*

155

Temple of Fortuna Virilis in Rome.[28] The ceiling compartments, containing scrolling acanthus, were of a type commonly employed by Roman architects (FIG 154), as were the pilasters, which featured similar decoration (FIG 155). The frieze of the chimney-piece (PLATE XXI, p. 174) was a faithful copy of the famous *Aldobrandini Wedding*, a fragment of a Roman fresco dating from the first century A.D. (FIG 156), while the painting of the Greek wedding in the apse (FIG 140, p. 157) was based on a marble relief discovered by Stuart on the Acropolis and illustrated in the *Antiquities of Athens* (FIG 157). The centaur tamed by love (FIG 144, p. 165) was clearly derived from a celebrated Antique Roman

155 Arch of the Sergii, as illustrated in Stuart and Revett, Antiquities of Athens, *IV (1816), chap.III, pl.III. The pilasters, with scrolling acanthus, are of a type commonly found in Classical architecture, providing the ultimate source for those in the Painted Room*

[28] David Watkin, *Athenian Stuart, Pioneer of the Greek Revival*, p.36

XVIII Spencer House, Painted Room, ceiling panel representing bacchantes playing musical instruments

XIX Spencer House, Painted Room, ceiling panel representing a shepherd led astray by bacchantes

XX Spencer House, Painted Room, ceiling panel representing dancing bacchantes. Wherever there is love, music and dancing are bound to follow

JAMES STUART

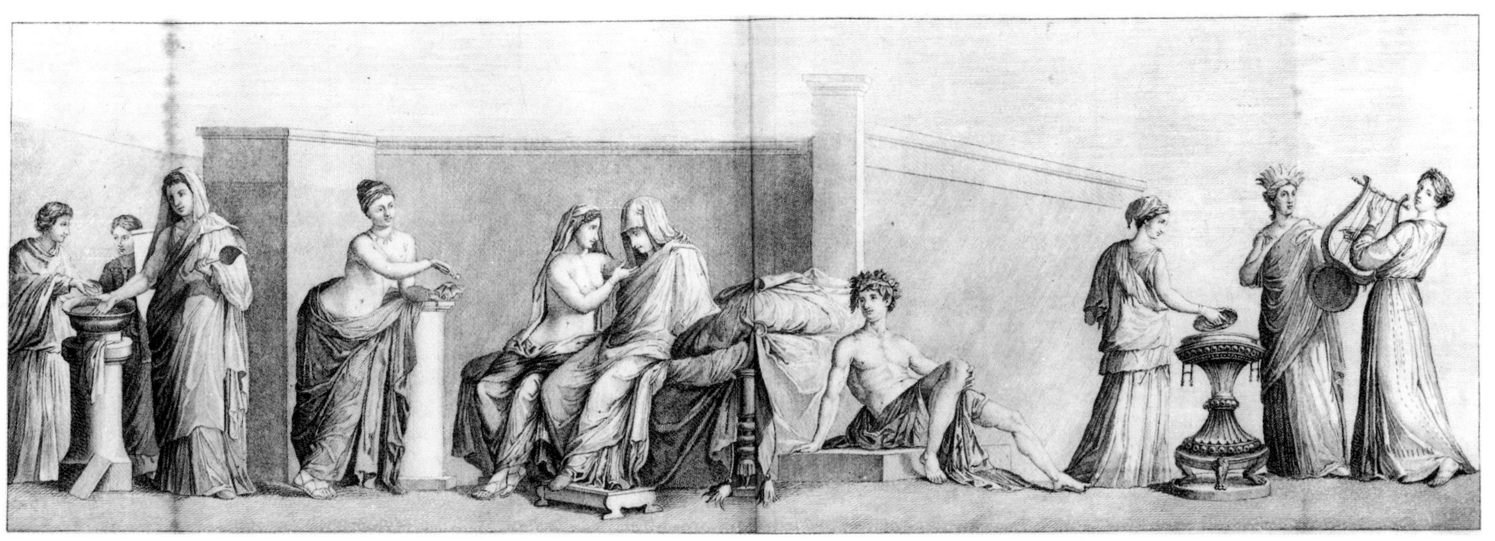

156 The Aldobrandini Wedding; *engraving by J. Mynde after Camillo Paderni, from George Turnbull,* A Curious Collection of Antique Paintings *(1741), pl.4. From the time of its discovery in the early seventeenth century,* The Aldobrandini Wedding *was regarded as one of the most precious examples of Classical painting. Numerous engravings were made, but the version at Spencer House (PLATE XXI,) was evidently taken from a painted copy, since the colours are close to those of the original. Several painted copies were in circulation in the eighteenth century; one hung in Goethe's house in Weimar, another in the London house of George Turnbull. It was from the latter copy that the present engraving was made*

157

157 Acropolis, Athens, relief representing an ancient Greek wedding, as illustrated in Stuart and Revett, Antiquities of Athens, *II (1789), p.VIII. The relief was evidently the source for the panel illustrated in Figure 140, p. 157*

158 The Borghese Centaur, *as illustrated in Paolo Alessandro Maffei,* Raccolta di Statue Antiche e Moderne, *I (Rome, 1704), pl.LXXII. This famous Antique statue was the source for the panel in Figure 144, p. 165*

XXI Spencer House, Painted Room, chimney-piece. The chimney-piece was a composite of diverse elements derived from the art and architecture of Greece, Rome, Renaissance Italy and seventeenth-century Flanders

158

159

161

162

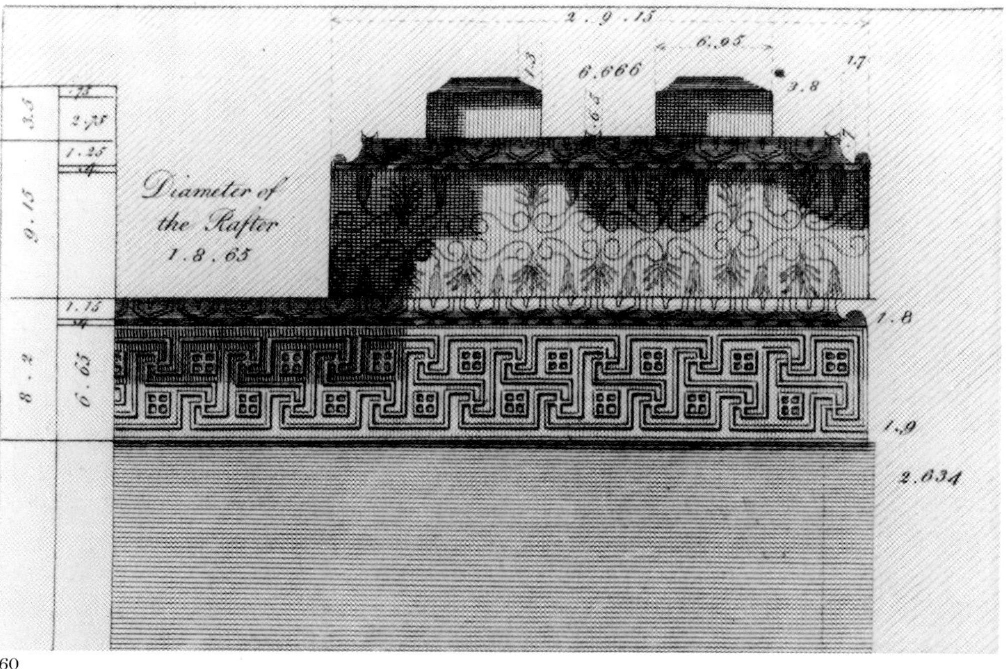

160

163

statue at the Villa Borghese (FIG 158), while that with the lyre and the piping Cupid (FIG 143, p. 160) may have been inspired by an Antique Roman sarcophagus at the Palazzo Giustiniani (FIG 159).[29] The allegorical panel of Honour and Virtue (FIG 147, p. 168) was taken from a Roman coin of the reign of the Emperor Galba (FIG 161),[30] while the unusual Greek fret on the overmantel (FIG 145, p. 166) was probably inspired by the frieze of the Theseum in Athens (FIG 160). The female figure in the panel representing the sacrifice to Cupid (FIG 141, p. 158) was apparently adapted from a Roman gem, as illustrated in de la Chausse's *Le Gemme Antiche Figurate* (1700) (FIG 163), while that in the sacrifice to Minerva (FIG 148, p. 169) may have been derived from Montfaucon's *L'Antiquité Expliquée* (FIG 162).[31] The altar in the sacrifice to Cupid was adapted from

[29] A similar centaur with lyre and piping Cupid appears on a Roman funerary cippus formerly in the Villa Borghese in Rome and now in the Louvre, which is illustrated in Enea Vico, *Le Imagini delle Donne Auguste Intagliate* (1557), frontispiece; Jean-Jacques Boissard, *I Pars Romanae Urbis Topographiae & Antiquitatum* (Frankfurt, 1597), pl.144; Bernard de Montfaucon, *L'Antiquité Expliquée*, 5, part I, pl.79

[30] The coin is likewise illustrated in Laurentius Beger, *Regum et Imperatorum*

159 Relief representing a musical centaur with lyre and piping Cupid, from a sarcophagus formerly at the Palazzo Giustiniani, Rome; engraving in Galleria Giustiniana, *2 vols (Rome, 1631), I, pl.xcc. The panel in Figure 143, p. 160, was clearly derived from some such source in the art of Antiquity*

160 Temple of Theseus, Athens, the frieze, as illustrated in Stuart and Revett, Antiquities of Athens, *III, chap.I, pl.VII. This unusual double Greek fret was reproduced by Stuart in the decoration of the overmantel in the Painted Room (FIG 145, p. 166)*

161 Coin of the reign of the Emperor Galba, as illustrated in Vincenzo Cartari, Le Vere e Nove Imagini de gli dei delli antichi *(Padua, 1615), p.517. The figures of Honour and Virtue were reproduced by Stuart in the panel in Figure 147, p. 168*

162 Roman gem representing a sacrifice, as illustrated in Montfaucon, L'Antiquité Expliquée *(1719), II, pl.xc, fig 2. The hooded figure reappears in the panel in Figure 148, p. 169*

163 Roman gem representing a sacrifice, as illustrated in Michelange de La Chausse, Le Gemme Antiche Figurate *(Rome, 1700), pl.2. The female figure in the ceiling panel in Figure 141, p. 158, is of the type illustrated here, commonly found in Classical representations of sacrificial scenes*

164 Roman marble candelabrum; engraving by Piranesi in Le Antichità Romane, *II (1756), pl.XXV. The motif of a putto terminating in scrolling acanthus is commonly found on the bases of Roman candelabra. Several examples were known. to the eighteenth century, and one of these must surely have been the source for the altar in the panel in Figure 141, p. 158. The candelabrum in Piranesi's engraving was displayed at the time in the church of Santa Costanza in Rome but has since been transferred to the Vatican Museum*

Romanorum Numismata (1700), pl.22; Montfaucon, op.cit., I, pl.ccx, fig.1

[31] The figure is of a common Classical type. Another example is illustrated in Leonardo Agostini, *Le Gemme Antiche Figurate* (Amsterdam, 1685), part I, pl.13

[32] Hans Ulrich Cain, *Römische Marmorkandelaber* (Mainz, 1985), pls 37–41, 93, 99–102

164

165

165 The Borghese Dancers, *as illustrated in Pietro Santi Bartoli,* Admiranda Romanarum Antiquitatum *(Rome, 1693), pl.63. This famous relief was almost certainly the source for the dancing figures in the panel in Plate* XX, *p. 173*

166

167

168

169

170

171

172

166 Roman marble relief of bacchantes and satyrs playing musical instruments, as illustrated in Michelange de La Chausse, Romanum Museum, *I, section II (Rome, 1746), pl.9. Bacchantes playing cymbals are often found in Antique sculpture and painting and were clearly the source for those in Plate XVIII, p. 173*

167 Detail of Roman marble relief with bacchante playing tambourine, as illustrated in Bartolomeo Cavaceppi, Raccolta di Statue, Busti, Bassirilievi ed altre Sculture Ristaurate, *3 (Rome, 1772), pl.33. The central bacchante in the panel in Plate XVIII, p. 173, was clearly derived from examples of this kind, which are common in Antique art*

168 Vatican Museum, Antique marble throne; engraving from Enio Quirino Visconti, Museo Pio Clementino, *7 (1782) pl.XLIV. During the period he spent in Rome, Stuart would almost certainly have seen the present throne, which was among the most prized examples of Antique furniture in the Vatican collections*

169 Ashmolean Museum, Oxford, Greek marble throne. As a leading authority on Antiquity, and more particularly ancient Greece, Stuart would certainly have been familiar with this celebrated example of ancient Greek furniture, which had formerly belonged to the Earl of Arundel

170 Spencer House, Painted Room, gilt-bronze candelabrum and stand; photograph of 1926. This remarkable piece of furniture was typical of Stuart's synthetic approach to design. The candelabrum was based on a reconstruction of the missing tripod from the Choragic Monument of Lysicrates (FIG 171). The griffins were derived from a Roman marble tripod in the Capitoline Museum (FIG 173). The pedestal was modelled on the bases of Antique candelabra (FIG 175)

171 Choragic Monument of Lysicrates, reconstruction of the missing torch, as illustrated in Stuart and Revett, Antiquities of Athens, *I (1762), p.36. The candelabrum in the Painted Room (FIG 170) clearly relates to this design*

172 Spencer House, Painted Room, gilt-bronze candelabrum; photograph of 1926

the bases of Classical candelabra (FIG 164).[32] The dancing bacchantes on the ceiling (PLATE XX, p. 173) were probably inspired by a famous Classical relief then in the Borghese collection in Rome (FIG 165), and those with tambourine and cymbals (PLATE XVIII, p. 173) likewise derived from Classical prototypes (FIGS 166 and 167). The furniture, too, was of Antique inspiration. The sofas and armchairs were clearly modelled on Classical marble thrones, such as those in the Vatican and Ashmolean Museums (FIGS 168 and 169 and PLATE XVII, p. 164). The gilt-bronze candelabra (FIG 170) were based on a reconstruction by Stuart of the missing tripod from the Choragic Monument of Lysicrates (FIG 171); the three addorsed griffins below were evidently derived from a

Classical tripod in the Capitoline Museum (FIGS 173 and 174);[33] and the incurved triangular pedestals with painted figures were modelled on the bases of Roman candelabra (FIG 175). Most striking of all, the giltwood candle-stand with addorsed sphinxes (FIG 177) was a near-replica of a Roman original recently excavated at Pompeii and displayed at the Museum of Antiquities at Portici, which the Spencers visited on their Grand Tour (FIG 176).[34]

The Painted Room was a bold statement of the new Neo-Classical aesthetic; indeed it is generally considered to be the first fully-integrated Neo-Classical interior in England, if not Europe, and has long been recognized as the forerunner of all the many Pompeiian and Etruscan rooms which followed in its wake. But it is noticeable also how much of the decoration was derived from intermediate sources in the art and architecture of the post-Classical period. Stuart was clearly inspired by the 'grotesque' interiors of Raphael, Giovanni da Udine and other artists of the Renaissance. Although ultimately of Classical inspiration, the pilasters used by Stuart were probably derived from Raphael's *Loggie* at the Vatican, as perhaps was the wave-scroll frieze (FIG 178). Raphael was likewise the source for the child and altar in the panel representing the sacrifice to Minerva (FIG 148, p. 169), which were copied more or less exactly from the famous *Sacrifice at Lystra* (FIG 179).[35] The female herms on either side of the chimney-piece (PLATE XXI, p. 174) looked back to the sculpture of the Renaissance and might well have been derived from the gate of the Villa Giustiniani in Rome (FIG 180). Two of the terracotta panels above the lintel were casts after original reliefs in marble by the seventeenth-century Flemish sculptor,

[33] H. Stuart Jones, *A Catalogue of the Ancient Sculptures Preserved in the Municipal Collections of Rome: The Sculptures of the Museo Capitolino* (Oxford, 1912), pl.9, fig.16. Two drawings of the tripod, which testify to the interest it aroused among artists, are registered with the *Census of Antique Art and Architecture Known to the Renaissance* [Berlin SMPK Kupferstichkabinett, Codex Berolinensis, f.48 v. B.. No. 120; Coburg Veste, Kupferstichkabinett, Codex Coburgensis, No. 73, 3]

[34] AP F41, GS to CH, Jan 1764

[35] A collection of engravings after Raphael's cartoons was listed among Lord Spencer's prints at Althorp in 1763 [AP F169]

173

174

173 Capitoline Museum, Rome, Roman marble tripod. The motif of three addorsed griffins used by Stuart in the design of the candelabra in the Painted Room (FIG 170) was derived from this source. The tripod was already on display in the Capitoline Museum at the time Stuart lived in Rome and the architect presumably made drawings of it which served as the basis of his later design. The use of the griffin represents a further play on the Spencer heraldry

174 Capitoline Museum, Roman marble tripod, as illustrated in Piranesi, Vasi, Candelabri, Cippi, Sarcofagi, Tripodi, Lucerne ed Ornamenti Antichi, *1 (Rome, 1778), pl.36. Piranesi's engraving is evidence of the interest aroused by the Capitoline tripod at this time and shows the artist thinking along similar lines to Stuart. In this imaginary composition the tripod has been adapted as a pedestal, surmounted by a vase from the Villa Albani*

175 Roman marble candelabrum; engraving from Bartolomeo Cavaceppi, Raccolta, *3 (1772), pl.58. It was from candelabra of this kind that Stuart derived the form and decoration of the pedestals in Figure 170*

175

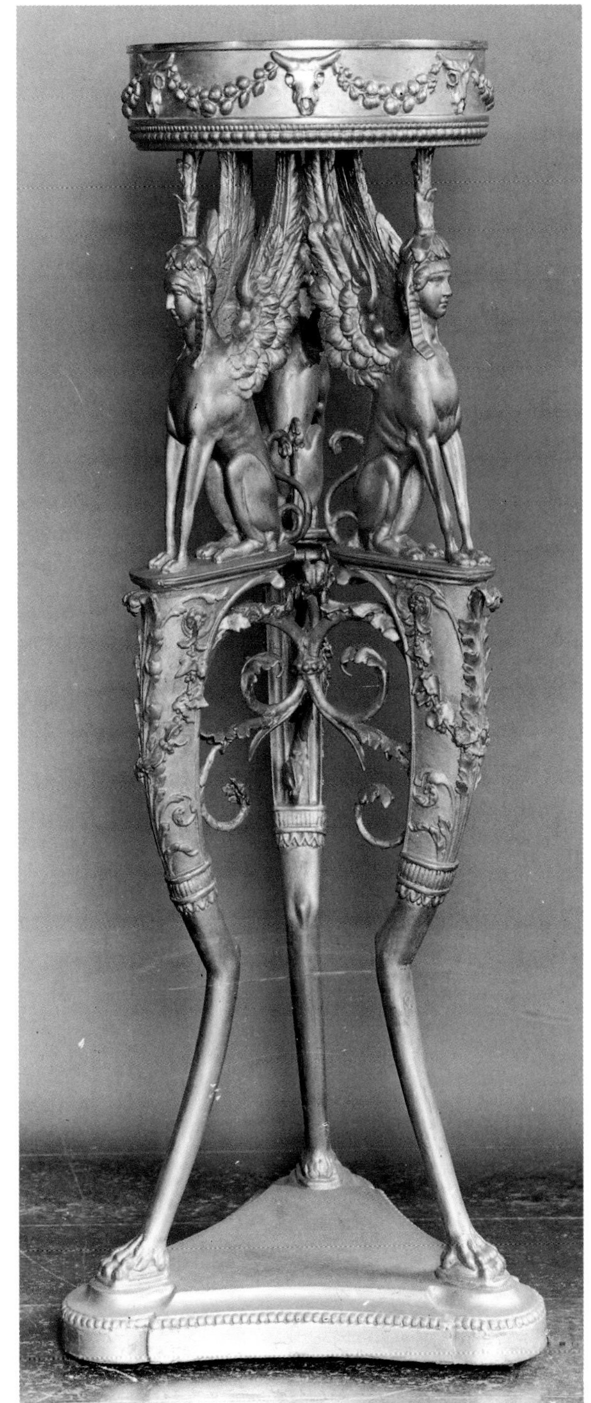

177

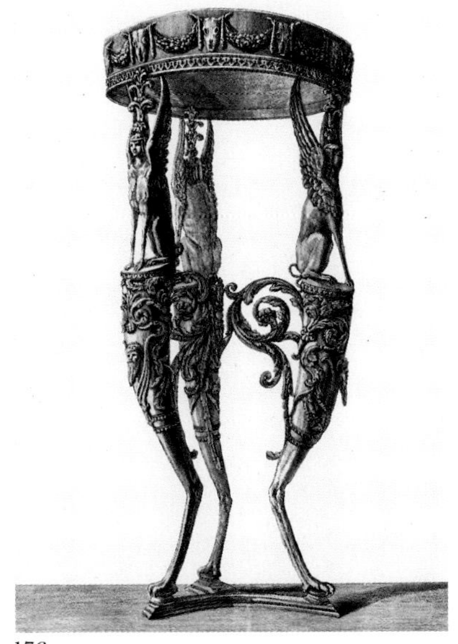

176

176 Roman bronze tripod, as illustrated in Piranesi, Vasi, Candelabri etc., *1 (1778), pl.44. The tripod in Piranesi's engraving had been excavated near Pompeii and was part of the collection displayed at the Museum of Antiquities at Portici, which the Spencers visited during their Grand Tour in 1763–64. It clearly provided the source for the magnificent giltwood candle-stand in Figure 177, probably designed by Stuart for the Painted Room*

177 Spencer House, Painted Room, giltwood candle-stand; photograph of 1926. An early example of the archaeological approach to furniture design, the present candle-stand was a near-replica of the celebrated Roman original in Figure 176

178

179

180

178 The Vatican, detail of the Loggie *by Raphael; engraving by Giovanni Ottaviani, from Camporesi,* Loggie di Rafaele nel Vaticano, *Part I (1772), pl. IX. The Vatican* Loggie *were among the most admired works of architecture in Rome and the pilasters and dado rail in the Painted Room were clearly inspired by this source (PLATES XIV and XV, pp. 162 and 163)*

179 Detail from The Sacrifice at Lystra, *by Raphael. The altar and child were reproduced in the ceiling panel illustrated in Figure 148, p. 169*

180 Villa Giustiniani, Rome, the gateway, as illustrated in Galleria Giustiniana, *2 vols (Rome, 1631), 2, pl. 160. This celebrated Roman landmark, since transferred to the Villa Celimontana, would appear to have been the source for the figures on either side of the chimney-piece in the Painted Room at Spencer House (PLATE XXI, p. 174)*

François Duquesnoy.[36] That in the centre (FIG 145, p. 166) was taken from a relief at the Palazzo Doria Pamphili in Rome (FIG 181), while the other (FIG 146, p. 167) was copied from the *Concerto d'Angeli* in the Church of the Santi Apostoli in Naples (FIG 182), although with customary nonchalance and wit Stuart took the liberty of substituting a bunch of grapes for the original scroll of music held by the putto on the left. It is interesting also that whereas the stands of the candelabra were Classical in almost every detail, the feet were of a type evolved in the seventeenth century, while the sofas and

[36] Mariette Fransolet, *François Duquesnoy, Sculpteur d'Urbain VIII 1597–1643* (Brussels, 1942)

armchairs clearly showed the influence of the Baroque and the Rococo in the curvilinear form of the frames. If, therefore, the Painted Room was Europe's earliest Neo-Classical interior, it also illustrates the limits of Neo-Classicism, or more properly its breadth. Indeed, if Stuart had wished to sum up the whole of the Western tradition in architecture, decoration, painting, sculpture and furniture, he could not have done so more effectively than in the Painted Room.

In addition to the state apartments Stuart was also involved in the decoration of the rooms along the north front where Lady Spencer had her bedchamber and closet. It is thought these rooms fulfilled a purely ceremonial function, providing an intimate yet sumptuous setting for the reception of close friends, and that in fact Lady Spencer slept

181

182

181 Galleria Doria Pamphili, Rome, Putti Tormenting a Goat, *marble relief, by François Duquesnoy (1597–1643). There are several known copies of this famous relief, which Stuart reproduced above the chimney-piece in the Painted Room (*FIG *145, p. 166)*

182 Church of the Santi Apostoli, Naples, Concerto d'Angeli, *marble relief, by François Duquesnoy. A detail of this relief was reproduced in the terracotta panel illustrated in Figure 146, p. 167 although with his customary nonchalance and wit Stuart substituted a bunch of grapes for the original scroll of music held by the lower putto*

183

184

183 Spencer House, Lady Spencer's Closet, chimney-piece; photograph of 1926

184 Spencer House, Lady Spencer's Bedchamber, chimney-piece; photograph of 1926. Set into the overmantel is a circular relief representing dancing bacchantes

185 Inlaid mahogany wardrobe, believed to have come from the private apartment of Lady Spencer at Spencer House. The wardrobe is part of a suite comprising a clothes chest (FIG 187), a washstand, a desk and two night tables. The design is architectural, with Corinthian-style colonettes supporting an entablature

186 Mahogany wardrobe, believed to have come from the private apartment of Lady Spencer at Spencer House. The massing and detailing of the wardrobe mark this out as an early example of Greek Revival furniture

185

186

187 Inlaid clothes chest, believed to have come from the private apartment of Lady Spencer at Spencer House

and dressed in a more modest but practical apartment on the floor above.

The Closet, adjoining the Music Room, had an elegant chimney-piece in Siena and white marble, Greek in inspiration and of architectural design, the jambs in the form of Ionic pilasters, the lintel carved with urns and festoons surmounted by a full Classical entablature (FIG 183). The plaster frieze followed the identical pattern to that in the Music Room (FIG 114, p. 139), while the walls were hung with crimson damask. The Bedchamber was likewise hung with crimson damask, and the chimney-piece, in Carrara marble, was surmounted by a circular relief representing dancing female figures in Classical drapery (FIG 184).[37] Among the contents of the apartment was a suite of mahogany furniture with Greek-fret inlay, comprising a large mahogany wardrobe with Corinthian colonettes (FIG 185), a chest (FIG 187), .a washstand, a writing table and a pair of bedside tables.[38] In addition there were one or more four-poster beds, upholstered *en suite* with the wall hangings, and a second mahogany wardrobe richly carved with anthemion ornaments and a bold Greek fret (FIG 186). Lady Spencer's apartment was skirted by a passageway, on the opposite side of which were two other rooms which might have been used by Lord Spencer, although nothing is known of their original decoration.

Having completed the decoration of the state and private apartments, Stuart turned his attention to the first-floor passageway (FIG 188). In a narrow space, chiefly used by servants, the architect managed to create an interior of considerable splendour, with a barrel-vaulted ceiling enriched with scrolling acanthus and other Classical ornaments. Few may have noticed, but here again Stuart indulged his love of the visual pun, for as a parting gesture, and as if to put his signature to the building, he discreetly added a row of tiny scallop shells at either end, symbols of his namesake, St James (FIG 189).

[37] The identical relief was used by Stuart as an overdoor at Montagu House and in the design of the organ case at Newby Hall

[38] The washstand was sold by the 8th Earl Spencer to the V&A in 1979 [W31 1979]

188

188 Spencer House, first-floor passageway. Within a narrow space, primarily intended for servants, Stuart managed to create an interior of considerable richness and beauty

189

189 Spencer House, first-floor passageway, detail of ceiling. The scallop shells were probably intended as a reference to Stuart's namesake, St James

17 SOME LIKELY EXECUTANTS

THERE ARE RECORDS of payments to Stuart from John Spencer's account at Hoare's Bank,[1] but unfortunately there is no mention in any of the Spencer papers of the craftsmen who worked under Stuart's direction. In the case of the Painted Room, it has sometimes been claimed that Stuart himself was responsible for the execution of the murals and inset painted panels. Arthur Young, who visited Spencer House shortly after its completion, asserted that the room was designed but also 'painted by Mr Steuart [sic]'.[2] Stuart was certainly capable of such work and did occasionally act as executant as well as designer,[3] but the decoration of the Painted Room displays such striking discrepancies in style and technique that if Stuart was to any extent involved, he must have received assistance from at least one other painter and probably several.[4]

Angelica Kauffmann, the best-known decorative painter of the period, can immediately be discounted, since she did not arrive in London from Rome until 1766. The same is true of her husband, Antonio Zucchi, another leading specialist in this area. A strong possibility, however, is Biagio Rebecca, a decorative painter from Italy, who settled in England in 1761 and worked with Stuart on comparable projects elsewhere, including Lichfield House in St James's Square where he produced a ceiling painting of a shepherd and bacchantes virtually identical to that on the ceiling of the Painted Room (PLATE XIX, p. 173, and FIG 190). Another candidate is Nicholas Dall, a muralist who worked under Stuart's direction at Shugborough in Staffordshire in 1764. There is Giovanni Battista Cipriani, another London-based Italian, who collaborated with Stuart on a scheme of painted decoration at a house in Portman Square and who was later commissioned to design Lord Spencer's funerary monument.[5] Another possibility is Charles Catton, who although primarily a coach painter, also worked on the decoration of interiors, being employed in this capacity by several leading architects, including Stuart himself, who used him at Greenwich. There is also a painter of heraldry, Edmondson, whose name is mentioned in a letter to the Spencers from Viscount Nuneham in connection with some unspecified scheme of decoration.[6] Yet another candidate is the painter Francesco Zuccarelli, a specialist in mythological landscapes, who might conceivably have been responsible for those on the north wall (PLATES XIV and XV, pp. 162 and 163), which follow his style and include a representation of Nessus and Dejanira, a subject he is known to have treated in an unidentified painting commissioned by Lord Spencer.[7]

For the plasterwork at Spencer House Stuart would almost certainly have chosen Joseph Rose, the same man employed by Vardy, for he had used him on his very first commission and turned to him again on subsequent projects, while for his own part Rose subscribed to *The Antiquities of Athens*. It is equally likely that the chimney-pieces were entrusted to the Flemish sculptor Peter Scheemakers, and perhaps his son Thomas, for both men collaborated with Stuart on numerous other projects. Indeed the elder Scheemakers worked with Stuart over a period of almost twenty years, and in two other instances produced chimney-pieces of near identical design to that in the Great Room,[8] while a catalogue of the contents of his studio reveals that he possessed several casts after Duquesnoy,[9] the sculptor whose work was reproduced in the terracotta panels in the

[1] HB, Account of JS, Ledger A, f.266, 24 Sept 1759, payment to James Stuart of £150; Ledger C, f.231, 29 May 1765, payment to Stuart of £100. The payments may also relate to Stuart's work at Wimbledon and it is possible that other, unrecorded payments were made to Stuart, since the sums here are below what might be expected given the scope of the architect's work and the far higher fees paid to Vardy

[2] Arthur Young, *A Six Weeks Tour through the Southern Counties of England and Wales*, p.359

[3] It should be noted that in 1768 Stuart exhibited three paintings at the Society of Artists on the same subject as the 'choice' panels in the apse of the Painted Room, namely a *Judgement of Paris*, a *Choice of Hercules*, and a *Judgement of Midas* [Algernon Graves, *The Society of Artists of Great Britain 1760–1791.... A Complete Dictionary of Contributors and their Work*, pp.247–9, Nos 215, 218, 219]

[4] The decoration of the room is attributed to Angelica Kauffmann and Antonio Zucchi in Edwin B. Chancellor, *The Private Palaces of London, Past and Present*, and Margaret Jourdain, *Decoration in England from 1660 to 1770*, pp.163, 178–9. However, neither painter was in England at the time the room was decorated

[5] Giovanni Battista Cipriani, *A Study of the Monument to John, 1st Earl Spencer, in the Church of St. Mary, Great Brington, Northamptonshire* [Ashmolean Museum 370:221]

[6] AP F114, GSH to GS, *c*1761

[7] In a letter to Lady Spencer from Naples dated 23 Jan 1770 [AP F117] Sir William Hamilton refers to a painting by Zuccarelli of *Nessus and Dejanira*, earlier commissioned by Lord Spencer. This, he reminds her, was based at his suggestion on a painting of *Glaucus and Scylla* attributed to Giulio Romano, then in the collection of Lady Betty Germain. It is possible that the painting by Zuccarelli was that which hung originally in the Dining Room at Spencer House, described by Arthur Young as representing 'a centaur carrying off a naked woman' [Young, op.

Painted Room. The gilt-bronze tripods in the Painted Room and other articles in this material have been attributed to the leading bronze founder Diederich Nicolaus Andersen, who in 1761 exhibited a related tripod after Stuart's designs at the Free Society of Artists,[10] although another possible candidate is William Palmer, smith and brass founder to George III, who subscribed to the *Antiquities of Athens* and produced a comparable range of furnishings for other Neo-Classical architects. Another figure who might have found employment at Spencer House was the carver and gilder John Adair, who worked under Stuart's direction on the decoration of Shugborough around the same time.

Chairs, tables and other articles of furniture were probably supplied by the partnership of John Gordon and John Taitt, well-known London cabinet-makers. Gordon produced a similar suite of seat furniture to that in the Great Room for another client, the Duke of Atholl, and had links to the Spencers through his close friendship with their comptroller, Thomas Townshend.[11] Together with John Taitt, whose name appears in a trade directory kept by Lady Spencer,[12] he carried out repairs and alterations at Spencer House in the 1770s, also working at Wimbledon, Althorp and other Spencer properties,[13] while in projects for Stuart's rival Adam, both he and Taitt showed their ability to respond to the most advanced Neo-Classical designs, producing furniture of comparable style and quality to that in the Painted Room.

190 Lichfield House, St James's Square, first-floor drawing room, ceiling painting by Biagio Rebecca. The painting is virtually identical to that in the Painted Room at Spencer House illustrated in PLATE XIX, *p. 173*

cit., p.355]. If so, it has since left the Spencer collection and remains untraced, although it is interesting to note that the Hunterian Collection in Glasgow has a painting by Zuccarelli representing *Hercules slaying the Centaur Nessus.* The painting of *Glaucus and Scylla* in the collection of Lady Betty Germain was sold following her death. Like the Zuccarelli, it cannot now be traced, having perhaps been reattributed. As further evidence that Zuccarelli might have painted the landscapes in the Painted Room, it is worth recording that the artist painted a view of Athens based on a plate in Stuart's *Antiquities of Athens* (I, pl.II), which was sold from the collection of Princess Louise, Duchess of Argyll, by Christie's, London, on 23 March 1973

[8] The chimney-pieces are at Lichfield House in London and Corsham Court in Wiltshire

[9] The casts are listed in the catalogue of the Scheemakers sale, Langford's, London, 6–7 June 1771, Lots 83, 85, 88 [Information supplied by Dr Ingrid Roscoe]

[10] Nicholas Goodison, 'Mr Stuart's Tripod', *Burlington Magazine* (Oct 1972), pp.695–705

[11] Thornton and Hardy, 'The Spencer Furniture at Althorp', section II, *Apollo*

[12] AP F200

[13] AP F195–F199

18 COSTS AND BENEFITS

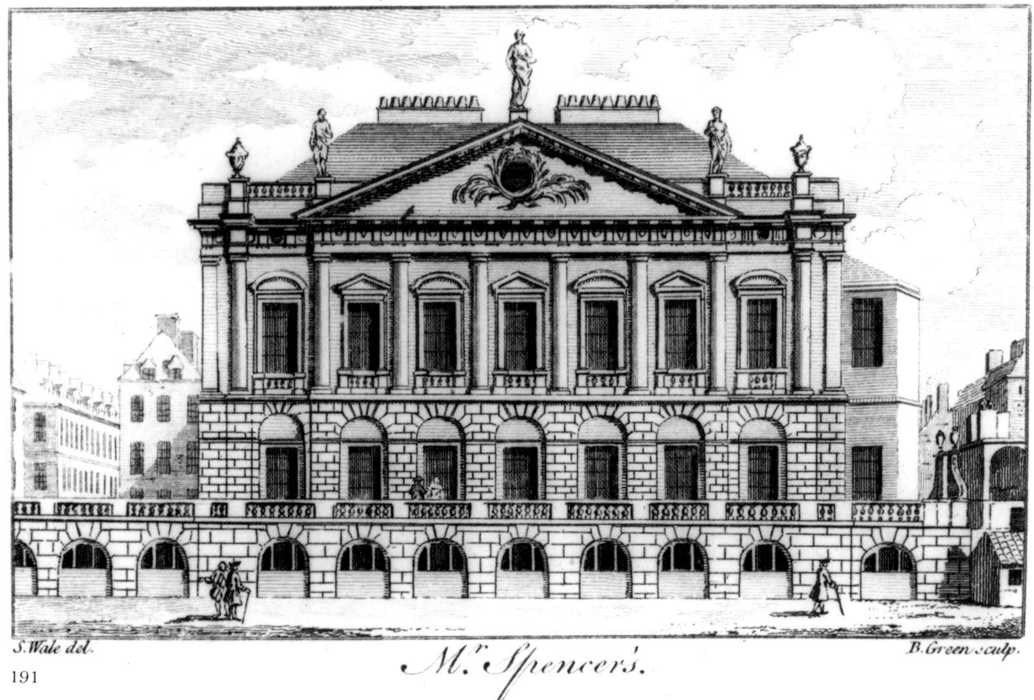

191

191 Spencer House, the west front; engraving by B. Green after S. Wale, from R. and J. Dodsley, London and its Environs Described *(1761), 3, p.65. Public interest in Spencer House was intense. The present engraving was published even before the building was fully completed*

192 Spencer House, north-west perspective; engraving by T. Miller after John Vardy, 1763. The dedication would indicate that Vardy and Lord Spencer remained on cordial terms despite Stuart's appointment

THE EXPENSE OF BUILDING Spencer House was enormous. The site alone had cost John Spencer £14,000, and when vouchers and other accounts were gathered together it was discovered that construction and decoration amounted to a further £35,000.[1] How much more was spent on paintings, objects and other ornaments can only be guessed. Rather astutely, however, Spencer approached the family trustees with the idea of selling them the property as a capital investment. For the discounted price of £32,000 the trust could acquire the house for the benefit of future generations of Spencers, while the Earl himself retained the right of residence for life. The trustees were easily won over. 'The propriety', they concurred, 'of purchasing a Town House for the Residence of so Noble and so Ancient a Family seems . . . unquestionable'.[2] The matter was referred to Chancery but quickly approved,[3] and in the summer of 1766 John Spencer received the sum of £32,000 in cash, free of all conditions.

Equally gratifying was the attention Spencer received when the house was unveiled. The construction of Spencer House generated enormous excitement. The building had barely risen above ground level when in September 1756 the diarist Mrs Delaney set out for Green Park in order, she wrote, 'to see Mr Spencer's house, which is begun and the ground floor finished . . . It will be superb when finished'.[4] As early as 1761, five years

[1] AP D31, D32

[2] AP D31

[3] PRO C33/425, fols 295, 340

[4] Lady Llanover (ed.), *The Autobiography and Correspondence of Mary Granville, Mrs Delaney*, 3 (1861), p.445

[5] AP F114, GBV to GS, 1763

[6] AP F41, CH to GS, 20 Mar 1764

[7] AP F101, GSH to GS, 23 Nov 1765

[8] The drawings exhibited by Vardy were as follows: *The first design intended for the house of the right Honourable Lord Viscount Spencer* [1762, No. 208]; *The north-west*

view of the same house, as at present executed [1762, No 209]; *The Plan and Ceiling of the alcove room on the ground floor, as designed and executed by Mr Vardy, at the Right Hon. Lord Spencer's in St. James's place* [1763, No. 194]; *The front of the alcove room of ditto* [1763, No. 195]; *The inside section of the alcove room at ditto* [1763, No. 196]; *The chimney for the great dining room, one pair of stairs* [1763, No. 197] [Algernon Graves, *The Society of Artists of Great Britain 1760–1791. . . . A Complete Dictionary of Contributors and their Work*, pp.266–7]

before the house officially opened, an engraving of the west front was published in a guide to London (FIG 191). The project was evidently a talking-point in London drawing rooms, for in 1763 the Spencers' friend, Lord Jersey, reported that at a dinner hosted by Lord Chief Justice Pratt the construction of the building had dominated the conversation.[5] Another friend, Lord Huntingdon, insisted on touring the house while work was still in progress;[6] yet another, Lady Nuneham, was said to be 'quite impatient for her visit to St James's Place'.[7] With Lord Spencer's permission Vardy exhibited a number of his designs at the Society of Artists, which only increased public curiosity (FIG 192),[8] and when the house finally opened in the spring of 1766 the whole of London society must have flocked to see it (PLATE X, pp. 78 and 79).

192

Inevitably there was a certain amount of adverse criticism. Some complained that the pediment was 'too large and heavy',[9] others that it was too 'lofty'.[10] Some thought the bay at the south-west corner upset the symmetry of the principal front, and that the addition of an entrance door would have improved the front's appearance.[11] Others complained that the columns were too massive and the order too severe;[12] that the basement was 'too large' and the *piano nobile* 'too small', so reversing the traditional 'subordination' of these elements.[13] There was criticism also that the north front remained unfinished.[14] Robert Adam, who gained admittance while his rival Stuart was still at work, described the interior as 'pityfullissimo'.[15] Another architect, John Gwynn, even proposed demolishing the building in order to use the site for the construction of a new royal palace.[16]

However, the overwhelming reaction was one of praise. Adam himself later conceded that at Spencer House, as in other projects, Stuart had 'with his usual elegance and taste . . . contributed greatly towards introducing the true style of antique decoration'.[17] Among Adam's surviving drawings is a sketch of one of the cornices at Spencer House.[18] The *Aldobrandini Wedding*, which Stuart had used to decorate the frieze of the chimney-piece in the Painted Room, was reproduced by Adam in identical fashion in published designs for a chimney-piece at St James's Palace.[19] Adam also made repeated use of the tripod devised by Stuart for the Painted Room, and in his designs for the decoration of an interior at Number 21 Portland Place he introduced the identical relief of Venus which Stuart had used in the Great Room, while the tea room he built at Moor Park in Hertfordshire was clearly based on Vardy's Palm Room.[20] Another leading architect of the period, Sir William Chambers, described the house as 'magnificent'.[21] The authors of *Vitruvius Britannicus*, a survey of the most admired buildings in England, devoted three full-size plates to the building (see endpapers).[22]

The house also found favour with a wider public. In a guide to London of 1761 it was said that of all the houses bordering Green Park, 'the most conspicuous by far is that lately built by Mr Spencer. Altogether it appears very noble'(PLATE VIII, p. 77).[23] The same comparison was made in another guide published in 1763, the author concluding that while other houses lining the park had merit, 'that newly erected by Mr Spencer, lately created Lord Spencer, is the most stately' (FIG 193, p. 194).[24] A guide for foreign tourists published the same year was equally enthusiastic, informing its readers in broken French that '*La Maison de Mylord Spencer est tres megnifique, & a la grande Appearance* [sic]'.[25] Writing in 1775, Walter Harrison described the house as 'most distinguished . . . not only exceeding magnificent in point of architecture, but also in the richness of its furniture'.[26] Another contemporary pronounced the decoration of the state apartments 'rich & in great taste'.[27] The statues and vases on the west front were especially admired. The authors of *Vitruvius Britannicus* pronounced the sculptor 'ingenious' and the sculptures 'masterly executed'.[28] Sir William Chambers likewise praised Spang's work,[29] while another contemporary remarked on the beauty of 'the figures and vases', which had, he declared, 'indeed a fine effect'.[30]

But the most fulsome praise came from Arthur Young, who in 1769 published a rapturous account of the house in a guide to the southern counties of England and Wales. Young had travelled hundreds of miles, looking at buildings of every description, but Spencer House was in his view unrivalled; his comments provide a fitting conclusion to this chapter:

> I do not apprehend there is a house in Europe of its size, better worth the view of the curious in architecture, and the fitting up and furnishing great houses, than Lord Spencer's in St. James's Place. Nothing can be more pleasingly elegant than the park front, which is ornamented to an high degree, and yet not with profusion; I know not in England a more

XXII *Spencer House, Entrance Hall, 1992. The plain stone colour of the walls, mixed on the evidence of paint scrapes, together with the stone-flagged floor and mahogany hall chairs complement the austere masculinity of the architecture. The new scheme deliberately reflects the eighteenth-century treatment of the hall as a transitional space between the hard architecture of the exterior and the richness of the principal rooms*

XXIII *Spencer House, Ante Room, 1992. The interior had been altered by Holland and there was never any question of reversing these changes. Instead the decoration represents a synthesis of eighteenth-century elements, Palladian as well as Neo-Classical, with complementary furnishings and works of art.*

[9] R. and J. Dodsley (publ.), *London and its Environs Described*, 6 vols (1761), 3, p.65

[10] Thomas Malton, *A Picturesque Tour through the Cities of London and Westminster*, p.108

[11] Dodsley, op. cit.

[12] Malton, op. cit.

[13] John Gwynn, *London and Westminster Improved* (1766), p.44n

[14] Dodsley, op. cit.; John Woolfe and James Gandon, *Vitruvius Britannicus*, IV (1767), p.6

[15] Penicuik MS, No. 4852, quoted in Thornton and Hardy, 'The Spencer Furniture at Althorp', section I, *Apollo*, p.451, n.21

[16] *A Plan of Hyde Park with the City and Liberties of Westminster &c shewing the Several Improvements Propos'd*, in Gwynn, op. cit., pl.I

[17] *The Works in Architecture of Robert and James Adam*, I (1778), p.5

[18] SJSM, *Adam Drawings*, 54, series 3 , No. 40

[19] 'A Chimney Piece designed for one of the rooms in St. James's Palace', in *The Works in Architecture of Robert and James Adam*, I (1778), No. V, p.IV. A manuscript drawing of a similar chimney-piece, believed to have come from the Adam architectural office and likewise decorated with a frieze copied from the *Aldobrandini Wedding*, is preserved in the Cooper Hewitt Museum 1938–88–5294

[20] Stuart used the identical configuration of palms in his design for the funerary

XXIV Spencer House, Staircase Hall, 1992. The redecoration is an accurate recreation of the original scheme, reflecting the transition from Vardy's lower well, with plain stone-coloured walls and stone-flagged floor, to the elaboration of the upper well, where Stuart perhaps intended the green walls to suggest a landscape setting for his 'temple interior', with festooned Ionic pilasters. The marble statuary recalls the Dilettanti's taste for fragments and representations of figures from the ancient world

beautiful piece of architecture. Nor is the fitting up and furniture of the rooms, inferior to the beauties of the outside. We were first shewn into Lord Spencer's library, which is 30 feet by 25; the ornaments exceedingly handsome. The chimney-piece very light, of polished white marble. On one side of the room hangs a capital picture of the nature of witchcraft; the expression and finishing is very great; and the extent of the painter's imagination striking, in drawing into one point such a multitude of the emblems of witchcraft, and all designed with a fine wildness of fancy. It is somewhat in the stile of Scarlatti.

From hence you enter the dining-room 46 by 24; exceedingly elegant: the decorations in the finest taste, and the richest of their kind; the ceiling and cornice of white and green, very beautiful. The slabs of Siena marble, large and finely veined. The chimney-piece, basso relievo, of white marble beautifully polished. On one side of it is a landscape, the killing of a dragon; the general brilliancy of which is very fine; and the trees beautifully expressed. On the other side is another yet more pleasing, the trees of which are likewise striking: the figures are a centaur carrying off a naked woman: her back appears, which is painted with a most delicate softness; she has a little slight drapery which is very elegantly designed, though perhaps not perfectly natural.

Next we entered the drawing-room, which is 24 by 21, clear of a noble bow window, parted from the room only by two pillars of most exquisite workmanship; they are carved in leaves, the thick foliage of which bends round in a fine arch from one to the other, in a taste that cannot be too much admired; on each side, in a semi-circular cove in the wall, an urn of white marble with basso relievos, very beautiful. Nothing can be more elegant than the chimney-piece; a fine border of Siena marble with a sweet festoon of flowers upon it in white marble polished; the ceiling, cornice, and ornaments of green and white and gold, and in a most delicate stile. Over the chimney, a picture of two usurers; great expression.

Returning, we next viewed the Attick story; the stair-case is in a very just taste, wide and lofty; the ceiling and ornaments green and white.

From the landing-place you enter first the music-room 25 by 23, the chimney-piece extremely light and elegant; on the left a small dressing-room very neat; chimney-piece very beautiful, the cornice of white polished marble, supported by pillars of Siena. This opens into the bed-chamber, 25 by 20. The beds and tables very finely carved and inlaid, the former of crimson damask, with coved tops, and extremely elegant. Returning to the music-room, you enter the grand dressing-room 25 by 23, which is fitted up with all possible taste; scarce anything can be more beautiful than the mosaic'd ceiling, the cornices and all the ornaments: the chimney-piece is exquisitely designed and admirably executed; it is of white marble wrought with the utmost taste, and beautifully polished; over the cornice are festoons of the lightest carving, and 2 eagles, with a very fine basso-relievo of carving in a glass in the center: the pictures are disposed with great elegance, and hung up by ribbons of gilt carving in the sweetest taste; among them are the following pieces:

Two old men's heads in the stile of *Rembrandt*; fine.
Ten pieces, companions, exceedingly beautiful; the colouring, attitudes, and drapery very striking; among them *Andromade*, Rape of *Europa*, *Venus*, *Neptune*.
A battle by *Borgognon*, very fine.
Madona, dark, but good.
Nativity, fine.
A *Christ*, ditto.
Holy family, pleasing, but the drapery not excellent.
Landscape, I imagine by *Claud Loraine*, fine.

Out of this room you enter the saloon 45 by 30, than which I never beheld one fitted up and furnished in a more exquisite taste; the ceiling, which is coved, is in mosaic'd compartments, green and white and gold; gilt medallions are let into it. The door-cases exceedingly elegant, their cornices supported by pillars most beautifully carved, and gilt with the same mixture of green as in the ceiling. The chimney-piece large, but very light; relievos of white polished marble, wonderfully elegant. Between the windows are two slabs very large, of the finest Siena marble, the frames carved in the most exquisite taste and richly gilded; they are beyond all comparison more beautiful and rich than any I have seen. The pier-glasses of a vast size, single plates, and the frames of admirable workmanship. The carving and gilding of the sofa frames in a stile and taste till now unknown. In the center of the room hangs an exceeding fine glass lustre. On each side the chimney is an historical landscape, one

monument of General Howe in Westminster Abbey and William Chambers did likewise in the Mosque in Kew Gardens

[21] Quoted in Albert Edward John, 7th Earl Spencer, 'Spencer House', Part I, *Country Life* (30 Oct 1926), p.664

[22] *Vitruvius Britannicus*, IV (1767), pls 37–40

[23] Dodsley, op. cit. These remarks were echoed a few years later by John Northoouck who wrote that of all the houses fronting the park 'the most conspicuous is that lately built by Lord Spencer' [*A New History of London, including Westminster and Southwark* (1773), p.720]

[24] *The Foreigner's Guide: Or, a necessary and instructive Companion Both for the Foreigner and Native, in their Tour through the Cities of London and Westminster* (1763), p.28

[25] Lerouge (publ.), *Curiosités de Londres et de l'Angleterre*, 2nd edn (Bordeaux, 1766), p.17

[26] Walter Harrison, *A New and Universal History, Description, and Survey of the Cities of London and Westminster, the Borough of Southwark, and their Adjacent Parts* (1775), p.530

[27] AP F101, GBV to GS, 1 Feb 1764

[28] *Vitruvius Britannicus*, IV, p.6

[29] 'The three figures placed on the Pediment of Mr Spencer's house, which are executed by the ingenious Mr Spang, are well composed for the purpose' [*Treatise on Civil Architecture*, p.63]

[30] Dodsley, op. cit.

[31] Arthur Young, *A Six Weeks Tour through the Southern Counties of England and Wales*, pp.354–61. The same account was published with the 3rd edn of 1772 and was extensively plagiarized in *A New and Compleat History and Survey of the Cities of London and Westminster* (1769), p.597

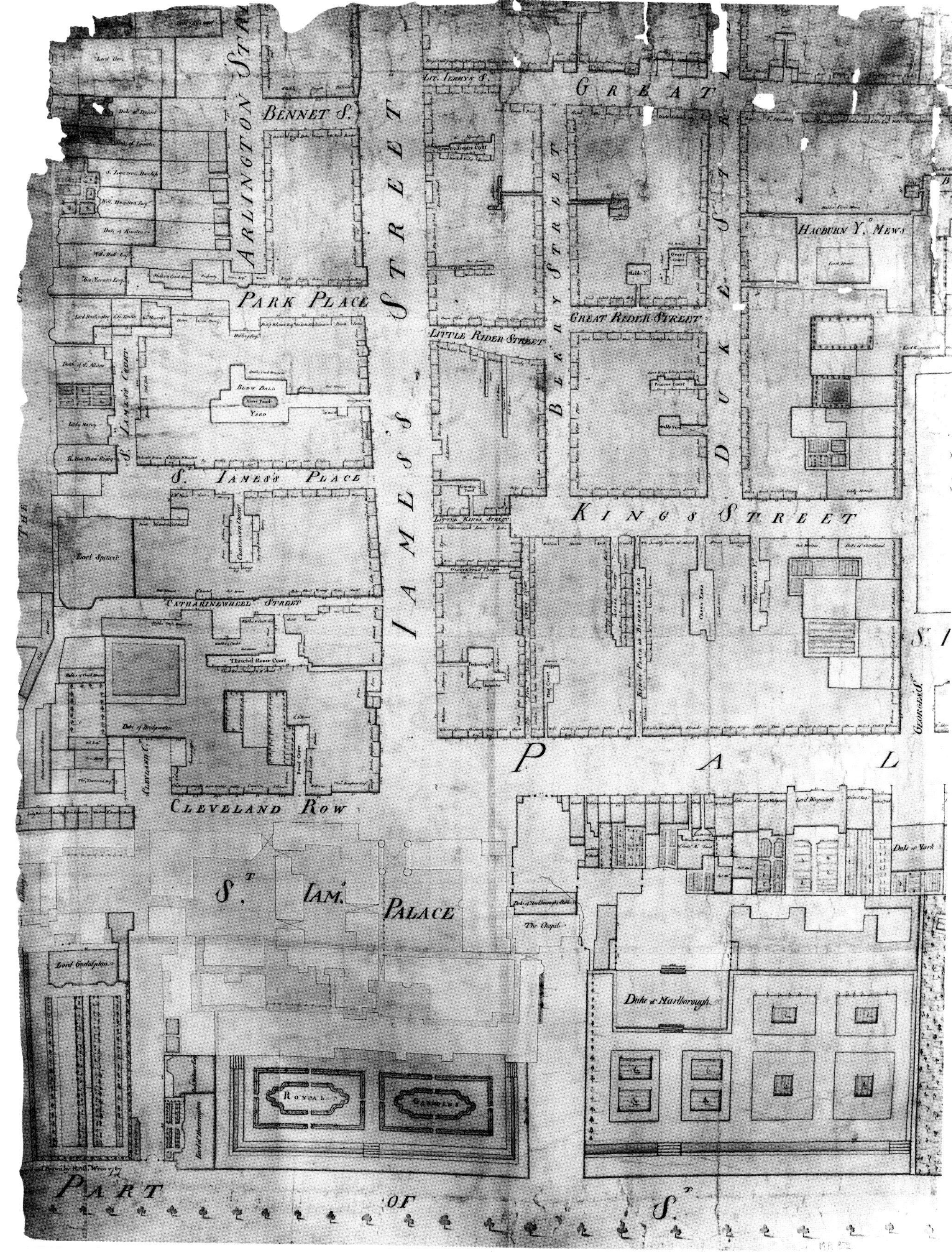
ARLINGTON STR
BENNET S.
LIT. JERMYN S.
GREAT
HACBURN Y.D MEWS
PARK PLACE
LITTLE RIDER STREET
GREAT RIDER STREET
BERRY STREET
DUKE
S.T JAMES'S COURT
BREW HALL
YARD
Princes Court
S.T JAMES'S PLACE
S.T JAMES'S STREET
KINGS STREET
LITTLE KINGS STREET
Earl Spencer
CATHARINEWHEEL STREET
Thatched House Court
Duke of Bridgewater
CLEVELAND C.T
CLEVELAND ROW
P A L
Lord Weymouth
Duke of York
S.T JAM. PALACE
The Chapel
Lord Godolphin
Duke of Marlborough
ROYAL GARDENS
PART OF S.T

193 Plan of St James's, by Matthew Wren, 1767. Spencer House is clearly marked, as are the houses and names of the Spencers' neighbours

Alexander and *Diogenes*; the expression good, but the colouring of both something of the Mannerist.

The next room is to me a phoenix, it is called the painted one; 24 by 22: on one side is a bow-window ornamented with the most exquisitely carved and gilt pillars you can conceive; the walls and ceiling are painted in compartments by Mr. Steuart, in the most beautiful taste; even the very scrolls and festoons of the slightest sort, which are run between the square and circular compartments, are executed with the minutest elegance: the ground of the whole is green; and the general effect more pleasing than is easily conceived. Nothing can be lighter or more beautiful than the chimney-piece; the frieze contains a most exquisite painting representing a clandestine marriage, which, without variety or glare of colours, has all the harmony of their utmost power: nothing can be finer than the drapery, which is designed with the justest taste, displaying the form of every limb through it in a most beautiful manner. The soft expression of the naked, and the beauty of the heads are very great. I should observe, that two of the small compartments of the wall are landscapes let into it with no other than the painted frame of the divisions: one represents a water-fall, and the other a bridge over a stream, both fine. The frames of the tables, sofas, stands, &c. &c. are all carved and gilt in the same taste as the other ornaments of the room, all with a profusion of richness, but with the utmost elegance. Remember to observe the peacock's feathers over one of the glasses, the turtles on a wreath of flowers, and the magpies on bunches of grapes: they are very beautiful, and the deception of the first extraordinary; the bold relief of such slight strokes does honour to the pencil of the artist. The looking-glass window is a piece of taste, and has an happy effect.

It would have been endless in each room to have mentioned *every* circumstance; but let me, in general, remark, that all I have attempted to describe are much superior to the idea you will have from my description; and all I have omitted to mention, in richness, elegance, and taste, superior to any house I have seen. The hangings, carpets, glasses, sofas, chairs, tables, slabs, every thing, are not only astonishingly beautiful, but contain a vast variety. The carving and gilding is all unrivalled; the taste in which every article throughout the whole house is executed, is beyond conception just and elegant: No expence was spared by the noble owner, and neither the brightest fancy nor the correctest judgement wanting to conduct the whole.[31]

PART III

A HOUSE IN TOWN

19 PLEASING COMFORTABLE SOCIETY

IT WAS NOT UNUSUAL in the eighteenth century for the wealthier members of the aristocracy to maintain at least three separate establishments: a house in the country, another in London and a third on the outskirts of the capital. The Duke of Northumberland divided his time between Alnwick Castle in Northumberland, Northumberland House in London and Syon Park in Middlesex. The Duke of Devonshire had the luxury of two country houses, Chatsworth and Hardwick in Derbyshire, a villa at Chiswick and Devonshire House in Piccadilly. So it was with the Spencers, possessed, as we have seen, of several residences other than Spencer House.

Like other members of the aristocracy the Spencers led a peripatetic existence, moving about the country according to a fixed routine established by long tradition. During the autumn and winter, from late September or October through to January or February, the family was at Althorp, where the Earl renewed his ties with the locality and indulged his love of fox-hunting, also hosting an annual house party at Christmas and New Year. In summer the Spencers visited their shooting estate at North Creake in Norfolk; they also made use of the house at Holywell, primarily as a stop-over on the road to Althorp but also as an operational base during election campaigns in St Albans. At other times they could be found at Wimbledon Park, relaxing and entertaining, staying for a week, a month, or simply the day or the afternoon. Owing to the Earl's ill health the family made frequent trips to Bath and other resorts, also staying on the country estates of friends and relations. They were likewise great travellers and generally spent a part of each year abroad, sometimes staying away for months at a time.

But for the greater part of the year the Spencers were in London, and the house in St James's Place was vitally important therefore as their principal headquarters. The Spencers generally arrived in town in January or February and remained there, with occasional excursions to Wimbledon, until July or August. This period of time, corresponding roughly to the first six to eight months of the year, gradually came to be known as the Season. It was the period in which Parliament was in session, with the Court in residence at St James's Palace. It was therefore a time to do business, especially political business; but it was also a time for pleasure, an opportunity to visit the theatre and the opera; to attend concerts and recitals; to stroll in St James's Park or the pleasure gardens at Ranelagh and Vauxhall; to shop for luxuries unavailable in the country; to participate in the excitement of sales at Christie's, Langford's and other London auction houses; to trade news and catch up on the latest fashions; to meet friends and make new acquaintances; to sit for one's portrait; to search for partners in marriage; to gather in clubs and coffee-houses; to sail on the Thames; above all to entertain and be entertained.

The mansions of the nobility played a vital role in the life of the London Season as a primary focus of social, political and cultural activity. Spencer House naturally occupied a pre-eminent position. The Spencers, as we have seen, had a vast network of relations and friends; they knew and were known to virtually everyone in fashionable society, including royalty, senior members of the aristocracy, artists and writers. In 1770 Lady Mary Coke

PAGE 196
David Garrick between Comedy and Tragedy, *by Sir Joshua Reynolds (Collection Lord Rothschild)* (*FIG 196, p. 200*)

194 James Cervetto (left) and Thomas Linley (right), from an early nineteenth-century engraving after a cameo by H. de Janvry. Cervetto and Linley were protégés of the Spencers; both performed and gave music lessons at Spencer House

recorded that Lady Spencer had given a mask at Spencer House, to which the whole of fashionable London would have flocked.[1] There are records of concerts being held at Spencer House, with performances by the virtuoso cellist James Cervetto (FIG 194).[2] To some extent also the house functioned as a private museum, in which interested strangers such as Arthur Young, and others more closely connected with the Spencers, could admire some of the finest works of art and furniture anywhere on public display.

And yet from their correspondence, and other documents of the period, it is clear the Spencers were in fact rather private people. Perhaps on account of the Earl's instinctive shyness, and his worsening health, they seem to have hosted rather fewer large-scale entertainments than might be supposed. On the whole the Spencers preferred more intimate gatherings, attended by a tight-knit circle of close friends and relations.

A member of this circle was Viscount Palmerston, a well-known connoisseur and collector, whom the Spencers met on the Grand Tour, and who claimed to have '*entrée libre*' to Spencer House.[3] Another was Caroline Howe, an eccentric figure rumoured to be the natural daughter of George I, who continued to wear the fashions of her supposed father's reign right up to the time of her death in 1814. In a letter of 1772, posted to Georgiana in France, she expressed impatience for her friend's return and the resumption of what she described as 'the pleasing comfortable society in which we have passed so many agreeable hours in St James's Place'.[4] Indeed she apparently kept a key to the door at the foot of the terrace leading through to Spencer House from Green Park, so that she could join her friends without the bother of a formal entrance.[5] Another frequent visitor was Rachel Lloyd, at one time housekeeper at Kensington Palace. Horace Walpole remarked that without her presence, Lady Spencer's receptions would be unworkable.[6] On one occasion, while the Spencers were travelling abroad, Miss Lloyd came to stay at Spencer house, being temporarily without accommodation. Her visit happened to coincide with a riot in which the house came under attack by the mob, although she was able to report, with evident relief, that being 'a very strong one indeed', it had not suffered any

[1] J. A. Home (ed.), *The Letters and Journals of Lady Mary Coke*, 3, p.235

[2] AP F184

[3] Brian Connell, *Portrait of a Whig Peer, compiled from the papers of the second Viscount Palmerston 1739–1802*, pp.61, 107

[4] AP F42, CH to GS, 25 Nov 1772

[5] AP F41, CH to GS, 16 Aug 1763

[6] W. S. Lewis, *The Yale Edition of Horace Walpole's Correspondence*, 32, p.178

195

196

195 Laurence Sterne (1713–68), by Sir Joshua Reynolds, 1760. Lord Spencer was one of Sterne's greatest patrons and he gave a dinner in his honour at Spencer House a short time before the writer's death

196 The actor David Garrick (1717–79) caught between the comic and tragic muses, by Sir Joshua Reynolds. The painting is based on a scene from Classical mythology, the Choice of Hercules, a subject treated in one of the panels in the Painted Room (FIG 142, p. 159). Garrick was a particularly close friend of the Spencers and a frequent visitor to the house in St James's Place

particular damage, and that the Spencers' comptroller Andrew Solinus had put up a brave defence.[7] The diarist, Lady Mary Coke, was likewise a member of the Spencer House circle, frequently calling at St James's Place, all too often to gamble, as in 1769 when, as she noted in her diary, she 'called on Lady Spencer, play'd two or three hands at quinze, & lost seven guineas'.[8] Another favourite was Viscount Nuneham, a noted connoisseur, who particularly enjoyed the atmosphere of Spencer House, finding in its warmth and simplicity a welcome respite from the pretentious posturing of the Court. Replying to a dinner invitation, which he reluctantly declined, Lord Nuneham declared, 'I give up all thoughts of the facetious conversation of the brilliant St James's circle without regret, but I have not an equal degree of philosophy when I think on the dinner in St James's Place'.[9] A particularly important member of the Spencer House circle was the writer Laurence Sterne (FIG 195). On one occasion, in the spring of 1767, he called at the house and breakfasted with Lady Spencer.[10] Shortly afterwards the Earl and Countess gave a dinner in his honour, inviting him to dine again in St James's Place a few weeks later.[11] The poet John Scott also dined at Spencer House,[12] and the artist Angelica Kauffmann called on the Spencers directly she moved to London from Rome.[13] Another great favourite was the actor David Garrick (FIG 196); indeed he called so often that on one occasion he felt obliged to apologize for his persistent appearances, promising Georgiana that 'As your ladyship has had for some time too much of my company I will keep from St James's Place as long as I possibly can'.[14]

But one must not forget that Spencer House was also a family home, occupied not only by the Earl and Countess but by their children. Georgiana bore her husband five children, three of whom survived, a boy and two girls. As youngsters their lives would largely have been spent on the second floor in a nursery which continued to function right up to the early part of this century. It was only after they reached the age of sixteen or so that they were able to participate fully in the life that went on in the state apartments.

The Spencers' son, George John (FIG 197), was born in September 1758 and although six weeks premature and very tiny and frail, he quickly gained in size and strength. The

King stood as sponsor at his christening and on his father's elevation to the earldom in 1765 he was granted the courtesy title Viscount Althorp, held ever since by Spencer heirs. In the same year he was placed in the hands of a private tutor, the eminent scholar Sir William Jones, and in 1770, at the age of twelve, he was sent to Harrow. Six years later he enrolled at Trinity College, Cambridge, graduating in 1778, after which he travelled on the Continent. In 1780, with the backing of his father, he was elected Whig M.P. for Northampton, subsequently exchanging this seat for that of Surrey, and in March 1782 he was appointed a Junior Lord of the Treasury. In the previous year he had married Lavinia Bingham (FIG 201, p. 215), eldest daughter of Charles Bingham, 1st Baron and later Earl Lucan of Castlebar, County Mayo, a prominent Irish peer and long-serving Whig M.P. News of the marriage reached the ears of Samuel Johnson, a close friend and protégé of the Binghams, who immediately wrote to congratulate the father of the bride. 'My Lord', he declared, 'Seldom has the cloudy atmosphere of my existence been more agreeably brightened than by the notification which your Lordship has been pleased to make to me of the approaching nuptials of your daughter . . . At the *Club*, it is not our custom to drink toasts . . . But this event, I suppose, will produce an extraordinary one – *To the felicity of Lord and Lady Althorpe.* Boswell no doubt, as "confirmation strong", of his honest zeal will pour a large libation of wine'.[15] The following year a son was born, so providing the Earl and Countess with their first grandchild while ensuring the succession in the following generation.

The Spencers' daughters were Georgiana and Harriet, born respectively in 1757 and 1761. Each received the education considered appropriate for girls of their station, studying French, Italian, Latin, drawing, music and dancing. The girls remained at Spencer House until they married, although they naturally continued to participate in the life of St James's Place. At seventeen Georgiana married William Cavendish, 5th Duke of Devonshire, head of one of England's wealthiest and most illustrious families. Harriet too made a favourable alliance, marrying Frederick Ponsonby, Viscount Duncannon, eldest son and heir of William 2nd Earl of Bessborough, another prominent Irish peer and politician, the wedding ceremony being conducted at Spencer House itself. Both sisters went on to become leading figures in society, but as we shall see, their lives were overshadowed by marital discord and a lengthening sequence of scandals involving unpaid gambling debts, flagrant adultery and a bewildering number of illegitimate children.

Spencer House also provided an occasional home for other members of the family. At one point Lord Spencer's mother was forced to take refuge in St James's Place after the Thames burst its banks and her own house in Richmond was flooded. On another occasion she came to stay when Georgiana sprained her ankle and was temporarily confined to bed. Georgiana's mother also made frequent appearances; indeed in the last years of her life she lived next door to Spencer House at Number 28 St James's Place,[16] which continued to be occupied by members of the Spencer family until the present century.

Spencer House was similarly home to the Spencers' servants. Indeed the latter made up the greater part of the household. There are no precise figures, but in comparable households a staff of forty or fifty was not unusual. It is some indication of the scale on which the Spencers lived that at a house party at Althorp in 1761 there were over 130 servants to only twenty-one guests.[17] The stables alone were manned by a staff of twenty-seven, and even when travelling the Spencers were well attended. According to Philip Changuion, chargé d'affaires in Naples at the time of the Spencers' Grand Tour, the Earl and Countess were accompanied by eight servants, a chaplain and a physician.[18]

[7] AP F42, CH to GS, 22 Sept 1772

[8] *The Letters and Journals of Lady Mary Coke*, 3, p.26

[9] AP F114, GSH to GS, 1767

[10] Walter Sichel, *Sterne: A Study, to which is added The Journal to Eliza* (1910), p.314

[11] Lewis Perry Curtis, *Letters of Laurence Sterne* (Oxford, 1935), pp.340, 342, 408

[12] AP F114, GSH to GS, 18 May 1780

[13] Lady Victoria Manners and G. C. Williamson, *Angelica Kauffmann, R.A., Her Life and Work* (1924), p.210

[14] David Garrick to GS, 6 Jan 1778, quoted in *Letters of David Garrick and Georgiana Countess Spencer 1759–1779* (1960), p.121

[15] Samuel Johnson to Charles, Baron Lucan, 1 Mar 1781, quoted in R. W. Chapman (ed.), *The Letters of Samuel Johnson*, 3 vols, 2 (1952), pp.410–11

[16] PRO MR 872

[17] AP F167

[18] PRO SPF 105/315, Changuion to Mann 19 July 1763 [SBFP]

197 Viscount Althorp with his sisters Lady Georgiana and Lady Henrietta-Frances (Harriet) Spencer, by Angelica Kauffmann, 1774

When crossing to Holland in 1756 they were said to have 'such a following of other attendants, that they had one pacquet boat for themselves, and another for their servants and baggage'.[19] From other records it is possible to form some impression of the composition of the Spencers' domestic staff. According to documents of the 1770s and 1780s the family was attended at various times by a steward; a comptroller; a groom of the chambers; a butler; two under butlers; three footmen attached to the service of Georgiana; two attached to the Earl, who was likewise attended by a valet; three footmen who served Lord Althorp; five or more housemaids, including two attached to Georgiana and a third to look after her younger daughter Harriet; a laundry maid; a porter; two cooks; a kitchen man; a baker; a confectioner; two kitchen maids; a dairy maid; three still room maids; a poulterer; a butcher; a coachman; an under coachman; a head groom; a steward of the stables; a farrier; a postilion; and two chairmen.[20]

Most of these servants would have accompanied the Spencers as they moved about the country, but a skeleton staff would always remain in each of the family's principal residences, primarily for reasons of security. It is not known where the Spencers' servants originated, but most would probably have been recruited from the countryside rather than the town, since country servants were considered cleaner, healthier, cheaper and more honest. It is likely also that some were recruited from the neighbourhood of Althorp and other family residences, since this provided additional security and was common practice. While almost all the Spencer servants were English, some from their names would appear to be foreign. Nor was this unusual. On her return from the Continent in 1762 Lady Mary Wortley Montagu was attended by an Italian, a Frenchman and a Prussian; and in 1766 the author of a satire on domestic service gave the following advice to the gentleman of fashion seeking to establish a household: 'Let his house be a pleasant *Babel* of all Tongues and Nations . . . let his Porter be a *Swiss*, the Cook a *Frenchman*, his Gentleman a *German*, his Butler an *Hollander*, his Coachman a *Swede*, his footmen *Austrians and Hungarians*'.[21] One of the Spencers' under-butlers was a certain François Panax, evidently a Frenchman or of French extraction, whose wife, 'Grizell', who worked as a laundry maid, may also have been from the Continent. Another foreign-sounding servant was the butler, Saulanic, and there was also a still-room maid, Anne Puttereaux, who like Panax probably came from France. There are only the most fragmentary records of the wages paid to servants,[22] but presumably they earned no less than the average since they worked in the household of one of the richest noblemen in England. Indeed they may well have earned more, since Spencer was renowned for his generosity to domestics and other retainers. On evenings when he entertained he generally allowed his staff a share of the liquor, a custom which on one occasion led to near-fatal consequences when two tipsy chairmen stumbled into a pond while transporting a guest home from dinner.[23] In addition to such privileges the Spencer servants also received a clothing allowance, and those who wore livery were supplied with the best that money could buy.[24]

[19] Alexander Fergusson (ed.), *Letters and Journals of Mrs Calderwood of Polton from England, Holland, and the Low Countries in 1756* (Edinburgh, 1884)

[20] AP F173

[21] *Directions to Lords and Ladies* (1766), p.15, quoted in Joseph Jean Hecht, 'Continental and Colonial Servants in Eighteenth-century England', in *Smith College Studies in History*, XL (Northampton, Massachusetts, 1954), p.1

[22] AP F187–F190

[23] *The Letters and Journals of Lady Mary Coke*, 4, p.100

[24] AP F186

20 UPKEEP AND MAINTENANCE

ARCHITECTURALLY THE HOUSE in St James's Place remained little altered during the remainder of the 1st Earl's lifetime, but there are records of various repairs and additions in the early 1770s.[1] A bricklayer, William Barlow of Duke Street, Grosvenor Square, was drafted in to carry out various works, including repairs to the chimney-stacks and paving, clearing a drain from the scullery and building wine bins in the cellar. A plumber, William Selby of Green Street, Grosvenor Square, overhauled the piping in the kitchen and scullery, among other essential repairs, while an ironsmith, William Palmer, was brought in in 1772 and again in 1773 to repair and replace defective ironwork, including locks, hinges, keys, bells, stoves, chimney furniture, kitchen equipment, travelling trunks, a water closet on the ground floor and 'a bell to Ring from my Lords Beadside to the Valletts Room in the Attick'. Palmer also supplied a set of keys for a 'Press in the Passage opposite the Tea Room' and another for a wardrobe on the 'Attick Storey where the servants cloathes are keeped', as well as 'a new double . . . key for Green Park & Door under Terras'. He made an additional charge for 'mendg a Lock for a press in the Nursery', and was also at work in the 'coal cellar', the 'larder', the 'Pastry Room', the 'Cooks Bedroom', the 'Confectioners Room', the 'Butlers Pantry', the 'Housekeepers Room', the 'Servants Hall', the 'maids room' and the 'Stuards Room', as well as the 'Musick Room' and 'My Lords Bed Chamber'. At the same time the house was repainted, possibly in consultation with Sir Robert Taylor, whose advice was sought in connection with some unspecified alterations to the staircase.[2]

The cabinet-makers and upholsterers, Gordon & Taitt, were called in repeatedly, supplying and repairing furniture as the need arose. In January 1772 they made a charge for 'Repairing & new Gilding the Hall Lanthorn in burnished Gold with a new plate of Glass for Do', to which was added 'a large pea green Balance Tassel & strong silk Line'. At the same time they repaired and regilt '3 side Lanthorns' in the 'Passage', presumably one of the corridors on the ground or first floors. They repaired and polished the twelve mahogany hall chairs, and made good the damage to a 'Porter's Chair'. Mirrors which had lost their lustre were resilvered and in some cases replaced; two clothes presses were supplied for 'His Lordships Dressing Room' and green lustring bags for the chandeliers. In February 1772 a length of 'Scotch carpetg' was used to patch the 'Dining Parlour Carpet', while in the Painted Room workmen made repairs to 'a Leather Case for the Tripod Stands', also supplying protective covers for the sofas and armchairs in crimson checked cloth lined with linen. In the Dining Room they serviced a table, a sideboard and a firescreen, and in the following month there was a charge for 'Altering a Carpet in My Ladys Dressing Room' and various works in 'My Ladys Maids Room'. The walls of the rear staircase were fitted with white deal battens and hung with new green baze, while the steps were lined with 'Wilton Carpet'. In June workmen were in the Great Room carrying out repairs to the giltwood pier tables, and there was also a charge for 'a neat inlaid firescreen, one side cover'd with her Ladyships Needlework'. At the same time the men dismantled and cleaned the hangings and curtains, billing the Spencers for 'taking down all the Damask Hangings & Window Curtains in general throughout the house, thoroughly cleaning & brushing Do'. Repairs were made to 'Lord Althorps bed', and in November the firm supplied a quantity of material and trimmings, including lace, braid and tassels, for '2 green lustring festoon window curtains new made up for My Lords Dressing Room'.

In 1773 the workmen returned; they repaired and restuffed a set of '6 Mahogany Gothick back Chairs' in Lord Althorp's room; they were engaged in the spring in 'laying down the Carpet & putting up the Window Curtains in My Ladys Great Dressing room', where they also attended to a 'Mahogany French elbow chair'; they carried out essential repairs to 26 beds and fitted 'new Lines & Tassels to 2 Window Curtains in My Lords Library'; they were at work in the 'Little Dining Parlour', and also in the 'Great Dining Parlour', where they polished the 'Leather Covers' on the chairs and serviced '3 Window Curtains'. The following year the firm supplied a quantity of furniture, including several music stands, a 'neat mahogany box for Lady Georgina [sic]', another for her sister Harriet, together with a 'strong chick hair mattrass' for her to sleep on. In addition there were charges made for 'sodering a brass branch for a lamp on the Great Staircase'; 'repairing the Jellasies [i.e. shutters] in the great Room'; supplying and installing a length of 'Scots carpeting for your Lordships dressing Room'; and 'a mans time repairing [wall] paper in Library'.

In addition to the cost of alterations and repairs, and the day-to-day running of the household, there was also the expense of local services, which were paid for out of rates levied by the Parish. Rubbish-collection, which was carried out by professional scavengers, was one such expense. Another was paving and street-lighting. In 1761 an Act established commissioners for paving, cleansing and lighting the streets of Westminster, including the Parish of St James's,[3] and in 1772 the Spencers received a demand in the sum of £37:10:0 for 'Paving, Repairing, Cleaning, and Lighting the Streets &c in the Parish'. Policing was also funded by means of a local rate. From the time of its constitution in 1685 the Parish of St James was provided with a watch house, although the vestry lacked the funds to maintain an effective watch. By an act of 1735 the vestry was granted powers to collect a rate for the maintenance of a regular body of some fifty 'Watchmen and Bedels', and surviving vouchers reveal that for the period 1771–72 the Spencers paid out £8:6:0. In 1774 an extra ten patrolling watchmen were appointed, equipped with rattles, carbines and cutlasses, and in 1793 their number was increased in response to an 'alarming Increase of a most daring and desperate set of Thieves, who are harbored in and nightly infest this parish'. In June 1796 the watch was again reorganized and improved, but it was not until 1829 that the parish watch in St James's came under the jurisdiction of the new Commissioners of the Metropolitan Police. Another rate was levied for the relief of the poor. In 1772 Lord Spencer's contribution was £37:10:0, and by 1774 the charge had risen to £39:10:0. There was also a tax on windows, which in the case of Spencer House worked out at £16 a year, as well as a levy on silver plate, calculated on the basis of weight. The Spencers declared some 4000 ounces and so received an annual demand of £10 in 'Plate Duty' during the period 1770–75. In addition there was ground rent to pay, which worked out at just over £120 a year, as well as land tax, which in 1771–72 amounted to almost £60; and in 1778 there was a charge of £15:9:0 for repairs and improvements to the local sewers.

Water at this time was supplied by a private enterprise, the New River Company, and was charged at a rate of £8 a year. The mains pipes were originally of elm. Later in the

[1] AP F199. Unless otherwise stated all information in this chapter is derived from this source

[2] Taylor's involvement in the works at Spencer House, and more particularly the Staircase Hall, is documented in letters in the Althorp Papers [AP F42, CH to GS, 9 Aug 1772; AP F43, CH to GS, 9 Mar 1773]. In addition there are records of a payment to Taylor of £200 from John Spencer's account at Hoare's Bank [HB, Account of JS, Ledger F, f.262, 27 Mar 1777]. However, there is nothing to indicate that Taylor was responsible for the decoration of the ceiling in the Staircase Hall, as claimed by the *Survey of London*, and the payment recorded at Hoare's may well relate to the works Taylor supervised at Althorp during the same period

[3] Information relating to local taxes and services is derived from *Survey of London*, XXIX, chap. II

century iron was introduced, although it was not until 1817, with the passing of the Metropolitan Paving Act, that water companies were compelled to substitute cast-iron for wood in every case.

A further expense was insurance. In 1774 the Spencers received a demand for £35, probably representing a fraction of the annual premium, which in view of the size of the house and the value of its contents must have been considerable.

Finally there was an annual charge for the pews which the Spencers rented in the parish church of St James's, Piccadilly. The Earl and Countess sat in Numbers 13–14 on the south side of the church, while keeping a seat for a footman in 'the Back Gallery Pew against the Wall for Servants'. Surviving vouchers for the period 1771–73 reveal that the total annual rental was £11:12:0.

21 END OF AN ERA

IN 1783, after long years of illness, Lord Spencer died at Bath. In his will[1] he left the sum of £10,000 to each of his daughters, together with minor bequests to loyal servants and friends; but the bulk of his estate, including the house in St James's Place, passed to his son Lord Althorp, who now succeeded as 2nd Earl.

Lord Spencer's widow, Georgiana, received a generous allowance and was granted the use of Holywell House, where she remained until her death in 1814 (FIG 198). In her final years she devoted herself to the care of her children and grandchildren, taking an increasingly active role in charity and religion. She lived very simply[2] but in a small way maintained her support for the arts. Under her supervision the house at Holywell was remodelled in the Gothic style, with advice from Lord Camelford who had assisted in the design of Strawberry Hill. At the same time the grounds were landscaped by Samuel Lapidge, a former associate of Capability Brown. Although Holywell remained the centre of her world, Georgiana continued to travel, both in England and abroad, and made regular visits to London, where she sometimes stopped at Spencer House. Records reveal that when staying in St James's Place she generally occupied an apartment on the second floor and received visitors in the Painted Room, although she occasionally slept in the Painted Room and received in the adjoining Great Room.[3] In the long run, however, her daughters grew jealous of this arrangement and Georgiana eventually took a rented apartment in Jermyn Street.

In 1803 Georgiana received a bequest from her old friend Rachel Lloyd comprising a large collection of historical manuscripts, and in the period that followed she devoted considerable time and energy to sorting and annotating these papers. One only wishes she had shown the same regard for her own papers and those of her husband, especially the building accounts and other precious documents relating to Spencer House; but whether from grief or indifference she decided instead to burn them, informing her daughter Harriet by letter that she had built a good-size bonfire for the purpose, and was making excellent progress, although there was such a 'cargo', as she expressed it, she could not be sure she would ever get through it all.[4]

198 Holywell House, St Albans; engraving by J. Storer after G. Shepherd, from The Beauties of England and Wales *(1806). The house dated back to Tudor times but was remodelled in the late seventeenth century by William Talman. Following the death of the 1st Earl Spencer, it was remodelled again for his widow in the Gothic style*

[1] PRO PROB 11/1111, ff.356–63

[2] AP F201

[3] In a letter to his mother, dated 13 Oct 1787, the 2nd Earl writes, 'I beg you would not think of lodging anywhere but in St James's Place, as it can be of no sort of inconvenience to me, I have directed the room where you slept before to be got ready for you to sleep in, & the bow-window drawing-room below stairs for you to sit & receive people in, as I may when I am there perhaps have some people of business to be with me in the Library, & all my papers &c are there; & it will be much better for you not to go to D:[evonshire] House, which would only mark more strongly why you were not there the last time' [AP F15]. In a second letter, dated 25 Dec 1788, the Earl suggests a slightly different arrangement: 'I hope Lavinia's coming to town will make no difference about your coming to St James's place, as we can very conveniently arrange an apartment for you there by your sleeping in the bow window room & having the great Room to sit in, or if you like it better sleeping in any Room you like up Stairs & sitting in the bow window room' [AP F16]

[4] Earl of Bessborough and Arthur Aspinall (eds), *Lady Bessborough and her Family Circle* (1940), p.3

PART IV

INTO THE NINETEENTH CENTURY

22 THE EPITOME OF THE CULTIVATED GRANDEE

HAVING COME INTO MONEY as a young man, the 1st Earl Spencer never understood the proper relationship between income and expenditure. As his grandson, the 3rd Earl, later remarked, he 'never put any restraint upon himself' and died 'very much in debt'.[1] However, through the acquisition of land and other investments, he had greatly increased the size of the Spencer estate and his son, the 2nd Earl, inherited a fortune estimated at between £40,000 and £60,000 a year (FIG 199). Quite apart from the purchasing power this gave him, it also conferred political power. Although he professed to have little taste for it, and never spent on anything like the same scale as his father, the 2nd Earl Spencer continued to finance elections in boroughs where the family traditionally held influence. At the same time he pursued a personal career in politics and, free from the restraints which had hampered his father's progress, he quickly rose to high office.

His career in the Commons naturally came to an end with his succession, when he was forced to relinquish his seat as M.P. for Surrey, but he immediately established himself as a leading figure in the Lords. Already, under Rockingham, he had served as a Junior Lord of the Treasury, and although he refused the honour, he was now offered the post of Lord Lieutenant of Ireland. Loyal to Fox and the Whigs, Spencer initially supported the policy of neutrality towards France, but in 1794 he crossed over to the Tory benches and in the coalition formed by Pitt was appointed Lord Keeper of the Privy Seal. Shortly afterwards he embarked on a diplomatic mission to Vienna in order to rally support against Napoleon, and although the mission failed, his efforts were rewarded the following December when he was appointed to the key post of First Lord of the Admiralty.

The task Lord Spencer faced was daunting. On land the French had proved themselves invincible. Revolutionary armies were pouring into Holland, Spain and Italy. One by one the members of the coalition formed against Napoleon in 1793 dropped away, and by 1797 Britain stood alone. The country's only hope was its navy. If Britain could establish mastery at sea the French might yet be checked.

Lord Spencer assembled his commanders, and in the selection and combination of officers showed remarkable vision and daring, particularly in the choice of a relatively junior seaman, Horatio Nelson, to head the Mediterranean fleet. In the months that followed Spencer directed a series of operations which remain among the most brilliant in the annals of naval history. In 1797 came news of stunning victories at Camperdown and Cape St Vincent, capped in 1798 by Nelson's triumph in the Battle of the Nile, which gave the British Navy undisputed control of the seas. The strain under which Lord Spencer lived at this time may be judged by the fact that when news reached London of Nelson's victory and Lady Spencer rushed to the Admiralty to congratulate her husband, she found him stretched out on the floor in a dead faint.

Aside from the sea battles he orchestrated, Lord Spencer also introduced a number of important reforms, earning widespread praise for his firm yet even-handed suppression of mutinies at Spithead and the Nore. In 1799, having allegedly refused the honour two

PAGE 208
A Meeting in the Park (*FIG 211, p. 225*)

199 George John, 2nd Earl Spencer, by John Singleton Copley. The portrait shows the Earl at the height of his power, wearing the robes of the Order of the Garter, with which he was invested in 1799 in recognition of his services as First Lord of the Admiralty

years earlier in favour of Admiral Howe, Lord Spencer was invested with the Order of the Garter.

When Pitt resigned in 1801 Lord Spencer followed him out of office, but it was remarked at the time that none of his predecessors had ever served so long during a time of war, and he took much of the credit when in the following year Napoleon was brought to the negotiating table at Amiens. As one commentator expressed it, Lord Spencer's period of office had been 'the most stirring, the most glorious in our naval history so that for him, more distinctly perhaps than for any other English administrator may be claimed the title of organizer of victory'.[2]

[1] Sir Denis Le Marchant, *Memoir of John Charles Viscount Althorp Third Earl Spencer*, p.xix

[2] *Dictionary of National Biography*, 53, p.355

In 1804 Lord Spencer returned to his political roots, rejoining the Whigs, and two years later, when the party came to power under Fox, he was rewarded with the post of Home Secretary. Had the Whigs remained in power Spencer would inevitably have continued to hold high office; he might eventually have become Prime Minister, but following the death of Fox the party largely collapsed and in March 1807 power passed to the Tories, who held on to office for over twenty years. Lord Spencer continued to sit in the Lords, and remained a senior party figure; but he gradually scaled down his political activities, and when the Whigs finally returned to power in 1830 he was already in his seventies, having long given up all thought of political office.

Like his father before him, the 2nd Earl Spencer was involved in a wide range of charitable works. It was largely through his efforts that the Northampton Infirmary was built. He was also a very keen sportsman, a life-long member of the Pytchley Hunt and for several years its Master. He had a parallel enthusiasm for shooting, sailing, sea-bathing, cricket and skating, even experimenting with hot-air ballooning.

But Lord Spencer's interests were chiefly of an intellectual and artistic nature. He was the epitome of the cultivated grandee: a Trustee of the British Museum; President of the Royal Institution; a Fellow of the Royal Society; Commissioner of the Public Records; and a founding member and first President of the Roxburghe Club. His greatest love was early printed books, of which he formed perhaps the finest private collection in the world. By the time of his death the collection totalled some 100,000 volumes, including more than sixty Caxtons; over 800 Aldines; the first three Mainz psalters and some fifty other specimens of presses associated with Gutenberg, Fust and Schoeffer; first editions of Chaucer, Shakespeare and Milton; 6000 volumes of Dante, including the first three editions of the *Divina Commedia*; the 1471 edition of Petrarch; and the earliest known edition of *Orlando Furioso*, published in 1516.

Music too was a passion. The Earl was himself an accomplished cellist and frequently took part in amateur recitals, likewise attending public concerts and the opera, while patronizing such leading composers as Valentino Nicolai and Tomasso Giordano. He also had a fondness for the theatre and was at one time associated with the literary club founded by Samuel Johnson. The fine and decorative arts were another abiding interest. The Earl took drawing lessons, regularly attended exhibitions, and followed the fashion for visiting the studios of famous artists. He took particular pride in the family collection, and began a catalogue of the paintings at Althorp, also supervising the cleaning of canvases and the regilding of frames. At the same time he made some notable acquisitions, including works ascribed to Raphael, Titian, Giulio Romano, Bronzino and Teniers. Under the influence of his father's old friend, Quentin Craufurd, he developed a particular interest in historical portraits, acquiring several outstanding examples by artists such as Philippe de Champaigne, Nicolas Maes, Corneille de Lyon and Rubens. Lord Spencer also continued the tradition of commissioning family portraits, turning to some of the leading exponents of the period, notably Reynolds, Phillips, Hayter, Shee and Copley. He commissioned landscapes from Jacob More and animal paintings from John Boultbee, also purchasing drawings by Alexander Cozens and Benjamin Robert Haydon.

Sculpture too was an interest. Indeed one of the Earl's first acts of patronage was to commission a monument to his father for the church at Brington, carved by Nollekens to a design by Cipriani (FIG 200).[3] He later commissioned a monument to his mother from

[3] AP G14, GJS to GS, 19 June 1786; AP G15, GJS to GS, 14, 28 June, 13 July 1786

[4] AP G100, G105, G121

[5] AP G157, G162, G165, G169

[6] AP G23

[7] AP G328

[8] AP G328, Accounts dated 24 Sept 1794, 5 Apr 1796

[9] AP G81, G161

[10] AP G129, G151, G159, G168

[11] AP F14–F18, L1–L2, L4

[12] AP F12, GJS to GS, 31 Mar, 4 Apr 1785; AP L1–L2, L10

Flaxman, to whom he had offered encouragement when First Lord of the Admiralty,[4] and like many prominent personalities of the period, he sat for his bust to Chantrey.[5] Spencer also patronized the gem-engravers Nathaniel Marchant,[6] James Tassie and Alexander Thompson, and at the same time made significant acquisitions in the area of jewellery and gold and silver plate.[7] During his diplomatic mission to Vienna he placed orders for porcelain with the Imperial Manufacture,[8] and he was also among the foremost English collectors of contemporary French furniture.

In the field of architecture Lord Spencer's tastes were eclectic, ranging from the Classical to the Gothic; he was less concerned with style than with comfort and practicality. But if he lacked the sophistication of his father, he was no less active as a patron and an insistence on quality led him to employ some of the foremost architects of the day, including Samuel Wyatt, Charles Heathcote Tatham,[9] Edward Blore[10] and Henry Holland. Under his direction the house at Althorp was radically transformed, and the grounds too were remodelled.[11] After fire destroyed the old Palladian mansion at Wimbledon he ordered the construction first of a temporary house and then of a picturesque Italianate villa.[12] He also built a house at Ryde on the Isle of Wight for use during the sailing season and financed the remodelling of Holywell for his mother. At Spencer House, too, there were changes, which will be discussed in detail in due course. First, however, it is necessary to examine the activities of Lord Spencer's family.

200 *Study by Giovanni Battista Cipriani for the funerary monument of the 1st Earl Spencer in St Mary's Church, Great Brington, carved by Joseph Nollekens, c1786. It was fitting that the monument should be carved by a sculptor whom in life the 1st Earl Spencer had patronized*

23 FAME AND NOTORIETY

IN MANY WAYS this was a time of rejoicing for the Spencers, a period of particular greatness. The Earl's elder sister, Georgiana, was widely regarded as one of the most beautiful and gifted women of her generation. She wrote and published poetry and was credited with a celebrated novel; she was a talented musician and singer, a leading hostess, a friend to many of the most eminent figures from the world of politics and the arts. Her husband, the Duke of Devonshire, was a senior statesman possessed of vast estates, palatial houses and priceless art treasures. She bore him three children, including an heir, the Marquess of Hartington, who later succeeded. Her elder daughter married Viscount Morpeth, later 6th Earl of Carlisle, while the younger girl became the wife of the distinguished diplomat Granville Leveson Gower, afterwards 1st Earl Granville.

Lord Spencer's younger sister, Harriet, was another leading figure in society, likewise admired for her beauty and wit. In 1793 her husband, Viscount Duncannon, succeeded as 3rd Earl of Bessborough, coming into considerable money and property, and after a distinguished career in the Commons became a senior member of the Lords. Harriet bore him four children, three sons and a daughter, each of whom achieved distinction. The eldest son, John, married a daughter of the Earl of Westmoreland and ultimately succeeded, occupying a succession of senior government appointments, including Home Secretary and Lord Lieutenant of Ireland. The second son, Frederick, married a daughter of the Earl of Bathurst and after a brilliant career in the army, received a knighthood, being appointed successively Secretary of State for War and the Colonies and Governor of Malta. The youngest son, William, married Lady Barbara Ashley Cowper, only daughter and heiress of the 5th Earl of Shaftesbury, and after long service as a Whig M.P. was raised to the peerage as 1st Baron de Mauley. The daughter, Caroline, married the future Prime Minister, William Lamb, eldest son of the 1st Viscount Melbourne.

The Earl himself seemed as successful in his private life as in his career as a public figure. His marriage could not have been happier. 'Lavinia', he once wrote, 'is really a charming creature and the more I live with her I think I am the more in love with her' (FIG 201).[1] The Countess was equally devoted. As a contemporary observed, 'She is like the most attentive servant and seems to watch every turn of his [Spencer's] countenance and does not let anybody do anything for him but herself'.[2] The marriage produced a total of eight children. A daughter, Sarah, married William Henry Lyttelton, 3rd Baron Lyttelton of Hagley, Worcestershire, a distinguished scholar and politician, and in later life served as Lady of the Bedchamber to Queen Victoria and Governess of the Royal Children (FIG 202). Another daughter, Georgiana, married Lord George Quin, younger son of the Marquis of Headfort, a senior courtier; George III and Queen Charlotte were her godparents. Lord Spencer's eldest son, Viscount Althorp, had a brilliant career in politics, serving for a time as Chancellor of the Exchequer and Whig Leader in the House of Commons. Another son, Robert, became a distinguished naval officer (FIG 203), serving with valour in the Napoleonic Wars; he was appointed successively Private Secretary and Groom of the Chamber to the Lord High Admiral, William, Duke of Clarence (later William IV), Commander of the Royal Sovereign Yacht and Surveyor-

[1] AP F12, GJS to GS, 14 Nov 1784

[2] Sir George Leveson Gower and Iris Palmer (eds), *Hary-O, The Letters of Lady Harriet Cavendish 1796–1809* (1940), p.187

201 Lavinia Bingham, wife of the 2nd Earl Spencer, by Sir Joshua Reynolds, 1781. The portrait shows Lavinia at the time of her marriage. As the wife of the 2nd Earl she established herself as a leading hostess and during her lifetime the house in St James's Place was frequently the setting for lavish entertainments

202 Reception of Louis Philippe by Queen Victoria, *by Franz Xavier Winterhalter, 1844. The painting shows Lady Sarah Spencer standing immediately behind the Queen's children, to whom she was governess*

201

202

203 Captain the Hon. Sir Robert Cavendish Spencer, by Thomas Phillips. A brilliant naval officer, Sir Robert seemed destined for the highest honours but his career was cut short when he died of a fever off the coast at Alexandria in 1830

General of the Ordnance, also receiving a knighthood. A third son, Frederick, also had a distinguished career in the navy.

The Spencers likewise drew credit from their cousins, the Poyntzes. Isabella Poyntz, daughter of Lord Spencer's uncle William Poyntz, married Viscount Dungarvon, afterwards 8th Earl of Cork, A.D.C. to George III, serving herself as Maid of Honour to Queen Charlotte. William's eldest son, also William, married the sister and sole heiress of the 8th Viscount Montagu. One daughter by this marriage married Brownlow Cecil, 2nd Marquess of Exeter, Grand Almoner at the Coronation of George IV; another married Robert Trefusis, 18th Baron Clinton, A.D.C. to the Duke of Wellington during the Peninsular War and Lord of the Bedchamber to both George IV and William IV.

Beneath the surface, however, there were tensions and the family was rocked by constant scandal and tragedy. Two of the Earl's children died in infancy. The younger of his two surviving daughters, Georgiana, died in childbirth while in her twenties; his second surviving son, Robert, died at sea in 1830 from a fever contracted off the coast of Egypt, and in the same year the youngest son, George, recently ordained as an Anglican minister, converted to Catholicism, later becoming a mendicant monk (FIG 204). The Duchess of Devonshire ran up gambling debts of over £100,000 and had an open affair with the future Prime Minister, Charles Grey, at that time a political novice seven years her junior, by whom she had an illegitimate daughter. She was banished for a time to the Continent and died while still in her forties. Her husband, it was discovered, already had an illegitimate daughter from a former liaison with a London milliner, and with the Duchess's full knowledge and consent began another, more serious affair with Lady Betty Foster, daughter of the eccentric Earl Bishop of Derry, who lived for a time at Devonshire House and bore the Duke a son and a daughter. Lord Spencer's younger

204 The Hon. George Spencer, in his later incarnation as Father Ignatius of Saint Paul; engraving from The Revd Father Pius Devine, Life of Father Ignatius of St Paul, Passionist *(Dublin, 1866). Having entered the Church of England as Rector of Brington, Lord Spencer's youngest son made a conspicuous conversion to Roman Catholicism, ending his days as a mendicant monk. Today there are moves to have him canonized*

sister, Harriet, was rumoured at various times to be the mistress of the Prince of Wales, the Duke of Cumberland and Richard Brinsley Sheridan. In 1792 she began a passionate affair with Granville Leveson Gower, the very man who later married her niece, Lady Harriet Cavendish, daughter of the Duchess of Devonshire. Granville was ten years her junior, but the affair lasted almost fifteen years and produced two children. To make matters worse Harriet's daughter, Caroline, deserted her husband, Lord Melbourne, placing herself under the protection of her lover, Lord Byron. Harriet became so agitated she burst a blood vessel and calm was not restored until Caroline was forcibly removed to Ireland, leaving Byron to the attentions of another of his many mistresses, Lady Oxford. Six years later Harriet was again embroiled in scandal when her namesake, Harriet Spencer, a great grandaughter of the 3rd Duke of Marlborough, became pregnant by her cousin, George Spencer Churchill, Marquess of Blandford. The girl was underage and unmarried, which only made her plight more desperate, and it was an act of mercy when Harriet stepped in and adopted the child herself, leaving the mother free to court and ultimately marry a nobleman from Germany.

Lord Spencer's maternal uncle, the Revd Charles Poyntz, also caused the family embarrassment. An incurable spendthrift, he mismanaged his finances to such an extent that at one point he was forced to flee the country in order to escape prosecution by his creditors. Years after his death the family was still trying to sort out his affairs. Mordaunt Poyntz, a cousin, likewise brought disgrace. A drunkard and a layabout, his misdemeanours were legion. On one occasion he scrambled on to a police cart carrying a prisoner to Reading Gaol and began to wave to passers-by shouting, 'Good-bye! Good-bye!', knowing full well that within minutes the story would be circulating in the neighbourhood of the Poyntz estate at Midgham. Eventually he drank himself into a state of lunacy and died, much to the family's relief, in 1820. A sister, also, showed a similar disregard for convention, beginning an adulterous affair with a younger son of the Marquess of Townshend, who was forced to fight a near-fatal duel with her husband.

There was scandal in Lavinia's family also. In 1793 her brother, Richard, eloped with Lady Elizabeth Belayse, wife of the future Duke of Norfolk, and in a highly-publicized trial was convicted of debauchery and fined £1000.[3] Although the couple later married (the bride being heavily pregnant at the time), they soon quarrelled and parted, Lady Elizabeth retiring to Paris.

[3] J. Ridgeway (publ.), *The Trial of the Hon. Richard Bingham for Criminal Conduct with Lady Elizabeth Howard, Wife of B. E. Howard Esq., Presumptive Heir to the Duke of Norfolk, and Daughter to the Earl of Fauconberg before Lord Kenyon and a Special Jury, Feb 24th 1794*

24 THE HOUSE UPDATED

BY THE TIME LORD SPENCER succeeded almost twenty years had elapsed since the construction of the house in St James's Place and in 1785 he decided to put in hand a programme of alterations and repairs. Henry Holland was the obvious choice as architect (FIG 205). He had already worked at Wimbledon and was soon to be employed at Althorp. He had recently completed the construction of Brooks's, the great Whig stronghold on St James's Street, and could count among his clients such distinguished figures as the Duke of Bedford, the Marquess of Stafford, Viscount Palmerston and the Prince of Wales, for whom he was currently remodelling Carlton House. His father, moreover, Henry Holland Senior, had worked for the 1st Earl Spencer, as had his father-in-law, the landscape designer, Capability Brown. Lord Spencer had particularly admired the alterations he had recently carried out at the house of a friend near Weymouth;[1] and there were political connections also, since both men had an interest in the borough of Okehampton.

205 Henry Holland. Under Holland's direction the ground-floor apartments at Spencer House were substantially remodelled. The architect was also responsible for the creation of the garden adjoining the terrace

In the spring of 1785 Lord Spencer and Holland toured Spencer House together and following this meeting a modest programme of refurbishment was put in hand, involving the renewal of paintwork and gilding in the principal apartments and repairs to furniture.[2] Later, however, Holland was able to persuade his client to embark on a far more ambitious scheme, involving structural as well as decorative changes, and in 1788 he returned to Spencer House together with an expert team of artist-craftsmen.[3] The works continued over a period of several years and it was 1796 before Holland received full and final payment of accounts totalling several thousand pounds.[4]

With a view to improving circulation and creating additional space for receptions, the Ante Room and Library were knocked together by means of a large door in the centre of the dividing wall. The Library chimney-piece, displayed by the door, was relocated on the north wall, and the same presumably happened in the Ante Room, although by the late nineteenth century the Ante Room chimney-piece had apparently been removed and has not been traced since. At the same time double doors were driven through the alcove in the Ante Room, providing direct access to and from the Staircase Hall, while the jib doors on either side, and the niches above, were blocked and covered over. Change of use required a change of furniture, and Holland introduced a suite of giltwood Louis XVI armchairs and sofas with characteristic tapestry covers, commissioned from the Parisian *marchand-mercier*, Dominique Daguerre.[5] The walls of the two rooms were hung with a matching green silk damask. Here, as elsewhere, fashionable draw curtains were substituted for the original festoons.

The removal of the Library chimney-piece from the east to the north wall involved the blocking up of the window in this position, and to compensate for the loss of light the window overlooking the Park was dropped to floor level to form a pair of French doors, a novelty at this time, giving direct access to the terrace. To preserve the symmetry of the west front, identical doors were added in the Palm Room, at the opposite end of the north-south *enfilade*.

The Dining Room, too, was substantially altered. The order of the columns and

[1] AP F12, GJS to GS, 11 July 1784

[2] AP F12, GJS to GS, 23 Apr 1785

[3] AP F15, GJS to GS, 10 Jan 1788; AP L1–L2, L10

[4] HB, Account of GJS, payments to Henry Holland spanning period 10 June to 29 Mar 1809 and totalling £40,908:0:9 (including work at Wimbledon and Althorp) in Ledgers H, ff.345, 347; I, ff. 131, 133, 137–139; K, ff.267, 270–71, 273; L, ff.108, 220, 227; M, ff.274, 276, 278; N, ff.284, 286, 288, 291, 292, 295, 298; O, ff.338, 340, 343; P, f.468; Q, f.508

[5] HB, Account of GJS, payments to Dominique Daguerre, 6 July 1796, 9 Jan 1797

The late HENRY HOLLAND, Esqr
View Hans Place.

206 Temple on the Ilyssus, Ionic Order, as illustrated in Stuart and Revett, Antiquities of Athens, *I (1762), chap II, pl. VI. Holland chose this order for the capitals of the columns in the Dining Room at Spencer House, replacing the original Roman Ionic capitals by Vardy (FIG 73, p. 110)*

pilasters was changed from Roman to Greek Ionic, with capitals, derived from the Temple on the Ilyssus (FIGS 73 (p. 110) and 206), finished to match the Carrara marble bases. The shafts were coated in yellow scagliola, richly veined to imitate Siena marble. At the same time the number of pilasters was reduced to four, correctly positioned *in antis* at opposite ends of the columnar screens. The walls were painted a pale shade of green, while the ceiling was painted to represent a sky. To improve the view and the lighting the casements were splayed, while the niches on the west wall were covered over. The original giltwood sideboards by Vardy were removed; in their place Holland substituted another pair in mahogany with gilt-bronze mounts representing the Spencer crest, clearly inspired by contemporary furniture in France. Between the windows the architect installed a matching pair of genuine Louis XVI pier tables, produced in France by the master *ébéniste*, Claude Charles Saunier, a protégé of Marie-Antoinette, and supplied by Daguerre (FIG 207). Holland also saw to the production of a large set of English hoop-back chairs in mahogany with leather seats, replacing the original suite.

With its conversion into a Library the Palm Room was likewise redecorated. Three new bookcases were introduced, the first in the centre of the north wall, the remaining pair on either side of the alcove. Suitable furniture was also brought in, replacing the original suite of giltwood chairs. On the first floor, Lady Spencer's Dressing Room was converted into a billiard room, the walls being hung with crimson damask. In the Great Room, too, the walls were hung with crimson damask, while the columnar doorcases on the north and south walls were replaced by simple architraves, supported by brackets, allowing for the installation of two large paintings salvaged from the fire at Wimbledon, *Liberality and Modesty* by Guido Reni and *Apollo crowning the Musician Pasqualini* by Andrea Sacchi, originally purchased by the 1st Earl Spencer.

Few further changes were made to the interior of the house during the 2nd Earl's lifetime, but one or two alterations are recorded in the Spencer papers and other documents of the period. In 1791 repairs were required in the Dining Room after one of the scagliola capitals came loose and fell crashing to the floor. As Lord Spencer reported to his mother, his daughter Sarah was playing in the room at the time and was very nearly killed. 'I had almost forgot to tell you', he wrote, 'of a most narrow escape that Sal had the other day from an accident that might have been fatal to her; she was playing about in the Dining Room here & the nurses & people were running about with her which shook the Room so that half one of the large scagliola capitals which had got loose without our knowing of it fell down & was dashed all to pieces within a foot or two of

207 Spencer House, Dining Room, a Louis XVI mahogany pier table with gilt-bronze mounts, by C.C. Saunier; one of a pair supplied by Dominique Daguerre for the Dining Room at Spencer House. The 2nd Earl Spencer was a leading collector of contemporary French furniture and filled the house in London with outstanding examples of this kind

where Sal stood; if she had been a little nearer the column she must inevitably have been killed, as the weight of the thing that fell was enough to have killed a man'.[6]

In 1802 a pier glass was imported from France for use in one of the ground-floor drawing rooms, supplied by Martin Eloy Liguereux, successor and former partner of Dominique Daguerre,[7] and in 1808 a new drawing room carpet was laid. To judge by a letter from Lord Spencer's daughter, Sarah, this seemingly minor event caused a considerable stir. 'The event of greatest importance I know of today', she informed her brother Robert, 'is the arrival and down-laying of a beautiful new carpet in the drawing-room below. It affords conversation to all the visitors and afforded Mama an excuse for turning out Lord Bulkley's great dog, whom he had brought in with him, two very good effects you will allow, to be produced by a new carpet. Alas, poor carpet! In how short a time will it be trod and spit upon by dogs and men, without scruple, and never thought of from week's end to week's end'.[8]

An event of far greater significance was the creation of the present garden to the west of the house at the foot of the terrace overlooking the park. For years the residents of St James's Place had been campaigning for the allotment of gardens, and in 1795 the Crown finally gave consent. Although the lease between Lord Spencer and the Crown was not drawn up until 1799, work went ahead on the construction of the garden in 1797.[9]

[6] AP F18, GJS to GS, 15 June 1792

[7] AP L10

[8] Lady Frederick Cavendish and Maud Wyndham (eds), *Correspondence of Sarah, Lady Lyttelton* (1912), p.9

[9] PRO CRES 6 / 85, pp.51, 79–86; CRES 6 / 88, pp.126–31; MPEE 54 (1) & (2); MPE 484, John Marquand and Thomas Leverton, *A Plan of the East Side of Green Park with the Line of the Proposed Inclosure for Gardens to the adjoining Houses; taken under the direction of John Fordyce Esq., Surveyor of His Majesty's Land Revenue*

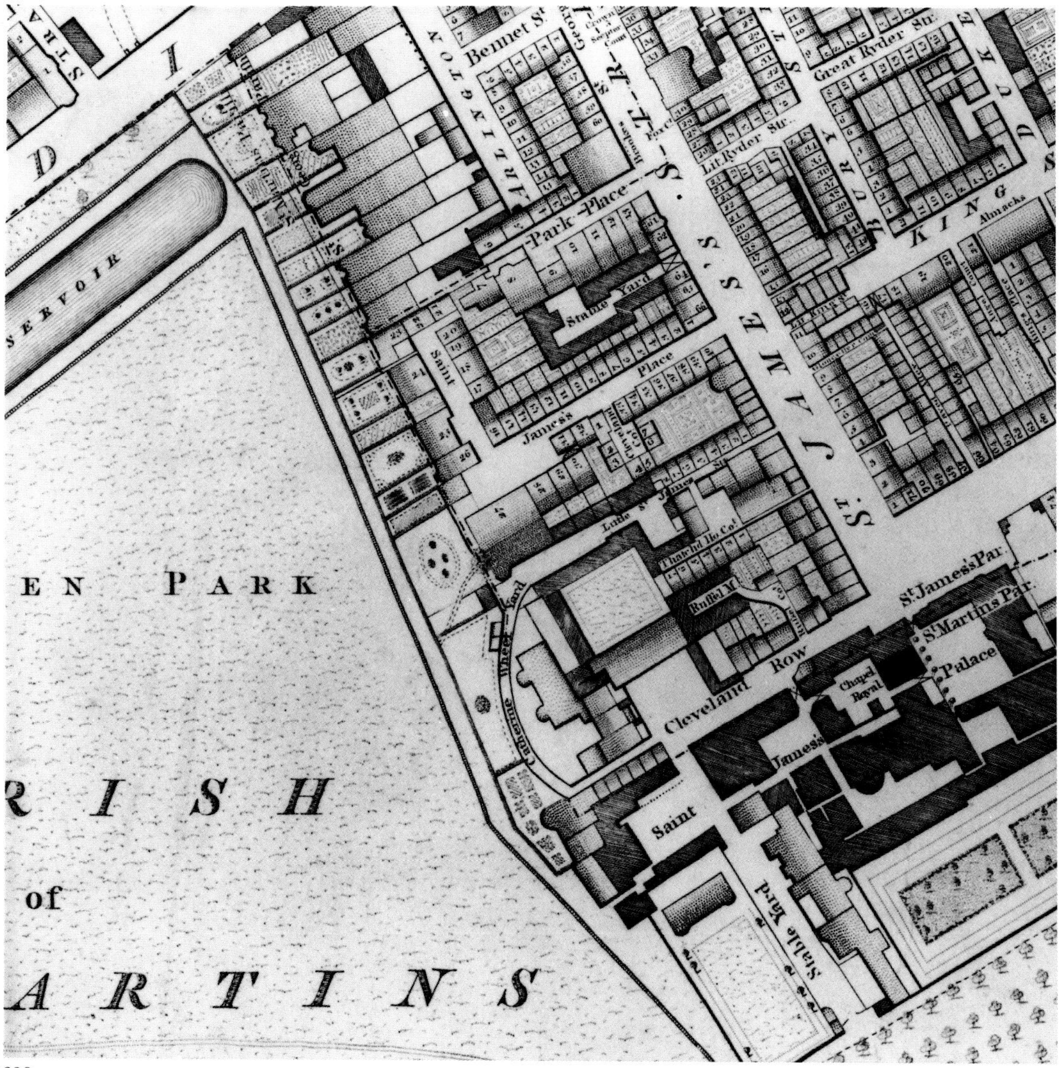

208

208 Map of London, Westminster, and Southwark, *by Richard Horwood, 1813, detail showing the garden of Spencer House shortly after completion*

209 *Spencer House, north-west view, c1800; aquatint by Thomas Malton, from* A Picturesque Tour through the Cities of London and Westminster *(1800), pl.96. The view shows the garden when newly laid out. In later years shrubs were planted along the fence on Queen's Walk, providing a greater measure of seclusion and privacy*

209

Contemporary plans show the original layout, formal yet relaxed, easing the relationship between the building and its surroundings (FIG 208).[10] The ground was levelled and turfed over to form an even lawn, while, in the centre, on axis with the house, an existing oval plantation was used as the basis of a conforming arrangement of flower-beds, crossed and encircled by gravel paths, with a meandering path to the south. For the purposes of security an iron railing was erected along the boundary with Queen's Walk while brick walls were built to north and south. Shrubs and trees were planted around the perimeter (FIG 209), although the original intention was to restrict growth on the west border, allowing a clear view of the house and garden from Green Park. In time, however, the shrubs grew tall and dense, screening the garden from public view and so providing a greater measure of privacy and seclusion. In addition, a flight of stone steps was added at the north end of the terrace, providing a direct link between house and garden.

Surviving accounts reveal that the cost of construction was in the order of £1,500, and that the works involved a mason, two bricklayers, an iron smith and a nurseryman.[11] The design was almost certainly by Henry Holland, through whom the workmen were paid; but one wonders to what extent the architect was guided by his clients, especially Lavinia, who had recently laid out a flower garden to her own designs at Althorp.

[10] In addition to the published maps which show the garden there are several manuscript plans, notably Horwood, *Plan of the Parish of St Martin in the Fields... 1799* [BL, Maps, K.Top. XXI–6]; Thomas Chawner, *Plan of St James's Palace, Marlborough House, York House, Bridgwater House, & the Improvements intended in St James's Street, Thatched House Court, etc, surveyed by Thomas Chawner 1834* [BL, Maps, Crace Collection, portfolio XII, No. 20]. Documents relating to the Office of Works buildings demolished to make way for the garden of Spencer House include John Marquand, *The names and occupiers of the low buildings in the Green Park, and the purposes for which they are now employed* [PRO MPE 495]; Block Plan of Spencer House and surrounding area [SJSM, 38/9]

[11] AP L10, Accounts of Nov 1797 (2)

210 Earl Spencer's St James's Park *[sic]; engraving c1810. The present view is one of many published in guide books to London in the eighteenth and nineteenth centuries*

The house continued to be much admired, with views appearing in many of the illustrated guides to London published during this period (FIGS 210–212). 'It is impossible', Thomas Malton wrote in 1792, 'not to be captivated with the appearance and situation of Earl Spencer's house seen across the lawn; and commanding a prospect of the western parts of the Park, with the Queen's house and garden. Spencer House is a noble structure of the Doric order, and has an imposing effect'.[12] For David Hughson, writing in the first decade of the nineteenth century, Spencer House was still, of all the houses fronting the park, 'the most worthy of notice'.[13] For a later writer, John Papworth, it was 'the most distinguished', a 'magnificent residence';[14] for another a 'splendid mansion'.[15] In a guide of 1825 the house was described as 'a beautiful building in the Grecian style of architecture', the statues 'commandingly graceful'.[16] The great British architect, Sir John Soane, directed his students to make drawings of Spencer House, which he afterwards used in lectures.[17] Furthermore, in 1795 he visited Spencer House to trace the plan of the Library (Palm Room), which he used as the basis of his own designs for a similar room at the house of the Duke of Leeds in St James's Square.[18]

Indeed it was the library which now attracted the greatest attention. Although the bulk of the Earl's collection was stored at Althorp, some of his greatest treasures were displayed at St James's Place. According to one source, the Palm Room contained 'the most select and valuable portion of his Lordship's Library including all the curious specimens of early printed books prior to the sixteenth century'.[19] The artist Benjamin Robert Haydon, who visited Spencer House the year before Lord Spencer died, was lost in amazement. Here, he exclaimed, were 'first editions, vellum copies, rare Boccaccios, unaccountable Dantes, impossible to be found Virgils, and not to be understood first editions of Homer'.[20] Even more explicit was the description provided by a French guide of the same date, which spoke of '*une bibliothèque qu'on peut regarder comme une des plus riches collections de livres de l'Europe. Elle contient particulièrement un grand nombre de manuscrits gothiques, des premières editions (princeps) de la Bible, des ouvrages imprimés par Caxton, par les Alde, par les Elzevirs*'.[21]

[12] Thomas Malton, *A Picturesque Tour through the Cities of London and Westminster*, p.108

[13] David Hughson, *London; being an accurate History of the British Metropolis and its Neighbourhood, to Thirty Miles Extent, from an actual Perambulation*, 6 vols (1805–9), 4, p.324; *Walks Through London* (1817), p.263

[14] John B. Papworth, *Select Views of London* (1816), pp.16–17

[15] C. F. Partington, *Natural History and Views of London and its Environs*, 2 vols (1834), 2, p.26

[16] John Harris (publ.), *London Scenes, or a Visit to Uncle William in Town; containing a description of the most remarkable Buildings and Curiosities in the British Metropolis* (1825), p.161

[17] SJSM, 17/3/7, 17/3

[18] SJSM, *Day Book*, entries for 16, 17 Jan 1795; *Notebook*, entry for 15 Jan 1795; *Journal*, entries for 16, 17 Jan 1795; Drawing in *Folio v*, 99, inscribed *Earl Spencer's Library* and in pencil *For the Duke of Leeds 17 January 1795*; Record drawing of same, dated 27 Feb 1808, in *Town Houses*, p.82

[19] George Baker, *The History and Antiquities of the County of Northampton*, 2 vols (1822–30), I, p.111

[20] Willard Bissell Pope (ed.), *The Diary of Benjamin Robert Haydon*, 5 vols (Harvard University Press, 1963), 4, p.106 [entry for 2 July 1833]

[21] Ernest Bourdin (publ.), *Guide Illustré du Voyageur à Londres* (Paris, c1851), p.134

211 A Meeting in the Park; *aquatint, 1806. In the nineteenth century, no less than the eighteenth, Green Park was a favourite parading ground for people of rank and fashion. Spencer House remained the primary architectural focus*

212 A Derby *vase decorated with a view of* Spencer House, *designed by* Bloor, *c1825. Almost eighty years after its construction Spencer House was still regarded as one of the principal sights of London*

212

25 ENTERTAINMENTS LARGE AND SMALL

LIKE HIS FATHER Lord Spencer was rather retiring. He had the temperament of a scholar. Balls and assemblies were a duty, not a pleasure; dancing was best avoided. By contrast Lavinia was extremely garrulous, an extrovert who loved the crowd. Entertainments at Spencer House were correspondingly varied, ranging from decorous dinner parties to the push and shove of crowded routs.

In 1790 the Spencers hosted an unusual event, when the younger members of the aristocracy were invited to St James's Place for a children's ball. In a letter to his mother the following day Lord Spencer provided an account of what was clearly a very successful occasion. 'We had a ball for children here last night', he reported, 'which went off vastly well, the supper was a very pretty idea of Lavinia's, each table representing some well known fairy tale which delighted not only the children but all the Fathers and Mothers excessively. There were about sixty boys & girls that danced, all between seven and twelve, except Amelia Sloper, who was above the age & a little boy of the D:[uke] of Athol's [sic] who was under it being only five years old, but a much better dancer than almost any of them'.[1]

In anticipation of another large event, a 'huge assembly' as he described it, the diarist Dr Burney was beside himself with excitement, expecting that as usual with receptions at Spencer House 'all London will be there'.[2] It was still the practice for women members of the aristocracy to hold a *levée*, or morning reception, and Lavinia was no exception. Her daughter, Sarah, described the scene as visitors streamed in from the cold and wet of a typical January morning. 'Mama's levée', she noted, 'is as usual frequented by all the usual visitors; they arrive cross as ten sticks, dripping, soaked through, and shivering in great coats, and snow shoes; and there remain for hours'.[3]

Lavinia also instituted a weekly *soirée*, held each Friday evening between ten and twelve, to which about 100 guests would come before moving on to assemblies at one or more of the other great London houses. Receptions of this kind were something of a novelty and aroused considerable comment. Once again Lavinia's daughter, Sarah, was on hand to record the immediate reaction. 'It was,' she observed, 'quite different from common parties for it was a talking party. I did not once hear those hated phrases "How suffocating!", "What a squeeze", "Have you been in the next room, it is even a worse crowd than this?" and so on, which I used to dread the sound of when I went out a few years since. Some people played at shilling whist, and some at billiards and most of them got together in little talking parties very comfortably'.[4] The diarist, Mary Berry, who also attended this inaugural reception, was equally impressed. 'In the evening', she noted afterwards, 'I went to Lady Spencer's before ten o'clock. An assembly in the drawing and billiard rooms of all the aristocracy of the Opposition. The rooms are uncommonly handsome, in the old style of carving, gilding, and damask, than which nothing invented since is handsomer. Everybody seemed pleased. Everybody prided themselves upon coming early, and it is to be repeated every Friday'.[5]

Music, too, played an important part in the life of Spencer House. Writing from

213 Samuel Rogers, by George Dance, 1795. Rogers was himself a resident of St James's Place and regularly called on his neighbours at Spencer House

St James's Place in the spring of 1785, the Earl informed his mother that, together with a family friend, he and Lavinia had been 'amusing ourselves with playing some trios composed last year for us by Nicolai, which are pretty enough & made a very good domestick way of passing the evening'.[6]

Spencer House also continued to provide a setting for important family events, as in 1805 when the Spencers' elder daughter, Sarah, celebrated her eighteenth birthday and the Countess gave a ball to mark her coming-out, a reception which one guest pronounced, 'very splendid'.[7] In 1815 the state apartments were thrown open for the marriage of Lavinia's niece, Lady Elizabeth Bingham, daughter of her brother Richard, to George Granville Harcourt, eldest son of the Archbishop of York, who conducted the ceremony. Six years later the Dining Room was cleared for the wedding of another of Lavinia's nieces, Georgiana, and the young Charles Nevill, with the Archbishop again presiding.

In old age the Spencers' youngest son, George, recalled that at the time he grew up the house in St James's Place had been a hive of activity, a place, as he expressed it, where 'the first society, whether of the political or the literary and scientific, were constantly received'.[8] The claim is supported by a diary George kept during this period, which survives among his papers in the archives of the Passionist Order. The diary is patchy and covers only a few short years, but it clearly demonstrates that during the Season the Spencers hosted lunch parties, banquets and other events almost every day of the week. Beyond this the diary also provides an occasional list of the Spencers' guests, who were indeed among the most eminent figures from the world of science, art, literature and politics. They included Sir Humphrey Davy; the chemists Hatchett, Barde and Wollaston; the engineer Sir Marc Isambard Brunel; the physiologist Alexander Wilson. There were famous geographers and explorers, such as Sir Edward Sabine and James Renell. Sir William Jones, who had tutored Lord Spencer as a youth, remained a life-long friend, as did other oriental scholars who were welcomed to St James's Place, among them William Marsden and David Pearce. The philosopher Sir James Macintosh was a frequent guest, as were the historian Henry Petrie, the essayist Sydney Smith, the critic Richard Sharp and the poets Henry Luttrell and Samuel Rogers a resident of St James's Place (FIG 213).

Classical scholars such as Frederick North and Peter Elmsley were naturally attracted to a house containing probably the most complete collection in London of early editions of the Greek and Roman classics. For the same reason Spencer House became a mecca for leading book-collectors, notably Richard Heber and Sir William Scott, while continuing to provide a rallying-point for senior members of the Whig party, including the future Prime Minister, Lord John Russell. The painter Thomas Phillips often dined with the Spencers, as did the sculptor Sir Francis Chantrey, and from the 2nd Earl's correspondence it is clear that Sir Joshua Reynolds was another frequent dinner guest. There are records also of the actress Eliza Farren dining at Spencer House, although by this time she had quit the stage to marry the Earl of Derby. Nelson, Collingwood and other heroes of the Napoleonic Wars were likewise regular guests.

Spencer House continued to be the scene of entertainments, large and small, until the death of Lady Spencer in 1831. After almost fifty years of marriage, 'half a century of blessings' as he described it,[9] Lord Spencer was unable to adjust to life alone and became increasingly withdrawn. He rarely ventured into society and almost never entertained. After mourning his wife for three years, he died at Althorp on 10 November 1834, his title and estates passing to his eldest son.

[1] AP F17, GJS to GS, 14 May 1790

[2] Burney to Madame d'Arblay, 7 May 1795, quoted in *Diary and Letters of Madame d'Arblay*, 7 vols (1854), 6, p.31

[3] Frederick Cavendish and Maud Wyndham (eds), *Correspondence of Sarah, Lady Lyttelton*, p.59

[4] Ibid., p.121

[5] Lady Theresa Lewis (ed.), *Extracts from the Journals and Correspondence of Miss Berry from the Year 1783 to 1852*, 3 vols (1865), 2, p.467

[6] AP F12, GJS to GS, 13 Mar 1785

[7] *An Irish Beauty of the Regency, compiled from 'Mes Souvenirs', the unpublished journals of the Hon. Mrs Calvert 1789–1822* (1911), p.45

[8] Quoted in Revd Fr. Pius Devine, *Life of Father Ignatius of St. Paul, Passionist (The Hon. & Rev. George Spencer)* (Dublin, 1866)

[9] Quoted in Albert Edward John, 7th Earl Spencer, 'Althorp, Northamptonshire, A Seat of the Earl Spencer', *Country Life* (18 June 1921), p.771

PART V

THE VICTORIAN AGE

26 A MOST THOROUGH KNOWLEDGE OF COWOLOGY

THE THIRD EARL SPENCER, better known under his previous title Lord Althorp, is a towering figure in the history of English politics. He was leader of the House of Commons, Chancellor of the Exchequer, architect of the great Reform Act and more than once was tipped as a possible Prime Minister. And yet it is probably true to say that there has never been a politician who so disliked politics, nor any who in early life showed so few signs of future greatness.

Lord Althorp was a slow developer; indeed his faltering intellectual progress as a child caused the family alarm. He found it hard to keep up with his fellows when sent away to Harrow and was eventually removed and placed under the direction of a private tutor. By 1800 he was ready to enroll at Trinity College, Cambridge, but as a nobleman he was naturally exempted from lectures and university exams, and initially paid little attention to his studies. However, there was no escaping the college exams and, having been warned by his parents that something more than a pass was expected, he settled down to a more industrious routine and to everyone's surprise was placed high in the first class. The following year he went one further, coming top of the college, an achievement unheard of in undergraduates of his background.

Althorp was clearly intelligent. And yet for all his academic distinction he showed little interest in anything of a cultural or artistic nature. Hoping to broaden his horizons, his parents sent him to Italy, but the effort was entirely wasted. Despite the very best introductions, he rarely ventured into Italian society and his one attempt to speak the language fell painfully flat. He toured the sights of Rome but was, in his own words, 'bored to death'.[1] Cutting short his visit, he returned to England by way of Switzerland, Germany and Holland, bypassing France altogether, 'in order', as he explained, 'to avoid seeing the galleries there'.[2] He arrived home safely, but with little to show for his time abroad except a few books for his father and a large Parmesan cheese.

The only pursuit for which Althorp had any real enthusiasm was sport, especially fox-hunting. He was riding to hounds from the age of five and at fifteen succeeded his father as Master of the Pytchley. Sport became an obsession, the sole topic on which he could be persuaded to speak. His cousin, Harriet Cavendish, described him as 'a zero in society',[3] a man, as she expressed it, 'whose soul is engrossed with one most uninteresting pursuit', who 'cares for neither Father, Mother, brothers, sisters or for anything on earth but that noble animal, a horse'.[4]

However, as heir to the Spencer title and estates, Althorp was expected to play some part in public life, and in 1804 he entered Parliament as M.P. for Okehampton in Devon, a borough controlled by his father. When the Whigs returned to power in January 1806, and his father became Home Secretary, Althorp was appointed a Junior Lord of the Treasury. Law required that ministerial appointees resign their seat and seek re-election. Rather than stand again for Okehampton, his father engineered his candidature for the seat of the University of Cambridge, left vacant by the death of Pitt. Although in the

PAGE 228
Ellen Terry, *by G. F. Watts, c1864 (FIG 222, p. 247)*

ensuing election Althorp was beaten into second position, in 1807 he fought a costly but ultimately successful campaign for the seat of Northamptonshire, which he held through seven successive parliaments.

Nevertheless, sport continued to dominate his life. It is said that he had horses stationed at ten-mile intervals along the road from London to Althorp and would gallop all night after the division of the House in order to be present for the meeting of the Pytchley the following morning. His sister, Lady Sarah, described his life at this time as one of 'flying from hunting to voting and from voting to hunting again'.[5]

His parents meanwhile were anxious to see him marry and father an heir, but he showed as little interest in the opposite sex as he had in the statues in the Vatican Museum. Eligible young ladies were paraded before him but nothing stirred. His thirtieth birthday came and went, and his parents began to despair. Finally, however, Althorp found a girl to his liking, Esther Acklom. She was neither beautiful nor graceful; on the contrary she was stout and clumsy. Nor was she especially intelligent or well-educated; Althorp's sister Sarah described her as 'a vulgar person and a spoilt child'.[6] Esther's ancestry was obscure and her connections far from brilliant. Although she was reputed to be rich, having inherited some 2,000 acres in Nottinghamshire, including a manor house at Wiseton, it was discovered that the property was heavily encumbered and in poor repair. But Althorp was in love, and in the spring of 1814 the couple were married, settling at Wiseton.

The following year Esther became pregnant but later miscarried. A second miscarriage followed in the summer of 1816 and the suspicion grew that she might be incapable of having children. In the autumn of 1817 Esther became pregnant again, and this time there was no miscarriage, nor any but the most promising signs, everything pointing to the birth of a healthy child, possibly an heir. 'I never saw her better in my life', Althorp wrote of his wife at this time, 'and I am therefore very sanguine as to the result'.[7] All hope was lost, however, when in June 1818 Esther was delivered of a still-born son, lapsing into a delirious fever, from which she died a few days later.

Althorp was inconsolable. He immediately resigned the mastership of the Pytchley and never hunted again. From this time forward he always wore black mourning clothes and for several months after Esther's death he lived in complete retirement at Wiseton. 'If it were not for my duty', he wrote to Lord Milton, 'I should like to shut myself up for the rest of my life'.[8] Esther's rooms were left exactly as they were the day she died. Wherever he went, Althorp took with him the pillow on which her head had rested in her final days, as well as her wedding ring, which he placed alongside his own.

Finally, in December 1819, Althorp emerged from retirement and returned to London to resume his duties in the House of Commons. Although never an extremist, he was considered a radical, campaigning hard for free trade, Catholic emancipation and the abolition of slavery in Britain's colonies. An opponent of repressive legislation, he angrily denounced the introduction of the Six Acts following the Peterloo massacre, and was fearless in his exposure of government corruption. At a time of acute distress and hardship, resulting from the long war with France and the immediate effects of the Industrial Revolution, he invariably took the side of the dispossessed.

From the time of his return to Westminster, Althorp's stature as a politician grew. He was twice invited to become party leader in the Commons, and when the offer was made a third time in May 1830 he accepted, taking much of the credit when, a few months later, the Tories were finally swept from office and the Whigs returned to power. Althorp was allegedly offered the premiership but declined in favour of Lord Grey (formerly the lover

[1] Ellis Archer Wasson, *Whig Renaissance, Lord Althorp and the Whig Party 1782–1845* (New York and London, 1987), p.13

[2] Ibid.

[3] Sir George Leveson Gower and Iris Palmer (eds), *Hary-O, The Letters of Lady Harriet Cavendish 1796–1809* (1940), p.192

[4] Ibid., p.186

[5] Wasson, op. cit., p.57

[6] Quoted in Lady Margaret Douglas-Home, *A Mere Miss Poyntz*

[7] Georgina Battiscombe, *The Spencers of Althorp* (1984), p.126

[8] Wasson, op. cit., p.97

of Althorp's aunt, the Duchess of Devonshire), accepting instead the office of Chancellor of the Exchequer while continuing to lead the party in the House of Commons.

Althorp's first step as Chancellor was to initiate a comprehensive programme of administrative reform, abolishing sinecures and over-paid appointments and generally improving the efficiency of government departments. But he is chiefly remembered for the crucial part he played in the preparation and passage of the Reform Bill in 1832, which greatly extended the suffrage, laying the foundations of the country's present democratic system. In the election that followed, Althorp was returned once more to Parliament for the newly-formed borough of South Northamptonshire and, although he resigned with Grey over the Irish Coercion Act in 1834, he was immediately reappointed as Chancellor on the formation of an alternative administration by Lord Melbourne, his cousin by marriage.

Althorp returned to Downing Street with extreme reluctance, for despite an obvious talent for politics, he positively hated the life of a politician. In later life he described his period as Chancellor as one of 'acute pain',[9] and at the time confided to a friend, 'My being in office is nothing more or less than a misery. I am perfectly sure that no man ever disliked it to such a degree as I do; and indeed, the first thing that naturally comes into my head when I wake is how I am to get out of it'.[10] Althorp's dread was such that he never brought his pistols to London for fear that he might suddenly be tempted to destroy himself in a fit of anguish.

His true love now was farming, which had taken the place of sport after Esther's death, and provided him with his main source of enjoyment and solace. He had always been an animal-lover and kept all manner of pets when at Harrow, but in an atavistic reversion to the ways of his ancestors, he now devoted every available moment to the breeding of short-horn cattle. Contemporaries were baffled. Here was a man at the top of the political ladder, a senior government minister from one of the great noble families of England, yet away from Westminster he would talk of nothing but livestock. A stranger who dined with him at this time afterwards noted, 'He is a most silent man – except about bulls and cows – only touch upon that and off he goes. His manners are plain to a degree. After dinner he gave us such a lecture about a said bullock who would be the finest extant animal but for a fault in his bottom. He talks certainly most learnedly about cattle, and has I suppose the most thorough knowledge of "cowology"'.[11] Any time spent away from farming was bitterly resented. It is alleged that a herdbook sat on Althorp's desk in Downing Street and that every Monday he received a detailed report on the calves born at Wiseton. It was duty alone which induced him to accept his reappointment as Chancellor in 1834, and when his father died a few months later, he seized on the event as a pretext for retiring from public life altogether.

[9] Sir Denis Le Marchant, *Memoir of John Charles Viscount Althorp Third Earl Spencer*, p.527

[10] Ibid.

[11] Douglas-Home, op. cit.

27 DEBTS AND RETRENCHMENT

THE SECOND EARL SPENCER had lived with little regard for economy and at various points had been forced to sell off important family assets. In 1789 he disposed of the estate at Okehampton, in Devon, and in 1811 auctioned off a collection of several hundred old master drawings. Following his mother's death he sold the house at Holywell, together with its contents, and from 1827 he leased the villa at Wimbledon, having previously disposed of the greater part of the furniture salvaged from the fire of 1785. Even so, he managed to leave debts of over half a million pounds. Annual interest payments on these debts came to £30,000, and since the estate as a whole brought in only £40,000, Lord Althorp, now 3rd Earl Spencer, had as little as £10,000 to cover expenses. Althorp alone absorbed some £5,000 a year and it was obvious that drastic action would have to be taken.

Directly he succeeded, the 3rd Earl Spencer put in hand a sweeping programme of austerity measures and by the time of his death had reduced the burden of debt to only a few hundred pounds. At Althorp he sold off outlying farms and leased the park to local farmers, while the deer, which had roamed there since Tudor times, were mounted on carts and sent as a gift to the king at Windsor. Little realizing their future value, Lord Spencer also disposed of the manors of Battersea and Wandsworth, and at the same time broke up the estate at Wimbledon, selling off land on the fringes while continuing to lease the villa and its immediate surroundings. Up and down the country small tracts of land were sold to the burgeoning railway companies. Lord Spencer even went so far as to auction off the contents of the house he had occupied in Downing Street when Chancellor of the Exchequer.

At the same time the Earl reduced his living expenses. As he wrote at the time, 'I have no desire to keep up the state of a great nobleman and shall be prepared to live very economically'.[1] He had never had much interest in the arts and added little to the family collection. Aside from a portrait of himself by Richard Ansdell, a kind of agricultural conversation piece in which he appears alongside his prize bull 'Firby' (FIG 214), Lord Spencer's only known contribution was a series of twenty-seven paintings of short-horn cattle, mostly by local artists. Nor did he indulge in any major building works, confining himself to the construction and refurbishment of a few utilitarian farm buildings.

For most of the year Lord Spencer lived at Wiseton, and although he continued to use the house at Althorp, having duties to perform as a magistrate in Northampton, he cut down on staff and closed the state apartments, installing himself in a modest suite off the principal circuit. As for the house in St James's Place, the Earl's first thought was to sell it. He had always hated London life and now saw 'no chance', as he expressed it, 'of either myself or any of my successors being in such circumstances as would justify me in having such a house'.[2] The property was actually put on the market, and several potential buyers expressed an interest, including two English Dukes and a foreign Prince. To add to its appeal Lord Spencer threw in three other buildings he owned in St James's Place, as well as the famous Marlborough diamonds and several old master paintings, all for £60,000.

[1] Georgina Battiscombe, *The Spencers of Althorp*, p.142

[2] Ellis Archer Wasson, *Whig Renaissance, Lord Althorp and the Whig Party 1782–1845*, p.329

But the scheme proved a failure and was ultimately abandoned. The census of 1841 reveals that the house was occupied at this time by Lord Spencer's younger brother Frederick and his family, attended by fourteen servants.[3] However, the Earl himself rarely used the house, staying there for only a few weeks in the year, usually in April or May. There is no record of any receptions and the only evidence of alterations is a bill from a firm of ironmongers for repairs to the grate in the Entrance Hall.[4]

In the last years of his life the Earl devoted himself to farming and agricultural reform. In 1837 he helped to found the Yorkshire Agricultural Society and the following year became the first president of the newly-instituted Royal Agricultural Society, serving again in this capacity in 1844. His love of cattle made him an obvious candidate for the presidency of the Smithfield Club, which he directed until his death, and his deep knowledge and experience of farming were translated into a series of highly-influential articles published throughout the 1830s and 1840s. Not the least of his achievements was the management of the farming estate at Holkham, the largest of its kind in England, for

214 John Charles, 3rd Earl Spencer (far left), with his prize bull 'Firby' at Wiseton, by Richard Ansdell R.A., 1843. The Earl had a passion for farming but little interest in art, and the present painting was virtually the only addition he made to the family collection

which he had complete responsibility during the minority of the 2nd Earl of Leicester.

Although more of a practical thinker than a speculative theorist, Lord Spencer took up the study of philosophy and religion and corresponded for many years with Henry Brougham. He also became a leading member of the Society for the Diffusion of Useful Knowledge, and it is some mark of his standing in scholarly circles that at one stage he was invited to stand as Chancellor of the University of Cambridge.

Inevitably he continued to be consulted in political matters and received repeated invitations to return to public life. Indeed, in quitting Melbourne's cabinet in 1834, he inadvertently brought down the government, for the King declared that without his presence the administration was unworkable. In 1835, following the collapse of the Peel ministry, an emissary was sent from London to try to persuade him to join a new administration, but by way of an answer the Earl simply gestured to some lambs gambolling in a field. 'Nothing', he declared, 'can induce me to leave them'.[5] In 1838, on the formation of a new ministry by Melbourne, Lord Spencer was offered the choice

215 Summer Fashions for 1842; *engraving published by tailors B. Read & Co., London and New York. The setting is Green Park, with the pediment of Spencer House clearly picked out on the horizon*

[3] PRO HO 107/736, Book 3, ff.19–20

[4] AP L10

[5] Battiscombe, op. cit., p.144

between the posts of Governor-General of Canada and Lord Lieutenant of Ireland, and in the following year there were calls for his appointment as Prime Minister, but he would not be tempted out of retirement.

Nor did Spencer ever remarry. In 1834, the year of his father's death, he proposed to his cousin, Isabella Poyntz, recently widowed by the death of her husband, Lord Clinton, but she refused him and he never again made any move in the direction of matrimony, resigning himself to a life without children and appointing his brother Frederick his heir.

Like his father and his grandfather before him, Lord Spencer suffered the agonies of gout. Applying the same drastic measures to his diet as he had to his finances, he adopted a punishing regime based on virtual starvation and total abstension from liquor. With scientific precision he weighed his food at every meal and, having partaken of his quota, bolted from the dining room to escape the temptation of a further helping. In the long run his health broke down, and when the end finally came, it came very quickly. In 1845, while officiating as steward at Doncaster Races, Lord Spencer was felled by a sudden collapse. He was rushed by carriage to Althorp, but never rallied and died a few days later. In his final hours he called for a locket containing a strand of his dead wife's hair. 'I promised her', he murmured, 'to die with it on'.[6] Another promise was fulfilled a few days later when, in accordance with his wishes, he was laid to rest alongside Esther in the family vault at Brington church. The couple had made a pact to position themselves this way in death, firmly believing that on the Day of Judgement they would thus rise together in heavenly reunion.

[6] Sir Denis Le Marchant, *Memoir of John Charles Viscount Althorp Third Earl Spencer*, p.562

28 A ROYAL FAVOURITE

216 Frederick, 4th Earl Spencer (1798–1857), by Stephen Catterson Smith P.R.H.A., *1849. The Earl was a senior courtier with a love of society and show. During his lifetime he hosted some memorable receptions in St James's Place*

THE FOURTH EARL SPENCER was the very opposite of his predecessor (FIG 216). By nature an extrovert, he loved to mingle in fashionable society and had a positive enthusiasm for public life. He had little interest in either sport or farming, and like many who inherit unexpectedly was rather extravagant, with an exaggerated sense of position and a tendency to overplay his role. It was typical of him that despite his brother's request for a simple funeral, he ordered the cortège to be preceded by a liveried footman bearing a coronet on a crimson velvet cushion. It was typical also that directly he inherited he discontinued the allowance formerly paid to his younger brother George. The sight of this exalted missionary, clad in his black habit and sandals, generally unwashed and unshaven, filled him with disgust and shame. The only time he ever showed his brother any kindness was when he agreed to pay his medical expenses after George contracted a near-fatal illness while tending to victims of the Irish famine.

The Earl had begun his career in the navy. He saw action in the Napoleonic Wars, was promoted Captain in 1822, and five years later was decorated for bravery after taking a leading part in the Battle of Navarino. In 1831, when it became apparent that he would probably inherit, he quit the navy for the safer world of politics, serving successively as M.P. for Worcestershire and Midhurst. In 1840 he was appointed Equerry to the Duchess of Kent and so began a brilliant career at Court. Following his succession, he was promoted Lord Chamberlain of the Queen's Household, a post he held from 1846 until 1848, serving concurrently as Councillor of the Duchy of Lancaster, and in 1854, having recently been awarded the Garter, he was appointed Lord Steward of the Household, retaining that position until his death.

Lord Spencer married twice. His first wife, whom he married in 1830, was his second cousin, Elizabeth Poyntz, daughter of William Stephen Poyntz, a nephew of the 1st Earl and Countess Spencer. Elizabeth died in 1851, but left her husband three children, a son and two daughters. The son, John Poyntz, was born at Spencer House in 1835 and eventually succeeded as 5th Earl Spencer. The elder daughter, Georgiana, died unmarried a short time before her twentieth birthday in 1852. The younger daughter, Sarah, also died unmarried, although in later life she became a close companion of the Prime Minister, Gladstone.[1] Lord Spencer's second wife, whom he married in 1854, was Adelaide Seymour (FIG 217), a descendant of the 1st Marquess of Hertford. The marriage produced two further children, a daughter, Victoria Alexandrina, born in 1855, and a son, Charles Robert, who followed in 1857. The daughter, to whom the Queen was sponsor, married William Mansfield, 2nd Baron Sandhurst, a high-ranking courtier and statesman.[2] The son eventually succeeded as 6th Earl Spencer.

217 Adelaide Seymour (1825–77), second wife of Frederick, 4th Earl Spencer, by Richard Buckner, 1858

Lord Spencer had a love of fine things and took enormous pride in his family inheritance. He had a particular *penchant* for porcelain, of which he formed a huge if somewhat miscellaneous collection, having the unusual ambition of owning at least one example of every manufacture. Through the acquisition of modern and historical portraits, he also made a significant contribution to the family picture collection, and at the same time made improvements to Althorp[3] and Spencer House,[4] neither of which had been touched since the lifetime of the 2nd Earl.

The works at Spencer House were especially extensive. The building meant a great deal to the Earl; he had strenuously opposed his brother's plans to sell the property and he now lavished several thousand pounds on a thorough-going programme of refurbishment. The architect he chose was Philip Hardwick, a leading professional, chiefly remembered today for the magnificent Euston arch, senselessly demolished in 1962. Hardwick, who also worked at Althorp,[5] was assisted at Spencer House by a local firm of decorators, Harmon & Sons of King St, St James's,[6] and by Giles Wakeling, upholsterer to the Admiralty.[7]

The terrace, which was found to be sagging, was buttressed (FIG 218). Gas lighting was introduced and plate-glass windows substituted for the original Georgian sashes. In an unusual display of reverence for the past the first-floor interiors were restored, particular attention being paid to the exact replication of the hangings and upholstery, but the ground-floor apartments were utterly transformed, passing from the cool Classicism of the early nineteenth century to the rich tones and elaboration of the Victorian period.

In the Staircase Hall the stone floor and steps were laid with a luxurious ruby-coloured

[1] *The Times* (1919), 10 Nov, p.20c; 12 Nov, p.17c

[2] Ibid. (1906), 15 Mar, p.10d; 19 Mar, p.6c; 19 Apr, p.6c

[3] AP L5

[4] AP L10–L11

[5] HB, Account of 4th Earl Spencer, Ledger 27, 18 July 1848, payment to Philip Hardwick of £3,546:16:5

[6] Ibid., 10 July 1846, payment to Harmon & Sons of £1646:9:6

[7] Ibid., 20 July 1846, payment to Giles Wakeling of £312:12:6

218 Spencer House, west front; photograph by Bedford Lemere, 1895. Visible in the photograph are the buttresses added to the terrace by Philip Hardwick and the plate glass windows so characteristic of the Victorian age

Saxony carpet with crimson rosettes. Similar carpets were laid in the Palm Room, Ante Room and Library; that in the Library had the additional feature of a central medallion framing Lord Spencer's cypher. The walls of the Ante Room and Library were decorated at first with panels of green lace paper framed by borders ornamented with ribbons, flowers and cable trimmings. Later, however, a rose-patterned paper was introduced, to be replaced in turn by panels of white watered satin paper framed by gilded fillets. The Dining Room, too, was repeatedly redecorated. In 1846 the walls were overlaid with panels of satin damask within ornamental borders; in 1851 sage-green flock paper was substituted, again in panels, with giltwood borders; and in 1856 the paper was stripped and the panelled walls painted a straw colour with the mouldings picked out in white.

As ever, the house continued to be admired. In a guide published around the time of the Great Exhibition the building was described as 'a noble palatial edifice'.[8] A French guide of the same date declared it, '*un beau modèle d'architecture*';[9] another described it as '*vaste et imposant*';[10] and in an Italian guide published in the 1840s the house was ranked among '*i principali . . . edifizi che apartengono a ricchi particolari*'.[11]

As a senior courtier and nobleman, Lord Spencer saw it as a duty to entertain and during his lifetime the house in St James's Place was the setting for many grand receptions. For one such event, in May 1856, the exterior of the building was adorned with an illuminated star, six feet high and powered by gas, superimposed with an anchor and the cypher of the monarch, VR.[12] The following spring the Earl hosted a reception attended by, among others, the Prince and Princess Edward of Saxe-Weimar, together with large numbers of foreign diplomats. In reporting the evening's proceedings, the *Morning Post* paid tribute to the beauty of Spencer House, 'all the magnificent saloons of which were on this occasion thrown open and brilliantly illuminated'.[13] But Lord Spencer's greatest triumph was undoubtedly the reception he gave in honour of the Queen the following July. A reporter from the *Morning Post* was again on hand to record this memorable event:

219 Mansions of Earl Spencer and the Earl of Ellesmere in the Green Park; *engraving by H. Adlard from* London Almanack for 1851. *For a hundred years Spencer House had been the most conspicuous building on the park, but it was dwarfed by Charles Barry's grandiose Italianate palazzo*

THE QUEEN AT SPENCER HOUSE

The Queen honoured the Earl and Countess Spencer with her presence at a ball given in honour of her Majesty, at Spencer House last evening.

The preparations for the reception of her Majesty were marked by all that princely liberality and good taste which distinguishes the household of our highest aristocracy. On the ground floor a suite of rooms were set apart for her Majesty's special service, and in the great ball-room up stairs a dais was erected, on which chairs of state were placed for the use of Her Majesty and the illustrious party by whom she was accompanied.

The whole mansion was illuminated with singular brilliancy, and the atmosphere was redolent of the choicest flowers, with which every available corner was studded.

The company honoured with invitations to be present began to arrive soon after nine o'clock.

Their Royal Highnesses the Duchess of Cambridge and the Princess Mary came shortly before 10 o'clock, attended by Lady Geraldine Somerset and Major Home Purves.

His Royal Highness the Duke of Cambridge, attended by Colonel Tyrwhitt, followed shortly afterwards.

His Serene Highness Prince Frederick of Holstein and Their Serene Highnesses the Prince and Princess Edward of Saxe-Weimar were among the early arrivals . . .

. . . The Queen arrived at 20 minutes after 10 o'clock. Her Majesty was accompanied by the King of the Belgians and the Princess Charlotte of Belgium, the Prince Consort, the Princess Royal, the Count of Flanders, and Prince Frederick William of Prussia.

The Queen was received in the entrance-hall by the Earl and Countess Spencer, whom her Majesty graciously saluted. The Duke of Wellington and the Marquis of Breadalbane were in attendance in their official capacities, and conducted the Sovereign to the apartments prepared for her reception.

Her Majesty entered resting on the arm of the King of the Belgians, the Earl Spencer conducting the Princess Charlotte of Belgium, and the Prince Consort leading the Countess Spencer. The Princess Royal followed with Prince Frederick William of Prussia.

After the lapse of a few moments the Queen ascended to the ball-room, the band playing the National Anthem. The Foreign Ambassadors and Ministers awaited her Majesty's arrival in brilliantly-decorated uniforms opposite the dais, and were graciously acknowledged by the Sovereign.

The Queen having taken her seat upon the chair of state, the other royal personages present assumed places on either side of Her Majesty, who for some moments engaged in animated conversation with the Countess Spencer, the Prince Consort meantime passing round the room, and graciously saluting the principal ladies present.

[8] H. G. Clarke & Co (publ.), *London as it is Today: Where to Go and What to See during the Great Exhibition* (1851), p.97

[9] L. Danel (publ.), *Londres et ses Environs* (Lille, 1851), p.54

[10] Ernest Bourdin (publ.), *Guide Illustré du Voyageur à Londres* (Paris, 1851), p.134

[11] *Descrizione di Londra* (Lucca, *c*1845)

[12] AP L11, Account from William Strode, gas fitter and engineer, 30 May 1856

[13] *The Morning Post* (28 May 1857)

[14] Ibid. (14 July 1857)

LONDON ALMANACK FOR 1851,

being three years afterLeapYear.

MANSIONS OF EARL SPENCER AND THE EARL OF ELLESMERE IN THE GREEN PARK.

At a given intimation from the Lord Chamberlain, the first quadrille was formed, her Majesty leading off with the Earl Spencer, and the Prince Consort dancing with the Countess Spencer. The following danced in the same set:–

Prince Fredk. Wm. of Prussia	...	Princess Charlotte of Belgium
Count of Flanders	...	Princess Royal
Lord Althorp	...	Princess Mary
Prince Edward of Saxe-Weimar	...	Duchess of Manchester
French Ambassador	...	Madame Van de Weyer
Count Chotek	...	Countess Persigny
Duke of Manchester	...	Lady Louisa Hamilton
Mr Thynne	...	Marchioness of Stafford
Viscount Castlerosse	...	Lady Clementina Villiers
Captain Seymour	...	Lady Cecilia Molyneux

Another quadrille having intervened, her Majesty commanded a third set and this time gave her hand to the Prince Frederick William of Prussia, the Prince Consort dancing with the Duchess of Wellington, the Earl Spencer with the Princess Charlotte of Belgium, Lord Althorp with the Princess Edward of Saxe-Weimar, the Duke of Manchester with the Countess Persigny, and Captain Seymour with the Duchess of Manchester.

The ball now became general, her Majesty remaining seated on the dais, and occasionally joining in the dance.

At midnight the Queen was conducted by the Earl and Countess Spencer to the banqueting-room, where a grand dinner was served on gold plate.

Her Majesty retired shortly before one o'clock, attended, as on her arrival, by the Earl and Countess Spencer, who, before the royal departure, received the Queen's gracious acknowledgements for the magnificent *fete* provided for the entertainment of her Majesty and her illustrious relatives.

The festivities were kept up some time after the Queen had taken her departure.[14]

To entertain on such a scale Lord Spencer was obliged to maintain a large body of household servants. A census return for the night of 20 March 1851 reveals that although the Spencers themselves were absent, the house was occupied by a staff of five: a porter, Thomas Noon, fifty years old and a native of Invernesshire; his wife, Jane, also a domestic servant, six years his senior and originally from Northumberland; a housekeeper, Rebecca Stone, thirty-nine years old and a spinster, who was born in Hertfordshire and had worked at Spencer House for a minimum of ten years; and two housemaids, both in their twenties and unmarried, the first a native of Suffolk, the other a Londoner from the parish of St Dunstan's.[15] How many more servants were present when the family was in residence can only be guessed, but thirty or even forty would seem a reasonable estimate.

The Earl's expenses must have been enormous and at various points he was forced to make economies. Over the years he sold off a number of old master paintings;[16] in 1850 he surrendered the southern portion of the garden of Spencer House to his neighbour Lord Ellesmere; and he also disposed of the land and livestock at Wiseton.[17] In the main, however, Lord Spencer managed to live within his means and on his death in December 1857 he left his son John with a handsome fortune, few debts and a title to which he had brought still greater lustre.

[15] PRO HO 107/1484, f.324

[16] AP L19, Nos 37, 88, 176, 183, 307, 326, 345

[17] BL Add MS 35,155, ff.90–91

29 THE RED EARL

220 John, 5th Earl Spencer, seated at his desk in the Palm Room, Spencer House. Originally a drawing room, the Palm Room was converted into a library during the lifetime of the 2nd Earl Spencer but by the end of the nineteenth century it was serving as an office

AT THE TIME he inherited the 5th Earl Spencer was only twenty-two years old, but he had already made a promising start to what was to be a brilliant career in politics. In 1856, fresh down from Cambridge, he stood for the seat of South Northamptonshire and was duly elected, entering the House of Commons as a Liberal M.P. under the leadership of Lord Palmerston. Following his succession he moved from the Commons to the Lords, and on the formation of Gladstone's first administration in 1868 he was appointed Lord Lieutenant of Ireland, a post he occupied for five years. It was in Ireland that Lord Spencer acquired the nickname 'the Red Earl', not, as is sometimes supposed, on account of his long red beard, but because of the resolute and often bloody means by which the security forces under his command cracked down on nationalist terrorism. In 1880 Lord Spencer was appointed Lord President of the Council, having particular responsibility for public education, and in 1882 was again appointed Lord Lieutenant of Ireland, serving in this post until 1885. The following year he once more assumed the duties of Lord President and from 1891 to 1895 served as First Lord of the Admiralty, spearheading the modernization of Britain's navy. In 1902, he was elected Liberal leader in the House of Lords, and it was rumoured at one time that he might become Prime Minister. Although in the last years of his life he suffered from ill health and was forced to retire from the party's front line, he always remained an influential figure.

Alongside his activities as a politician Lord Spencer also did service at Court. As the son of a former Lord Chamberlain, he was already well known to the royal family. His aunt, moreover, Lady Lyttelton, had served for many years as governess of the royal children, and in 1859 the Earl himself was appointed Groom of the Stole to Prince Albert, acting in this capacity until the Consort's death in 1861. The following year he was granted the same position in the household of the Prince of Wales, later Edward VII, and although he resigned his duties in 1866 in order to concentrate on politics, he served the royal family again from 1901 to 1907 as Privy Seal to George, Prince of Wales, afterwards George V.

Following in the tradition of his ancestors, Lord Spencer took a leading part in the affairs of Northamptonshire; he chaired the Quarter Sessions in Northampton and from 1872 was Lord Lieutenant of the county, serving concurrently as Chairman of the County Council. He was likewise active in charity, taking a particular interest in the Northampton Lunatic Asylum, although on one occasion he came dangerously close to joining the inmates. Strolling alone in the grounds one day, he was accosted by two newly-appointed keepers. 'Now, now', said one, 'you come back quietly with us'. 'But my good man', the Earl protested, 'I'm Lord Spencer!' To which the keepers automatically replied, 'That's what they all say here'.[1]

Agriculture was another abiding interest, and in 1898 the Earl was elected President of the Royal Agricultural Society. He also found time for foreign travel and generally spent a part of each year abroad, journeying on the Continent but also to more distant destinations, including America and Canada. Sport, too, was a favourite pastime. As an undergraduate he had hunted with the Cambridgeshire, and during his period in Ireland he often rode out with the Meath, the Ward and the Kildare, while at Althorp he was three times Master of the Pytchley. At the same time he developed an enthusiasm for rifle-shooting and was a founder member and one-time President of the National Rifle Association, frequently taking part in the annual shooting match between the Commons and the Lords.

As head of the family it was Lord Spencer's duty to father an heir, and in 1858, a year after his succession, he married. His choice fell on Charlotte Seymour, a cousin of his step-mother (FIG 221). The same age as himself, Charlotte was considered one of the beauties of the day; the Irish dubbed her 'Spencer's Fairy Queen'. She was cultivated, with a deep interest in the arts and a lively engaging manner which won her many friends and admirers. Sharing many of her husband's interests, she was a great source of companionship and support. The marriage also strengthened the Spencers' ties at Court, since one of Charlotte's sisters, Eliza, wife of the 3rd Viscount Clifden, was Extra Lady of the Bedchamber to Queen Victoria, while another, Augusta, had married a younger son of the 1st Marquess of Ailesbury, who in 1880 became Vice Chamberlain. Sadly, however, the marriage produced no chidren, and Lord Spencer eventually appointed his half-brother, Bobby, his heir.

Despite an excellent education, Lord Spencer was far from bookish. A friend, Margot Asquith, claimed that she had never seen him open a book, let alone read one, and whether in jest or genuine ignorance he once referred in conversation to 'that book *Jane Eyre*, you know, by George Eliot'.[2] However, in matters relating to art he was not without knowledge or discernment and patronized a number of leading painters, among them Leslie and Watts.

Lord Spencer also took an active interest in architecture. Directly he inherited he embarked on an extensive programme of alterations at Althorp, involving the refurbishment of the interior and the creation of a formal garden by Teulon. A few years later, in

[1] Georgina Battiscombe, *The Spencers of Althorp*, p.234

[2] Margot Asquith, *More Memories* (1933), p.87

[3] AP L5–L6

[4] AP L11–L13

[5] AP L11, Frederick Sang to Charlotte, Countess Spencer, 20 May 1873

[6] HB, Account of 5th Earl Spencer, Ledger 11 (1), 13 Dec 1873, payment to Frederick Sang of £800

221 Charlotte Seymour, wife of the 5th Earl Spencer, by Sir Thomas Alfred Jones. Charlotte was one of the beauties of the age and a leading political hostess

1876, he ordered further changes, calling on the services of the well-known architect John MacVicar Anderson, under whose direction the interior was again remodelled.[3]

At Spencer House, too, there were changes.[4] The building had lost none of its power to impress; an architect of the period was quite overcome by 'the great architectural merits of this historical and celebrated Anglo-Italian mansion, which for sober dignity and Palladian proportions stands unrivalled amongst the West End palazzi'.[5] However, in 1873 the Earl judged it appropriate to redecorate and turned for advice to Frederick Sang.[6] Sang was a fashionable London architect and painter, a regular exhibitor at both the Royal Academy and the Royal Society of British Artists, with a clientele of wealthy and aristocratic patrons, including the Marquess of Salisbury and the Earl of Derby. He also had dealings with the Royal Exchange and the Carlton Club and in 1873, the year he was approached by Lord Spencer, there was a public showing of his designs for the reorganization of the government offices in Whitehall. Sang had lived for a time on the Continent, and his work owed much to the prevailing style in France, an eclectic blend of diverse forms and ornaments principally inspired by the art and architecture of the seventeenth and eighteenth centuries. He was apparently recommended to Lord Spencer by a colleague, the Parisian upholsterer and decorator, Barbier, successor to the firm of Chabert and Meurice, who had previously supplied materials for Althorp[7] and was himself to be involved in the works at Spencer House.[8] It was Sang's idea to restore the architectural decoration of the house to what he believed to be its original mid-eighteenth century appearance, suggesting that the ceilings be painted with elaborate Italianate frescoes. He was particularly concerned that the ceiling of the Dining Room should be painted in this way, and spelt out his plans in some detail. 'As to the treatment of the interior', he wrote, 'and in this particular instance of the Dining Room I could recommend no other but the style of the period of the erection of the building and the decorations in vogue from 1700 to 1750 i.e. in the effective and beautiful manner of J. B. da Novarra who about that time carried out some of the best work in Rome such as the vaults and ceilings of the Church of the Apostles'.[9]

The idea that Spencer House might resemble some late Baroque Italian Church did not find favour. Although Sang claimed to have discovered traces of such a scheme under subsequent coats of paint,[10] having in reality uncovered Holland's painted sky, Lord Spencer would not be swayed. Another of Sang's suggestions was similarly rejected, namely that the stone floors in the Entrance Hall, Staircase Hall and ground-floor passageway be replaced in richly coloured marbles – red, green, black and grey – on a variety of different patterns.[11] In the end Sang had to content himself with supervising the implementation of a very different scheme, equally sumptuous but more in line with the tastes of his clients, which was devised by his colleague Barbier.[12] Confining themselves to the Ante Room, Library and Dining Room, the Spencers created a sequence of interiors which would not have looked out of place in the Paris of Napoleon III. The Ante Room and Library were decorated *en suite*, with wall hangings of green *brocatelle* on a lozenge pattern, pleated in the corners, matched by elaborately draped curtains and *capitonné* chair covers of the identical fabric, the niches in the Ante Room being lined with crimson velvet (FIGS 59, 64 and 226, pp. 101, 104 and 253). A contrasting colour scheme was chosen for the Dining Room, where the walls were hung with a yellow silk damask, spotted in gold and framed by cable borders, while matching curtains with tasselled tie-backs were applied to the windows overlooking the park (FIG 66, p. 106).

The house in St James's Place continued to play a vital role in the social and political life of London. The Earl, it was said, 'exercised magnificent hospitality',[13] and his wife established herself as one of the great hostesses of the day. Under her auspices the house became a 'rallying-point of fashion', the state apartments 'thronged with the famous men and women of the time'.[14] The house was especially important as a focus of political activity, a 'great centre of Liberal hospitality', as the Countess of Warwick expressed it,[15] frequently providing the setting for meetings of the Liberal Cabinet. In 1888 the Spencers hosted a famous reception to muster support for the Home Rule Bill, an event, it was said, which 'baffled description' and 'created the greatest excitement in social circles'.[16] Although

[7] AP L6, ff.229–31

[8] HB, Account of 5th Earl Spencer, Ledger 11 (1), 8 Sept 1874, payment to Barbier of £1344 11s

[9] AP L11–L13

[10] In a letter to Lord Spencer Sang wrote, 'In removing the old coats of paint I have discovered the old ornamental painting of panels &c exactly of the style and manner proposed in my design. I have left some of them untouched for your Excellencys inspection' [AP L11, 6 Nov 1873]

[11] AP P19

[12] An album of watercolour drawings by Barbier relating to the redecoration of the ground-floor apartments at Spencer House in the 1870s survived among the Spencer papers until the lifetime of the 7th Earl, but it has not been possible to trace this document, which may perhaps have been sold

[13] *Dictionary of National Biography*, entry for 5th Earl Spencer

[14] Edwin Beresford Chancellor, *The Private Palaces of London, Past and Present*, p345; *The Morning Post* (2 Nov 1903)

[15] Frances, Countess of Warwick, *Afterthoughts* (1931), p.250

[16] Lady St Helier, *Memories of Fifty Years* (1909), p.253

[17] E. W. Hamilton to J. R. Dasent, 10 Mar 1882, quoted in Peter Gordon, *The Red Earl: The Papers of the Fifth Earl Spencer 1835–1910*, 2 vols (Northampton, 1981–86), 1, p.19

[18] Quoted in Gordon, op. cit.

[19] Sir George Leveson Gower, *Years of Content 1858–1886* (1940), p.5

[20] Royal Archives, Diary of George, Duke of York, entry for 16 Feb 1893

[21] Ibid. [attached cutting]

[22] Christopher Simon Sykes, *Private Palaces: Life in the Great London Houses*, p.301

[23] *The Morning Post* (21 July 1881)

[24] William Clowes & Sons (publ.), *Catalogue of an Art Exhibition at Spencer House by the Kind Permission of Earl Spencer K.G. in aid of the East London Branch of the Girls' Friendly Society . . . 16th-22nd March 1887*

[25] *The Morning Post* (20 May 1895)

[26] PRO RG11/128, f.71

222 Dame Alice Ellen Terry, by George Frederick Watts, c1864. At a charity concert at Spencer House in 1895 the actress was among the principal performers

some stayed away, many more attended, 'alive to a little civility', as one contemporary observed, 'especially from a house like Spencer House'.[17] According to Lord Elcho, the house in St James's Place was one of Lord Spencer's greatest political assets. Enumerating his claims to consideration, he argued that the Earl had three key advantages, namely 'station, wealth, and a large Whig house in the centre of London'.[18]

An invitation to dinner at Spencer House was especially prized. The Earl had a colossal appetite and for a number of years employed the celebrated French chef, Monsieur Beguinot, who had formerly worked for the duc de Morny, illegitimate half-brother of Napoleon III. Beguinot had the temperament of a true artist, living only for his work. When asked by Lord Spencer how he wished his rooms to be decorated, he begged that one be fitted out with rich mahogany furniture and dark red hangings providing the necessary inspiration for '*un grand dîner sérieux*', while the other should be decorated in white and pale blue, '*plutôt propice pour quelque combinaison amusante et frivolé*'.[19]

Among the beneficiaries of Lord Spencer's hospitality was the young Duke of York, afterwards George V, who dined at Spencer House in February 1893.[20] According to a newspaper report, the band of the Royal Marine Light Infantry played throughout dinner in an adjoining room, and there was a party afterwards for a hundred guests.[21] Another royal visitor was the Duke of York's father, the Prince of Wales; indeed, in the period following the death of Prince Albert, Spencer House was one of the few London mansions the Queen would allow him to visit. As the sovereign expressed it herself in a letter to Lord Granville, 'The Queen thinks that with the exception of Lord Granville, Lord Palmerston, and possibly Lord Derby, and the three or four only great houses in London, Westminster House, Spencer House, and Apsley House, the Prince and Princess of Wales should not go out to dinners and parties, and not to *all* these in the *same* year.'[22]

Spencer House also continued to provide a setting for important family events, as in 1881 when the Earl's sister, Victoria, married Lord Sandhurst. The ceremony itself took place in St James's Piccadilly, but afterwards bride and groom returned to Spencer House, together with family and friends, including the Prince and Princess of Wales, Princess Mary and the Duke of Teck, while in the garden the Band of the Scots Guards 'performed an excellent programme of music'.[23]

On occasion the house was thrown open for charity events. In 1887 the state apartments were used for an art exhibition in aid of the East London branch of the Girls' Friendly Society. Inaugurated by Lord and Lady Spencer, the exhibition was held under the patronage of the Princess of Wales and Princess Christina of Schleswig-Holstein, featuring jewellery and plate, miniatures, drawings, porcelain, lace embroidery, fans and decorative objects, lent by, among others, Queen Victoria, the Prince of Wales, the Duke of Cambridge, the Duke of Wellington and other members of the royal family and aristocracy. The exhibition was evidently a success, for the catalogue quickly sold out and had to be reprinted.[24] A few years later, in May 1895, the Spencers hosted a charity concert for the Hoxton Working Men's Club and Soup Kitchen, which featured performances by Ellen Terry (FIG 222) and Letty Lind.[25]

Although childless, the Spencers maintained a large establishment. The census of 1881 reveals that they were attended at this time by no fewer than twenty-nine servants.[26] The stables in Catherine Wheel Yard were manned by a coachman, George Cheris, fifty-two years old and a widower, who came originally from Hampshire and worked in conjunction with a groom, Ernest Callow, a married man in his early twenties, whom the Spencers had recruited from the neighbourhood of Althorp. In addition there were five other servants, simply described as 'helpers', all of whom were bachelors from outside

London, ranging in age from twenty-three to thirty-eight. In the main body of the house there was a resident steward, James Wilson, thirty-five years old and married, from Petersham in Surrey; a valet, John Harland, also married, thirty-one years old and a native of Stroud in Gloucestershire; an under-butler, Theodore Gillingham, forty-five years old, from Shaftesbury in Dorset; a porter, Christopher Churchill, a married man in his fifties who came originally from Carton in Wiltshire and had worked at Spencer House for at least ten years; and three footmen, all in their twenties and unmarried, from outside London, assisted by a junior domestic, Alfred Gibbons, likewise a bachelor, twenty years old and a native of Leeds in Kent. The housekeeper was the same Rebecca Stone who had held this position for over thirty years, having worked at Spencer House for at least forty. Now approaching her seventy-sixth birthday, she remained a spinster. Working under her control were two kitchen maids, three laundry maids, a still-room maid and seven other assorted maidservants. With the exception of Jane Churchill, wife

223 Spencer House, Palm Room; photograph of c1890. As the photograph reveals, the original furniture from the Palm Room had been removed

of the porter, all the female servants were unmarried; most were from outside London and in their twenties or early thirties. One, Emma Dunkley, came from the village of Brington near Althorp. Others were from as far afield as Scotland and the north of England. There were far fewer servants when the Spencers were away, of course, although five was apparently considered the minimum and the number could rise to eight.[27]

Large households were by now becoming a thing of the past. Along with other great landowning families, the Spencers saw their income dwindle as a result of the agricultural depresssion which began in the late 1870s. Prior to the depression rents from their estates were calculated at between £40,000 and £50,000 a year, but by 1885 the total had dropped by some 40 percent to around £25,000. Althorp was especially hard hit, rents declining from £21,000 in 1890 to £12,000 in 1895. At the same time the value of land was plummeting, forced down by panic selling, and the Spencers saw their principal asset reduced to a fraction of its former worth. To make matters worse, the family also lost out in the collapse of Barings Bank.

In 1879 the Earl was forced to borrow £15,000, and in 1885 he took out an additional loan of £40,000. At the same time he scaled down his living expenses, but it soon became obvious that a larger sacrifice was required, and in 1892 he sold the famous library assembled by the 2nd Earl, which was acquired by the widow of a leading industrialist, John Rylands, and presented to Manchester University.

The sale raised over £200,000, and enabled Lord Spencer to install electric light at Spencer House,[28] but his financial difficulties continued and he therefore resolved to lease the property and move to more modest accommodation. Indeed as early as 1886 he had instructed his solicitor to seek out a suitable tenant. The property market was then severely depressed and, as the solicitor explained, finding a tenant of sufficient means was 'no easy matter. . . . Nearly everyone is so poor now, nothing seems to sell or let'.[29] However, in 1889 Spencer House was taken for a spell by an unnamed American, recorded only as a 'yankee',[30] and from this time onward the Earl and Countess lived there only intermittently, the building being occupied by a succession of remarkable and sometimes improbable tenants.

[27] PRO RG10/135, f.57 [1871]; RG12/86, f.9 [1891]

[28] AP L13

[29] W. S. Forster to Earl Spencer, 20 June 1886, quoted in Gordon, op. cit., 2, p.36

[30] Earl Spencer to Earl Granville, 22 Dec 1889, quoted in Gordon, op. cit., 2, p.163

30 THE GREAT BARNATO

SPENCER HOUSE found its most colourful tenant in Barnie Barnato, otherwise known as the Great Barnato, a famous tycoon and one of the richest men in Victorian England (FIG 224). Through business dealings in South Africa involving diamonds, gold, real estate and banking, Barnato had built up a colossal fortune estimated in the tens of millions. He was an elected member of the Cape Legislative Assembly and a founder and Life Governor of de Beers. He owned newspapers, breweries and race-horses; there was a park in Johannesburg that bore his name. He had links with royalty and was the toast of the world's stock markets. The Lord Mayor of London gave a banquet in his honour, and in 1895, the year he moved to Spencer House, he was reckoned to be the most highly-paid businessman in England, reputedly earning a full five pounds for every minute of his working day.

But there was another Barnie Barnato, or Barnett Isaacs to give him his true name, a poor boy from London's East End, born into a penniless Jewish family in 1852. His father was a second-hand clothes merchant and as a boy Barnato received only the most rudimentary education, leaving school at the age of thirteen in a state of semi-literacy. At first he worked as a bouncer in a local pub for, although he was woefully short-sighted and only five feet three inches tall, he was remarkably strong and nimble on his feet. Daniel Mendoza, the famous Jewish prize-fighter, was a boyhood idol and at one stage Barnato considered a career in professional boxing. He also toyed with the idea of becoming an actor, modelling himself on Edmund Kean and Henry Irving, and memorizing speeches from Shakespeare; but the closest he came to Stratford-upon-Avon were the music halls of Whitechapel, and his most serious role was that of a clown-cum-acrobat in a tight-rope and juggling act he devised with his brother Harry. It was at this point, as a means of attracting an audience, that Barnett Isaacs took the more flamboyant name Barnato.

The stage act was not a success, and to supplement his earnings Barnato was forced to run errands for local tradesmen. For a time he plucked chickens for a Kosher poultry butcher, and when a barrow was available he would hawk old clothes and fruit in Petticoat Lane and Hatton Garden. But already he was dreaming of better things. A cousin had recently embarked for South Africa, sending back glowing accounts of the country's wealth and prospects and, as soon as he had scraped together the money, Barnato bought a one-way ticket and joined him. Some twenty years later he had amassed a fortune reckoned at over £20,000,000.

Barnato was not only rich; he was also lucky in love. In his wife, Fanny, he found the perfect partner. His physical ideal, he once confided, was Queen Boadicea, and Fanny was certainly stout. She was also Jewish, and in quick succession brought forth three healthy children, including two sons. In June 1894 the family moved to London, for Barnato had plans to branch into Europe. They lodged at first in rented accommodation in Curzon Street, but Barnato was determined to build a house of his own and by the following year had acquired a large freehold site on Park Lane belonging to the Duke of Westminster.

Barnato was not the first of the so-called Randlords to move to Park Lane; Beit and

"Barney" Barnato.

224 'Barney' Barnato; *drawing by H. Furniss, c1895. Born into a penniless Jewish family in the slums of Whitechapel, Barnato rose to become one of the wealthiest businessmen of his generation. In 1895 he took a lease on Spencer House, but his tenancy came to an abrupt and dramatic end when he was drowned at sea in mysterious circumstances in 1897*

Robinson had both established footholds here. But in architecture, as in business, Barnato meant to outdo his rivals. Passing one day in front of Dudley House, the property taken by Robinson, Barnato sneered to a companion, 'I'd half a mind once to buy that property. It's got such a splendid place for the baby's perambulator'.[1] He was equally withering about the house of Alfred de Rothschild in Piccadilly. Rothschild was regarded as an authority in artistic matters and his house was considered the *nec plus ultra* of architectural propriety; but Barnato was unimpressed. When it was suggested to him that he might seek Rothschild's advice in connection with his own building plans, he laughed, 'I don't need *his* help. Why, his house would go into my hall!'[2]

[1] Stanley Jackson, *The Great Barnato* (1970), p.164

[2] Ibid., p.163

225

Barnato planned to build on a monumental scale. The house dreamt up by his architect, T. H. Smith, was a Renaissance palace, approximating in style to a Loire chateau, five storeys high with a central top-lit staircase, the exterior encased in finest Portland stone (FIG 225). The ball room alone covered 2,000 square feet, and no expense was spared in construction.[3] Before acquiring the site, which in itself cost £30,000, Barnato received a letter from the Duke of Westminster's land agent asking for an assurance that he would spend at least another £20,000 on the projected house. 'Tell the Duke', Barnato replied, 'that I plan to spend that on the stables alone'.[4]

[3] *The Builder* (10 Oct 1896)

[4] Jackson, op. cit., p.162

225 Palazzo Barnato, Park Lane; illustration from The Builder *(10 October 1896). Inspired by the châteaux of the Loire, Barnato's Park Lane mansion was one of the last great houses to be built in London. Barnato himself never lived there and the building has since been demolished*

It was estimated that the house would take two years to build, and since Barnato's lease in Curzon Street was coming to an end, he cast about for another house to rent in the interval. He first approached the Duke of Wellington, offering to rent Apsley House but, as the Duke was still in residence and had never expressed the slightest intention of moving, Barnato's impertinence met with a stiff refusal. Not long afterwards, however, his eye fell on Spencer House, which was available for rent and which in addition to the splendour of its architecture had one other key advantage. As Barnato expressed it in a newspaper interview, 'It's not a bad position. Exactly half-way between the Prince of

226

226 Spencer House, Ante Room; photograph by Bedford Lemere, 1895. The photograph shows the room as decorated by Barbier twenty years earlier. The walls were hung with green brocatelle, while the niches in the alcove were lined with crimson velvet. The Louis XVI seat furniture had probably been introduced by Henry Holland

227 Spencer House, Great Room, looking south; photograph by Bedford Lemere, 1895. Prominent in the photograph are the paintings by Guercino acquired by the 1st Earl Spencer through Gavin Hamilton. Electricity had been installed in 1892 and dozens of light bulbs are visible above the cornice. The seating furniture would originally have been backed up against the walls

Wales in Marlborough House and the P.M. in Arlington Street'.[5] Barnato was prepared to pay the whole rent at once, and as Spencer confided to Rosebery, 'I felt I ought not to refuse so good an offer'.[6]

It is unlikely the Prince of Wales or Lord Salisbury ever visited Spencer House during Barnato's occupation; but if they had they would have found themselves surrounded by a very different crowd from that at the Court and Westminster. With the bounteous hospitality for which he was famous, Barnato threw open the state apartments to people from his own world; to bookies and jockeys, actors and impresarios, boxers and journalists, orthodox rabbis and impoverished Jewish scholars.

Barnato had little appreciation of art; he only ever bought one painting, a study of sheep, and when asked why he had chosen it replied, 'Because one of them looks like me'.[7] However, he was greatly taken by the state apartments, especially the Painted Room, where he liked to stand at night with his back to the fireplace, admiring his surroundings. At other times, however, he could be found in less reverent mood, walking about the state apartments on his hands, a trick remembered from his days as an acrobat, bringing squeals of delight from his children. Although proud of his connection with the house, he was never overawed. Nor did he ever lose sight of his own considerable achievements and position. On one occasion he was summoned to Marlborough Street Magistrates Court in order to vouch for a friend facing bankruptcy charges. When asked by the judge where he lived, he loudly replied, 'Spencer House'. Astonished, the judge exclaimed, 'But that's Lord Spencer's house. Are you his major-domo?' 'No', Barnato bellowed, 'I'm my own bloody domo!'[8]

Barnato had never lost his love of the theatre; nor had he given up the ambition of becoming an actor. During his time at Spencer House he worked on a play based on his own life, assisted by a professional playwright, Haddon Chambers. Chambers later recalled that during meetings at Spencer House, Barnato would strut about the rooms acting out scenes from his colourful past. Barnato had hopes of staging the play at the Criterion. If necessary, he declared, he would buy up the theatre and form his own company; but the play was never written, let alone performed.

About the time Barnato moved to Spencer House his business fortunes began to dwindle. As they did so he took to drink and suffered bouts of delirium in which he imagined that money was turning to dust in his hands and that the walls were encrusted with diamonds, which he would try to prize free with his finger-nails. In June 1897, having travelled out to the Cape, he was returning by steamship to England when, in mysterious circumstances which were never clarified, he fell into the sea and was drowned. The Johannesburg stock exchange ceased trading for a day as a mark of respect; thousands turned out for the funeral at the Jewish cemetery in Willesden. The chateau in Park Lane, so close to completion, was snapped up by the Sassoons, and a remarkable chapter in the history of Spencer House came to an abrupt and dramatic end.

[5] Ibid., p.164

[6] Earl Spencer to Earl of Rosebery, 8 Sept 1895, quoted in Peter Gordon, *The Red Earl: The Papers of the Fifth Earl Spencer 1835–1910*, 2, p.36

[7] Jackson, op. cit., p.163

[8] Ibid., p.190

31 SPENCER COUSINS

SPENCER HOUSE was next let to Lord Spencer's cousin, the Duke of Marlborough, and his American-born wife, Consuelo Vanderbilt, daughter of the famous railway millionaire. It was the Marlboroughs' intention to remain at Spencer House for the Season only, partly to entertain during this, the year of Queen Victoria's Diamond Jubilee, but primarily for the purposes of parturition. The Duchess was heavily pregnant, and it was felt that she should give birth in suitably august surroundings. The Duke was hoping for an heir and his dreams were fulfilled when on 18 September 1897 the Duchess was safely delivered of a boy in Lady Spencer's Dressing Room, which had been converted as a bedroom.

The Marlboroughs' marriage was not a happy one, however, and later ended in divorce; it was said the Duke only married Consuelo in order to finance the restoration of Blenheim. Nonetheless the Duchess had the fondest memories of her time in St James's Place. In her memoirs she recalled that the birth of her son was a particularly joyful moment, although she claimed to have been troubled by a spectre from the past:

> On September 18, 1897, my first son was born. We had taken Spencer House, overlooking Green Park, for the event. It was fitting that Churchills should be born there, since they were descendants of the Spencer family . . . Spencer House was an eighteenth-century mansion partly decorated by the brothers Adam [sic]. As the bedrooms were small, I occupied a corner drawing-room and from my bed could see the fine gallery with the vista of a further room painted in the Pompeian style. There were nights when a cold draught would wake me; it was as if a presence had glided through the room. My mother, who had come from America to be with me, professed to have seen a ghost.[1]

Another important event was the famous fancy-dress party at Devonshire House, which took place a short time earlier. Guests were required to wear 'allegorical or historical costume of the period before 1815', and the Marlboroughs joined with others in forming a procession representing the court of Catherine the Great, with the Duke as French Ambassador and the Duchess as Lady-in-Waiting to the Empress. Both were splendidly arrayed. The Duke wore a straw-coloured velvet costume, copied from a genuine Louis XV original, over a white and gold damask waistcoat, the whole set off by elaborate embroidery with silver, pearls and diamonds (FIG 228). The outfit was produced by the celebrated French *couturier*, Worth, who afterwards recalled that it had taken several dress-makers the best part of a month to complete and was probably the most expensive commission he ever received. 'When I came to make out the bill', he confessed, 'I was almost afraid to begin it'.[2]

The Duchess was equally captivating, her hair hooped and powdered, her rounded figure cleverly concealed by a magnificent pale green satin dress richly embroidered with garlands of roses and resplendent jewellery, including a diamond girdle (FIG 229). Other guests at the ball included the Prince and Princess of Wales, the Duke and Duchess of York and other members of the royal family, together with all the most prominent figures from politics, diplomacy and the upper reaches of the aristocracy. The event was still fresh in the Duchess's mind more than half a century later when she recalled how, as

[1] Consuelo Vanderbilt Balsan, *The Glitter and the Gold* (1953), p.97

[2] Sophia Murphy, *The Duchess of Devonshire's Ball* (1984), p.63

[3] Vanderbilt Balsan, op. cit., p.96

dawn broke over London, she walked back to Spencer House through Green Park still wearing her eighteenth-century ball gown, causing astonishment among the homeless community camped out on the grass:

> The fancy dress ball at Devonshire House was a fitting climax to a brilliant season. The ball lasted to the early hours of morning, and the sun was rising as I walked through Green Park to Spencer House, where we then lived. On the grass lay the dregs of humanity. Human beings too dispirited or sunk to find work or favour, they sprawled in sodden stupor, pitiful representatives of the submerged tenth. In my billowing period dress, I must have seemed to them a vision of wealth and youth, and I thought soberly that they must hate me. But they only looked, and some even had a compliment to enliven my progress.[3]

228 The Duke of Marlborough in the costume he wore to the Duchess of Devonshire's fancy dress ball, 1897. The costume was an exact replica of a Louis XV original, made by the great French couturier Worth. 'When I came to make out the bill', Worth confessed, 'I was almost afraid to begin it'

229 Consuelo Vanderbilt, Duchess of Marlborough, dressed as the wife of the French Ambassador to the Court of Catherine the Great, 1897. Although seven months pregnant at the time, the Duchess's rounded figure was cleverly disguised by her costume

228

229

PART VI

THE TWENTIETH CENTURY

32 AN ENIGMATIC BARON

IN 1901 SPENCER HOUSE was let to Mrs Ogden Goelet, wife of a prominent New York property developer.[1] Mrs Goelet had come to London for the Season and was probably introduced to the Spencers by the Duchess of Marlborough, being a close friend of the Vanderbilts. Mr Goelet, who is chiefly remembered for the fact that he owned two steam yachts, each over 300 feet long, apparently remained in New York. Little is known of Mrs Goelet's tenancy, but she would probably have felt at home amid the Greek Revival decoration of the Stuart rooms; she later buried her husband in a Greek Revival mausoleum.[2]

In the early part of 1902 Spencer House was let again,[3] but by the autumn it had been vacated and the Spencers decided to return. However, it was about this time that the Countess was suddenly taken ill. Cancer was diagnosed and the celebrated woman physician, Dr Mary Scharlieb, was summoned to Spencer House, where a two-hour operation was performed.[4] The Countess responded well, but the following June she was caught in a sudden downpour while travelling in an open carriage and quickly developed pneumonia, leading to an attack of paralysis. For four months she lay at Spencer House but her condition steadily deteriorated and on 31 October she died. Lord Spencer had less need than ever of a grand London mansion and in 1905 Spencer House was let to an Austrian nobleman, the Baron de Forest.[5]

The Baron de Forest is something of an enigma. He was born in 1879, but it is not known where; nor is it known who his true parents were. He is said to have been the adopted son of the German Jewish railway millionaire, Baron de Hirsch,[6] yet he was educated at Eton and Christchurch and does not appear to have had any sort of Jewish upbringing. Nor is there any mention of him in biographies of Hirsch, who was himself an orthodox Jew and an ardent Zionist. Presumably he inherited a share of Hirsch's fortune, for his own wealth was colossal. By the time he was thirty he had amassed a priceless art collection, and during the time he lived at Spencer House he also rented Stowe in Buckinghamshire while maintaining a large estate in Austria. His connection with Austria is unclear; in 1899 he was granted the title Baron de Forest by the Emperor Franz Josef, but the following year he became a naturalized British citizen and applied successfully for his title to be officially recognized by Queen Victoria. Cementing his ties with the Establishment, he joined the Prince of Wales's Own Norfolk Artillery Militia, later serving with the Staffordshire Imperial Yeomanry, and in 1904, after a mysterious first marriage annulled the previous year, he married the daughter of an English peer, Lord Gerard, by whom he had two sons. At the same time he pursued a career in politics, not, as one might expect, on the Tory side, but as an 'advanced radical'.[7] In 1910 he was elected to the Kennington division of the London County Council, a position he held until 1913, and from 1911 to 1918 he was M.P. for West Ham. During the First World War he fought on the side of the Allies and saw action in France, but he later cut his ties with England and emigrated to Liechtenstein, where in 1920 he was granted the title Count de Bendern, relinquishing his Austro-Britannic barony. In 1932 he became a naturalized citizen of the principality and in 1936 was appointed Diplomatic Councillor,

[1] AP L13, Memorandum, 26 July 1901

[2] Robert Stern *et al*, *New York 1900: Metropolitan Architecture and Urbanism 1890–1915* (New York, 1983), p.131

[3] Peter Gordon, *The Red Earl: The Papers of the Fifth Earl Spencer 1835–1910*, 2, p.37

[4] Mary Scharlieb, *Reminiscences* (1924), p.176

[5] AP L13, *Schedule of repairs and alterations agreed to be done at Spencer House, St James's SW under the agreement between the Rt. Honble Earl Spencer KG and the Baron de Forest dated May 26th 1905*

[6] Information on the Baron de Forest is principally derived from back copies of *Debrett's* and *Dod's Parliamentary Companion*

[7] *Dod's Parliamentary Companion* (1912 edn), p.270

[8] Edwin Beresford Chancellor, *The Private Palaces of London, Past and Present*, pp.343–4

[9] Ibid., p.342

PAGE 258
Spencer House, the Palm Room in use as a typing pool (FIG 256, p. 289)

230 Spencer House, Painted Room, c1908. The photograph shows the interior cleared of its Neo-Classical furnishings and decorated with pieces from the collection of its then occupant, the Baron de Forest

after which time nothing more is heard of him until his death at Biarritz in 1968, recorded only in the *New York Times*.

The Baron lived at Spencer House until shortly before the outbreak of the First World War, filling the state apartments with some of his many art treasures (FIG 230). A visitor noted portraits by van Dyck in the Ante Room, together with works by Turner, Greuze, Cuyp and Holbein; paintings by Jan Steen and Ter Borch in the Library; and in the Dining Room a famous pair of Boulle armoires, formerly belonging to the Duke of Hamilton, accompanied by a *Holy Family* by Murillo, a portrait of the Duchess of Buckingham by van Dyck and a study of a boy with a flute by Frans Hals.[8]

The house still had the power to impress. The historian Edwin Beresford Chancellor, who visited the building in 1908, was particularly struck by the Painted Room and in one of the most purple passages of a particularly purple period in English prose declared, 'When we enter this apartment we seem to be stepping back two thousand years; we are no longer in a London reception-room; we are in the *tablinium* in the house of Marcus Lucretius, or in one of the remarkable painted chambers in the dwelling of Meleager; that red light in the sky is not the sun setting over the trees of the Green Park, but the afterglow of some great eruption of Vesuvius! If a door open, surely Glaucus or Diomed or the blind Nydia will appear! It is truly a room in which to dream of the past'.[9]

33 INCOMPARABLE SHIRT-FRONTS, MIRACULOUS COLLARS

In 1910, as the Baron de Forest was entering his fifth year of residence, there came word from Althorp that Lord Spencer had died. The Earl had been in poor health for several years. In 1904 he suffered a heart attack and the following year a stroke. In 1908 he was obliged to resign as Lord Lieutenant of Northamptonshire and on 13 August 1910 he suffered a second stroke, which proved fatal.

As expected, Lord Spencer was succeeded as 6th Earl by his half-brother Bobby. Short in stature, yet trim and immaculately groomed, Bobby Spencer was the model of an Edwardian dandy. He prided himself on a physical resemblance to Charles I and was widely regarded as one of the best-dressed men of his generation (FIG 231). A contemporary remarked with awe on his 'incomparable shirt-front, his irreproachable cuffs, and his miraculous collar'.[1] Yet beneath this foppish exterior was a shrewd and serious character, gifted and ambitious.

In 1880, fresh down from Cambridge, Spencer was elected Liberal M.P. for North Northamptonshire, a seat he held until 1885 when he successfully contested Mid-Northamptonshire. Although he was defeated in the election of 1895, and failed to win the seat of East Hertfordshire in 1898, he was again returned for Mid-Northamptonshire in 1900. At the same time he pursued a career at Court, where family connections, combined with his own charm and energy, guaranteed him swift promotion. In 1886 he was appointed Groom-in-Waiting to the Queen, and from 1892 until 1895 he served as Vice-Chamberlain, rising to Chamberlain in 1905 following the accession of Edward VII. Since by tradition the Chamberlain was always a peer, Spencer was now created Viscount Althorp, a title to which he had an obvious claim as heir to the Spencer earldom, and departed the Commons for the Lords. When George V came to the throne in 1910 Spencer was retained as Chamberlain, serving in this capacity until 1912 when he resigned in favour of his brother-in-law, Lord Sandhurst. In his final years he was showered with honours, including the Garter.

In 1887 Spencer married Margaret Baring of the well-known banking family, a daughter of the 1st Lord Revelstoke, Director of the Bank of England, and a sister of the distinguished writer, Maurice Baring. Margaret was not only rich but beautiful, intelligent and cultivated, a gifted musician and linguist. Once again the marriage brought the Spencers closer to the royal family, for Margaret's younger sister, Susan, later served as Maid of Honour to Queen Victoria and was married to the royal physician, Sir James Reid.

Margaret bore her husband six children, three boys and three girls. The eldest boy eventually succeeded as 7th Earl Spencer and, with the Prince of Wales as sponsor, was christened Albert Edward John, although from the earliest times he was known to the family as Jack. From Harrow he went to Trinity College, Cambridge, and on the

[1] Sir Henry Lucy, quoted in Georgina Battiscombe, *The Spencers of Althorp*, p.241

[2] *The Times* (1928), 13 Feb, p.12d; 14 Feb, p.13g; 16 Feb, pp.14c, 19d; 17 Feb, p.16c; 25 Feb, p.15c

[3] Ibid. (1955), 10 May, p.13c; 12 May, p.12c; 13 May, p.13b

[4] Ibid. (1906), 5 July, p.12e; 6 July, p.10b; 10 July, p.10b

[5] Sir Almeric Fitzroy, *Memoirs*, 2 vols (1925), 2, p.579

[6] Royal Archives, Diaries of George V and Queen Mary

231 An Expert in Ceremony; *caricature of Charles Robert, 6th Earl Spencer, by Spy, from* Vanity Fair. *The Earl was famed for the height and stiffness of his collars, which the present caricature scarcely exaggerates*

outbreak of war joined the 1st Life Guards. Wounded in action, he was transferred from the front in 1917 and served for the remainder of the war as A.D.C. on the King's personal staff. In 1919 he married Lady Cynthia Hamilton, a distant cousin, daughter of the 3rd Duke of Abercorn, by whom he had two children, including a son, so ensuring the succession in the next generation.

Lord Spencer's second son, Cecil, attended the Royal Naval College at Osborne and Dartmouth, where he studied alongside Prince Edward, later Edward VIII, and in 1912 joined the navy. He served with distinction during the First World War and was awarded both the *Croix de Guerre* and the Distinguished Service Cross. A Lieutenant-Commander while still in his twenties, he accompanied the Prince of Wales on his official tour of Australia and New Zealand in 1920, and seemed destined for the highest honours, but was killed in a riding accident in 1928.[2]

Lord Spencer's youngest son, George, also entered the navy but retired at the rank of Sub-Lieutenant, and after a brief spell in the army moved abroad, banished, it is said, for some unspecified breach of conduct. Having married twice and fathered two children, he died in 1982.

Of the Spencer girls the eldest, Delia, was a brilliant musician like her mother, a student and later a Fellow of the Royal College of Music. In 1914 she married Colonel the Hon. Sidney Peel, younger son of the 1st Viscount Peel, who after a distinguished career as a soldier, barrister, M.P. and Foreign Office Adviser, was created a Baronet in 1936. Delia was herself appointed Woman of the Bedchamber to H. M. Queen Elizabeth The Queen Mother, accompanying the royal family on their post-war tour of South Africa, and in 1950 became a Dame Commander of the Victorian Order. Lord Spencer's second daughter, Lavinia, married Luke White, 4th Baron Annaly, a hero of the First World War, and served for a time at Court as Extra Lady-in-Waiting to H. M. Queen Elizabeth The Queen Mother when Duchess of York.[3] The youngest daughter, Margaret, to whom Queen Alexandra was sponsor, was born in 1906 and became a brilliant pianist, studying for a time at the Conservatoire in Paris. She later married the Hon. Henry Montagu Douglas-Home, younger son of the 1st Earl of Home and brother of the future Prime Minister, Alec Douglas-Home.

Tragically Margaret's mother died in childbirth with her,[4] and at forty-nine Bobby Spencer was left alone to bring up the family. His eldest daughter, Delia, gradually assumed the responsibilities of mother and hostess, but family life never regained its former spirit. Although he continued to discharge his public duties, Bobby became increasingly depressed and withdrawn. He never remarried and for the rest of his life always wore some token of mourning. He could not bear to hear his wife's name mentioned and a painful silence was maintained even by his children.

In 1914 the Baron de Forest departed Spencer House and the Spencer family returned to St James's Place. The Earl complained to a friend that he had found the interior 'in a state of indescribable filth',[5] but order was quickly re-established and the following year the house was visited by George V and Queen Mary.[6] The Queen was known for her love of art and architecture, but also for her habit of acquiring other people's belongings; if anything caught her fancy she would simply let drop a compliment and the hapless owner would have little choice but to make her a present of it. Those in the know generally took the precaution of hiding their best belongings, and one wonders whether the Spencers did likewise. Another royal visitor to Spencer House was Queen Alexandra, godmother to the Earl's youngest daughter, whose arrival in St James's Place also caused alarm. Although in her seventies, and quite deaf, the Queen insisted on a full guided tour, and after escorting her around the house, bellowing at the top of his voice, the Earl was so exhausted he retired to bed.[7]

During the early part of the First World War the house remained open and in use. Lord Spencer's son, Cecil, spent two weeks' leave there in January 1915.[8] However, the state apartments were kept shut, except on rare occasions, with their contents under wraps, and when it finally became apparent that the war would not be won as easily or as quickly as most had imagined, Lord Spencer offered the house to the Government rent-free for the duration.[9]

Quite apart from the slaughter, the war had a devastating effect on the economy and radically transformed the social order. When the fighting ended Lord Spencer found himself in the same precarious position as other members of the aristocracy, who had seen their wealth and status dramatically eroded. The process of decline had begun much earlier of course, long before the conflict in Europe. From the time of the Reform Act the aristocracy had been losing political power, while the Industrial Revolution led to a steady reduction in the value of land, on which their wealth and position had always depended. The agricultural depression of the 1870s and 1880s was another blow, and the value of land was forced down further by the wave of panic-selling which followed the announcement of Lloyd George's budget proposals in 1909. Equally damaging was the introduction in 1889 of death duties, which were substantially stiffened in 1894. The Spencers saw their own land holdings decline by almost 30 per cent, while the death of the 5th Earl left a crippling tax bill. Paintings were sold;[10] expenses were trimmed; but in the end the family was forced once more to give up its London house and in 1920 the property was let to Prince and Princess Christopher of Greece.[11]

[7] Lady Margaret Douglas-Home, *A Mere Miss Poyntz*

[8] *Priscilla Napier, A Memoir of the Lady Delia Peel, born Spencer, 1889–1981* (Norfolk, 1984), p.90

[9] *The Times* (27 Sept 1922), p.12d

[10] AP L19, Nos 20, 33, 300

[11] AP L14, Memorandum of 10 May 1920

34 A PRINCE AND HIS PRINCESS

232 Prince Christopher of Greece in the uniform of a Greek General. The Prince moved to Spencer House following his marriage to Nancy Leeds, widow of an American tin-plate millionaire

233 Princess Christopher of Greece. The photograph carries a loving inscription to the Prince

PRINCE AND PRINCESS CHRISTOPHER were an unusual couple, even by the standards of the 1920s. The Prince was immaculately royal (FIG 232). His father was King George I of the Hellenes, his nephew George II. His mother was a Romanov, a niece of Tsar Nicolas I, and he was likewise related to the English royal family through his paternal grandfather, King Christian IX of Denmark, father of Queen Alexandra. The Princess came of less exalted stock. She had entered the world as plain Miss Nancy Steward, the daughter of a small-time businessman in Cleveland, Ohio (FIG 233). She was eight years the Prince's senior, although she claimed to be four years younger, and had been married twice before. Her first husband was a Mr George E. Worthington, whom she divorced. Her second was William B. Leeds, a tin-plate manufacturer, who on his death in 1908 left a fortune estimated at £40,000,000. From a grand apartment on New York's Fifth Avenue, Nancy moved to London a short time before the First World War. When a charity event arranged by a group of aristocratic ladies went disastrously wrong, Nancy stepped in with a five-figure cheque and immediately became an accepted member of fashionable society. Her generosity reached the ears of Prince Christopher, who was also in London at this time and after a whirlwind romance he proposed. Society gossips made the obvious connection, and there can be little doubt that Nancy's money was later used to fund the anti-Republican activities which for a short while kept Prince Christopher's nephew, George II, on the Greek throne. The Prince, however, preferred to reflect on Nancy's charm and kindness rather than her millions. 'She was pretty rather than beautiful', he mused in his memoirs, 'On the surface she reminded one of a Dresden china figure with her fair hair, small regular features and flawless pink and white colouring. But underneath it she had an exceptionally keen brain, a tremendous sense of humour and the kindest heart in the world.'[1]

Nancy naturally accepted the Prince's proposal. The Prince was young and dashing with a romantic past and provided an immediate entrée to the highest social circles. Indeed Nancy later managed to marry off a son from her previous marriage to Prince Chistopher's niece, Princess Xenia, a member of the Russian royal family. But at this point the war intervened and it was not until 1920 that Nancy and the Prince were finally united. Immediately after the wedding the couple settled at Spencer House and for a time maintained a busy social life, although rather unusually for newly-weds they kept to separate rooms, the Princess sleeping alone in Lady Spencer's Dressing Room. However, it was fast becoming apparent that the Princess was not at all well, and in 1923 cancer was diagnosed. The patient was never informed; the truth was deliberately kept from her, and the Prince continued to dine out with friends and attend receptions, in an effort, he claimed, to maintain the illusion that there was nothing seriously the matter. But from this time forward the Princess never stirred from her bed, and it was here on 29 August 1923 that she died.

The funeral over, Prince Christopher packed up his belongings and departed for New York.[2] Not long afterwards he married again, his second wife being the daughter of the duc de Guise, pretender to the French throne. Although in later life he became a Major-General in the Greek Army, he died in Athens in January 1940 and so was spared the worst of the Second World War. As for Nancy's son and his wife the Russian princess, their marriage soon foundered and ended in divorce.

[1] Prince Christopher of Greece, *Memoirs* (Plymouth, 1938), p.121

[2] *The Times* (1923), 30 Aug, p.11a & c; 3 Sept, p.9g; 7 Sept, p.13a & b

35 THE CURATOR EARL

234 Albert Edward John, 7th Earl Spencer, by Augustus John. The Earl never liked this portrait but it captures exactly his gruff demeanour and strong sense of family honour

235 Lady Cynthia Hamilton, wife of the 7th Earl Spencer, by Sir William Nicholson, 1932. For a brief time the Countess presided over the house in St James's Place, where in 1924 the Earl's younger sister Margaret had her coming-out party

THE DEATH OF PRINCESS CHRISTOPHER had been preceded by that of Lord Spencer, who died in September 1922[1] to be succeeded by his eldest son. In many ways the 7th Earl Spencer stands outside the Spencer tradition. He was a Tory, not a Liberal; he never stood for Parliament, never held political office and never served at Court; he had opted for the army over the navy, and although he hunted in his youth, he later abandoned the sport. Of all the Spencers, however, there was surely none who better understood his family history or so revered his ancestors.

Jack Spencer has gone down in history as 'the Curator Earl'. Although active in many other areas, especially charity and local politics in Northamptonshire, most of his life was devoted to the arts and more particularly the consolidation and expansion of the Spencer collection. He began, and largely completed, the monumental task of sorting the family archives, which he generously placed at the disposal of scholars. He opened the house at Althorp to the public and frequently gave tours and lectures, also lending paintings,

[1] *The Times* (27 Sept 1922), p.12d

234

235

jewellery and other works of art for public exhibition in museums all over England. He carefully researched the history of the Spencer family and published learned articles in a wide range of periodicals. He edited a collection of letters between Georgiana, 1st Countess Spencer, and the actor David Garrick, and added to the famous gallery of historical portraits at Althorp, while commissioning new works from such distinguished artists as Augustus John (FIG 234), Sir William Nicholson (FIG 235) and William Orpen.

236 Spencer House, Entrance Hall; photograph of 1926. Few changes were made to the room during the refurbishment that followed the 7th Earl's succession, but the heads of the niches were painted with scallop shells

For almost twenty years he was a member of the Standing Commission on Museums and Galleries, while serving concurrently on the Board of Trustees of the Wallace Collection and the Advisory Council of the Victoria and Albert Museum, of which he was at one time Chairman. He was likewise Chairman of the Royal School of Needlework, and like many aristocratic gentlemen of his generation was himself an able needleworker, attending personally to the historic textiles at Althorp. He was at the same time a patron of both the Northampton Museum and the Northamptonshire Antiquarian Society, also playing a leading part in the affairs of the Society of Dilettanti, the Walpole Society and the Roxburghe Club.

The Earl had a special attachment to the house in St James's Place and, although the odds were heavily against him, with death duties and other financial worries to contend with, he resolved to move back there when the property was vacated by Prince Christopher, and immediately put in hand a programme of alterations and repairs.[2] The interior of the house was little changed since the lifetime of the 5th Earl Spencer; the fabrics were faded and worn, the paintwork and gilding in poor repair. Estimates were sought from two leading decorating companies, Lenygon & Morant and W. Turner Lord & Co. Lord Spencer chose the latter, and by the summer of 1924 work was well advanced. Under the Earl's guiding hand, the state apartments were transformed, the exuberance of the late nineteenth century giving way to a more stringent formality and restraint. The Entrance Hall was repainted, with scallop shell decoration added to the heads of the niches (FIG 236). The Ante Room was hung with green silk damask, with matching curtains cut to a simple design, while the niches in the alcove were stripped of their crimson velvet lining and painted (FIG 237). A few pieces of good Georgian furniture were substituted for the former miscellany of French and Oriental items. The Library was decorated *en suite* (FIG 238), while in the Dining Room the hangings were removed and the walls and columns painted over in ivory (FIG 239). The Palm Room, too, was given a coat of off-white paint, and in the first-floor apartments fitted carpets were taken up and the original floorboards exposed. Chairs were reupholstered and placed against the walls. In the Great Room the hangings were replaced by pale green panelling, while columnar doorcases were reinstated on the north and south walls, replacing the originals removed during the occupation of the 2nd Earl (FIG 241, p. 272). Significantly, the original Bolognese pictures were removed to Althorp; connoisseurs no longer admired such works and they were replaced by smaller paintings, principally portraits by Rubens and other artists whose reputation remained undimmed.

The restoration was far from academic and was clearly inspired by a vision of the eighteenth century peculiar to the period; but in its own way it was scholarly and correct, as one would expect from a man of Lord Spencer's erudition. The Earl himself was clearly proud of his achievement, publishing a four-part article on the house in *Country Life* in 1926, complete with photographs which today provide a valuable record of the interiors as they appeared at this time (FIGS 236–242, pp. 269–73).

The house was newly decorated when the state apartments were thrown open for a party to mark the eighteenth birthday of Lord Spencer's youngest sister, Margaret. A

[2] AP L14

237

237 Spencer House, Ante Room; photograph of 1926. The decoration of the interior had been greatly simplified, with plain Georgian furniture substituted for the French and Oriental miscellany of earlier years

238 Spencer House, Library; photograph of 1926. The Library and Ante Room were decorated en suite, with green damask wall hangings, and the placing of furniture reveals the 7th Earl's admiration for the formal arrangement typical of Georgian interiors

239 Spencer House, Dining Room; photograph of 1926. In a return to the practices of the eighteenth century the walls had been stripped of their yellow damask hangings

238

239

240 Spencer House, Lady Spencer's Dressing Room; photograph of 1926. The interior once again evoked the atmosphere of an eighteenth-century salon

241 Spencer House, Great Room; photograph of 1926. Lord Spencer dispensed with hangings, possibly for reasons of economy, and the walls were panelled and painted pale green. The original Bolognese pictures, so admired by previous generations, were considered unworthy and removed to the private quarters at Althorp. On the north and south walls reconstructions of Stuart's missing doorcases were substituted for the more modest doorcases introduced by the 2nd Earl Spencer

242 Spencer House, Painted Room; photograph of 1926. All the original Neo-Classical furnishings had been reinstated

240

241

débutante facing her first London Season, Margaret was understandably nervous; many of the guests were unknown to her. But the event was a great success. A dinner for eighty was held in the Dining Room, followed by jazz and Viennese waltzes in the Great Room, with an orchestra playing until dawn. A less agreeable event occured in 1925 when burglars broke in and tried to make off with a number of art treasures. No doubt they were disturbed for they only managed to take one painting, a landscape by Jacob More, which they promptly discarded in the garden of Bridgewater House.[3]

In 1926 Lord Spencer received a visit from George v and Queen Mary. Evidently impressed by the recent works, the Queen noted in her diary that with the Earl as their guide, she and the King had toured the state apartments, which she thought 'very fine'.[4] The King, too, enjoyed his visit, but he was surprised to discover that after all the trouble and expense of the refurbishment of Spencer House the Earl was planning to move. Indeed he had already signed a lease and, stranger still, the tenant was a club for ladies.[5]

[3] AP L21, No. 213

[4] Royal Archives, Diary of Queen Mary, entry for 19 Dec 1926

[5] Royal Archives, Diary of George v, entry for 19 Dec 1926

242

36 YEARS OF ECLIPSE

243 Spencer House, north front; photograph of January 1942. The photograph shows the effects of enemy bombing, the walls blackened by smoke and most of the windows blown out and boarded up

BY THE LATE 1920s the cost of maintaining a grand London mansion had risen to prohibitive levels; in some cases it could be as much as £20,000 a year.[1] People with far greater fortunes than Lord Spencer were beginning to sell up and move to more modest accommodation. The London mansion no longer played the same central role in politics, power having passed to a new class whose members preferred to do business in the debating chamber rather than the drawing room. The difficulty of finding staff, and the gradual breakdown of the Season and other social traditions, hastened the process of decline, and with historic buildings legislation still in its infancy, the mansions began to tumble. Demolition began even before the First World War. Harcourt House went in 1906, Harewood House in 1908 and Buckingham House was destroyed the same year. So too was Cumberland House, while Camelford House followed in 1913. But the inter-war years were especially destructive. Devonshire House was sold to developers in 1920 and demolished five years later to make way for an eight-storey apartment block. Grosvenor House came down in 1927 to be replaced by the eponymous hotel, and Dorchester House suffered the same fate in 1929. The same year saw the destruction of Aldford House, while the 1930s witnessed the tragic loss of Norfolk House and Chesterfield House, together with the mutilation of Lansdowne House.

Lord Spencer held out as long as possible; reluctantly he sold off a group of old master paintings and family portraits.[2] But in the end he was forced to accept defeat. He could not bear to sell the house and would never have allowed it to fall into the hands of developers, but in 1926, a short time before the royal visit, he signed a lease with the Ladies' Army and Navy Club. The Club remained in occupation until shortly after the outbreak of the Second World War[3] and during this period carried out extensive alterations, including the construction of a large iron and glass conservatory on the terrace and a two-storey extension over the south and east wings, providing additional bedrooms. The changes were not entirely sympathetic. The two-storey extension was faced on one side in lavatory brick and on the other in deep red sand cement. But there was little Lord Spencer could do. He had at least guaranteed the house's survival. As an

244 The Marlborough Room, Althorp, 1960. Visible in the photograph is the chimney-piece from Lady Spencer's Dressing Room and armchairs from the Great Room

extra precaution he had emptied the interior of its contents, including pictures, furniture and every kind of object likely to be damaged, all of which were packed up and sent to Althorp for safe-keeping, taking their place in the public and private apartments (FIG 244). The company of these treasures was some consolation but, as Lord Spencer probably guessed, neither he nor any of his immediate descendants would return to live at Spencer House again.

In the autumn of 1940 the Blitz began, and several great London houses were hit (FIG 243). An oil bomb severely damaged the Adam rooms at Number 20 St. James's Square, while Montagu House in Portman Square was gutted, the splendid Stuart rooms reduced to rubble and ash. Some of the most memorable photographs of the war show the King and Queen examining the damage inflicted on Buckingham Palace. Indeed the great London houses became a symbol of resistance. After a particularly heavy raid Lady Londonderry joked defiantly that 'a flying bomb made for Londonderry House, but on seeing it swerved to the left over the Park, and exploded near the Serpentine.'[4]

Fearing for the safety of Spencer House, Lord Spencer took drastic action and ordered all the interior fixtures to be prized from the walls and ceilings and transported to Althorp. Chimney-pieces, door cases, doors, even chair rails and skirting boards were all

[1] Christopher Simon Sykes, *Private Palaces: Life in the Great London Houses*, p.328

[2] AP L19, Nos 38, 67, 73, 74

[3] 1943 is the date given in *Survey of London* [p.521]

[4] James Lees-Milne, *Prophesying Peace* (1977), p.93

245

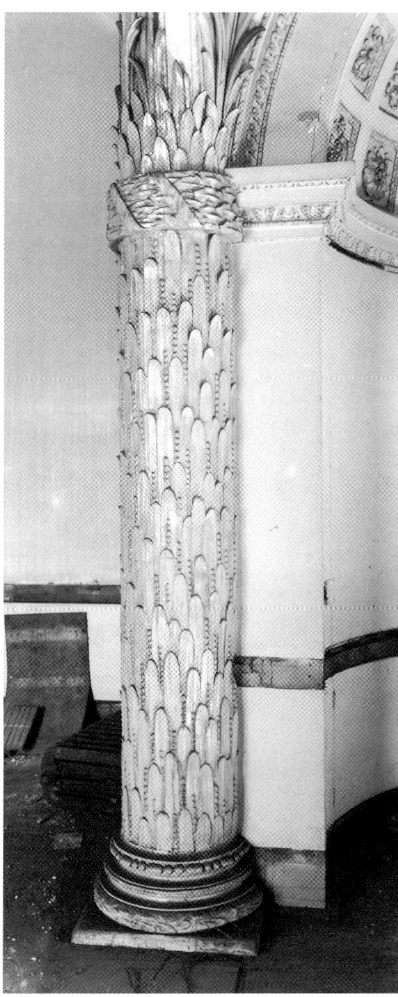
246

247

dismantled (FIGS 245 and 246). So too were the inset panels in the Painted Room. Lord Spencer even tried to remove the plaster reliefs from the ceiling of the Great Room but these were discovered to be attached by metal braces to the brickwork and could not be shifted. The whole operation took several days, but by the evening of 12 May 1941 all the various fixtures had been loaded into vans, and the following morning, after travelling through the night, the convoy reached Althorp.

The wisdom of Lord Spencer's action was immediately revealed. Indeed the packers were still at work when, shortly after midnight on the night of 10–11 May, a high explosive 500 kilogram bomb fell on Bridgewater House a few yards to the south.[5] Quite apart from the damage this caused at Bridgewater House itself, the stables of Spencer House were wrecked and the force of the blast shattered windows along the south and west fronts of the main building, causing particular damage in the Painted Room. In a separate incident the building immediately to the north of Spencer House, also Spencer property, took a direct hit and was totally destroyed (FIG 247). With each falling bomb the fabric of Spencer House was weakened. Plasterwork was shaken from the walls and in December 1941 Lenygon & Morant were called in to prop up the ceiling in the Painted Room, which by now was on the point of collapse (FIG 245).[6] To add to Lord Spencer's troubles, the government authorized the removal of the original eighteenth-century gates on to the terrace, which were carted away for scrap in January 1943.[7] A few months

245 Spencer House, Great Room with view through to Painted Room; photograph of 1944. Visible through the open door is the scaffolding erected to support the ceiling of the Painted Room. The original dado rail and skirting in the Great Room had been removed

246 Spencer House, Palm Room; photograph of 1944. The photograph shows the interior stripped of its dado rail and skirting

247 Spencer House, north-west view; photograph of 1950. The photograph shows how narrowly the house escaped destruction, a bomb having flattened the building immediately to the north. The conservatory erected on the terrace by the Ladies' Army and Navy Club had somehow survived intact

248

248 Spencer House, Entrance Hall; photograph of 1946. Although the building was now deserted, signs of its wartime occupation were everywhere in evidence

later in August, the young James Lees-Milne, Historic Buildings Secretary of the National Trust, was invited by Lord Spencer to survey the damage and afterwards wrote an evocative description of his torch-lit tour of the battle-scarred remains:

> At 6 I joined Lord Spencer at Brooks's and he took me to Spencer House overlooking the Green Park. He brought torches because it is quite dark inside. All the windows have of course been blown out. The house suffered most severely from the bad raid in April 1941 when I watched the corner house, which also belonged to Lord Spencer, burn to the ground. Incendiary bombs have destroyed parts of the top floor, and a blast has torn away the stucco from many ceilings.

The Painted Room, he continued, was 'now alas badly damaged', the ceiling 'almost totally down', but in the manner of all great ruins the building retained a poignant beauty. 'It is a wonderful house', Lees-Milne concluded.[8]

As in the First World War, large private houses in London were put to alternative uses. Wimborne House became the headquarters of the Invalid Comforts Section of the Prisoners-of-War Department of the British Red Cross, while at Londonderry House the gilded state apartments were converted into a military garrison with troops in every room and the famous Great Gallery made over to 'an exhibition of worn-out lorry tyres'.[9] Spencer House joined the list of requisitioned mansions and during the latter part of the war did service as the central office of the nation's nursing services (FIG 248).[10]

5 WPL, Civil Defence Records 142, 3/948, 3/1568

6 AP L14

7 James Lees-Milne, *Ancestral Voices* (1975), p.148

8 Ibid., pp.231–2

9 Lees-Milne, *Prophesying Peace*, p.123

10 According to *Survey of London*, the nursing services remained at Spencer House until 1948

249

250

251

252

249 Spencer House, Dining Room; photograph of c1955. This was the state of dereliction to which the house had been reduced by the time work began on its refurbishment by Robert Atkinson & Partners

250 Spencer House, Music Room; photograph of c1955. The interior was as far removed as it is possible to imagine from the splendid setting for concerts orginally devised by James Stuart

251 Spencer House, Lady Spencer's Dressing Room; photograph of c1955. By this time the chimney-piece and other fixtures had been installed by Lord Spencer at Althorp (FIG 244, p. 275)

252 Spencer House, Great Room; photograph of c1955. Little remained of the original decoration besides the plasterwork

253 The Great Room, Spencer House; photograph of c1948. The photograph shows the interior laid out as an exhibition gallery by the building's then occupants, Christie's

By the time the war ended the house was in a state of utter dereliction. Photographs of the period show the garden overgrown, the facades blackened by smoke and the interiors stripped of ornament (FIGS 245–247). Yards of electric cable hung from the ceilings (FIGS 249–252), with rubbish piled in corners. In some rooms the walls had been pasted over with simple lining paper (FIG 252). Painted signs provided a grim reminder of the building's former use (FIG 248).[11]

To return to Spencer House was unthinkable. Lord Spencer faced acute financial difficulties; indeed at one point during the war he had seriously considered handing over Althorp to the National Trust. He therefore cast about for a tenant. Few individuals in the immediate post-war period had the means or the inclination to take on a house this size, especially one requiring such extensive repair. On the other hand, however, the market was full of companies looking for temporary accommodation to replace premises destroyed during the war, and in 1948 Lord Spencer succeeded in leasing Spencer House to the auctioneers Christie's, whose sale-rooms in King Street had been flattened in the Blitz and were currently under reconstruction. A clean-up operation was hurriedly put in hand. The state apartments on the first floor were converted into exhibition galleries, with sales being held in the rooms below, generally conducted from a podium in the Dining Room. A small collection of surviving photographs in the archives at Christie's show furniture, porcelain and other items laid out on display in the Great Room (FIG 253)

253

and Lady Spencer's Dressing Room. While the main body of the house was let to Christie's, the stables, which had suffered irreparable damage in the Blitz, were pulled down and replaced by the present garages and maisonettes built by the firm of W. Curtis Green Son & Lloyd. On the instructions of Lord Spencer a plaque was added to the principal facade, carved in relief with a scrolling 'S' surmounted by an Earl's coronet.

Christie's eventually returned to King Street and in 1956 a new lease was signed with

[11] Archives of Syborn & Atkinson, photographs, 80415–80425

254

255

254 Spencer House, Great Room; photograph of 1956. Floor-to-ceiling partitions had been used to create three separate offices in the largest of the first-floor apartments

255 Spencer House, Entrance Hall; photograph of 1956. The window on the south wall, which formerly provided a view over the internal courtyard, had been filled with the metal doors and supra-portes of a high-speed elevator

XXV Spencer House, Dining Room, 1992. The interior evokes the period of the Regency, with elements that also look back to the mid-eighteenth century. Holland's scagliola columns have been restored and Vardy's original sideboards are once more in place. On the north wall hangs the painting by Gavin Hamilton commissioned by the 1st Earl Spencer, Agrippina with the Ashes of Germanicus, *which was sold by the late Earl but acquired by the Tate Gallery and placed here on loan. The wall colour recreates Holland's green, rather than Vardy's darker sage*

XXVI *Spencer House, Library, 1992. The interior is conceived as an early nineteenth-century gentleman's study, with portraits of the Spencers lining the walls. The chimney-piece is a replica of Vardy's eighteenth-century original*

XXVII Spencer House, Palm Room, 1992. No less resplendent than in the eighteenth century, the Palm Room still has the power to astonish. The original colour scheme has been restored, and replicas have been made of Vardy's palm-leaf seating furniture. The white and gilt finish of the frames, which complements the architectural treatment, is an authentic reconstruction, based on evidence from a pair of original chairs, now in the Boston Museum of Fine Arts, Massachusetts

XXVIII Spencer House, Lady Spencer's Dressing Room, 1992. The interior is largely as it was in the days when Georgiana, Countess Spencer, received here and serves once more as a place of entertainment. The walls are hung with crimson figured damask, woven to an authentic eighteenth-century pattern and to the original twenty-one inch width. Copies of the original giltwood fillets masking the tacks have been recarved, as have the original doorcases

XXIX Spencer House, Palm Room, replica of original armchair, 1992. The replica follows exactly the exuberant palm-leaf decoration of the original seating furniture, providing the necessary complement to the ornamental plasterwork and joinery of the room. The new seating furniture, comprising four armchairs, two window seats and a sofa, has been carved by Ben Bacon, painted and gilded by Clare Kooy-Lister and upholstered by Peter Thuring

XXX Spencer House, Music Room, 1992. This room was subdivided when in office use, and suffered heavy losses. All the missing woodwork has been recarved by Dick Reid, including the skirting mouldings, chair rail, doorcases and window architraves. Scrapes revealed no evidence of gilding, so the plasterwork and joinery have been painted off-white, and the walls are now a period 'Wedgwood' blue although it is possible that the room was originally hung with damask

256 Spencer House, Palm Room; photograph of 1956. First a drawing room, then a library, afterwards a study, the Palm Room was now a typing pool

the British Oxygen Company which at the same time took possession of Bridgewater House. Both buildings were thoroughly overhauled, in similar style, by the leading commercial architects, Robert Atkinson & Partners, better known for their modernist office blocks than the conservation of historic buildings. Floor-to-ceiling partitions were erected in the Great Room (FIG 254) and the Dining Room, each divided to form three separate offices. In the Entrance Hall the recess on the south wall was filled with the metal doors and supra-portes of a high-speed elevator (FIG 255). Swing-doors were driven through the walls of the ground- and first-floor passageways. The internal courtyard became a repository for single-storey lavatory pavilions and soaring lift-shafts. Lord Spencer's Room was transformed into a typing-pool (FIG 256), while Lady Spencer's Dressing Room was refurbished as a plush executive office. Lord Spencer must have thrown up his hands but the house had at least been preserved and the structure stabilized, while the Painted Room was restored and Georgian-style sashes reinstated on the north and west fronts.[12]

The lease issued to BOC was for forty-two years, but by 1961 the company was ready to move and in May of that year the remainder of the lease was offered for sale.[13] Although they had not yet found a buyer, in September 1962 BOC vacated the building. The following year, however, the lease was taken by the Intelligence Unit of the *Economist* magazine.[14]

The *Economist* was still at Spencer House in 1975 when Lord Spencer died.[15] The Countess had preceded him by four years,[16] but there were two surviving children, a daughter, Anne, and a son, Edward John, generally known as 'Johnnie'. Anne had married a naval officer, Christopher Wake-Walker, son of a famous Admiral. Johnnie, who now succeeded as 8th Earl Spencer, had originally planned on a career in the Army and after a spell at Eton entered the Royal Military College at Sandhurst, afterwards serving in the Royal Scots Greys. Following the war, however, he resigned his commission and embarked on a career at Court, serving successively as Equerry to George VI and H.M. The Queen. In 1954 he quit the Court and took up farming, enrolling at the Royal Agricultural College at Cirencester. In the same year he married. His wife, only seventeen at the time of her engagement, was the Hon. Frances Roche, younger daughter of the 4th Baron Fermoy. The marriage ended in divorce and by the time of the 7th Earl's death the couple had separated, but Frances bore her husband four healthy children, a boy and three girls. The boy, Charles (b.1964), eventually succeeded as 9th Earl Spencer. The eldest girl, Sarah (b.1955), married Neil McCorquodale, a Lincolnshire landowner and farmer. The second girl, Jane (b.1957), married Sir Robert Fellowes, afterwards appointed Private Secretary to The Queen and Keeper of The Queen's Archives. But it was the youngest daughter, Diana (b.1961), who achieved the greatest fame when, in July 1981, at St Paul's Cathedral, she married the Prince of Wales.

The Royal Wedding was witnessed by millions and immediately catapulted the Spencers into the limelight. It was front-page news, therefore, when a short time later the *Economist* announced that it was planning to move from Spencer House and was seeking a buyer for the remainder of its lease. One rumour had it that the house was earmarked as the future London residence of the Prince and Princess of Wales.[17] *The Times* reported that the National Trust was interested in acquiring the building as a possible headquarters.[18] It was suggested also that the house might be purchased by the Getty Museum for the exhibition of works of art blocked for export to the United States.[19] In the end, however, after months of speculation, the property was purchased by the J. Rothschild group of companies, and work began immediately on one of the most ambitious restoration programmes of recent years.

[12] Ibid., Robert Atkinson drawings 230/3 – 230/6; RIBA (Portland Place), Dove Brothers working drawings

[13] The advertisement is preserved in WPL [Spencer House file]

[14] *The Field* (3 Jan 1963)

[15] *The Times* (12 June 1975), p.20g

[16] Ibid. (6 Dec 1972), p.19f; *Who Was Who*, VII (1971–80), p.746

[17] *Daily Telegraph* (24 Nov 1981)

[18] *The Times* (20 Dec 1982); *Daily Telegraph* (20 Dec 1982). The rumour was scotched in *The Times* (30 Jan 1983)

[19] *Daily Telegraph* (12 Apr 1983)

PART VII

THE HOUSE REVIVED

37 A PIONEERING CONCEPT

THE J. ROTHSCHILD GROUP already had a connection with St James's Place. In 1982 the Chairman, Jacob Rothschild, had moved his offices into Number 5 St James's Place, since which time the company had steadily expanded, occupying Numbers 12–15, 29, 32–33, and 39–40. Indeed, such was the Rothschild presence that people sometimes jokingly referred to the street as St Jacob's Place. Most of the company's premises were listed, dating like Spencer House from the eighteenth century. Through refurbishment work the company had gained valuable experience, and its achievements to date had been widely praised. However, the project to restore Spencer House was of another order of magnitude.

257

The company's plan was to restore Spencer House as a commercial venture, selling or letting the building when the project was completed; it had not yet taken the decision to occupy the building itself. But this was never a straightforward commercial exercise. Lord Rothschild freely admits that the decision to take on Spencer House was largely a romantic one, inspired by the love of a great historic building he had known since childhood. His primary aim was to rescue Spencer House from long decline and restore the building in a manner consistent with its unique historical and architectural importance. Nonetheless, as Chairman of a public listed company, with responsibilities to over 15,000 shareholders, he had to ensure that the project was commercially viable. But how was this to be achieved? It was conventional wisdom that restoration of the kind he envisaged was neither profitable nor practical. The costs were enormous and market interest doubtful. Nor was it immediately apparent how an eighteenth-century mansion could be restored to anything like its original appearance and still meet the needs of the modern age.

Lord Rothschild, however, took a different view. He not only thought the project feasible; he believed he could reverse the logic of the market. When he looked at Spencer House he saw not an office building of so many square feet, but a unique work of art, the architectural equivalent of an old master painting. Far from being a loss to set against profits, high-quality restoration might be the very means of achieving financial as well as aesthetic success.

In a sense Lord Rothschild could not have chosen a less promising candidate. As it stood, Spencer House was a text-book example of the old approach to the commercial redevelopment of historic buildings: the interior missing many of its original fixtures; the floors laid with contract carpeting and lino; rooms divided by partitions, with swing-doors, modern radiators, and fluorescent lighting; the internal courtyard crammed with lift shafts, lavatory blocks, water tanks, and machinery.

No in-depth survey had yet been carried out, but already a schedule of dilapidations had set the minimum cost of refurbishment at £250,000, a figure later revised to nearer half a million pounds. One had only to look at Spencer House to realise the scale of the problem. Throughout the building there were visible signs of structural movement as indicated by cracks and fractures around door and window openings, uneven floors, and walls that were out of alignment. Railings and other external ironwork were generally

PAGE 290
Spencer House, west front, detail of the statue of Flora (see above)

corroded, and rusting had led to discolouration and damage of stone copings. Cracks had developed in the stone cladding to the north and west fronts, and pieces of stone were beginning to come loose from the cornices. The statues on the pediment were badly weathered (FIG 257), as was the carved decoration to the pediment and entablature (FIG 258). The stone steps leading down to the basement area from St James's Place were supported by means of a single metal plate which was itself badly rusted, while the old coal vaults beneath the pavement were running with damp, most having lost their doors.

257 Spencer House, west front, detail of statue of Flora. Through long exposure to the elements, the statues on the west front were severely eroded

258 Spencer House, west front, detail of soffit below pediment. A few sections of the the carved decoration were dangerously weathered by wind and rain. Where this posed a threat to the structural integrity of the facade, carving was removed and replaced with replica work (FIG 264, p. 309)

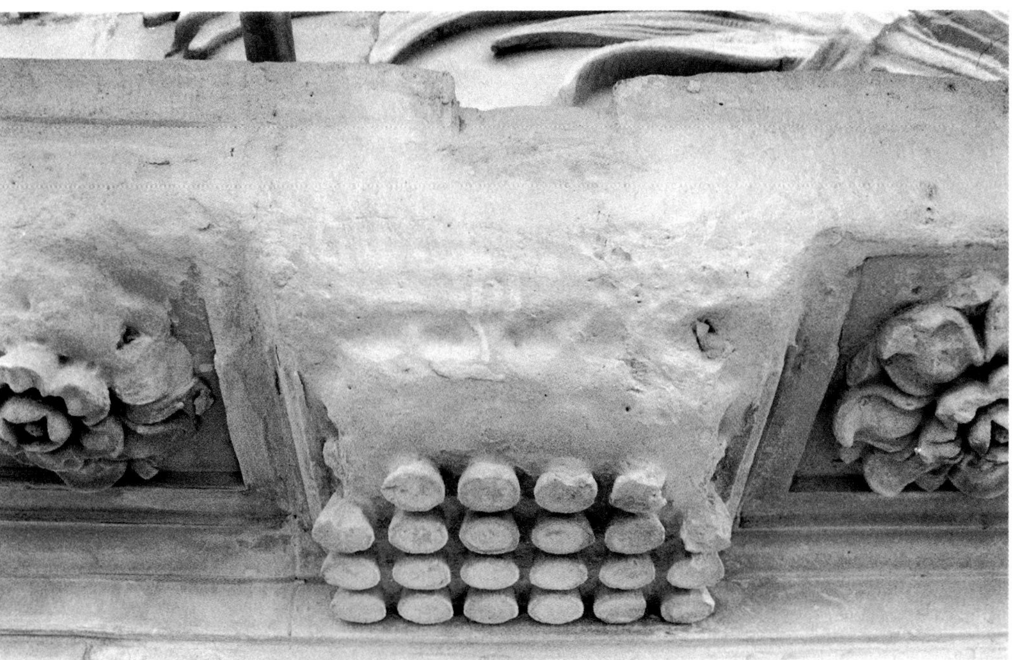

258

Water had penetrated the building at second-floor level, and a defective gutter had led to flooding and related damage in both the Painted Room and the Palm Room.

An added problem was the lease and the question of planning consent. The lease acquired from the *Economist* was due to run until only December 1997, without any option to renew. Indeed the lease might terminate sooner, in 1990, when the original grant of planning consent for office use was due to expire and the building would in theory revert to residential use. If the grant was not renewed the company would forfeit the last six years of its tenancy. Nor was this unlikely. During and immediately after the Second World War, Westminster City Council had given consent for many residential buildings in the area to go over to commercial use. This was an emergency measure designed to alleviate the problems faced by City companies whose premises had been destroyed or badly damaged in the Blitz. Now, however, the planning authorities were actively seeking to convert back as many of these buildings as possible. The company was well aware of this. It was no secret that the *Economist* had tried, but failed, to negotiate an extension of office use prior to selling the lease.

The odds were daunting. Even among Lord Rothschild's colleagues there was scepticism. As one senior director remarked of his first site visit, 'It was like looking at the original white elephant'. But for Lord Rothschild the challenge was irresistible, combining as it did his two great passions and those of his Rothschild ancestors: business and the arts. There may even have been an element of family one-upmanship, since Lord Rothschild was taking on a building given up for lost by the *Economist*, of which his cousin, Evelyn de Rothschild, was Chairman.

For a time the company explored the idea of a joint venture, first with Peter de Savary and afterwards with Stanhope Securities and Trafalgar House, but by October 1985 Lord Rothschild had decided to go it alone. A committee was formed, chaired by Lord Rothschild himself but with three other members of the company to help steer the project: Clive Gibson, a fellow director, whose father, Lord Gibson, was at that time Chairman of the National Trust; Paddy Drummond, the company's property director; and Moira Mullen, another long-serving member of the Rothschild team, who took responsibility for day to day management. All three shared Lord Rothschild's passion for Spencer House and were to play a vital role in the coming restoration programme.

Work, in fact, was already underway. In February 1985, a month after taking on the lease, the company had commissioned a feasibility study from Rolfe Judd, a London-based architectural practice with particular expertise in the commercial redevelopment of historic buildings. The practice had recently been involved in the refurbishment of Number 11 St James's Place and already had some knowledge of Spencer House itself, having examined the building the previous year on behalf of Peter de Savary. Rolfe Judd were first instructed to explore the possibility of restoring the building as a private residence in accordance with the proposed change of use. Plans were drawn up and advice was taken from leading estate agents, but the response was discouraging. Who, after all, could afford to live in such a house? The only likely candidate was a foreign head of state or a member of a ruling family. Anyone of this sort would probably feel that the exposed position of the house, originally a key advantage, did not provide adequate privacy and security, while accommodation on the second floor, originally the Spencers' private quarters, was a little modest, an interesting reflection on changing attitudes to domestic comfort. Hotel use was considered, as was embassy use, but in the end it became apparent that the best and perhaps the only viable scheme was for the house to continue in use as a single occupant office building. Recognizing the problems this would raise at the planning level, the company made informal approaches to the relevant authorities, who indicated that if a scheme of exceptional merit was presented they might reconsider their position. On this basis the company instructed Rolfe Judd to draw up the necessary plans.

The first step was a structural survey, conducted by S. B. Tietz & Partners, a firm of engineers with some thirty years' experience, having worked on a wide range of historic buildings including Warwick Castle and the Banqueting House in Whitehall. No attempt was made at this stage to examine the underlying fabric of the building, but Tietz could find no visible signs of recent foundation movement. Despite appearances Spencer House was in sound condition, remarkably so for a building of its age. The only immediate problems were the south and east wings, where the original eighteenth-century walls were beginning to give way beneath the weight of the vertical extensions added in the 1920s, and the floor loadings, which would need to be increased to meet modern-day requirements for office use.

Lord Rothschild had already decided that the restoration of the interior, including the state apartments, would be entrusted to David Mlinaric. By training an architect, Mlinaric had come to specialize in interior design, earning a reputation for historical sensitivity combined with flair and imagination. For clients such as the National Trust he had worked on some of the most important historic buildings in England and had recently masterminded the restoration of the British Embassy in Paris. To ensure consistency between the structural and decorative sides of the project, Mlinaric was involved from the outset and advised throughout. Advice was also sought at this stage from John Cornforth, a leading architectural historian with specialist knowledge of eighteenth-century interior decoration. Cornforth was acting adviser to the Foreign Office on the refurbishment of Britain's embassies and had recently worked with David Mlinaric in Paris.

At Mlinaric and Cornforth's suggestion the company commissioned a report on the building's architectural history. I myself was fortunate enough to be given this assignment, having worked in a similar capacity on the Paris Embassy project. Six months were set aside for research, allowing for in-depth study in archives and libraries. At the same time a microscopic analysis was made of the paintwork in the state apartments to determine the prior use of colour and gilding, a task entrusted to Tom Helme, an expert on historic paints who had trained at one time with David Mlinaric and was now an adviser to the National Trust. Findings varied from room to room, but on the whole there was good surviving evidence of paintwork and gilding dating back to the construction of the house. There was also the surprise discovery that the walls of the Palm Room were of hessian-backed paper stretched taut over rough timber panelling; that the soffit of the first-floor landing in the principal staircase was of timber rather than plaster; and that under several layers of modern paint the old scagliola on the columns and pilasters in the Dining Room had survived intact.

Research offered valuable clues, but it could not provide solutions to the essential questions which inevitably arise whenever a great historic building is restored. To what point in time should Spencer House be restored? Should it, in fact, be restored to any one particular period, or might not the restoration reflect the building's long and complex history? How far should the restoration be taken? Should all parts of the building be restored or simply certain areas? Should every missing feature be replaced, or merely a selection?

All these questions would be debated at length in the weeks and months ahead. One of the most exciting aspects of the restoration were the sometimes heated discussions in which opposing ideas were batted back and forth. But by now, a consensus was beginning to develop and in July 1986 the architects were ready with a scheme which provided some tentative solutions.

It was immediately recognized that the building could not be restored to its original mid-eighteenth century appearance. In the first place there was insufficient evidence, and secondly it would involve the reversal of all the ground-floor alterations carried out by Henry Holland, a major English architect who had played a particularly significant role in the building's development. In the case of the west front, for example, it was possible to put back the original sash windows by Vardy, and so restore the facade's original appearance, but this would have meant removing Holland's French doors, which, beyond their historical and architectural importance, were extremely useful in providing access to the terrace.

But how far did one take this principle? Did the changes made by Philip Hardwick in the 1840s not also have historical validity? Should the plate glass windows on the north front be retained? Should the draught lobby in the Entrance Hall be preserved? Indeed, might not the principle of integrity be applied to the alterations carried out in the 1920s and 1950s? Were these not equally a part of the building's history? Did they not constitute a document, however grim, of a particular moment in the building's development and the development of architecture generally?

After long discussion it was agreed that architecturally the house would be restored as far as possible to its original appearance, retaining Holland's alterations. Attention would naturally be focused on the state apartments, but in all areas of the building original features would be retained and restored.

Rolfe Judd had never faced a challenge like it. Their brief, in essence, was to restore Spencer House to the appearance of an eighteenth-century nobleman's palace while equipping it for use as an office block that could meet the needs of the twentieth and even the twenty-first centuries. To help devise a solution they turned once more to S.B. Tietz & Partners, also seeking advice from Voce Case & Partners, a firm of mechanical and electrical engineering consultants with particular expertise in historic buildings. The Leonard Stace Partnership joined the project as quantity surveyors, having worked already on numerous restoration programmes, including Hertford House, home of the Wallace Collection.

Rolfe Judd came up with two alternative schemes. In the first, the main offices would be concentrated in the old servants' quarters and private family apartments. The state apartments would be used as offices for senior directors and their immediate staff, also providing the setting for lunches, company receptions and meetings. The internal courtyard would be cleared, making it possible, on the north side, to open up the original window in the Entrance Hall. Although it was necessary to retain the courtyard extension to the west, this would be rebuilt on a reduced scale so that it no longer rose above the level of the Venetian window in the Staircase Hall. The original eighteenth-century walls of the south and east wings would be preserved, and the vertical extensions of the 1920s demolished. In their place new extensions would be built, sufficiently light that they posed no threat to the underlying fabric and suitably proportioned and detailed, with brick and stone facades to match the originals below. The only overtly modern feature would be a transparent glass walkway hugging the walls of the south and east wings, cantilevered off the new extensions. This was a space-saving measure, designed to release the whole of the area behind for office use. The walkway would naturally impinge on the courtyard but, being transparent, the structure of the south and east wings would still remain visible. Two new lifts would be discreetly introduced adjacent to the Entrance Hall, and plant and machinery would be carefully concealed on the roof and in the basement.

The second scheme was identical to the first save for the treatment of the south and east wings. By demolishing and completely rebuilding these areas the architects could engineer an additional 1,500 square feet of office space while the facades still followed the design of the originals.

According to Leonard Stace, the cost of the first scheme was somewhere in the order of four million pounds. The second would be nearer four and a half million. However, neither estimate allowed for decoration and furniture, and there was also the cost of the lease to consider, as yet an unknown quantity.

The time had come for the company to make a decision and Lord Rothschild called a meeting of the executive committee. There were only three real options. The first was to give up the project altogether and try to sell the few remaining years of the lease or surrender the property to the Spencer Trustees. The second was to proceed on a speculative basis with no guarantee of finding a buyer or tenant. The third option was to develop the building for the company's own use, thereby rationalizing its existing office arrangements. Persuading the committee that the project could be brought in on time and budget was hard enough. Making the financial case was harder still. A firm of independent advisors had warned that neither of the two schemes proposed by Rolfe Judd would ever make money. In his own mind, however, Lord Rothschild, remained convinced that the project was viable. He favoured the first and more sensitive of the architect's two schemes and urged his colleagues to press ahead with the development of the building as the company's headquarters. By the end of the meeting the committee had been won over.

Before a planning application could be submitted it was necessary to work up the plans in greater detail. The first step was a comprehensive photographic survey in which every ceiling and wall in the building was minutely recorded. Engineers from Tietz then proceeded to carry out a full structural survey. Bore holes were sunk in the basement to establish ground conditions, and trial pits were excavated to explore the foundations. Core samples were taken from the brickwork, while a comprehensive borescope survey was made using fibre optics to investigate the internal condition of the walls. The whole surface of the courtyard was removed to expose the underlying construction. Inside the building all the floorboards were taken up, and for six weeks investigators picked their way through the timbers, plotting the position of every beam and joist, assessing the condition and individual strengthening requirements of every member. A temporary superstructure was erected over the roof and the internal construction investigated. Samples of timber were sent away for tests, while a search was carried out for rot, infestation and asbestos. Advice was sought from Bob Hayes, a conservation engineer and technical adviser to the National Trust, on the practical methods of guaranteeing a stable indoor enviroment during the project. Relative humidity and temperature levels had to be managed to prevent mould and rot infestation, and the potentially disastrous effects of expansion and contraction of the building's fabric.

The structural survey turned up some interesting discoveries. In the Dining Room it was found that the floor was supported in part by single timbers measuring up to forty feet in length. Above the Great Room the shell of an earlier ceiling was discovered, indicating that Vardy had already made a start on the decoration of this room at the time he was superseded by Stuart. The old ice house was unearthed in a vault beneath the pavement in St James's Place, while a well was discovered at the foot of the old servants' staircase at the south-west corner of the building. The removal of floorboards revealed the original pugging, or floor filling, varying in composition according to location, with a mixture of lime and horsehair in some rooms, straw and lime in others, and seashells in the state apartments, all of which was carefully bagged up and replaced when the survey was completed. Amid the jumble of obsolete and obsolescent services, ducts were discovered above the ceiling of the Great Room, introduced in the 1840s by Philip Hardwick to carry away fumes from the gasoliers. Another surprise discovery was an old leather shoe nailed to a joist beneath the floor of the Painted Room, presumably left for good luck.

The survey also confirmed that the house was of excellent construction, supported below by substantial brick step foundations resting on firm, sandy clay with safe bearing pressures of up to two tonnes per square foot. The walls of the south and east wings were of solid masonry construction with complete bricks and no rubble in-fill. The brickwork in the north and west wings was of snap-header construction, with whole bricks spaced at regular intervals reaching back into the fabric behind. The timbers were of good, solid redwood and, in accordance with the highest eighteenth-century standards, the principal beams were lodged at either end in arched recesses within the brickwork, allowing for air to circulate, so providing protection against rot.

Nonetheless there were problems. Water penetration had led to an outbreak of dry rot in the area above the ceiling of the Great Room directly behind the relief of Bacchus. There were also areas of wet rot in the Painted Room, the Palm Room, and on the second floor of the west wing. Rising damp was discovered in the area beneath the terrace, compounded by water penetration from above. Some of the principal timber members were showing signs of splitting, partly because of earlier cutting and notching to accommodate services, and partly because of the dessicating effects of modern heating.

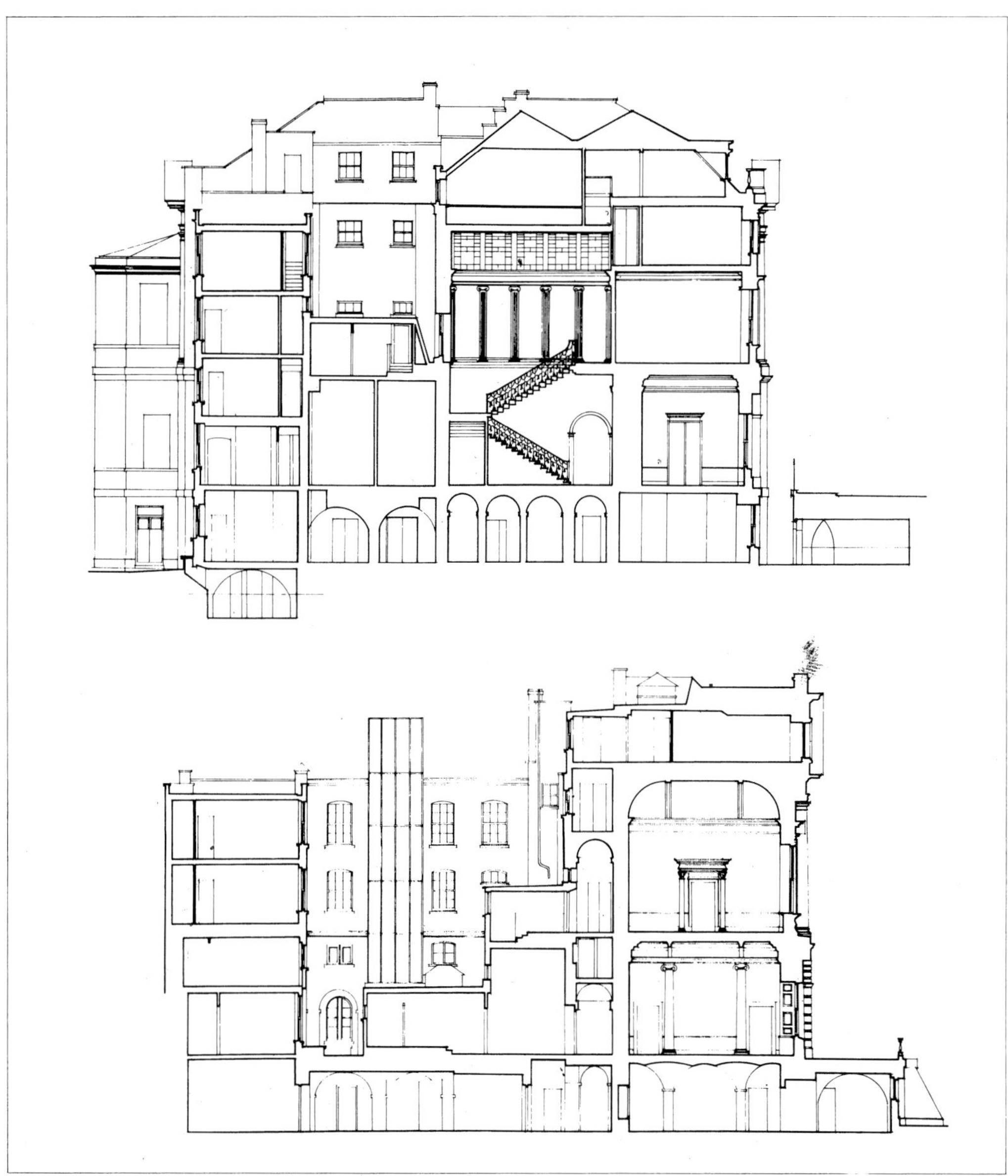

259a & b

259a Spencer House, south-north section prior to restoration. The courtyard is occupied by extensions added in the 1950s (see FIG *261a)*

259b Spencer House, east-west section prior to restoration. Clearly visible are the ill-proportioned vertical extensions added to the south and east wings in the 1920s, together with courtyard extensions and a lift shaft introduced in the 1950s (see FIG *261b)*

Although adequate in some areas, floor loadings would generally have to be increased by as much as 100 per cent and sometimes more.

While engineers from S. B. Tietz considered these problems, Voce Case continued its investigation into the question of services. A survey was conducted to establish more precisely the building's thermal and accoustic characteristics. Closed circuit television was used to investigate flues and drains, as Voce Case began to look more closely at the question of routeing and the positioning of plant and machinery.

But now came a change of plan (FIGS 259 and 261). In September 1986, at the suggestion of David Mlinaric, the company appointed Dan Cruickshank, an expert on eighteenth-century construction, to advise on architectural detailing. Doubts had been raised about the modern glass walkway in the internal courtyard, which some believed ran contrary to the spirit of the project and which would immediately be visible to visitors through the Entrance Hall window, providing an inappropriate overture. Cruickshank saw the possibility of keeping the walkway but building the outer wall in brick and stone

260 Spencer House, east wing, detail of new passageway showing original courtyard wall. The passageway was added to improve circulation and maximize available floor space for office use. The original walls were preserved within, fully-exposed to provide a tangible link with the past

261a Spencer House, south-north section after restoration. Visible at ground-floor level is the newly-built facade of the west wing of the courtyard, modelled on a house in Bloomsbury Square by Isaac Ware. The 1920s vertical extension above the south wing has been rebuilt along more sympathetic lines using a light-weight steel and concrete frame with traditional brick and stone facades. An internal walkway has been created by bringing forward the line of the north-facing wall

261b Spencer House, east-west section after restoration. The new elevation of the south wing of the courtyard matches the original at ground-floor level, while the upper storeys are proportioned and detailed in sympathy

261c Spencer House, plan of ground floor after restoration

261d Spencer House, plan of first floor after restoration

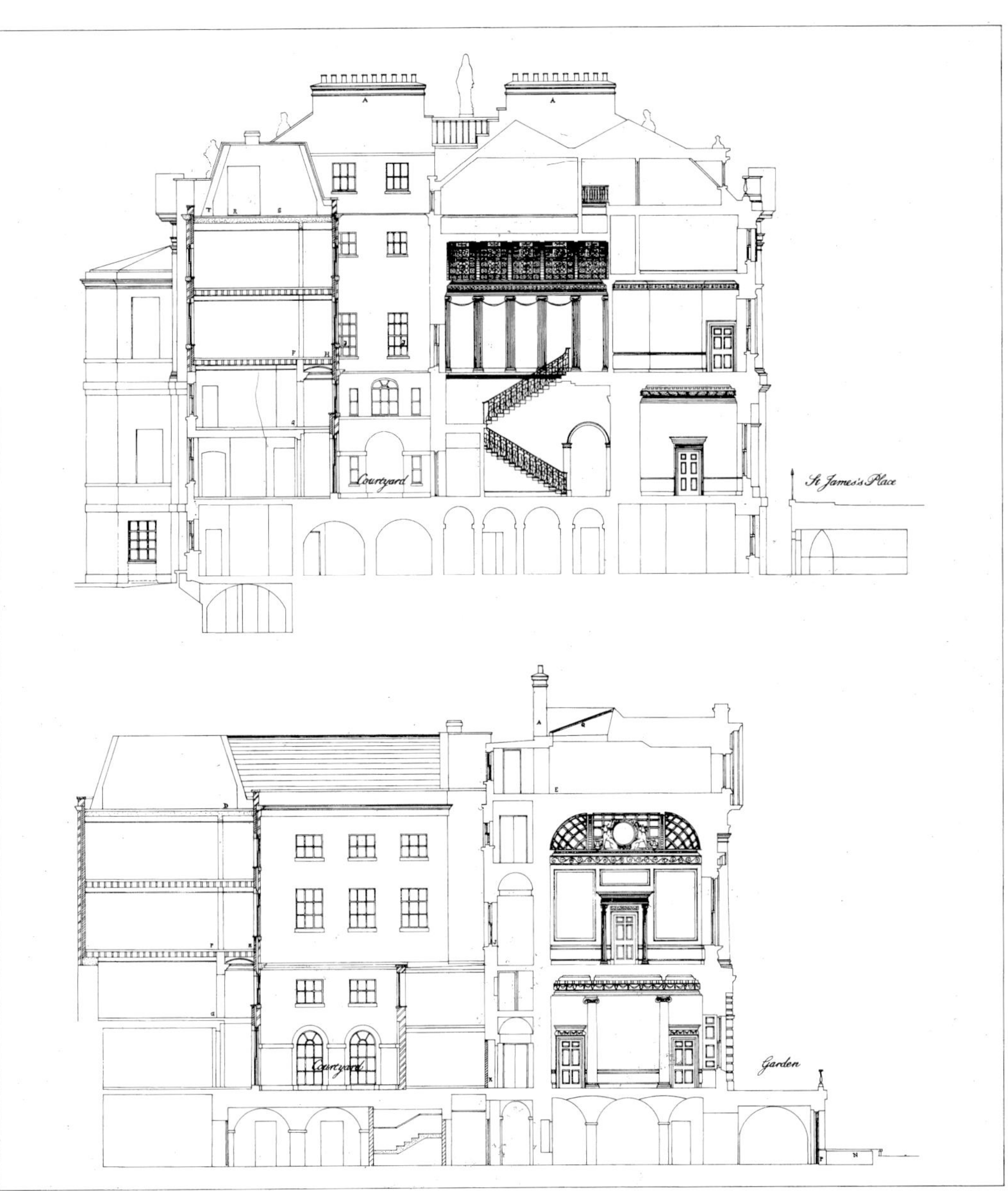

261a & b

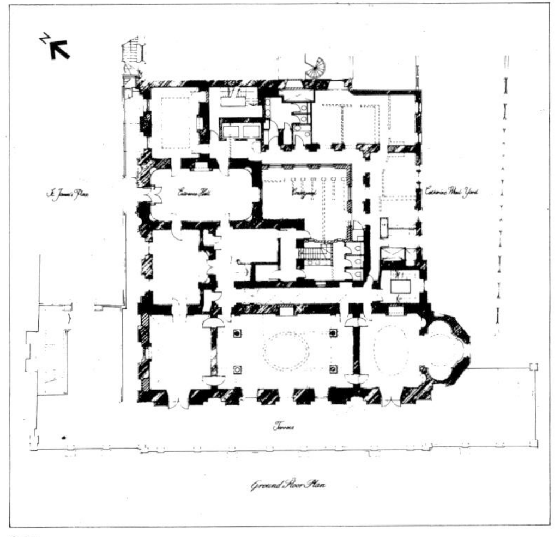

261c

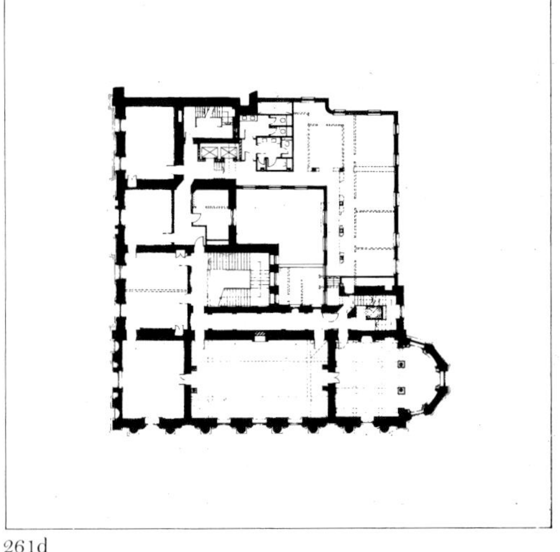

261d

to match the design of the original elevation, which would still be preserved within, fully exposed as before (FIG 260). The idea met with general approval, as did Cruickshank's plan to redesign the facade of the new extension on the west side of the courtyard, which was modelled on the street front of a house in Bloomsbury Square by John Vardy's contemporary, Isaac Ware.

To assist in the process of developing and approving ideas the company also appointed an expert panel of advisers, who met at regular intervals throughout the project. The panel was chaired by Colin Amery, architectural correspondent for the *Financial Times*; the other members being John Cornforth, introduced earlier in this chapter; John Harris, former keeper of the RIBA Drawings Collection; Gervase Jackson-Stops, architectural adviser to the National Trust; and Peter Thornton, Curator of the Sir John Soane Museum. At the same time the company sought to involve the planning and listed buildings authorities more closely in the consultative process. John Martin Robinson of English Heritage became effectively part of the team, playing a vital role both at the planning stage and during the works themselves. Through close collaboration potential areas of contention were avoided in advance and there developed a spirit of cooperation far removed from the fraught and sometimes adversarial atmosphere which often bedevils the restoration process.

Certain problems would only be solved on site later, but by October 1986 the company and its advisers had developed the key outline solutions and a formal application was submitted, followed in January by a full stripping-out schedule itemizing every feature to be removed or retained. The company presented its plans to leading amenity groups, including the Ancient Monuments Society and the Georgian Group, and approval was unanimous. Even now, however, it was far from certain that the project would go ahead, for the company had applied not merely for an extension to existing planning consent but for office use in perpetuity, seeing this as the only way of safeguarding its investment, as well as the building's long-term future. Nor had anything final been agreed with regard to the lease.

Fortunately, however, all these hurdles were overcome. In February 1987 the Spencer Trustees approved the company's scheme and agreed to grant a 120-year extension to the lease. In March, English Heritage approved the listed building application, and in May the planning application was passed by Westminster City Council. Within a month workmen were already on site.

38 RESTORING THE FABRIC

262 Spencer House, west front, detail of statues and vases on pediment. The statues and vases were considered an integral part of the building's original fabric. Despite their badly weather-beaten condition they were retained and treated in situ with an approved stone-hardener to guard against further erosion

IN SCALE AND COMPLEXITY the restoration of Spencer House was no less an undertaking than the building's original construction. The project involved literally hundreds of companies and individuals from every branch of the building industry, as well as related trades and professions, the principal contractor being Wates Special Works, whose previous projects ranged from the Royal Naval College at Greenwich to Unilever House.

Over a year had been set aside for preliminary investigations, a fact to which many attribute the project's eventual success. Owing to the detailed survey there were few surprises of the sort which sometimes cause major delays. Nevertheless, there were decisions to be made on site each day. Indeed some of the most urgent problems had yet to be fully resolved at the time work began.

Chief among these was the problem of floor loadings. In the past timbers had been strengthened by means of external steel plates, but reinforcement of this kind was no longer permitted in the building. The authorities required that the outward appearance of timbers remain unchanged. The only solution was internal strengthening. This could best be achieved by cutting a channel along each timber, into which high tensile steel rods would be inserted, bonded by means of a hard-setting epoxy resin. However, the technique had only ever been used in the country, since in London the stricter constructional bye-laws precluded the use of epoxy resin as a strengthening material, because it lacked the proper fire-resistance potential for burning one hour without softening. The only way forward was to create a new resin which met the required standard, and fire tests were immediately put in hand, eventually resulting in the development of a formula which burnt like timber, the charring providing a similar degree of insulation.

But other difficulties now arose. Internal reinforcement had never been used to strengthen timbers by anything like the extent required at Spencer House, and although trials established that the job could be done, the physics were such that, in some cases, timbers would have to be grooved to within 2.5cm of their bottom surface in order to accommodate the necessary quantity of strengthening material. This in turn raised the obvious practical problem of how to support the timbers during the actual strengthening operation. If any of the timbers deflected, the damage to the ornate ceilings below would be disastrous. Fortunately, however, a solution was found. By suspending the timbers from simple A-frames it was possible to support them from above: ancient technology in the service of high-tech engineering.

In some cases, where no other method was possible, external steel reinforcement was permitted, and in the area over the Great Room, where many of the original timbers had already been replaced, new steel beams were introduced alongside the remaining timbers. But this was no easy operation. There were eight beams in all, each measuring nine metres in length and weighing half a tonne. The beams had to be hoisted to roof level and lowered vertically through a narrow skylight before being gently manoeuvred into place by hand using a simple block-and-tackle system. One slip and the beams would have plunged through the floor, bringing down the ceiling of the Great Room and probably the Dining Room as well. There were three men on site to steer and twelve anxious spectators. Luckily the operation was performed without mishap.

A solution was also needed to the problem of the proposed brick walls to the walkway in the courtyard. Traditional masonry walls, built off the courtyard construction, were out of the question; the weight could not have been sustained by the supporting piers in the basement. Instead, therefore, a framework of steel was erected, cantilevered off the existing brickwork of the south and east wings, and the new facade wall applied in the way of a veneer. This solved the difficulty but with comical results, since for structural reasons the upper facade had to be applied first, with the lower facade following, creating the illusion of a construction project outside the bounds of gravity and physics.

Only a week into the project a decision was taken to remove the Victorian buttresses to the terrace wall, creating added difficulties for the engineers (FIG 218, p. 239). The buttresses had been introduced to counter the outward movement of the terrace, which was due to the spreading of the vaults within, and some other system had to be devised, invisible with time and conceived in such a way as to cause minimum disturbance to the existing fabric. If work elsewhere on site was not to be delayed, a solution had to be found in only two weeks. Partners at Tietz remembered this as a time of frantic activity, but as the deadline loomed the problem was at last overcome. Their proposal was to pin the terrace wall to the main body of the house by means of long steel rods, embedded in a special grout, passing horizontally through diamond-drilled boreholes between the vaults. To hold the rods in place, each would be bonded at the terrace wall end to vertical steel stanchions encased within the wall, running down to a concrete thrust-block several feet below ground level. The principle was simple, but the practical difficulties immense. Each of the rods was six metres long, while the area through which they passed allowed for a margin of error in the drilling of only half an inch. In order to stabilize the terrace during the pinning operation, each rod had to be thoroughly secured before work began on the insertion of the next. The vermiculated stone cladding to the piers was carefully removed before drilling and afterwards replaced, with any damage made good through the piecing-in of replica work. Once again there was considerable tension on site, but the results are outstanding. Looking at the wall today, one would never guess that the original fabric had in any way been disturbed.

To tackle the problem of the dry rot discovered above the Great Room ceiling advice was sought from a specialist consultant, Brian Ridout. It was crucial to avoid hacking out the enriched plaster decoration, and Ridout proposed a less drastic remedy whereby the dry rot fungus was slowly starved of moisture, while the surrounding area was kept properly ventilated. Only where the structural integrity of primary beams was affected was timber cut away, the work being carried out from above.

The installation of services was particularly problematic. The building had to be equipped with every modern device: telephones and fax machines, televisions and data communications. It required total rewiring and plumbing, a new heating system, and air conditioning for the south and east wings. All of this would have to be achieved, moreover, with minimum disturbance both to the outward appearance and the internal structure of the building. It had already been established that plant would be located on the roof and in the basement. Roof-level plant was positioned above the new extensions over the south and east wings, cleverly screened by traditionally-detailed mansards. An LEB substation was created in one of the old coal vaults beneath the pavement in St James's Place, while another of the vaults was used to house a back-up generator. The routeing of cabling and pipework was achieved by installing two vertical risers in the south and east wings connecting at every level with horizontal circuits, known on site as the 'race tracks', which ran below the passageways ringing the central courtyard. The principle of minimum impact was carried through to the appearance of the interiors. Even in secondary areas strip-lighting and bulkheads were rejected in favour of up-lighters, table lamps and traditional wall-lanterns. On the front steps in St James's Place the original lamps were converted back from electricity to gas.

The servicing of the state apartments was especially challenging. In place of external radiators, low temperature radiant panels were fixed to the walls between the dado rails and skirting, which, when painted over, were indistinguishable from traditional timber panelling. Additional heat was provided by means of convectors under grilles in the floor, discreetly positioned in the window embrasures. Telephone, data and electrical connections were provided by means of socket panels concealed beneath the floorboards, scaled down in size to fit the limited space available between the timbers. In place of conventional smoke detectors a vacuum-driven system was devised with hidden pipes in the ceilings carrying air from the rooms to remote sampling units, which were in turn linked to the fire alarm panel in the basement.

Although largely devised by Voce Case, these highly-complex systems were installed by Benham Building Services Ltd, a firm with its own record of achievement, having

263 Spencer House, west front, detail of stone repairs below entablature. Some of the original metal cramps bonding the Portland stone cladding had rusted, causing cracks to develop. In all such cases affected stones were removed and replaced

XXXI Spencer House, Dining Room, restoration of scagliola coating to columns. Restorers had to strip away several layers of paint to reveal the original scagliola applied to the shafts. Expert polishing in the traditional manner, using pumice-stone, brought back the former colour and lustre

XXXII Spencer House, Dining Room, restoration of gilding to cornice. Working from paint-scrapes and documentary evidence, it was possible to determine the original allocation of colour and gilding in the state apartments

XXXIII Spencer House, Dining Room, restoration in progress. Modern pipework and electrical and data cabling have been installed under the floors throughout the principal rooms, and new floors laid using English oak boards of varying widths. The existing ceiling gilding has been cleaned and renewed in part, but the wall painting and polishing of the scagliola columns, and the installation of replica doorcases, remains to be done

XXXV *Spencer house, Lady Spencer's Dressing Room, replica of original chimney-piece (detail of drop), carved by Peter Coates of the Dick Reid Workshop, 1992. Both chimney-piece jambs are embellished with magnificently carved trails of fruit, flowers and nuts, the iconography clearly relating to the themes of love and fecundity*

LEFT
XXXIV *Spencer House, Lady Spencer's Dressing Room, replica of original chimney-piece (detail of frieze), carved by Charles Gurrey of the Dick Reid Workshop, 1992. This work-in-progress photograph reveals the frieze at different stages of completion; the fully carved and polished eagle's head contrasts with the incomplete carving of the foliage and climbing rose. The quality of work rivals that produced in the eighteenth century*

xxxvi Spencer House, Great Room, replica of original chimney-piece, carved by the Dick Reid Workshop, 1992. The Bacchic frieze, derived from the Choragic Monument of Lysicrates in Athens, was an appropriate centrepiece for a room chiefly devoted to hospitality. Nearly 8,000 man hours of masonry and carving were required to complete the new chimney-piece

worked on such major historic buildings as Buckingham Palace and the Royal Academy.

The restoration of the stonework was undertaken by Gilbert & Turnbull, a long-established firm which had previously worked on various National Trust properties, as well as St Paul's Cathedral and Windsor Castle. On close examination it was discovered that the cracks on the north and west fronts were due to rusting of the underlying metal cramps, whose original protective coating of lead had failed. In all such cases affected stones were replaced, not with cement mortar but with genuine Portland stone, carefully honed to the right dimensions (FIG 263, p. 304). Although badly weathered, the statues on the pediment were considered an integral part of the building and were therefore retained, being treated *in situ* with an approved ethyl sylicate stone hardener to guard against further erosion (FIG 262, p. 301). The carved decoration of the pediment and entablature, damaged in part by defective guttering, was replaced where necessary (FIG 264). To restore the stone to its proper marble-like brilliance, the facades were cleaned using the water jet method, with a soft sand spray limited to areas with ingrained grime. Gilbert & Turnbull also took responsibility for relaying the floor of the internal courtyard and the basement passageways in traditional York stone, elements of which were found under the concrete coating of the 1950s. The restoration of the original stone staircases was carried out by another firm, J. Bysouth, who patiently stripped away the accumulated

264 Newly-carved mutule and metope, used to replace damaged sections of the soffit to the pediment on the west front

layers of modern emulsion paint and lino, an operation lasting several weeks in asphyxiating dust and heat.

The removal of the lift shafts in the courtyard revealed extensive damage to the original brickwork. It was hoped that enough original bricks could be salvaged from small-scale demolition works to patch the gaps, but most were too badly damaged to be reused. In the end, therefore, salvage bricks were brought in from other sources, hand-picked for size and colour. A similar problem was faced in the construction of the new brick walls in the courtyard. Outside salvage bricks of suitable condition could not be found in sufficient quantities and the walls were eventually built using modern mixed stock bricks containing the same basic colours of pink and yellow found in the originals.

Pointing, too, was a difficult area. The original brickwork had been laid in the traditional manner with a fine, quarter-inch joint of lime mortar. Workmen on site found it virtually impossible to work to the old eighteenth-century standard and a compromise had to be found. In the end the bricks were laid in modern cement, with joints a respectable 7–9mm. The joints were then raked out to allow for the insertion of a small quantity of lime mortar, creating the appearance of traditional pointing. To heighten the effect a coin was used to score each joint, imitating the penny-struck method by which eighteenth-century bricklayers achieved such excellent definition and modelling.

Particular delicacy was required in the pointing of the new brick arches above the windows, and the workmen agreed to use lime putty, but, as they soon discovered, the bricks quickly absorbed the small amount of moisture in the putty, making the task unmanageable. Again, however, a solution was found, borrowed once more from the eighteenth-century. Rather than lay the bricks dry the workmen soaked them in water first and laid them damp.

The roof of the building was re-tiled with traditional blue slate from Wales, the original pattern having previously been recorded in photographs. All external ironwork was thoroughly repaired and repainted, the colour inspired by the original steel-blue gates and railings at the Spencers' country seat at Althorp.

By now a start had been made on the joinery contract, awarded to Ashby & Horner, a firm established around the same time Spencer House was built. It was hoped that enough of the original eighteenth-century floorboards could be salvaged to relay the floor of at least one of the principal apartments, ideally the Painted Room, but in the end new oak floorboards were laid throughout, cut to random widths and polished with natural wax to achieve an authentic pale eighteenth-century colour. At the same time Ashby & Horner made up replicas of the original mahogany doors and other missing elements. Even in the secondary areas traditionally-detailed joinery was produced to preserve continuity. Where original features survived they were carefully restored, and in one or two cases later elements were retained, including the Victorian draught lobby in the Entrance Hall, which still served a useful purpose, and the columnar doorcases in the Great Room, introduced by the 7th Earl Spencer in the 1920s and based on the missing Stuart originals (FIG 241, p. 272).

The company had given an undertaking to reproduce all the original carved decoration to joinery in the state apartments, but at the time work began it was not yet clear how this could be accomplished. Modernism, with its insistence on mechanization, had dealt a crippling blow to traditional architectural craftsmanship in England and it was thought at first that the company would have to go abroad to find the necessary skills. Lord Rothschild, however, was determined to find the skills at home, and the company eventually made contact with Dick Reid, a carver from York. Reid had trained in the 1950s, afterwards setting up a workshop of his own, and as one of only a tiny number of carvers struggling through the 1960s and 70s was largely responsible for keeping traditional skills alive in this area. In the early 1980s, with architectural conservation moving into the ascendant, Reid came into his own, winning commissions for replica carving at Fairfax House, Nostell Priory and York Minster, as well as new work at Henbury Rotunda and the British Ambassador's residence in Tokyo.

Reid had the reputation of being able to work from photographs. At Chatelherault in Scotland he had recreated an entire ceiling from a single illustration in *Country Life*. The company had already gathered together an extensive collection of photographs showing the state apartments at Spencer House prior to the removal of fixtures in 1941. These

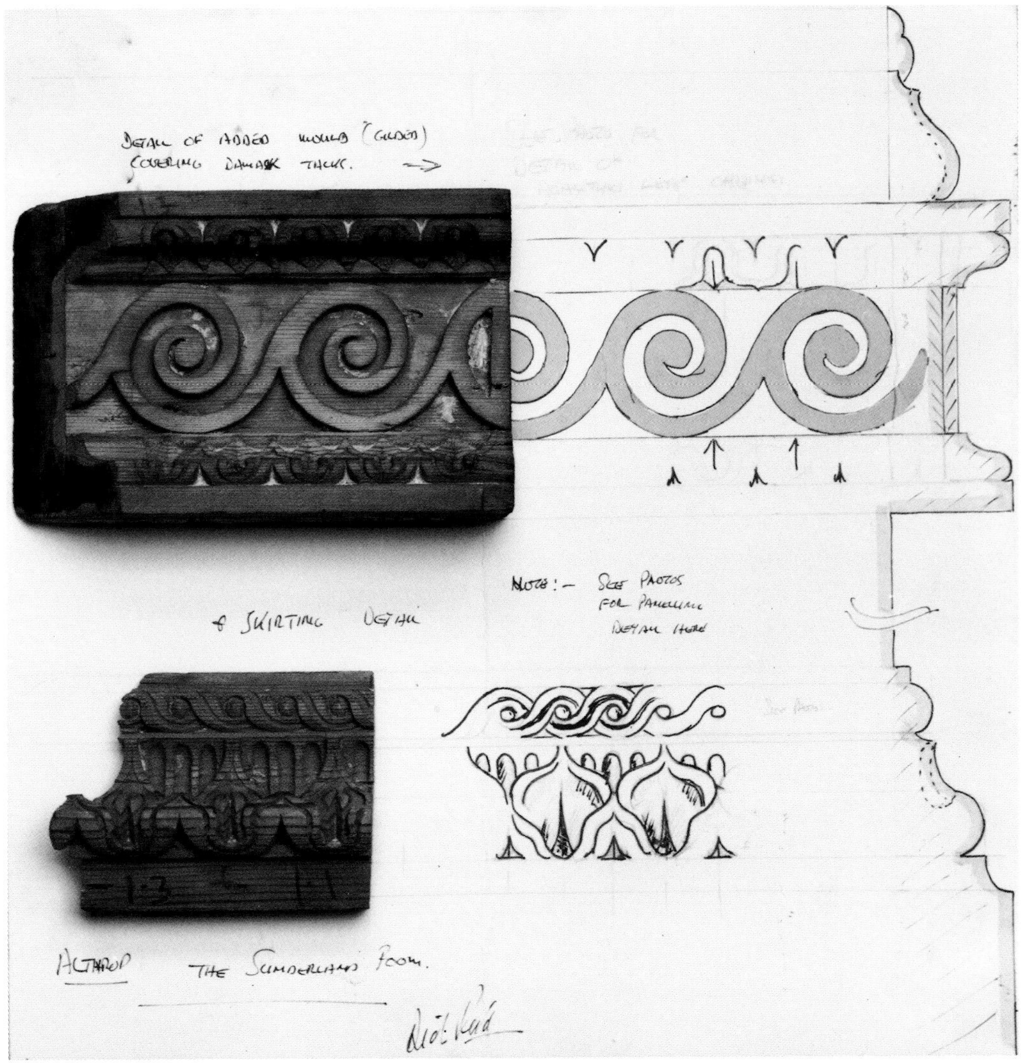

265 Sections of original dado rail and skirting from the Music Room, accompanied by full-scale working drawings by Dick Reid

would have been sufficient for Reid to do a creditable job, but were the actual fixtures not still at Althorp?

Earlier Lord Rothschild had written to Lord Spencer, who generously gave consent for company representatives and a team from Rolfe Judd to travel down to Althorp to examine and record the missing Spencer House fixtures. The first task was to locate these elements, which was no easy matter. In the Marlborough Room alone, the team found sections of the skirting and dado rail from Lady Spencer's Dressing Room, the doorcases from the Dining Room, and sections of the dado rail from both the Dining Room and the Library. In the end, however, virtually every piece was traced. Photographs were taken, together with measurements and impressions, and following his appointment to the project Dick Reid made his own trip to Althorp to carry out further investigations (FIG 265).

Having assembled the evidence, a decision had to be made as to the technique Reid used. The economical option was to replicate the carving in composition from specially-carved moulds, but Reid was convinced that only hand-carved timber would produce a truly satisfactory result. Although some minor repetitive work was eventually produced from moulds using expanded polyurethane foam, virtually all the carving was executed in the traditional manner using fine-grained pine. With the company's backing, Reid

266

267

assembled a team of twenty-two carvers based in York, London and Essex. Every feature was faithfully reproduced to the original design, and the results have been outstanding. If the original carver, Thomas Vardy, could somehow travel forward in time, he would surely find the work as good as any produced under his own direction when the house was first built (FIGS 266 and 267).

Another issue, still unresolved at the time work began, was the replacement of missing chimney-pieces. As a principal focus of the state apartments, it was vital that these should be of a suitable kind. One option was genuine antique chimney-pieces approximating in date and style to the missing originals. Another was unobtrusive marble slips of modern manufacture. Eventually, however, it was decided to copy the originals, which in scale, form and iconography were integral to the rooms.

266 Installation of replica dado rail in the Palm Room

267 Piecing-in and refining a missing section of the carved timber surround to a window in the Great Room

268 Sculptor Peter Coates at work on the replication of the original chimney-piece from Lady Spencer's Dressing Room. Coates works from a plaster cast made from moulds taken on site at Althorp

The original chimney-pieces were mostly of white statuary marble from the famous quarries at Carrara in Italy. The quarries were still in operation, but the expense and difficulty of acquiring marble from this source was immense. One suggestion was that the replicas be made up in plaster or timber and afterwards painted in *faux marbre.* Trials were also carried out using a similar but less expensive marble from Portugal. It soon became clear, however, that only true Carrara would yield up the proper definition and finish, and Reid himself travelled out to the quarries to exercise some personal persuasion. The period he spent there was brief but rich in incident, as anyone can imagine who has ever done business of this kind in Italy. In fact Reid found it almost as difficult to extract a quantity of unhewn marble as the 1st Lord Spencer and his contemporaries had found it to buy up Antique sculpture. However, by the time he returned to England he had negotiated the acquisition of no less than ten tonnes of the finest Carrara.

It was now that the really demanding work began. The original chimney-pieces had been carved by some of the greatest of all eighteenth-century sculptors. Would Reid and his team, with relatively little experience of marble, having specialized in timber and stone, succeed in reproducing the extraordinary quality of the eighteenth-century carving? Slowly at first, but with growing facility and confidence, the carvers set to work. Operating in exactly the same way as their eighteenth-century predecessors, they divided

269 Spencer House, Library, detail of replica chimney-piece. The frieze, carved by Charles Gurrey, captures exactly the spirit of the best eighteenth-century craftsmanship

270 Spencer House, Library, detail of replica chimney-piece. The lion head and drapery of Vardy's original chimney-piece at Althorp have been reproduced with absolute fidelity

themselves into teams. Those with a background in masonry prepared the underlying fabric, trainee carvers worked on runs of mouldings and other repetitive details, while the most skilled members of the workshop tackled the fine figures and ornaments adorning the friezes and jambs. At the time of writing work continues. The last of the chimney-pieces is due to be completed in 1994, but Dick Reid's carvers have already proved their worth. The quality of their work is breathtaking, faithful to the original yet remarkably free, with the same spirit of vitality which characterizes the best eighteenth-century carving (FIGS 268–272, pp. 313–17).

Another success has been the replication of the original gilt-metal door furniture, with its distinctive scrollwork escutcheons and handles in the form of human masks. The replicas were produced in moulds, from carvings prepared once more by Dick Reid, and have been used throughout the state apartments, a tribute to their designer James Stuart and to the 1st Earl Spencer, whose family name, like Stuart's, is recalled by the S-shaped scrolls.

For all the difficulties encountered on site, which also included a bungled attempt by the resident caretaker to abscond with panels from the Painted Room, the project ran extremely smoothly. By June 1988, a year after work began, the first part of the contract had been completed, and a start could be made to the long-awaited decoration of the interior.

271 Spencer House, Great Room, detail showing figures from the frieze of the replica chimney-piece, carved by Charles Gurrey. Copied from Stuart's original at Althorp, the frieze ultimately derives from the Choragic Monument of Lysicrates in Athens

272 Spencer House, Great Room, detail of replica chimney-piece. Peter Coates has recreated the original capitals with miniature masks of Apollo framed by Hellenistic scrollwork volutes

39 DECORATION

THE RESTORATION of historic interiors can never be exact. However conclusive the evidence, however scientific the analysis, interpretation inevitably introduces a subjective element, so that in the end restoration speaks as much of its own time as of that which it aims to revive. Just as today we look back on the restoration work of the past and clearly see reflected the aesthetic preferences and scholarly prejudices of the period, so, perhaps, in future years, the restoration of Spencer House will be viewed in this way, as a late twentieth-century meditation on the eighteenth-century past, reflecting not only the state of knowledge but also the personal tastes of those who participated.

So far as decoration was concerned, the project was always clearly led by one man, David Mlinaric. Having cast his eye over the house, and the evidence produced by research, Mlinaric immediately understood that while in some areas it might be possible to produce a close approximation to the original scheme, in others a freer interpretation was necessary. But this had always been his strong point. Through long experience Mlinaric had developed a unique ability to work from the most fragmentary clues, relying on intuition and an informed sense of period to produce historically convincing, visually harmonious interiors. As far as possible Mlinaric would aim to recreate the original decoration and atmosphere of the state apartments; even in the secondary areas he adopted a traditional, if simplified, approach. But he would also contribute something of his own, adding a further layer to the building's already complex character.

Although mindful of questions of sequence and overall harmony, Mlinaric approached each room on an individual basis, giving careful consideration to the findings from Tom Helme's paint analysis and other historical clues provided by documentary research.

In the Entrance Hall the walls had at some stage been replastered, leaving no trace of earlier paintwork, but in the niches Helme found the remains of a stone-coloured scheme which appeared to be original. The entablature was discovered to have been off-white, and the same colour was found on the cast of Antinous and the surviving joinery, except for the skirting which had originally been painted off-black. Although no early paintwork was found on the ceiling, it could safely be assumed that the colour had originally been off-white to match the entablature. The interior as a whole was largely intact; apart from the 1950s stone floor and the Victorian draught lobby, it was virtually unaltered since the house's construction, and since the evidence from paint scrapes was more or less conclusive, Mlinaric decided to follow the original scheme (PLATE XXII, p. 191).

The Morning Room was more problematic. Scrapes revealed that the ceiling was originally off-white, but the date of the panelling remained uncertain. Nothing, therefore, could be confirmed about the original decoration of the walls. Mlinaric used what evidence there was as the basis of an imaginative reconstruction of the room's original scheme, keeping to off-white for the ceiling, cornice and joinery, while choosing an eighteenth-century stone colour for the panelling. (PLATE IX, p. 77)

In the Staircase Hall the evidence was far more complete, enabling Mlinaric to produce a close approximation to the original scheme: stone to the walls at ground-floor level; green to the walls above; a brighter green to the ceiling; the skirting dark grey; and all other details in timber and plaster picked out in white. Several colours were found on the balustrade, including crimson and bronze, but the earliest was a traditional steel-blue, overlaid with *trompe-l'oeil* drapery, and this was reproduced (PLATE XXIV, p. 192).

In the Ante Room, as in the Entrance Hall, the walls had been replastered, but Helme found traces of a dark-green colour in the apse. This, however, was hard to date, and evidence relating to the ceiling and cornice was equally confusing, although it appeared that gilding had not originally been used. There was never any question of restoring the room to the Vardy period, Holland's late eighteenth-century alterations having been retained, and Mlinaric therefore devised a scheme which used a late eighteenth-century shade of yellow for the walls to evoke the Holland period, while the existing white and gilt decoration of the ceiling, cornice and apse was retained and renewed where necessary (PLATE XXIII, p. 191).

The Library presented similar problems. The room had been remodelled by Holland, but nothing was known of the architect's original scheme. The walls had been replastered and evidence relating to the ceiling was hard to interpret. The only clue was a bill for wall paper in the Spencer archives, but this referred to work in the 1770s, predating Holland's involvement. In the end Mlinaric chose a broad-striped paper in two shades of green, specially printed by Coles to a traditional pattern dating from the turn of the nineteenth century. No early gilding having been found, the plasterwork and joinery were painted white, with the ground to the frame of the central ceiling compartment picked out in blue, the one trace of early colour discovered here (PLATE XXVI, pp. 282–283).

In the Dining Room paint scrapes revealed the colours used by both Vardy and Holland. In view of the structural alterations carried out by Holland, it was the latter's scheme which Mlinaric followed: a soft green for the walls; the frieze the same colour with the mouldings picked out in white; the joinery white and gilt; and the shafts of the columns and pilasters in Siena scagliola. The only departure was the treatment of the ceiling. Although the central section had been replastered, the areas at either end retained their original paintwork, apparently off-white without any gilding. According to tradition, however, the central section of the ceiling had been decorated by Holland with a painted sky. Any attempt at restoration would have been a leap in the dark, and Mlinaric therefore decided to retain the existing scheme of white and gold (PLATE XXV, p. 281).

Another dilemma was presented by the Palm Room. Despite the introduction of Holland's French doors, the original architectural decoration by Vardy was still essentially intact. In this, his most important room, it was decided to restore the original scheme: the walls sage-green; the joinery and decorative plasterwork white and gilt; the coffering in the alcove with elements of pink (PLATE XXVII, pp. 284–285).

Although evidence of gilding on most of the decorative plasterwork in the room existed, the precise distribution and quantity of gilding on the palm columns was unknown owing to alterations that had been done in the past. The present solution was reached by a series of experiments which suggested that the weight of gold on the columns should reflect the solid gilding of the frieze and a joint decision was taken on this basis. For the adjoining ground-floor passageway Mlinaric devised a more sober scheme, based on the discovery that the walls had originally been a stone colour, with the ceiling white and the skirting off-black (FIG 58, p. 100).

Of the first-floor interiors, the Music Room, at the head of the stairs, provided very little information, having been stripped of its architectural features and then partitioned. Only the cornice remained, and even this was incomplete. The room had probably been decorated originally with fabric hangings, but there was no documentary evidence of

273 Spencer House, Great Room, restoration in progress. Work has been completed on the paintwork and gilding to the ceiling, cornice and joinery, but the crimson damask wall hangings and window curtains have yet to be installed

this, and the walls themselves had been replastered. Paint scrapes to the frieze showed no signs of early gilding, suggesting to Mlinaric that the decoration of the room had originally been marked by restraint, and he therefore opted for simple painted wall surfaces, selecting an eighteenth-century shade of blue, with the ceiling, frieze and joinery off-white (PLATE XXX , p. 288). A similar approach was also taken to the interiors which had originally served as Lady Spencer's bedchamber and closet, adjoining the Music Room to the east.

In the Great Room and Lady Spencer's Dressing Room the case was overwhelming for a return to the original Stuart scheme, with wall hangings of figured silk damask. Green was believed to have been the original colour, for threads of green silk had been found on an original sofa from the Painted Room, and it was thought likely that the furniture for these three first-floor interiors had been upholstered *en suite.* However, research showed that at some point before 1846, possibly as early as the eighteenth century, both the

274 Work underway on the restoration of the Painted Room. All the inset panels have been removed for off-site conservation, while the shafts to the columns are ready for gilding

Great Room and Lady Spencer's Dressing Room had been hung with crimson silk damask, and the same material was known to have been chosen by the 1st Earl Spencer's wife for the walls of her bedchamber and closet. After consulting with the advisory panel, crimson damask rather than green was selected (PLATES XXVIII and XXXVII, pp. 286–287 and 325). Analysis of the paintwork to the Dressing Room ceiling revealed that the earliest and possibly the original colour of the roundels was blue, with the rest of the paintwork in buff, white and pink, the mouldings being picked out in gilt. Despite initial uneasiness, Mlinaric decided to reproduce this vivid polychrome scheme. In the Great Room also there was good surviving evidence of the original colours used by Stuart in the decoration of the ceiling (FIG 273), a combination of blueish-greens with white and gilt which the architect had used for the decoration of a ceiling in the Tower of the Winds at Shugborough. It was through paint analysis also that the discovery was made that the plaster medallions above the cornice, white for a hundred years or more, had originally been painted in imitation of bronze. All these findings were incorporated, with only minor deviations, into the final scheme of restoration (PLATE XXXVII, p. 325).

In the first-floor passageway traces of green were found on the walls, similar to the colour in the Staircase Hall, but these could not be dated with accuracy and Mlinaric decided to follow a similar scheme to that in the ground-floor passageway: the walls a stone colour and the skirting off-black. Early coats of off-white distemper were found on the ceiling and this was repeated (FIGS 188 and 189, p. 185).

The Painted Room presented a particular problem in that the original pale-green ground to the murals had been painted over in a darker shade during the refurbishment of the 1950s (FIG 274). To try to remove the later layer of paint was a risk no one was prepared to take, and simple surface cleaning was recommended. The frames of the inset panels and the shafts of the columnar screen were regilded, while all areas of plain white paintwork were renewed.

Before the decoration could begin a decision had to be made about the stripping of existing paintwork and gilding. Owing to pollution, buildings in London have always been redecorated more often than those in the country, and after more than 200 years the original plasterwork and joinery at Spencer House were caked in paint, the mouldings having lost all definition. Some would argue that accumulated layers of paintwork are part of the history of a building, almost in the way of living tissue, and, as Tom Helme's analysis had shown, they also fulfil a vital documentary role. But was there really any point in keeping layers of paint at the expense of the outstanding quality of the original carving and modelling? What would be the effect, moreover, when the old, paint-clogged work was seen alongside the new crisp carving by Dick Reid and his team?

The issue was debated at length, but eventually it was agreed that where overpainting had caused disfigurement, stripping would be allowed. The approach was different in every room. In the Great Room, for instance, only the window shutters were stripped, while in the Palm Room paint was removed from every element (FIG 275). In each case, however, a section of the original paintwork was retained and simply painted over so as to preserve the 'archaeology' for future generations to study, the location of these sections being carefully recorded. In some rooms, where the quality was adequate, existing gilding was retained, providing continuity with the past. In the Great Room, for example, it was possible to retain as much as 70 per cent of the existing gilding.

275 The Palm Room during stripping. All surfaces shown have been sprayed with a stripper which softens and loosens the paintwork. The dark patches are caused by oils in the paint rising to the surface. After stripping, the plaster palm fronds were repaired where necessary

276 Expert plasterer Mark Davis puts the final touches to hand-modelled replicas of missing rosettes from the frieze below the dome of the Palm Room alcove

Work could now proceed, directed by Mlinaric through the principal decorating contractor, C. Tavener & Son, specialists in the restoration of historic interiors. Most of the stripping was undertaken by Stewart Restoration Systems with results which fully justify the enormous amount of time and effort which went into this delicate operation. Particularly satisfying was the stripping of the paintwork to the soffit of the first-floor landing in the Staircase Hall, which brought back to life the superbly crafted carving of the underlying timber. Equally successful was the stripping of the columns and pilasters in the Dining Room, a task undertaken by a scagliola expert, Michael Koumbouzis, who, having first removed the surface paintwork, used a traditional pumice-based polish to restore the original lustre to the shafts.

Great care was taken to ensure that proper materials were used in the stripping process, but in some cases the team was caught out by surprise discoveries. Scrapes taken from the alcove in the Palm Room indicated that the shafts of the columns were of solid timber, but stripping revealed that those on the screen wall had previously been replaced using resin composition. A timber stripper was used, containing chemicals which caused an adverse reaction in the resin, and it therefore became necessary to recarve the shafts in timber, a job entrusted to Dick Reid. Another surprise discovery was made in the Staircase Hall, where stripping revealed that the wave-scroll frieze had originally been

made from two different materials. The section adjoining the top flight of stairs was of hand-carved timber, being liable to damage and close examination, while the other sections, being out of reach and further from view, were of moulded plaster, presumably an economy measure.

The sub-contract for painting and gilding was awarded by Tavener's to Hare & Humphreys, whose previous projects included work at Windsor Castle and St James's Palace. Before any painting could begin, however, repairs were necessary to the plasterwork, and Tavener's turned to the father-and-son team of Tommy and Mark Davis, traditional craftsmen who worked in the manner of eighteenth-century *stuccatori*, modelling and restoring plaster ornaments on site (FIG 276). In the Palm Room it was necessary to renew the existing drum walling, and specialist sub-contractors, Albert E. Chapman Ltd, took on the job. The timber panelling was cleaned and consolidated; a new covering of hessian was added; and hot size glue was pasted over the surface, causing the hessian to shrink as it dried, so achieving the proper taut finish.

Now the painters and gilders could set to work. Their immediate task was to prepare all surfaces. Timber and plaster areas were carefully rubbed down, paintwork was cleaned with sugar soap, and the walls were cross-lined using linen-backed paper. To achieve an authentic matt paint finish, Hare & Humphreys used a white flat oil, stained by hand to a specific shade of off-white and afterwards tinted to the required colour using only pure pigments. The gilding was of the best 23.25 carat gold, and traditional English oil gilding was used rather than water gilding as practised on the Continent. Where applied to areas with existing gilding, the gold was carefully toned down with a tinted parchment size. In the Great Room the original bronzed finish to the allegorical reliefs was reproduced by applying a coat of gold size, overlaid with silver leaf and glazed with a bronze powder varnish. In some areas graining was used to simulate mahogany. The doors leading through to the Ante Room from the Staircase Hall were treated this way, as were two of the doors in the Entrance Hall. Again, traditional materials were used: a compound of powder earth pigments bound with beer and finished with an oil and resin overglaze. The painting of *trompe-l'oeil* drapery on the balustrade of the main staircase was executed by decorative artists Alan Dodd and Richard de Baer (FIG 283, p. 340).

Silk for the hangings in the Great Room and Lady Spencer's Dressing Room was specially woven on traditional Jacquard looms by an English manufacturer, Richard Humphries. The looms, dating from the early nineteenth century, were designed to weave to the narrow twenty-one inch width which was one of the key characteristics of eighteenth-century weaving. The pattern chosen for the hangings was derived from a genuine fragment of eighteenth-century Pavia damask belonging to John Cornforth, which had to be analysed, thread by thread, and the findings translated into the perforated cards which are used to regulate the looms during the weaving process. Great care was taken in the dyeing of the silk to achieve an authentic eighteenth-century shade of crimson, while Dick Reid was commissioned to replicate the original giltwood fillets, used to mask the tacks holding the hangings in place, which survived at Althorp.

The restoration of the murals in the Painted Room was tackled by Anthony Miloserdovs, assisted by Suzie Kennard. In addition to the problem of colour, the 1950s retouching had involved the use of a non-porous paint. As a result of flooding, blisters had formed where moisture was unable to escape, while in other areas water damage had caused severe discolouration and the formation of a white salty crust. The murals were first washed down with a solution of distilled water and pH-neutral cleansing agent, gently applied with a natural sponge. Liquid nylon was then injected into the areas affected by

XXXVII Spencer House, Great Room, 1992. As in the eighteenth century, the Great Room serves as the setting for grand receptions and is likewise a gallery containing fine paintings of the sort admired by the 1st Earl and Countess Spencer. The columnar doorcases installed in the 1920s have been retained, and the walls are hung with the identical figured damask used in Lady Spencer's Dressing Room. The reliefs above the cornice are painted once more in imitation of bronze and all the missing woodwork has been recarved

XXXVIII Spencer House, Painted Room, south-west view, 1992. Stuart's original Neo-Classical seating furniture, sold from Althorp to the Victoria and Albert Museum after the death of the 7th Earl Spencer, has been reinstated, with specially-woven green silk damask covers. The murals and inset panels have been cleaned and conserved and the integrity of the interior restored

xxxix Spencer House, Painted Room, apse end, 1992. Stuart's original Neo-Classical sofas and chairs, designed on a curve to stand against the wall of the apse, have been reinstated. The new upholstery follows the slimmer lines appropriate to eighteenth-century seating furniture and has re-established the balance between the frames and the seats (undertaken by Peter Thuring, with advice from the Victoria and Albert Museum)

blistering and the paintwork carefully pressed back into place. Where the original painted decoration could not be saved, tracings were taken through acetate and any lost features faithfully copied. The inset panels also required attention and were removed for off-site conservation by Clare Wilkins. It was immediately discovered that at some point in the past, probably during the refurbishment of the 1950s, some of the panels had been removed from their original supports and laid on aluminium backing with a tar-like glue. These, and certain other panels, were relined. After surface cleaning all previous retouching was carefully removed and any damage made good.

While deciding his approach to paintwork, gilding and wall hangings, David Mlinaric had naturally considered the question of window curtains, the choice of cut and fabric being governed by the same desire for historical and visual consistency. In the Entrance Hall and Staircase Hall, Mlinaric followed eighteenth-century practice, dispensing with curtains altogether, so as to enhance the proper architectural character of these interiors. In the Ante Room, Library and Dining Room, which evoked the Holland period, draw curtains were used, such as Holland favoured in place of festoons. The fabrics Mlinaric selected were of French manufacture, consistent with Holland's francophile leanings, and in each case the colour and material were carefully chosen to suit the character of the room: a patterned silk for the Ante Room; plain blue baize for the Library; and brown mohair cut velvet for the Dining Room. In the Palm Room draw curtains were used for the Holland French doors, although the fabric, a green silk damask, was dyed to key in with the colour of the walls, which looked back to Vardy. For the window in the alcove, an original eighteenth-century feature, Mlinaric appropriately chose a simple silk festoon curtain, and in the first-floor apartments he likewise opted for festoons so as to underscore the mid-eighteenth-century character of these interiors. The curtains selected for the Music Room were of red moreen, those in the Painted Room of green silk damask, woven once more by Richard Humphries to the Pavia pattern. In the Great Room and Lady Spencer's Dressing Room the curtains were naturally *en suite* with the crimson damask wall hangings.

By the spring of 1989 work was well advanced, and the following autumn the decoration of the state apartments was nearing completion. The interiors had been painted and gilded, hangings were in place, and curtains were being installed. But, so far as furniture and pictures were concerned, the project was far from over. Indeed it had barely begun.

40 TEMPLE OF THE ARTS

IT WAS THE COMPANY'S original intention that the state apartments should serve as directors' offices, and a healthy debate had begun on the relative merits of 'Milanese Modern' and 'Banker's Georgian' for the furniture, but all such discussions were suddenly brought to an end by a change of plan. Lord Rothschild had always hoped that Spencer House might occasionally be used for conferences, receptions and other events, but if it were possible somehow to develop these activities on a commercial basis, the viability of the project would be greatly enhanced. The building had already been equipped to cater for fairly large-scale company entertainments; no significant alterations were required, and in January 1989, after preliminary discussions with the Spencer Trustees, the company applied for planning consent, which was granted the following April.

Effectively the state apartments would now be serving their original purpose, and this made it possible to take their restoration one step further by installing furniture of the kind used originally. A budget of some three million pounds was established, but with prices soaring for top-quality eighteenth-century English furniture, it was realized that this would never be sufficient and a three-part strategy was developed. In addition to any purchases it made, the company would seek to borrow furniture from public and private collections, while attempts were made to replicate the more important pieces originally from the house. With the state rooms due to open in the summer of 1990, there was an urgent need for action and the company set to work at once. Two leading experts were called in to work with Mlinaric: Christopher Gibbs, a London dealer with special knowledge of the eighteenth century, and John Harris, who had formerly worked with the advisory panel. Celia de la Hey, an architectural writer with particular expertise in the sphere of conservation, was also appointed to coordinate the project.

In seeking out loans the company was especially keen to borrow original pieces from the house. The bulk of these were at Althorp, but over the years various items had been sold to public museums. Following the death of the 7th Earl Spencer, the Victoria and Albert Museum had acquired the armchairs and sofas from the Painted Room, principally at the instigation of Peter Thornton, at that time Keeper of the furniture and woodwork department, and his colleague John Hardy, in the then-distant hope that the furniture might one day return to Spencer House. The suite was displayed in the library at Kenwood House, a Neo-Classical interior designed by James Stuart's contemporary, Robert Adam, but would it not look better, did it not indeed belong, in the interior for which it was expressly designed?

Another important piece in the Museum's collection was an original sideboard from the Dining Room designed by Vardy. This had been removed during the alterations carried out by Holland, later finding its way on to the market, and its pair had followed a similar route, finally being acquired by the museum of decorative arts at Temple Newsam House in Leeds. Although the Dining Room had been redecorated to the Holland period, any reservations regarding historical consistency were far outweighed by the exciting prospect of completing a two-part reunion, bringing the sideboards together after long years of separation and returning them to their intended architectural setting.

277 Spencer House, Lady Spencer's Dressing Room, replica chimney-piece and eighteenth-century engraved steel grate and fire irons. Throughout the state apartments genuine Neo-Classical fire grates have been acquired by the company to complement the replica chimney-pieces

Preliminary enquiries were made and the response was encouraging. There was by now a consensus in the museum world that objects should ideally be displayed in their proper historical context, and both the Victoria and Albert Museum and Temple Newsam were keen to see the Spencer House furniture reinstated, as was English Heritage, custodians of the Stuart sofas and armchairs at Kenwood. However, there were obvious conditions attached: public access; tight security; and a stable physical environment.

The company had already agreed to open the house to the public one day a month and was happy to extend this arrangement. Security was never an issue. With twenty-four hour surveillance, an infra-red alarm system, smoke and water detectors, and a host of back-up devices, Spencer House was as safe as any museum. Although window blinds were required, the glazing already contained an ultraviolet filter to guard against light damage.

Far more daunting was the question of humidity controls. It is difficult enough to create a stable environment in a museum dedicated solely to conservation; at Spencer House, the frequent use of the state rooms, for a variety of functions, greatly complicated the situation. Bob Hayes and Voce Case had already been recalled to devise a system for regulating humidity levels, but it was not immediately apparent how this could be achieved without introducing large and obtrusive humidifiers to each room. The decoration of the state apartments was newly completed and the floorboards could not be lifted without damage, being laid with traditional tongue-and-groove joints. In any case, every inch of available space below was already taken up with pipework and wiring. After a lengthy period of research and experiment, Voce Case finally adopted an ingenious, if somewhat incongruous, solution, making use of technology developed for freshening vegetable displays in supermarkets. Compact ultrasonic humidifiers were installed beneath the existing floor grilles, allowing water vapour to be dispersed into the atmosphere at room temperature, rather than as steam, and these were fed by a miniature water pipe threaded behind the skirting, leading down to a reservoir in the basement equipped with a pump. The convector fans beneath the grilles were adapted to distribute the water vapour, while a pre-set computerized control system ensured that the level of relative humidity remained steady at an optimum constant of 55 per cent.

An additional condition was that tables, chairs and sofas should not be used. Since the state apartments were to be thrown open for banquets, receptions and tours, the only solution was to place the furniture behind protective barriers. In the Painted Room the company had to give an assurance that drinking, dining and smoking would not be permitted. Any disadvantage, however, was fully compensated by the rewards when, after a long, sad absence, Vardy's Dining Room sideboards and Stuart's Painted Room sofas and armchairs finally returned.

Even now, however, there were problems to be faced. During the period of their separation the Vardy sideboards had been regilded in different ways, and to reconcile their disparate appearance the company turned to Peter Thuring, a furniture restorer recommended by the National Trust. It was Thuring, too, who tackled the complex difficulties presented by the condition of the Painted Room seating furniture. At some stage, possibly during the early nineteenth century, the frames of the sofas and armchairs had been stripped back to the timber and regilded; a surprisingly coarse first layer of gesso concealed early damage and repairs to the wood. With more layers applied in subsequent restorations, the original crispness of the carving had been obscured. Wholesale stripping and re-gilding was out of the question, running contrary to the Victoria and Albert Museum's conservation policy, but it was agreed that one armchair should be treated in this manner, to reveal the quality of the original carving (FIG 278).

An added problem was the clash between the red 1950s upholstery and the predominantly green paintwork of the room. The width and pattern of the fabric were wrong for period, and the seats and backs overstuffed. The earliest covers had probably been green, since threads of green silk were found attached to the remains of the original upholstery tacks. When these were held up against the surviving areas of un-retouched green in the Painted Room itself, especially the scrolling acanthus on the pilasters, the colours were found to match and it was decided, therefore, to reupholster the entire suite in green silk damask, specially dyed and woven by Richard Humphries. With advice from Frances Collard at the Victoria and Albert Museum, Thuring restuffed the seats and backs, restoring their original slender profile. The shafts of eighteenth-century nails found in the seat rails established that close nailing, rather than silk braid, was the correct way to finish the covers, while holes in the frames confirmed that there should also be tufting. Bolsters for the sofas, were inspired by designs in mid-eighteenth-century pattern books.

In addition to original pieces of furniture, the company also negotiated the loan of items of conforming style and date. The National Trust generously agreed to lend a magnificent giltwood side table from Wimpole Hall in Cambridgeshire, attributed to the architect Sir William Chambers, whose praise of Spencer House was noted in an earlier chapter. The table is remarkably close to documented pieces by James Stuart and makes an impressive addition to the decoration of the Ante Room. Lord Rothschild himself made loans from his own private collection, including a marquetry cylinder bureau of the Louis XVI period which stands in Lady Spencer's Dressing Room, and a pair of giltwood 'Atheniennes' with Louis XVI ormolu candelabra displayed in the Painted Room, replacing the original painted torchères removed to Althorp.

Meanwhile a start had been made on the second aspect of the furnishing programme, the replication of original furniture. The intention was to copy select items which, in their design and iconography, were integral to the rooms. Having already made such an outstanding job of recarving the architectural decoration, Dick Reid was asked to undertake the first and most daunting task of copying Stuart's magnificent pier tables and glasses from the Great Room. The vast pier glasses, designed to reflect the paintings which faced them, were crucial to Stuart's concept of the interior as a private art gallery. The frames of the glasses and tables, adorned with amorini, garlands of roses and other attributes of Venus, echoed the symbolism of the plaster decoration to the ceiling. The Spencers again gave support to the project by allowing Reid to draw, measure and photograph the originals at Althorp, even lending the workshop an actual garland from one of the pier tables (FIG 279).

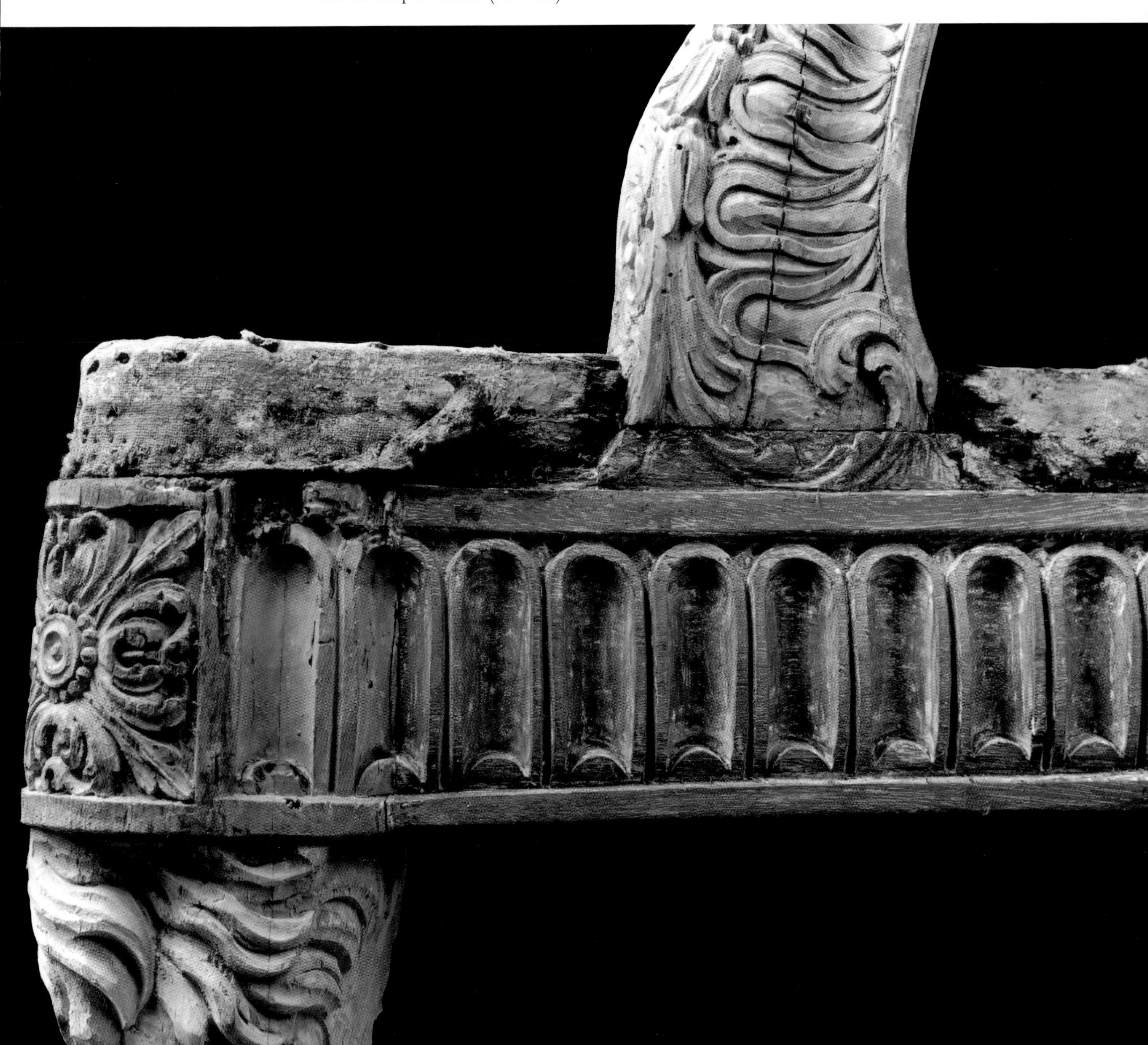

278 Detail of frame of original Stuart armchair from the Painted Room. Stripping revealed early damage and repairs to the lime wood frame, including the piecing-in of a new fluted seat rail in mahogany. The crispness of the original carving is evident on the arm, leg and corner rosette

A particularly exciting opportunity arose when, in 1990, a pair of armchairs originally from the Palm Room came up for auction at Sotheby's in New York. They were immediately recognized by John Hardy, but were unfortunately beyond the allocated budget. Luckily, however, the armchairs were acquired by Christopher Gibbs and a colleague, Jonathan Harris, and when placed temporarily in the Palm Room the effect was overwhelming. Every experiment with alternative furniture had failed, and the company decided to commission replicas. With the consent of Harris and Gibbs, one of the armchairs was sent to the studio of Ben Bacon, a Canadian-born carver with extensive experience in replication work and a special knowledge of English eighteenth-century furniture. It was an ideal project for Bacon, who had trained initially under the Italian chairmaker, Liberti. Vardy's chair had been stripped of all its original paintwork and gilding but this only made it a better model, since the original eighteenth-century carving was fully exposed. Bacon set to work at once to produce four armchairs, and the results were superb.

Meanwhile the sale of the armchairs in New York had alerted the Boston Museum of Fine Arts to the true identity of a pair of chairs in its own collection. Since the chairs had never been stripped, the conservation department was able to carry out tests to establish the original finish. Microscopic analysis revealed traces of lead-white under an eighteenth-century blue, indicating that the frames had probably been painted white with the palm fronds and other carved detail picked out in gilt, matching the original decoration of the Palm Room dado. It was the hoped-for outcome, and for an authentic reconstruction of the finish, the replicas were entrusted to an expert gilder, Clare Kooy-Lister, well known for her work for the National Trust and English Heritage. The upholstery was tackled once more by Peter Thuring, using the same green silk damask as the Palm Room curtains. In 1992, the completed armchairs were finally installed and it is no exaggeration to say that they transformed the room. They have since been joined by copies of two windowseats from the same suite at Althorp, reproduced by Bacon with the Spencers' cooperation, and there are plans to extend the project further. The missing sofa from the suite has been traced to a private collection in England and with the consent of the owner, Bacon is already at work on a replica which will stand, as Vardy intended, in the centre of the north wall directly opposite the palm tree columns.

The same team is also currently working on copies of the original arm chairs and side chairs from the Great Room and Lady Spencer's Dressing Room, examples of which survive at Althorp and the Victoria and Albert Museum. The frames, like the originals, will be white and gilt, complementing the dados, with covers of crimson damask to match the wall hangings and window curtains.

To complete the Great Room, crystal chandeliers have been made up to an eighteenth-century pattern by the London firm of R. Wilkinson & Sons. These magnificent full-scale copies provide a reminder of the 'exceeding fine glass lustre' described here by Arthur Young in 1769, and are fitted with tiny low wattage bulbs to simulate the effect of candlelight.

The third part of the project, the purchase of suitable antique furniture, has been equally successful. With their knowledge of the market, Christopher Gibbs and John Harris initially set their sights on New York, where they scoured the showrooms of all the major dealers. The expedition produced some exciting acquisitions. Prominent among these was an assortment of eighteenth-century marquetry furniture, ideal in date and style for Lady Spencer's Dressing Room, having a delicate, almost feminine character which would surely have appealed to the 1st Earl's wife, Georgiana. The furniture

279 Dick Reid (right) and carver José Sarabia discuss the replication of the original Stuart pier glasses and tables from the Great Room. The photograph shows work in progress on the frames for the pier glasses and on one of the decorative swags from the pier table

includes a pair of side tables by John Cobb of *c*1760; a pair of corner cupboards of *c*1770 attributed to the celebrated cabinet makers Ince and Mayhew, whose greatest patron was George Spencer, 4th Duke of Marlborough, a cousin of the 1st Earl Spencer; and a beautiful jardinière by the leading *ébéniste* of the pre-Revolutionary period, Weisweiler. Also from New York is the mahogany kneehole desk in the Ante Room, similar to pieces by Vile and Cobb in the Royal Collection and at Chatsworth, and a desk chair in the style of William Hallett. Both provide the perfect complement to the robust Palladian design of the room's architectural decoration.

Outstanding pieces were also found in London. For the Library the company acquired a pair of elegant early nineteenth-century bookcases which, with a Regency drum table from New York, add to the impression of a gentleman's study. In the Entrance Hall a suite of plain mahogany sun-back chairs underlines the austerity of this severe Classical interior. Several splendid looking glasses have been acquired, including a giltwood girandole of *c*1765 attributed to William France (FIG 280), a close associate of Robert Adam, which hangs in Lady Spencer's Dressing Room. This has been paired with a replica carved by Clifford Wright, and it is scarcely possible to tell the two apart. Perhaps the most exciting acquisition was a suite of mahogany chairs, now in the Ante Room, which had earlier been sold from Althorp and are believed to have been made for the 1st Earl Spencer by William and John Gordon. Dating from around 1760, these chairs may well have been intended for use at Spencer House, and by a remarkable stroke of fortune a matching armchair has been discovered and acquired in Paris.

So often the restoration of eighteenth-century buildings is spoilt by inappropriate floor coverings, especially fitted carpets, which were more or less unknown in England before the turn of the nineteenth century. In the state apartments at Spencer House it was decided to opt for the traditional solution of bare boards and loose Oriental rugs. In general antique rugs have been used, carefully chosen for colour, quality and wear. Their rarity gives them an importance and interest consistent with their surroundings. Among the best is the rug in the Palm Room, produced in Agra around 1860 and an exceptionally fine example of this sought-after manufacture. In the case of the Great Room, no carpet could be found of adequate size and quality, so it was decided to commission a new carpet, currently being woven in Turkey to an authentic seventeenth-century Persian pattern.

Spencer House was originally conceived as a setting for fine works of art and the company was determined to seek out paintings and sculpture of exceptional quality, preferably having some historical or stylistic connection with the original collection. Among the most significant acquisitions were the two Neo-Classical paintings which hang today on either side of the chimney-piece in the Great Room. Originally commissioned for Houghton Hall, they were produced by Cipriani, the artist who designed the 1st Earl Spencer's funerary monument, and the style and subject matter reflect the same fascination with Antiquity which characterizes the room. Their size, moreover, echoes the scale of the paintings which hung here originally, while the frames, specially carved by Arnold Wiggins and Sons Ltd, are copies of the original Great Room picture frames designed by James Stuart to match the door and window surrounds (FIG 281).

A significant historical link with the original collection was made when the company purchased a second, signed version of a painting well known to the eighteenth century: Carlo Maratta's *Introduction of the Marchese Pallavicini by the Artist to the Temple of Virtù* (PL XXIII, p. 191).[1] The composition, with the poet and patron of the arts, Niccolo Maria Pallavicini (1650–1714) led by Apollo to the Temple of Fame, was inspired by the Andrea Sacchi which the 1st Earl acquired at vast expense in 1758, and which had earlier belonged to Pallavicini himself.[2]

Another important acquisition was the giant bust of the Roman Emperor Lucius Verus which presides over the Entrance Hall, a further reminder of the 1st Earl Spencer's passion for Antiquity and his particular admiration for Classical sculpture. The company has also made a special point of purchasing Spencer family portraits, examples of which are displayed in various parts of the house, including a mezzotint of the 1st Earl's wife which hangs in the Library, together with a group portrait of the Society of Dilettanti, of which the Earl himself was a prominent member.

As with the furniture, the company has sought to supplement its purchases with loans from public and private collections. It was especially thrilling to discover that Gavin Hamilton's *Agrippina*, commissioned by the 1st Earl Spencer during the period of Spencer House's construction, was held in store at the Tate Gallery. The Trustees gave consent for the painting to be lent and today it hangs in the Dining Room, possibly its original location. The painting is especially well-suited to hang here for in the background is a Classical building modelled on the Temple of Fortuna Virilis in Rome, the source for the

280 Spencer House, Lady Spencer's Dressing Room, detail showing a giltwood girandole of c1765, attributed to William France. To make up a pair, a copy of the girandole was commissioned from Clifford Wright. The girandole is displayed against the crimson silk damask specially woven to an original eighteenth-century pattern by Richard Humphries. The hangings are framed by replicas of the original giltwood fillets used to mask the tacks holding the fabric in place, carved by Dick Reid

281 Carver Ben Bacon at work for Arnold Wiggins & Sons on the replication of the original Stuart picture frames from the Great Room

design of the Dining Room frieze. Five works originally commissioned by George III from Benjamin West have been lent from the Royal Collection, and the Royal Academy has made frequent temporary loans, including a celebrated portrait of William Chambers by Joshua Reynolds, a close friend and protégé of the 1st and 2nd Earls Spencer, and a portrait of the sculptor Joseph Wilton, who worked on the construction of Spencer House under Vardy. Due to Lord Rothschild's close personal involvement with Waddesdon Manor, the National Trust agreed to lend a set of four full-length female portraits by Reynolds for the Great Room. As with the Ciprianis, the dimensions of these paintings recall the originals they replace.

Lord Rothschild has himself lent paintings, among them a landscape by Ruysdael and a peasant scene by van Ostade, which hang in Lady Spencer's Dressing Room. Similar paintings are known to have hung here originally, and the double-stacked picture-hang is likewise of eighteenth-century inspiration. Another major loan, again from a private collector, is the centaur which stands in the Staircase Hall, a full-scale copy by the eighteenth-century sculptor Cavaceppi of a famous Antique original in Rome, which the 1st Earl Spencer would certainly have seen and admired on the Grand Tour. The company has also welcomed loans from the art trade, among them an outstanding painting by Murillo, *St Joseph with the Christ Child*, which hung for a time in the Dining Room.

Finally, and not inappropriately, Spencer House has at times provided a sanctuary for works of art displaced by restoration projects elsewhere. Thanks to the generosity of the Whitbread family, a fine collection of eighteenth-century paintings and furniture was placed on loan during the refurbishment of Southill Park, while Sir George Christie lent an equally fine selection of paintings from his own collection at Glyndebourne during the reconstruction of the famous opera house.

41 CONCLUSION

A CONCLUSION is in one sense premature. Work on Spencer House continues. Appropriate late eighteenth-century planting is planned for the garden, and the decoration of the state apartments constantly evolves as fresh opportunities arise to purchase and borrow suitable furniture and works of art. But already one can speak of lasting achievements.

In architectural terms the project has been hailed as one of the most successful ever undertaken. Once again the house achieves that perfect fusion of the fine and decorative arts to which the 1st Earl Spencer and his architects originally aspired. Now, as in the eighteenth century, the state apartments provide a showcase in which it is possible to admire some of the finest works of art and furniture anywhere on public display in an architectural setting of incomparable beauty and sophistication.

Equally important, the house now has a role, a living function. While retaining the atmosphere of a private residence, it serves as a place of business and a focus of social, cultural and political activity, just as it did originally. In December 1989, the Great Room provided the setting for a dinner held by the Society of Dilettanti, which two centuries earlier had played such a vital role in the design and construction of the house. The dinner was attended by the Prince and Princess of Wales, and it was the Princess, a direct descendant of the 1st Earl Spencer, who opened the building officially in 1990. Since then there have been countless receptions, as well as concerts, lectures, tours and other events. In July 1990 the Nato summit lunch was held at Spencer House, attended by the British Prime Minister and other world leaders, and the following year the house was chosen again for the G7 summit lunch. In August 1992 the state apartments were thrown open for a dinner, hosted by all the living British Prime Ministers, to celebrate the 40th anniversary of the accession of Her Majesty The Queen, who was joined on this occasion by senior members of the royal family (FIG 282).

The success of the Spencer House project clearly demonstrates that high-quality restoration can be acheived within a commercial framework and points the way to greater cooperation between architects and historians, planners and developers. Valuable discoveries have been made and existing ideas and techniques refined, while vital training has been provided in traditional craft skills. The restoration of Spencer House, no less than its construction, is a paradigm of what can be achieved through architecture and offers hope to all who love historic buildings.

282 Her Majesty The Queen arrives at Spencer House on the occasion of a dinner held in her honour by past and present prime ministers to celebrate the fortieth anniversary of her accession to the throne. The Queen with the Prime Minister, John Major, and Lord Rothschild

OVER PAGE
283 Spencer House, Staircase Hall. The balustrade was restored to its original steel-blue colour, with trompe-l'oeil drapery by decorative artists Alan Dodd and Richard de Baer

APPENDICES

I Spencer Family Tree

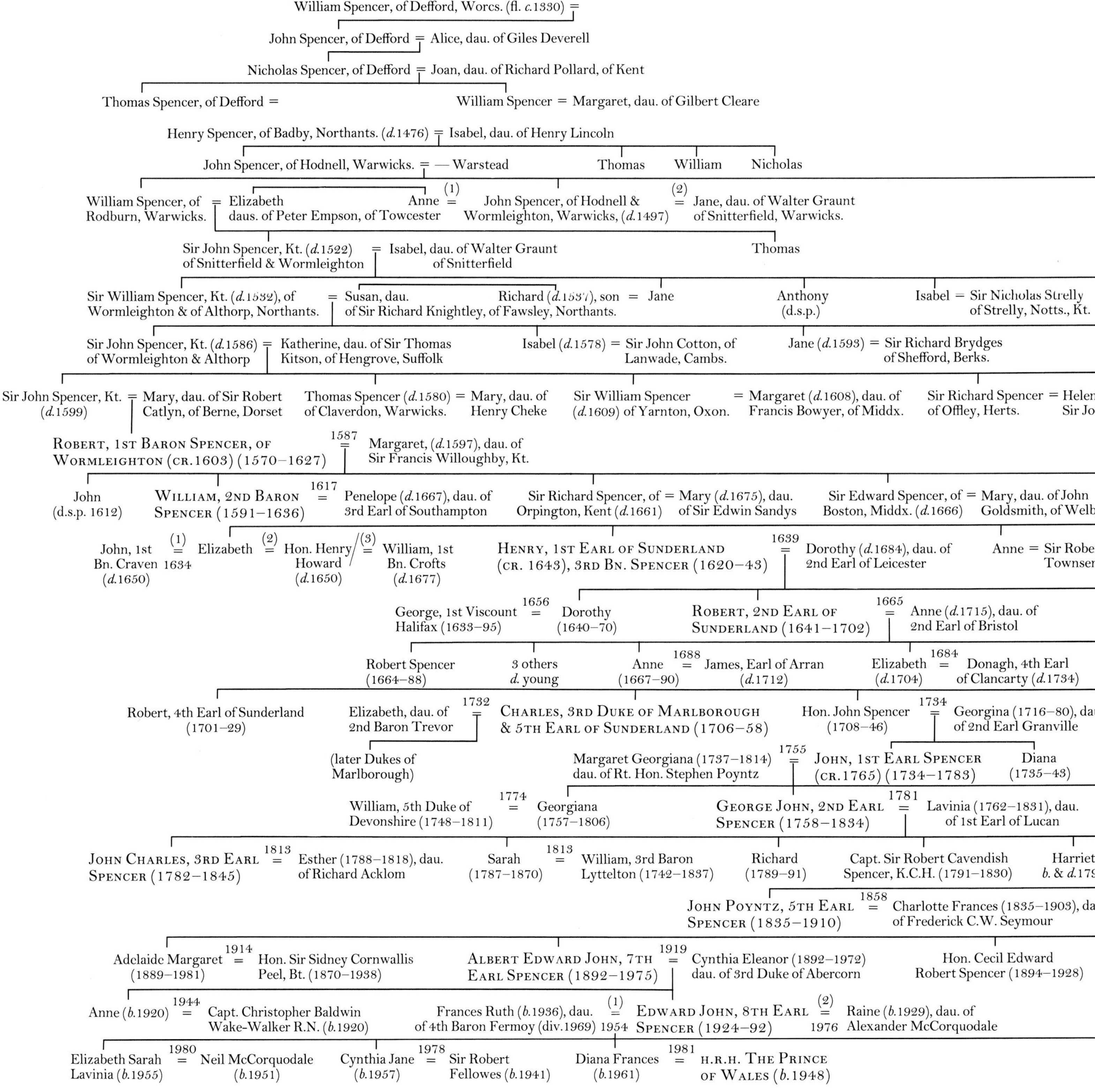

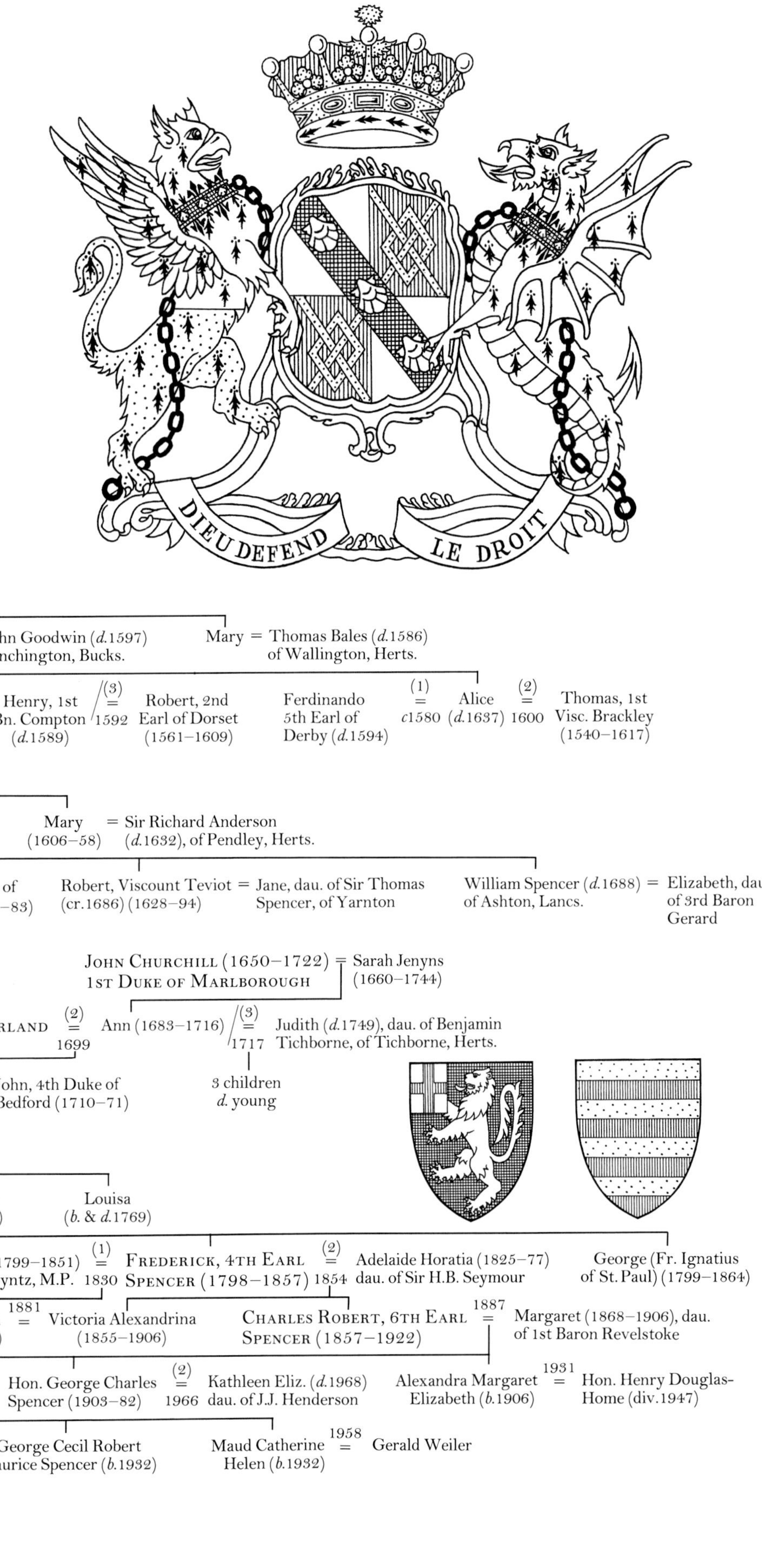

Thomas Spencer, of Badby & Everdon = Margaret Smith of Wold

Dorothy = Sir Richard Catesby (*d.*1553) of Legers Ashby, Northants.

Dorothy (*d.*1575) = Thomas Spencer (*d.*1576) of Badby & Everdon — Anne = Sir John Goodwin (*d.*1597) of Winchington, Bucks. — Mary = Thomas Bales (*d.*1586) of Wallington, Herts.

Elizabeth = George, 2nd Bn. Hunsdon (*d.*1603) — William, 3rd Bn. Monteagle (*d.*1581) (1) = *c*1575 Anne (*d.*1618) (2) = Henry, 1st Bn. Compton (*d.*1589) / (3) = 1592 Robert, 2nd Earl of Dorset (1561–1609) — Ferdinando 5th Earl of Derby (*d.*1594) (1) = *c*1580 Alice (*d.*1637) (2) = 1600 Thomas, 1st Visc. Brackley (1540–1617)

Elizabeth (*d.*1618) = 1607 Sir George Fane (*d.*1640) of Buston, Kent — Margaret (*d.*1613) — Mary (1606–58) = Sir Richard Anderson (*d.*1632), of Pendley, Herts.

Alice (*b.*1625) = Henry, 1st Earl of Drogheda (*d.*1676) — Margaret (1627–93) = 1655 Anthony, 1st Earl of Shaftesbury (1621–83) — Robert, Viscount Teviot (cr.1686) (1628–94) = Jane, dau. of Sir Thomas Spencer, of Yarnton — William Spencer (*d.*1688) of Ashton, Lancs. = Elizabeth, dau. of 3rd Baron Gerard

Penelope (*d.* an infant)

John Churchill (1650–1722) 1st Duke of Marlborough = Sarah Jenyns (1660–1744)

Arabella (1673–98), dau. of 2nd Duke of Newcastle (1) = 1695 Charles, 3rd Earl of Sunderland (1675–1722) (2) = 1699 Ann (1683–1716) / (3) = 1717 Judith (*d.*1749), dau. of Benjamin Tichborne, of Tichborne, Herts.

Anne (1702–69) = 1720 William, 1st Viscount Bateman (*d.*1744) — Diana (1710–35) = 1731 John, 4th Duke of Bedford (1710–71) — 3 children *d.* young

Henrietta Frances (1761–1821) = 1780 Frederick, 3rd Earl of Bessborough (1758–1844) — Charlotte (1765–66) — Louisa (*b.* & *d.*1769)

Georgiana Charlotte (1794–1823) = 1814 Lord George Quin (1792–1888) — Georgiana Eliz. (1799–1851) dau. of Willm. Poyntz, M.P. (1) = 1830 Frederick, 4th Earl Spencer (1798–1857) (2) = 1854 Adelaide Horatia (1825–77) dau. of Sir H.B. Seymour — George (Fr. Ignatius of St. Paul) (1799–1864)

Georgiana Frances (1832–52) — Sarah Isabella (1838–1919) — William, 2nd Baron Sandhurst (1855–1921) = 1881 Victoria Alexandrina (1855–1906) — Charles Robert, 6th Earl Spencer (1857–1922) = 1887 Margaret (1868–1906), dau. of 1st Baron Revelstoke

Lavinia Emily (1899–1955) = Luke, 4th Baron Annaly (1885–19) — Barbara, dau. of Benjamin Blumenthal (div.1962) (1) = 1931 Hon. George Charles Spencer (1903–82) (2) = 1966 Kathleen Eliz. (*d.*1968) dau. of J.J. Henderson — Alexandra Margaret Elizabeth (*b.*1906) = 1931 Hon. Henry Douglas-Home (div.1947)

George Cecil Robert Maurice Spencer (*b.*1932) — Maud Catherine Helen (*b.*1932) = 1958 Gerald Weiler

Charles Edward Maurice 9th Earl Spencer (*b.*1964) = 1989 Victoria, dau. of John Lockwood

Kitty Eleanor (*b.*1990) — Eliza Victoria (*b.*1992) — Catya Amelia (*b.*1992)

Key: d.s.p.: decessit sine prole (died without issue) Bn.: Baron Visc.: Viscount cr.: created

II Spencer House building accounts

Vouchers and other documents relating to the construction of Spencer House were retained by the Spencers until at least June 1766, when they were gathered together and submitted to an auditor of the Inner Temple, Thomas Parker.[1] Thereafter they appear to have been either lost or destroyed, possibly in the aftermath of the death of the 1st Earl Spencer, the bulk of whose papers were burnt by his widow. The accounts are no longer in the Spencer archive;[2] nor are they mentioned in the first recorded catalogue of the archive published in 1871.[3] The 7th Earl Spencer could find no trace of the papers when researching his article on Spencer House for *Country Life* in 1926,[4] and had still not found them when in 1964 he published his own summary catalogue of the family archive.[5] Neither the Inner Temple nor the Middle Temple has any record of the papers of Thomas Parker, the auditor who examined the Spencer House accounts in 1766;[6] and the accounts do not appear alongside Parker's affidavit in the Public Record Office.[7] However, in the archives of Hoare's Bank in Fleet Street, where the 1st Earl Spencer kept an account, there are records of payments which Spencer made through his architect John Vardy to various artists and craftsmen during the period the house was being built. The records cover the early stage of construction, spanning the period 25 February 1757 – 27 July 1759, although there are payments after that date to Vardy alone ending on 2 April 1765, shortly before the architect's death. Although incomplete (work on the house continued until the spring of 1766), the records at Hoare's are extremely valuable in that they supply the names of at least some of the contractors involved in the project, as well as approximate dates and figures. Not all the contractors have been identified; it would be particularly interesting to discover the identity of Robert Friend, who was clearly a major player, his fees totalling more than £1000. However, many were leading figures and these are dealt with in detail in the main text, while footnotes provide suggestions in cases where the identity of contractors is in doubt.

Accounts

1 Ledger Y, fol.251
[February-June 1757]

	£
February	
25 To John Vardy's bill to John Devall	500
March	
2 To John Vardy's bill to John Palmer	9 : 7 : 0
9 To Do – to Col. Geo Gray	221 : 6 : 8
16 To Do – to James Eves	807
April	
21 To John Vardy's bill to Robert Friend[8]	200
May	
6 To John Vardy's bill to Thomas Vardy	100
21 To John Vardy's bill to John Hutchins	24
28 To John Vardy's bill to John Devall	1000
To Do's rect	200

2 Ledger Z, fol.157
[June–October 1757]

June	
27 To John Vardy's rect	400
30 To Do's bill to Fra Benson	157 : 10 : 0
July	
23 To John Vardy's bill to John Spencer	150
September	
10 To John Vardy's bill to John Raven	9
16 To Do – to John Devall	500
17 To Do – to Ed: Gray	200
October	
3 To John Vardy's bill to Thomas Vardy	100

3 Ledger Z, fol.158
[October 1757–March 1758]

October	
22 To John Vardy's bill to John Devall	200
November	
2 To John Vardy's bill to James Eves	455
7 To Do – to Edward Gray	100
8 To John Vardy's bill to John Spencer	100
11 To John Vardy's bill to Thomas Vardy	200
1758	
January	
25 To John Vardy's bill to Daniel Fenton	22 : 15 : 0

4 Ledger Z, fol.159
[March–July 1758]

March	
15 To John Vardy's bill to Edward Gray	545 : 17 : 0
18 To Do's bill to John Spencer	559
29 To Do – to John Palmer	81 : 15 : 0
30 To Do – to Henry Crowder[9]	23
" To Do – to Thomas Vardy	243 : 15 : 0
April	
4 To John Vardy's bill to Edward Eves [?]	386
15 To John Vardy's bill to Robert Friend	100
May	
13 To John Vardy's bill to Robert Friend	100
June	
8 To John Vardy's bill to John Devall	400
10 To Do – to Do	770 : 8 : 0
20 To Do – to John Marshall[10]	215 : 10 : 0
July	
1 To John Vardy's bill to Mr Friend	100
8 To Do – to John Davis	50

5 Ledger Z, fol.160
[July–November 1758]

July	
12 To John Vardy's bill to Mr H. Spang	50
August	
11 To John Vardy's bill to Robert Murry	25

19 To John Vardy's bill to Robert Friend 50
22 To Do – to Thomas Vardy 100
26 To Do – to Edward Gray 100
" To Do – to John Devall 200

September
30 To John Vardy's bill to Daniel Fenton 8 : 8 : 0
" To Do – to Edward Gray 300
" To Do – to Robert Friend 100

October
2 To John Vardy's bill to Mr John Spencer 200
17 To John Vardy's bill to John Davis 50

6 Ledger Z, fol.161
[November 1758–April 1759]

November
25 To John Vardy's bill to Robert Friend 100
27 To John Vardy's bill to Thomas Vardy 100
29 To Do – to John Devall 500
" To Do – to Edward Gray 200

December
19 To John Vardy's bill to John Coultarte[11] 100
20 To Do – to Henry Spang 100
23 To Do – to Edward Gray 100
" To Do – to Joseph Rose 50

1759
January
3 To John Vardy's bill to T. Vardy 400
19 To John Vardy's bill to Joseph Carr 20
31 To John Vardy's bill to R. Murry 20

February
3 To John Vardy's bill to Robert Friend 50
12 To John Vardy's bill to Joseph Wilton 30
15 To Do – to John Hutchinson[12] 8 : 10 : 0
17 To Do – to Joseph Rose 30

7 Ledger A, fol.266
[May–September 1759]

May
11 To John Vardy's bill to Robert Friend 60
12 To Do – to John Devall 300
16 To Do – to Edward Gray 100
17 To Do – to Richard Coventry 59 : 9 : 0
" To Do – to Thomas Vardy 200
22 To John Vardy's bill to John Palmer 50
25 To Do – to Thomas Clark 100

June
1 To John Vardy's bill to Mr Spencer 50
4 To John Vardy's bill to Robert Friend 50
" To Do's bill to George Marshall[13] 30

July
27 To John Vardy's bill to Robert Friend 100

8 Ledger A, fol.267
[October 1759–February 1760]

October
13 To John Vardy's bill to Robert Friend 50

9 Ledger A, fol.268
[March–October 1760]

May
23 To John Vardy 1000

June
30 To John Vardy 1000

10 Ledger B, fol.385
[January–May 1762]

February
26 To John Vardy 96 : 8 : 10

11 Ledger C, fol.231
[February–June 1765]

April
2 To John Vardy 1139 : 10 : 0

Notes

[1] AP D31; PRO C33/425, fols 295, 340

[2] Every attempt has been made to trace the Spencer House accounts among the surviving Spencer papers in the Manuscripts Department of the British Library, the Northamptonshire County Record Office and the Muniment Room at Althorp, but without success. Nor is there any reference to the papers at the Royal Commission on Historical Manuscripts

[3] Alfred J. Horwood, 'The Manuscripts of the Right Honourable Earl Spencer at Spencer House, St James's', in *Second Report of the Royal Commission on Historical Manuscripts* (London, 1871), pp.12–20

[4] Earl Spencer, 'Spencer House, St. James's Place', *Country Life* (30 Oct, 6 and 13 Nov 1926)

[5] Earl Spencer, 'Spencer MSS. The Archives of the Spencer Family belonging to Albert Edward John, 7th Earl Spencer', *Bulletin of the National Register of Archives* (Historical Manuscripts Commission, No. 13, 1964), pp.21–6

[6] I am grateful to Ian Murray and Lesley Whitelaw, librarians respectively of the Inner Temple and the Middle Temple, for their help in trying to trace the Parker papers

[7] PRO C31/161

[8] There are records of earlier payments to this individual from an account kept by Vardy at Drummonds Bank, related perhaps to some other joint project (DB, Account of John Vardy, 1755)

[9] Ibid. (1754)

[10] A cabinet-maker and upholsterer by this name is recorded at Walker's Court, Knave's Acre, Golden Square, in 1749 (*Dictionary of English Furniture Makers*) and in a trade directory kept by Georgiana, Countess Spencer (AP 200)

[11] Possibly related to Richard Coultart, a carver registered in the Parish of St George's, Hanover Square, in 1767, and at Park Street, Grosvenor Square, in 1774 (*Dictionary of English Furniture Makers*)

[12] Possibly the upholsterer John Hutchinson, engaged on the decoration of Audley End, Essex, in *c*1762–71 (Ibid.)

[13] Possibly the furniture-maker of this name, active around 1772

III Pictures in my Dressing Room in London

One of the few surviving documents relating to the early history of Spencer House is a memorandum drawn up by Georgiana, Countess Spencer, listing the paintings in her Dressing Room.[1] The memorandum, entitled *Pictures in my Dressing Room in London*, is undated, but was probably drawn up around 1770[2] and agrees in most particulars with Arthur Young's description of *c*1769 (see chp. 18, p.190–95), although discrepancies suggest that the hang of paintings was subject to change. In the eighteenth century the attribution of works of art had not yet become the exacting business it is today, and several of the paintings which Lady Spencer believed to be by the great European masters have since been shown to be the product of their studio or followers.[3] Nonetheless, the memorandum is valuable in that it indicates the kind of paintings thought suitable for a lady's dressing room at this time, while demonstrating how seriously Lady Spencer took the study of art and history. One can easily imagine the Countess, on days when she received, regaling her guests with the information she had gathered on the subject-matter of her paintings and the biographical details of their supposed authors.

Pictures in my Dressing Room in London

Landscape by Nicolo Poussin over the Chimney the Spy's returning from the promis'd Land[4]

A Madona & Child by Guido Rheni Scholar to Hannibal Carraci of the Bolognese School[5]

A Salutation by Parmigiano He Studied after Coreggio & was of the Lombard School[6]

A Courtezan by Titian He was scholar to John Bellini & of the Venetian School[7]

The marriage of St Catherine by Carlo Dolci a Florentine[8]

The Offering of the Shepherds by Valerio di Castella, of the Genoese School scholar to Biscaina[9]

A St Catherine by Leonardo da Vinci a Florentine[10]

A girl by Reubens, of the Flemish School[11]

A Holy Family by Frederick Barocio, he studied from Coreggio & was of the Lombard School[12]

A Holy Family by Albano, he was of the Carraci School[13]

A St Francis by Guido Rheni[14]

A Landscape by Salvata Rosa, a Neapolitan[15]

A St Sebastian by Guercino of the Caracci School[16]

A Holy Family by Carlo Marat, a Scholar of Andreo Sacchi[17]

6 peices by Teniers of the Flemish School, he was a scholar of Reubens[18]

4 peices D^{o} by Paulia Lucia Gentile[19]

Notes

1 AP F169

2 One of the paintings listed, Barocci's *Holy Family*, is thought to have been acquired in 1769 and since the Countess moved from Spencer House in 1783 following the death of her husband, the memorandum must have been drawn up between these two dates

3 Kenneth Garlick, 'A Catalogue of Pictures at Althorp', *Walpole Society*, 45 (1974–76) (hereafter referred to as 'Garlick')

4 Francois Millet (1642–79), *The Promised Land*, oil on canvas, $37\frac{1}{2}'' \times 52\frac{1}{2}''$ (Garlick, No. 458). The painting is almost certainly the 'Landscape with Figures', then believed to be by Nicolas Poussin, which the 1st Earl Spencer acquired at the Sir Luke Schaub sale in 1758 (*A Catalogue of the Grand and Capital Collection of Italian, Flemish and Dutch Paintings of the Hon. Sir Luke Schaub, lately deceased* (Langford, London, 26–28 April 1758), 1st Day, No. 49, price £48 6s). The painting was ascribed by Arthur Young to Claude Lorraine (Young, op. cit., p.358) and by Horace Walpole, who saw it at Althorp in 1760, to Gaspard Dughet (Paget Toynbee (ed.), 'Horace Walpole's Journals of Visits to Country Seats &c', *Walpole Society*, XVI (1927–28), p.31, but it has since been reattributed to Francois Millet

5 Guido Reni (1575–1642), *The Virgin and Child*, oil on panel, $19\frac{1}{4}'' \times 15\frac{1}{2}''$ [enlarged to $22'' \times 17''$] (Garlick, No. 510). The painting had previously hung at Althorp, where it was listed in the inventory of 1746 (AP L15, *A Catalogue of the Pictures at Althorpe and Wimbleton [sic] belonging to the late Honble. Mr Spencer*), and was much admired by Horace Walpole, who possessed a copy by Sassoferrato (*Visits to Country Seats*, p.31)

6 Gerolamo Mazzola Bedoli (*c*1500–69), *The Annunciation*, oil on panel, $33'' \times 23''$ (Garlick, No. 40). The painting had previously hung in the 'Picture Closett' at Althorp, where it was noted by Knapton as the work of Parmigianino in the inventory of 1746. The painting was still at Althorp in 1760, when it was noted by Horace Walpole, again as the work of Parmigianino (*Visits to Country Seats*, p.31), but it has since been reattributed to Gerolamo Mazzola Bedoli

7 Titian (*c*1487/90–1576), studio of, *Portrait of a Young Woman*, oil on canvas, $35'' \times 25''$ (Garlick, No. 644)

8 Carlo Dolci (1616–86), *Marriage of St Catherine*, oil on canvas, $28'' \times 23''$ (Garlick, No. 130). The painting was acquired by the 1st Earl's father from George Knapton in 1740 (AP L15, receipt from Knapton dated 23 Nov 1740 in the sum of £80 for 'a Picture of Carlo Dolci representing a mariage of St. Caterine') and was noted by Knapton in the 'Picture Closett' at Althorp in the inventory of 1746. It was sold by the 8th Earl Spencer to Colnaghi in 1982 (Alexandra Artley and 'Thomas Dibdin', 'Restoration Comedy', *Harpers and Queen* (April 1987), p.172; Simon

Blow and Alexandra Artley, 'A Tale of Two Houses', *Connoisseur* (June, 1991), p.62)

[9] Valerio Castelli (1625–59), *Adoration of the Shepherds*, oil on canvas, oval, 26″ × 40″ (Garlick, No. 82). The painting does not appear in the inventory of 1746 and may therefore have been acquired by the Spencers themselves, possibly during their visit to Italy in 1763–64

[10] Unlisted in Garlick, but noted by Knapton in the inventory of 1746, when it was hanging in the Green Room at Althorp

[11] Sir Peter Paul Rubens (1577–1640), *Daughter of Balthasar Gerbier*, oil on canvas, 26″ × 21″ (Garlick, No. 571). The painting was acquired by the 1st Earl Spencer at the Sir William Hamilton sale, Prestage's, London, 20 Feb 1761 (*A Catalogue of well-known and approved Collection of Pictures [i.e. that WH]... which will be sold by Auction by Messrs Prestage and Hobbs... on Friday and Saturday the 20th and 21st of February 1761*, 1st day, lot 78)

[12] Federico Barocci (*c*1535–1612), *Holy Family*, oil on canvas, $23\frac{1}{2}$″ × 17″ (Garlick, No. 23). During their tour of Italy in 1763–64 the Spencers acquired a work by this artist described by their travelling companion David Garrick as 'a very good sketch of a Picture by Baroche' (David Garrick to the Duke of Devonshire, Abano, 25 June 1764, quoted in *Sir Brinsley Ford Papers*). However, on the evidence of a receipt in the Spencer archive, now apparently lost, Garlick identifies the present painting as one which the Spencers acquired through the agency of Matthew Nulty in Rome in 1769 at a price of £50

[13] Francesco Albani (1578–1660), *Holy Family*, oil on canvas, $14\frac{1}{2}$″ × $11\frac{1}{4}$″ (Garlick, No. 3). The painting had been inherited from Sarah, Duchess of Marlborough and formerly hung in the 'Picture Closett' at Althorp, where it was noted by Knapton in the inventory of 1746. It was sold by the 8th Earl Spencer to Colnaghi in 1982 (Artley and 'Dibdin', op. cit., p.172; Blow and Artley, op. cit., p.62)

[14] Guido Reni (1575–1642), school of, *St Francis*, oil on canvas, 17″ × $12\frac{1}{2}$″ (Garlick, No. 522). The painting formed part of the Sunderland collection and was ascribed to Reni by Knapton in the inventory of 1746, when it was hanging in the 'Picture Closett' at Althorp

[15] Unidentified

[16] Guercino (1591–1666), *St Sebastian and the Angels*, oil on copper, $17\frac{1}{2}$″ × 13″ (Garlick, No. 247). The painting is almost certainly the *St Sebastian* by Guercino which the 1st Earl Spencer acquired at the Sir Luke Schaub sale in 1758 (*A Catalogue of the Grand and Capital Collection of Italian, Flemish and Dutch Paintings of the Hon. Sir Luke Schaub, lately deceased etc.*, 26–28 Apr 1758, 1st day, No. 52)

[17] After Carlo Maratta (1625–1713), *The Flight into Egypt*, oil on copper, 23″ × $18\frac{1}{2}$″ (Garlick, No. 438). The painting is thought to be a copy, possibly by a pupil, of a famous original by Maratta now in the Galleria Nazionale in Rome. It formed part of the Sunderland collection and was ascribed to Maratta by Knapton in the inventory of 1746, when it was hanging in the 'Picture Closett' at Althorp. The painting was still at Althorp in 1760, when it was noted by Horace Walpole (*Visits to Country Seats*, p.31)

[18] David Teniers the younger (1610–90), *Perseus and Andromeda, Triumph of Venus and Cupid, Leander Dead, Neptune's Car perturbed by a Crocodile, Triumph of Amphitrite, Rape of Europa*, oil on copper, $8\frac{1}{2}$″ × 20″ (Garlick, Nos 630–35). The prior history of the paintings is unknown and it is possible that they were acquired by the Spencers themselves. The set was broken up when in 1985 *Leander Dead* was sold through Sotheby's by the 8th Earl Spencer (Artley and 'Dibdin', op. cit., p.172; Blow and Artley, op. cit., p.63)

[19] Louis Cousin, called also 'Gentile' (1606–67), *The Triumph of Venus, The Triumph of Amphitrite, The Triumph of Arion, The Triumph of Galatea*, oil on copper, $8\frac{1}{2}$″ × 20″ (Garlick, Nos 109–12). The paintings form an obvious set with the preceding works by Teniers and may have been acquired in 1766, the date which appears on the reverse side of *The Triumph of Venus*

IV Views of Spencer House

The following is a list of paintings, drawings and engravings showing views of Spencer House from the time of its construction to the mid-nineteenth century.

Paintings and Drawings

North-west View of Spencer House, unattributed, watercolour drawing, *c*1780 [GLRO, Maps and Prints, Westminster DD, 5386]

Spencer House, by R. B. Schnebbelie, pen and ink, *c*1798 [GLRO, Maps and Prints, Westminster DD, 5411]

West Front of Spencer House, office of Sir John Soane, watercolour drawing, *c*1809 [SJSM, 17/3/-]

West Front of Spencer House, office of Sir John Soane, watercolour drawing, *c*1817 [SJSM 17/3/7]

St James's Place (north front of Spencer House), by C. J. Richardson, watercolour drawing, 1819 [GLRO, Maps and Prints, Westminster DD, 5342]

Elevation of Lord Spencer's in the Green Park, unattributed, watercolour drawing, *c*1820 [GLRO, Maps and Prints, Westminster DD, 5409]

Lord Spencer's, by C. J. Richardson, watercolour drawing, July 1828 [GLRO, Maps and Prints, Westminster DD, 5394]

Spencer House, unattributed, pen and ink, *c*1840 [GLRO, Maps and Prints, Westminster DD, 5385]

Engravings

Mr Spencer's, engraved by B. Green after S. Wale, in R. and J. Dodsley, *London and its Environs Described*, 6 vols. (1761), 3, p.65

To The Rt Honble Ld Visct Spencer this North West View of his House in St. James's Place is Humbly Inscribed by his most Obedient and most Humble Servant John Vardy... 1763, engraved by Thomas Miller after John Vardy, 1763 [copy in GLRO, Maps and Prints, Westminster DD, 15430]

The West Front of Ld Spencers House to the Green Park, drawn and engraved by John Vardy, 1763 [copy in GLRO, Maps and Prints, Westminster DD, 5387]

The North Front of Ld Spencers House in St James's Place, drawn and engraved by John

Vardy, 1763 [copy in GLRO, Maps and Prints, Westminster DD, 5389]

The Ground Plan of the Rt Honble Ld Spencer's House in St James's Place, drawn and engraved by John Vardy, 1763 [copy in GLRO, Maps and Prints, Westminster DD, 5392]

Front to St. James's Park [sic] of the Rt. Honble Earl Spencer's, engraved by M. Darly after J. Gandon, in Woolfe and Gandon, *Vitruvius Britannicus*, IV (1767), pls 39–40

Front to the Street of the Rt Honble Earl Spencer's, engraved by M. Darly after J. Gandon, in Woolfe and Gandon, *Vitruvius Britannicus*, IV (1767), pl.38

Plan of the Ground Floor of Ye Rt Honble Earl Spencer's, engraved by M. Darly after J. Gandon, in Woolfe and Gandon, *Vitruvius Britannicus*, IV (1767), pl.37

Spencer House, aquatint, 29 Nov 1800, published in Thomas Malton, *A Picturesque Tour through the Cities of London and Westminster* (1800), pl.96 [coloured version of the above in WPL, Box 35, No. 15a]

Earl Spencer's, St James's Park [sic], engraved by James Peller Malcolm after R. B. Schnebbelie, published by Malcolm, London, 16 Jan 1798, and in Malcolm, *Malcolm's Views within Twelve Miles Round London* (1810) (penultimate plate); *Londinium Redivivum*, IV (1802–07), p.246; *Malcolm's One Hundred and Nineteen Views* (1836), pl.33

Earl Spencers St James's Park [sic], line engraving, *c*1800 [untraced; copy in GLRO, Maps and Prints, Westminster DD, 5406]

West Front of Earl Spencer's House, St. James's Place, London, engraved by J. Storer after Hodgetts, in T. F. Dibdin, *Bibliotheca Spenceriana*, 4 vols (1814–15), I (1814), p.IX

View from the Library Window, Spencer House, St. James's Place, engraved by J. Storer after Hodgetts, in Dibdin, op. cit., I, p.383

Homer, Chimney Piece Ornament in the Library at Spencer House, From the Sculpture of Scheemaker, engraved by S. Freeman after W. Alexander, in Dibdin, op. cit., IV (1815), p.587

Earl Spencer's House, Green Park, engraved by E. Byrne after J. P. Neale, published by John Harris, St Paul's Church Yard, London, 1 Mar 1815, and in Revd Joseph Nightingale, *The Beauties of England and Wales*, x, part III (1815), opp. p.638

Earl Spencer's House, Green Park, drawn and engraved by W. Wallis, published by W. Clarke, New Bond Street, London, 1 Feb 1817, and in David Hughson, *Walks through London*, 2 vols (1817), 2, p.263

Lord Spenser's House [sic], line engraving, published in *London Scenes, or a Visit to Uncle William in Town; containing a description of the most remarkable Buildings and Curiosities in the British Metropolis* (1818), opp. p.273 (opp. p.161 in 1825 edn)

Earl Spencer's House, line engraving, in Samuel Leigh, *Leigh's New Picture of London* (1818), opp. p.81

Earl Spencer's House, line engraving, published in *The Picture of London for 1820* (1820), opp. p.122

Earl Spencer's House, line engraving, in John Britton, *Britton's Original Picture of London* (1826), p.287

Earl Spencer's House, Green Park, engraved by T. Barber after Thomas H. Shepherd, published by Jones & Co, Temple of the Muses, Finsbury Square, London , 1831, and in Shepherd, *London and its Environs in the Nineteenth Century* (1829–31), p.114

Earl Spencer's House, Green Park, engraved by J. Shury, *c*1834, published in C. F. Partington, *Natural History and Views of London and its Environs*, 2 vols (1834–35), 2, p.27

Spencer House, line engraving in Samuel Leigh, *Leigh's New Picture of London* (1834), opp. p.164 (opp. p.172 in 1839 edn)

Spencer House, Green Park, steel engraving, *c*1850, published in *The Penny Magazine* [copy in GLRO, Maps and Prints, Westminster DD, 25426]

Mansions of Earl Spencer and the Earl of Ellesmere in the Green Park, engraved by H. Adlard, published in *London Almanack for 1851* [copy in GLRO, Maps and Prints, Westminster DD, 14188]

GENERAL VIEWS

Paintings and Drawings

Green Park, English School, *c*1760 [Coll. Earl Spencer]

Green Park, by David Turner, oil on canvas, *c*1800 [ex. Coll. Earl Spencer; purchased by 7th Earl Spencer from Leggatt Brothers 1922; listed in Garlick, No. 647]

Green Park, by J. Curtis, oil on canvas, *c*1800 [National Trust, Anglesey Abbey]

Engravings

View of the Queen's Walk in the Green Park, engraved by Storer after E. Dayes, published by L. Stockdale, Piccadilly, London, 15 Apr 1797, and in Hunter, *The History of London and its Environs*, 2 vols (1811)

View of the Lodge in the Green Park, aquatint, *c*1800 [copy in GLRO, Maps and Prints, Westminster DD, 26235]

A Meeting in the Park, aquatint, 1806 [copy in Museum of London, A18101];

The Bason in the Green Park, St. James's, coloured aquatint, published by Rudolph Ackermann, 101 Strand, London, 1 Oct 1810, in No. 22 of *Ackermann's Repository of the Arts*, and in Papworth, *Select Views of London* (1816), pl.IX

Summer Fashions for 1842 . . . View, St. James's from Green Park, London, coloured engraving, published by B. Read & Co, 12 Hart Street, London, and Broadway, New York, 1842 [copy in Guildhall Library]

Destruction of the Victoria and Albert Balloon on Monday Evening June 16th 1851, aquatint, published by Ackermann & Co, 96, Strand, London, 1851 [copy in WPL, Box 35, No. 12b]

V Spencer House: A bibliography 1761–1851

Between the time of its construction and the Great Exhibition of 1851 Spencer House featured in no fewer than thirty-four guides to London and Great Britain, including several published either abroad or in England for the foreign market. The following is a chronological list:

Dodsley, R. and J., *London and its Environs Described, containing an Account of whatever is most remarkable for Grandeur, Elegance, Curiosity or Use in the City and in the Country Twenty Miles around it*, 6 vols (1761), 3, p.65

The Foreigner's Guide: Or, a necessary and instructive Companion Both for the Foreigner and Native, in their Tour through the Cities of London and Westminster (1763), p.28

Lerouge (publ.), *Curiosités de Londres et de l'Angleterre*, 2nd edn (Bordeaux, 1766), p.17

Young, Arthur, *A Six Weeks Tour through the Southern Counties of England and Wales*, 2nd edn (1769), pp.354–61; 3rd edn (Bordeaux, 1772), pp.110–15

A New and Complete History and Survey of the Cities of London and Westminster (c1769), pp.596–7

Noorthouck, John, *A New History of London, including Westminster and Southwark, to which is added a General Survey of the whole; describing the Public Buildings, Late Improvements, &c* (1773), p.720

Harrison, Walter, *A New and Universal History, Description, and Survey of the Cities of London and Westminster, the Borough of Southwark, and their Adjacent Parts* (1775), p.530

Walpoole, George Augustus, *The New British Traveller; or a Complete Modern Universal Display of Great-Britain and Ireland* (1784), p.268

Bowles, Carington, *New London Guide; being an Alphabetical Index to all the Streets, Squares, Lanes, Courts, Alleys, Docks, Wharfs, Keys, Stairs, &c., Churches, Chapels, and other Places of Worship; Villages, Hamlets, Hospitals and Public Buildings of every Denomination, in and within Five Miles of the Metropolis* (c1786)

Malton, Thomas, *A Picturesque Tour through the Cities of London and Westminster* (1800), p.108

Malcolm, James Peller, *Londinium Redivivum, or an Ancient History and Modern description of London*, 4 (1802–07), p.246

Hughson, David, *London; being an accurate History of the British Metropolis and its Neighbourhood, to Thirty Miles Extent, from an actual Perambulation*, 6 vols (1805–09), 4, p.324

Nightingale, Revd James, *The Beauties of England and Wales*, x, part III (1815)

Papworth, John B., *Select Views of London* (1816), pp.16–17

Hughson, David, *Walks through London* (1817), p.263

Leigh, Samuel, *Leigh's New Picture of London* (1818), p.275

Harris, John (publ.), *London Scenes, or a Visit to Uncle William in Town; containing a description of the most remarkable Buildings and Curiosities in the British Metropolis* (1818), p.88; (p.219, 1839 edn)

Shepherd, Thomas H., *London and its Environs in the Nineteenth Century* (1829), p.111

Partington, C. F., *Natural History and Views of London and its Environs*, 2 vols (1834), 2, p.26

Leigh, Samuel, *Leigh's New Picture of London* (1834), p.209; (p.219, 1839 edn)

Descrizione di Londra (Lucca, c1840), p.337

Reynolds, John, *The New Picture of London* (c1850), p.89

Cradock & Co, *London Life As It Is; or a Hand-Book to all the Attractions, Wonders and Enjoyments of the Great City* (c1850), p.56

Cradock & Co, *Londres en 1851: ou Vue Complète de la Metropole de l'Empire Britannique* (1851), p.45

Piper, W. & T., *The English and Continental Guide to London* (1851), p.85

Clarke & Co, H. G., *London as it is Today: Where to Go and What to See during the Great Exhibition* (1851), p.97

Danel, L., *Londres et ses Environs* (Lille, 1851), p.54

Bourdin, Ernest, *Guide Illustré du Voyageur à Londres* (Paris, c1851), p.134

VI Restoration and furnishing of Spencer House

Freeholders

The Trustees of The 8th Earl Spencer's Marriage Settlement

Leaseholders and clients

THE J. ROTHSCHILD GROUP
Lord Rothschild
Clive Gibson
Patrick H. Drummond
Moira Mullen
Henry Wrong
Stephen Jones
Celia de la Hey
Philippa Hart

Honorary advisory panel

Colin Amery
John Cornforth
John Harris
Gervase Jackson-Stops
Peter Thornton

Decoration and furnishing

MLINARIC, HENRY AND ZERVUDACHI LTD
David Mlinaric
Hugh Henry
Jane Rainey
Mary Birley

Professional team

ARCHITECTS
ROLFE JUDD
Donald C. Hands
Michael J. Trickett
Keith J. Hills
Jane Harris
John R. Sinclair
Judith Patrick
Jan Burne
David Smith

STRUCTURAL ENGINEERS
S. B. TIETZ & PARTNERS
James I. Hardwick
Alan S. Mansell
Michael A. Bekhor

QUANTITY SURVEYORS
LEONARD STACE PARTNERSHIP
Richard C. Gough
Paul K. Stratton
Kevin P. J. Casey

MECHANICAL & ELECTRICAL CONSULTANTS
VOCE CASE & PARTNERS
John R. Case
Stephen J. Westbrook

MAIN CONTRACTOR
WATES SPECIAL WORKS LTD
Martin J. Peat
Michael Love
David Maddams
Jeff Barley
David Smith

Consultants

SPECIAL ARCHITECTURAL ADVISER
Dan Cruickshank

ARCHITECTURAL CARVING
Dick Reid

FURNITURE
Christopher Gibbs
John Harris

GARDEN
Mary Keen

ENVIRONMENTAL CONTROL
COLEBROOK CONSULTING LTD
Robert J. Hayes

SECURITY
HARVEY SECURITY ASSOCIATES
Roy Harvey

TIMBER DECAY
RIDOUT ASSOCIATES
Brian V. Ridout

Research

HISTORICAL RESEARCH
Joseph Friedman

HISTORIC PAINT ANALYSIS
Tom Helme

GARDEN RESEARCH
Anne Chandos-Pole
SELL WADE POSTINS
Todd Longstaffe-Gowan

ADDITIONAL RESEARCH (FURNITURE)
John Hardy

Professional advisers to freeholders

SURVEYORS
DRIVERS JONAS
Robin T. Bishop
Elizabeth de Burgh Sidley
Nicholas J. Shepherd
Robert J. Stuart

SOLICITORS
FRERE CHOLMELEY
G. Hugo Southern
Sophie Hamilton

Professional advisers to clients

SURVEYORS
MORGAN GRENFELL LAURIE
John W. Lockhart
A. Martin Burkitt

SOLICITORS
STONES PORTER
Robin W. Assael

SURVEYORS/RIGHTS OF LIGHT
MICHAEL BROOKS & ASSOCIATES
Michael J. Brooks

Statutory authorities

ENGLISH HERITAGE
John Martin Robinson
WESTMINSTER CITY COUNCIL
Stephen Rankin (Planning)
Paul Velluet (Listed Buildings)
Brian McDade (District Surveyor Services)

Amenity societies

ANCIENT MONUMENTS SOCIETY
THE GEORGIAN GROUP
SAVE BRITAIN'S HERITAGE

Specialist contractors

ARCHITECTURAL CARVING
DICK REID STUDIOS AND WORKSHOP
Charles Gurrey (Marble carving)
José Sarabia (Timber carving)

DECORATION AND GILDING
C. TAVENER & SON LTD
Roger E. Tavener
Nigel J. Chadwick

STONEWORK
GILBERT & TURNBULL LTD
Dennis S. Whittome
Anthony Povey
David Povey
J. BYSOUTH
George W. Sumners
Mark Smith
Gary Bainbridge

PAINTING RESTORATION
Clare Wilkins

GARDEN CONSTRUCTION
LANDSCAPE MANAGEMENT
Nicholas G. S. Lawrence

Joinery sub-contractor

ASHBY & HORNER JOINERY LTD
Alfred F. Foulkes
Peter L. Salter
Anthony Swain
George H. Toomey
Terence Willard
Patrick E. Gowing
Peter Overton
Peter Murphy

Mechanical and electrical sub-contractor

BENHAM BUILDING SERVICES LTD
Brian Smith
Norman Morley (Mechanical)
Patrick Coulsdon (Mechanical)
Roger Furness (Electrical)
Andrew Long (Electrical)

Specialist sub-contractors

DECORATION AND GILDING
HARE & HUMPHREYS LTD
Peter J. Hare
Paul C. Humphreys
David Johnston

MURAL RESTORATION (PAINTED ROOM)
Anthony Miloserdovs
Suzie Kennard

SCAGLIOLA
THE SCAGLIOLA COMPANY
Michael Koumbouzis

SPECIALIST PLASTERERS
T. H. DAVIS & CO
Tommy Davis
Mark Davis

ARCHITECTURAL CARVING
Anthony Harrington
T. Hilliard

PAINT STRIPPING
STEWART RESTORATION SYSTEMS LTD
Malcolm Stewart

SILK WEAVING
HUMPHRIES WEAVING COMPANY
Richard Humphries

SILK HANGING
Michael Jewiss
Rosa Manzano

TROMPE L'OEIL PAINTING
Alan Dodd
Richard de Baer

CONSERVATION OF ROOFLINE STATUES
CONSERVATION SPECIALISTS
Deborah A. Carthy

DRUM WALLING, PALM ROOM
ALBERT E. CHAPMAN LTD.

Furniture & furnishings

COPIES OF ORIGINAL FURNITURE DESIGNED BY JOHN VARDY AND JAMES STUART
Ben Bacon (Carving)
Clare Kooy-Lister (Gilding)
Peter Thuring (Gilding and Upholstery)
DICK REID STUDIOS & WORKSHOP
José Sarabia (Carving)

CONSERVATION AND UPHOLSTERY OF PAINTED ROOM FURNITURE
Peter Thuring

COPIES OF ORIGINAL PICTURE FRAMES DESIGNED BY JAMES STUART
ARNOLD WIGGINS & SONS LTD
Michael Gregory
Susan May

CHANDELIERS FOR GREAT ROOM AND PAINTED ROOM
R. WILKINSON AND SONS LTD
Peter Prickett

Principal sub-contractors and suppliers

VENTILATION DUCTWORK
Adrian Sheet Metalworks Ltd

FIRE ALARM
AETP Systems Ltd

EXTRACT FANS
Airquipment Ltd

C.W.S. BOOSTER PUMP SET
Allan Aqua-Systems Ltd

KITCHEN GALLEYS
Alternative Plans Ltd

SPENCER DOOR FURNITURE
Architectural Hardware Ltd

SANITARYWARE
Armitage Shanks Ltd

AUTOMATIC CONTROLS
Berkley Environmental Systems Plc

METALWORK
Bradwell Engineering (UK) Ltd

SECURITY SYSTEMS
Britannia Security Systems Plc

ROOF LANTERN LIGHTS
British Patent Glazing Co Ltd

CARPETS
J. Bullman & Sons (Carpet Contractors) Ltd

VARIABLE AIR VOLUME TERMINALS
Carrier Distribution Ltd

CHANDELIER HOOKS
Chandelier Cleaning & Restoration Services Ltd

CHILLER UNIT
Climate Equipment Ltd

CAST IRON RADIATORS
Clyde Combustions Ltd

BRONZE FLOOR GRILLES AND SOLRAY HEATING PANELS
Comyn Ching & Co. (Solray) Ltd

MECHANICAL COMMISSIONING
Commtech Ltd

CHIMNEY LININGS
Country Warmth Ltd

ASPHALT ROOFING
Coverite (Asphalters) Ltd

WALL PLASTERING
Croydon Plastering Ltd

PICTURE RAIL IRONMONGERY
Danico Brass Ltd

PAINTING & DECORATING
T. J. Day

BRICK SUPPLIER
Deben Builders Merchants Ltd

FAN COIL UNITS
Diffusion Environmental Systems Ltd

TERRAZZO FLOORING
Fieldmount Terrazzo Ltd

AIR HANDLING PLANT
Fischbach Ventilation Ltd

H.W.S. CIRCULATING PUMPS
Grundfos Pumps Ltd
BUILDERS' WORK
Hampshire Chasing Ltd
BOILERS AND HOT WATER HEATERS
Hamworthy Engineering Ltd
CIRCULATING PUMPS
Holden & Brooke Ltd
RADIATORS
Hudevad Britain Ltd
ULTRASONIC HUMIDIFIERS AND REVERSE OSMOSIS PLANT
J.S. Humidifiers
EMERGENCY LIGHT UNIT
J.S.B. Ltd
SOOT WASH
Jaconello (London) Ltd
COOLING TOWER
John M. Fuller Ltd
DEMOLITION
John F. Hunt Demolition Ltd
FLOOR DUCT HEATING SYSTEMS
Kampmann (U.K.) Ltd
IRONMONGERY
Laidlaw & Thomson Ltd
STRUCTURAL STEELWORK
Lancaster Construction Ltd
STRUCTURAL CONCRETE
Laxbeam Ltd
ROOF SLATING
London Welsh Slate Roofing Company Ltd
GRANOLITHIC PAVING
Malcolm MacLeod & Co Ltd
MARBLE VANITORY TOPS AND FLOORING
Mandale Mining Co Ltd
HUMIDIFICATION WORKS
A. G. Manly & Company Ltd
UNINTERRUPTED POWER SUPPLY SET
Merlin Gerin Ltd
DAMP-PROOF RENDERING
Metropolitan Services (Proofings Ltd)
BUILDING MANAGEMENT SYSTEM
Microtech Building Management Systems Ltd
GENERAL STEELWORK
M. I. W. Fabrications Ltd
MAIN CONTROL PANEL
Norlight Panels Ltd
BRICK MANUFACTURERS
Northcote Brick Co
PLASTIC COMPOSITE MOULDINGS
Oakleaf Reproductions Ltd
FIBROUS PLASTER CORNICES
Ornate Plastering
PROPRIETARY SUSPENDED CEILINGS
Phoenix Interiors Plc
C.W.S. STORAGE TANK
A.C. Plastics Ltd
LIFT MANUFACTURER
Porn & Dunwoody (Lifts) Ltd
WATER LEAK DETECTION SYSTEMS
Raychem Limited
BRICKWORK
Robert H. Prescott
RAISED ACCESS FLOORING
ARI Propaflor Ltd
CHIMNEY POTS
Redbank Manufacturing Ltd
CARPENTRY
R.K. Construction (London) Ltd
GOLD LEAF SUPPLIER
Richard Lingwood Ltd
EXTRACT FANS
Roof Units Group
MARBLE WORK
J. Rotherham Ltd
TIMBER RESTORATION AND FLOOR STRENGTHENING
RTT Restoration Ltd
PIPEWORK LAGGING
Seftacraft
SECONDARY GLAZING
Selectaglaze Ltd
SCAFFOLDING
SGB Plc
WALL AND FLOOR TILING
C. J. Sims
UV FILTER GLASS
Solaglass Laminate
BRICK POINTING
Spooner Bros
KITCHEN HOODS
Stott Benham Ltd
TERRACE RESTRAINT WORKS
Structoplast Contracts Ltd
SUPPLY AND REFURBISHMENT OF ELECTRIC AND GAS LANTERNS
Sugg Lighting Ltd
STANDBY GENERATOR
Swan Generators Ltd
LEADWORK
T. & P. Lead Roofing Ltd
UNDERPINNING AND GROUNDWORKS
Thundercrest Ltd
ELECTRICAL ACCESSORIES
Wandsworth Electrical Ltd
AIR HANDLING UNITS
Waterloo Ozonair
KITCHEN EQUIPMENT
Welequip Ltd
YORK STONE PAVEMENTS
Westminster City Council
EXTRACT FANS
Woods of Colchester Ltd

Utilities

BRITISH GAS PLC
BRITISH TELECOM
LONDON ELECTRICITY

VII Lenders of works of art

Spencer House gratefully acknowledges the generosity of the following lenders:

The Royal Collection

Public institutions and charitable trusts

Leeds City Art Galleries
The National Trust – Waddesdon Manor (The Rothschild Collection)
The National Trust – Wimpole Hall
The Peter Moores Foundation
The Royal Academy
The Tate Gallery
The Victoria and Albert Museum

Private collections

Michael Chamberlayne
Glyndebourne (Sir George Christie)
The Trustees of Rothschild Family Settlements
Thoresby Park
Mr & Mrs Samuel Whitbread

The fine art trade

Artemis Ltd
Christopher Gibbs Ltd
Harari & Johns Ltd
Daniel Katz Ltd
Meissner Fine Art and BNP Art

VIII Use of Spencer House

Since 1990, the Principal Rooms have been available for government, corporate and private events, under the management of Spencer House Limited. They are also open to the public on most Sundays of the year. The Grant Leisure Group acted as consultants in the setting up of both the banqueting and the public opening activities. Outside the Principal Rooms, the office areas are occupied by the J. Rothschild group of companies.

Director

Stephen Jones

Curatorial

Celia de la Hey
Philippa Hart

Administration

John Johnston
Howard Meadows

Banqueting

Richard Waddington
Steven Lattimer
Nanette Reast
Vincent O'Toole
Daniel Collins
Fergal O'Cainan
Aurea Gurdon

BIBLIOGRAPHY

The present bibliography provides a list of some of the more useful books and articles consulted in the preparation of this study. For reasons of space all but a handful of the illustrated books through which attempts have been made to trace the sources of Spencer House's design have been omitted. For a more extensive bibliography in this area the following studies are recommended:

Archer, John, *The Literature of British Domestic Architecture* 1715–1842 (1985)

Crook, J. Mordaunt, *The Greek Revival, Neo-Classical Attitudes in British Architecture 1760–1870* (1972)

Harris, Eileen, *British Architectural Books and Writers 1556–1785* (C.U.P, 1990)

Haskell, Francis, and Nicholas Penny, *Taste and the Antique* (1982)

A separate bibliography of guide books in which Spencer House is specifically mentioned is provided in Appendix v. This covers the period from 1761 to 1851. Unless otherwise stated, all printed material was published in London.

Adam, Robert, *Ruins of the Palace of the Emperor Diocletian, at Spalatro, in Dalmatia* (1764)

Adam, Robert, and James, *Works in Architecture*, 3 vols (1778–1822)

Adams, Bernard, *London Illustrated 1604–1851: A Survey and Index of Topographical Books and their Plates* (1983)

The Age of Neo-Classicism, exh. cat., 14th exhibition of the Council of Europe, 1972

The Ageless Diamond, exh. cat., Christie's, 1959

Agnew's, *Dealer's Record* (1967–81)

Alston, R. C. *et al*, *A Checklist of 18th-Century Books containing lists of subscribers* (1983)

Amelung, Walther, *Die Sculpturen des Vaticanischen Museums*, 2 vols (Berlin, 1903–08; 1935–36)

The Annual Biography and Obituary of 1831, Part I, No.1 [Obituary of the Rt. Hon. Capt. Sir Robert Cavendish Spencer]

Antichità di Ercolano, 8 vols (Naples; 1755–92)

The Architectural Review, 'Lansdowne House, Berkeley Square' (January 1910), pp.19–26

Armstrong, Sir Walter, *Sir Joshua Reynolds at Althorp House* (*c*1905)

Artley, Alexandra, and 'Thomas Dibdin', 'Restoration Comedy', *Harpers and Queen* (April 1987), pp.170–73

Ashurst, John, 'Conserving Stone', *The Architects' Journal (Renovation Supplement)* (29 June 1988), pp.36–7

Askwith, Betty, *The Lytteltons, A Family Chronicle of the Nineteenth Century* (1975)

– *Piety and Wit, A Biography of Harriet, Countess Granville 1785–1862* (1982)

Asquith, Margot, *More Memories* (1933)

Baker, George, *The History and Antiquities of the County of Northampton* 2 vols (1822–1830)

Baker, George Pierce (ed.), *Some Unpublished Correspondence of David Garrick* (Boston, 1907)

Bamford, Francis, and Duke of Wellington (eds), *The Journal of Mrs Arbuthnot 1820–32*, 2 vols (1950)

Baring, Maurice, *Cecil Spencer* (1929)

– *The Puppet Show of Memory* (1932)

Barker, Godfrey, 'The Spencer Line', *Connoisseur* (July 1981), pp.179–83

Barkley, Harold, 'A Kent-Vardy Collaboration', *Country Life* (13 October 1960), p.791

Barrett, Charlotte F. (ed.), *Diary and Letters of Madame d'Arblay*, 3 vols (1890–91)

Bartoli, Pietro Santi, *Admiranda Romanarum Antiquitatum* (Rome, 1693)

Bates, L. M., *Somerset House: Four Hundred Years of History* (1967)

Batey, M., 'Nuneham Park, Oxfordshire. The Creation of a Landscape Garden', *Country Life* (5 September 1968), pp.540–42

Bathurst, Earl of, *The Earl Spencer's and Mr John Warde's Hounds 1739–1825* (Cirencester, 1932)

Battiscombe, Georgina, *The Spencers of Althorp* (1984)

Beard, Geoffrey, *Decorative Plasterwork in Great Britain* (1975)

– *The Work of Robert Adam* (1978)

– *Craftsmen and Interior Decoration in England 1660–1820* (1981)

Beard, Geoffrey, and Christopher Gilbert, *Dictionary of English Furniture Makers 1660–1840* (1986)

Beck, Herbert, and Peter C. Bol, *Forschunge zur Villa Albani Antike Kunst und die Epoch der Aufklarung* (Berlin, 1982)

Beer, Sir Gavin de, 'Voltaire's British Visitors', in *Studies on Voltaire and the Eighteenth Century* (Institut et Musée Voltaire, Geneva, 1957)

Beeton, Isabella Mary, *The Book of Househo Management* (1861)

Bellaigue, Geoffrey de, 'George IV and French Furniture', *Connoisseur*, 195, No.784 (June 1977), pp.116–25

Belli Barsali, Isa, *Ville di Roma* (Milan, 197(

Bénézit, E., *Dictionnaire Critique et Documentaire des Peintres, Sculpteurs, Dessinateurs et Graveurs*, 10 vols (Paris, 1976)

Benson, Arthur Christopher, and Viscount Esher (eds.), *The Letters of Queen Victoria 1st series [1837–61]*, 3 vols (1907)

Bessborough, Earl of, *Enchanted Forest* (1984)

Bessborough, Earl of (ed.), *Georgiana: Extracts from the Correspondence of Georgiana, Duchess of Devonshire* (1955)

Bessborough, Earl of, and A. Aspinall (eds. *Lady Bessborough and her Family Circle* (1940)

Bibliotheca Sunderlandiana, Sale Catalogue o the Truly Important and Very Extensive Library of Printed Books Known as the Sunderland or Blenheim Library, sale cat., Puttick and Simpson, 1–12 December 1881

Binney, Marcus, *Sir Robert Taylor, From Rococo to Neo-Classicism* (1984)

Birkenhead, Sheila, *Peace in Piccadilly: The Story of Albany* (1958)

Blomfield, Reginald, *A History of Renaissance Architecture in England 1500–1800* (1897)

Blow, Simon, and Alexandra Artley, 'A Tale of Two Houses', *Connoisseur* (June 1991), pp.58–66

Bluche, François, *La Vie Quotidienne de la Noblesse Française au XVIIIe Siècle* (Paris, 1973)

Blunt, Anthony, *The Paintings of Nicolas Poussin, A Critical Catalogue* (1966)

– *Nicolas Poussin* (1967)

Blunt, Reginald (ed.), *Mrs Montagu, 'Queen of the Blues', Her Letters and Friendships from 1762 to 1800*, 2 vols (1923)

Blyth, Henry, *Caro, The Fatal Passion, The Life of Lady Caroline Lamb* (1972)

Bober, Phyllis Bray, and Ruth Rubinstein, *Renaissance Artists and Antique Sculpture* (O.U.P., 1986)

Bol, Peter C. (ed.), *Forschungen zur Villa Albani, Katalog der Antiken Bildwerke 1*, 3 vols (Berlin, 1989–92)

Bold, John, *John Webb: Architectural Theory and Practice in the Seventeenth Century* (1989)

Bolton, Arthur T., 'Lansdowne House, Berkeley Square', *Country Life* (15 November 1913), pp.III–VI

– 'James Stuart at Portman House and Spencer House', *Country Life* (1 May 1915), p.6*–11*

– 'Hagley Park, Worcestershire', *Country Life* (16 October 1915), pp.520–28

– 'Lichfield House, No. 15 St James's Square', *Country Life* (12 May 1917), pp.2*–6*

– 'Home House, No. 20 Portman Square, London', *Country Life* (15 November 1919), pp.624–9

– *The Architecture of Robert and James Adam, 1758–94*, 2 vols (1922)

– *Lectures on Architecture by Sir John Soane* (1929)

– 'Lansdowne House, A Great London House Reconstructed', *Country Life* (11 May 1935), pp.490–95

Bottari, Giovanni Gaetano, *Musei Capitolini*, 4 vols (Rome, 1750–82)

Bourke, Algernon, *The History of White's*, 2 Vols (1892)

Bradshaw, John (ed.), *The Letters of Philip Dormer Stanhope, Earl of Chesterfield*, 3 vols (1892)

Britton, John, and E. W. Brayley (eds), *Beauties of England and Wales*, 18 vols (1801–15)

Bruce, Lord Charles, *The Althorpe Library* (Northampton, 1900)

Buckle, George Earle (ed.), *The Letters of Queen Victoria*, 2nd series [1862–85] (1926); 3rd series [1886–1901] (1928)

The Builder (10 October 1896)

The Building Times, 'Rebuilding of Lansdowne House' (July 1935), pp.2–6

Burke's Peerage & Baronetage, 105th edn, 4th impression (1980)

Burke's Royal Families of the World (1977)

Burlington, Richard Boyle, Earl of, *Fabbriche Antiche Disegnate da Andrea Palladio Vicentino* (1730)

Bussche, Josef Van den, C.P., *Ignatius (George) Spencer Passionist (1799–1864): Crusader of Prayer for England and Pioneer of Ecumenical Prayer* (Leuven University Press, 1991)

Butler, I., *Rule of Three* (1967)

Cain, Hans Ulrich, *Römische Marmorkandelaber* (Mainz, 1985)

Calder-Marshall, Arthur, *The Two Duchesses* (1978)

Calloway, Stephen, *Twentieth-Century Decoration: The Domestic Interior from 1900 to the Present Day* (1988)

Campbell, Colen, *Vitruvius Britannicus*, 3 Vols (1717–25)

Camporesi, Pietro, *Loggie di Rafaele nel Vaticano* (Rome, 1772)

Cannon, Garland, *Oriental Jones, A Biography of Sir William Jones 1746–1794* (1964)

Cannon, Garland (ed.), *The Letters of Sir William Jones*, 2 vols (Oxford, 1970)

Cartari, Vicenzo, *Le Vere e Nove Imagini de gli dei delli antichi* (Padua, 1615)

Cartwright, Julia, *Sacharissa: Some Account of Dorothy Sidney, Countess of Sunderland, Her Family and Friends, 1617–1684* (1893)

Cash, Arthur H., *Laurence Sterne, The Later Years* (1986)

Cavaceppi, Bartolomeo, *Raccolta di Statue, Busti, Bassirilievi ed altre Sculture Ristaurate*, 3 Vols (Rome, 1768–72)

Cavendish, Lady Frederick, and Maud Wyndham (eds), *Correspondence of Sarah, Lady Lyttelton* (1912)

Cecil, Lord David, *The Young Melbourne and the Story of his Marriage with Caroline Lamb* (1939)

Chambers, Sir William, *A Treatise on Civil Architecture* (1759)

Chancellor, Edwin, B., *The Private Palaces of London, Past and Present* (1908)

– *Disappearing London* (1927)

Chandos-Pole, Annie, *Preliminary Report and Proposal for the Garden of Spencer House*, [unpublished] (August, 1987)

Chapman, R. W. (ed.), *The Letters of Samuel Johnson with Mrs Thrale's Genuine Letters to Him*, 3 vols (1952)

Charleston, R. J., *Pottery and Porcelain at Althorp* (n.d., copy in Northampton Library)

– 'Porcelain in the Collection of Earl Spencer at Althorp, Northamptonshire: 1. English Porcelain', *The Connoisseur* (January 1967), pp.8–14

– 'Meissen and Other German Porcelain in Earl Spencer's Collection at Althorp', *The Connoisseur* (February 1969), pp.69–75

Charlton, John, *Lancaster House* (HMSO, 1954), 2nd edn (1957)

– *Marlborough House* (HMSO, 1962)

Chippendale, Thomas, *The Gentleman and Cabinet-Maker's Director*, 3rd edn (1762)

Clark, Anthony M., *Pompeo Batoni: A Complete Catalogue of his Works* (Oxford, 1985)

Clifford, Timothy, 'Mr Stuart's Tripod and a Candelabrum', *Burlington Magazine* (December 1972), p.874

Climenson, Emily J. (ed.), *Elizabeth Montagu, The Queen of the Blue-Stockings, Her Correspondence from 1720 to 1761*, 2 vols (1906)

Cokayne, George Edward, *Complete Peerage*, Vicary Gibbs (ed.), 12 Vols (1910)

Collard, Frances, *Regency Furniture* (1986)

Collins, Arthur, *A History of the Noble Family of Carteret* (1756)

Colonna, Gustavo Brigante, *Porporati e Artisti nella Roma del Settecento* (Rome, n.d.)

Colson, Percy, *A Story of Christie's* (1950)

Colville, O., *Duchess Sarah* (1904)

Colvin, Christina (ed.), *Maria Edgeworth, Letters from England 1813–44* (1971)

Colvin, H. M. (ed.), *History of the King's Works*, v (1976)

Colvin, H.M., *Biographical Dictionary of*

British Architects 1600–1840, 2nd edn (1978)

Connell, Brian, *Portrait of a Whig Peer, compiled from the papers of the second Viscount Palmerston, 1739–1802* (1957)

Constable, W. G., *John Flaxman 1755–1826* (1927)

Corbett, Julian S. (ed.), 'Private Papers of George, second Earl Spencer, first Lord of the Admiralty 1794–1801', *Navy Records Society*, I (1913); II (1914)

Corley, Brigitte, *Lichfield House, 15 St James's Square* (Privately printed, 1983)

Cormack, Malcolm, 'The Ledgers of Sir Joshua Reynolds', *The Walpole Society*, XLII (1968–1970), pp.105–69

Cornforth, John, 'Stafford House Revisited', *Country Life* (7–14 November 1968), pp.1188–91, 1257–61

– 'Old Grosvenor House', *Country Life* (15 November 1973), pp.1538–41

– *English Interiors 1790–1848: The Quest for Comfort* (1978)

– 'Newby Hall, Yorkshire', *Country Life* (7–14 June 1979), pp.1802–06, 1918–21

– 'Devonshire House, London', *Country Life* (20 November 1980), pp.1894–7

– *The Inspiration of the Past* (1985)

Cornforth, John, and John Fowler, *English Decoration in the 18th Century*, 2nd edn (1978)

Cowper, C. S. (ed,), *Diary of Mary, Countess Cowper, Lady of the Bedchamber to the Princess of Wales 1714–20* (1864)

Croft-Murray, Edward, 'A Drawing by "Athenian" Stuart for the Painted Room at Spencer House', *British Museum Quarterly*, XXI, No.1 (March 1957), pp.14–15

– *Decorative Painting in England 1537–1837*, 2 vols (1962–1970)

Croker, John W. (ed.), *The Letters of Mary Lepel, Lady Hervey* (1821)

Crook, J. Mordaunt, *The British Museum* (1972)

Cross, Wilbur L., *The Life and Times of Laurence Sterne*, 3rd edn (Yale University Press, 1929)

Cruickshank, Dan, 'Tracing a Palladio Elevation', *The Architectural Review*, CLXXV, No.1045 (March 1984), pp.44–7

– 'Adapt and Survive', *The Architects' Journal (Renovation Supplement)* (29 June 1988), pp.22–9

– 'Master of the Art of House Carving', *The Architects' Journal (Renovation Supplement)* (22 March, 1989), pp.34–7

– 'Remaking a Historic Room', *The Architects' Journal (Renovation Supplement)* (22 March 1989), pp. 24–31

Cruickshank, Dan, and Peter Wyld, *London, The Art of Georgian Building* (1975)

Cruickshank, Dan, and Neil Burton, *Life in the Georgian City* (1990)

Curtis, Lewis Perry, *Letters of Laurence Sterne* (Oxford, 1935)

Cust, Lionel, *History of the Society of Dilettanti* (1898)

Dalton, R., *Antiquities and Views in Greece and Egypt* (1752)

Dasent, Arthur Irwin, *The History of St. James's Square and the Foundation of the West End of London* (1895)

– *The Story of Stafford House* (1921); 2nd edn (1927)

De Hirsch, Baron Maurice, *A Worldwide Philanthropic Empire: The Life Work of Baron Maurice de Hirsch*, exh. cat., Nahum Goldman Museum of the Jewish Diaspora, Tel Aviv, 1982

De l'Orme, Philibert, *Le Premier Tome de l'Architecture de Philibert de l'Orme* (Paris, 1568)

De' Rossi, Domenico, *Studio di Architettura Civile*, 3 vols (Rome, 1702–21)

Debrett's Peerage & Baronetage (1990)

Desgodetz, Antoine, *Les Édifices Antiques de Rome* (Paris, 1682)

Devine, Revd Fr Pius, *Life of Father Ignatius of St. Paul, Passionist (The Hon. & Rev. George Spencer)* (Dublin, 1866)

Dibdin, Thomas Frognall, *Book Rarities; or a Descriptive Catalogue of some of the most curious, rare, and valuable Books of early date; chiefly in the collection of the Right Honourable George John, Earl Spencer, K.G.* (1811)

– *Bibliotheca Spenceriana; or a Descriptive Catalogue of the Books Printed in the Fifteenth Century and of Many Valuable First Editions, in the Library of George John Earl Spencer K.G.*, 4 vols (1814–15)

– *A Catalogue of the Valuable Duplicates of a Nobleman's Library ... which will be sold by Auction on Tuesday May 9 1815 and Three following Days, by R. H. Evans, at his House, No 26 Pall Mall* (1815)

– *Aedes Althorpianae; or an Account of the Mansion, Books, and Pictures at Althorp, the Residence of George John, Earl Spencer, K. G.*, 2 vols (1822)

– *A Descriptive Catalogue of the Books printed in the Fifteenth Century lately forming part o[f] the Library of the Duke di Cassano Serra, and now the property of George John, Earl Spencer, K.G.* (1823)

– *Reminiscences of a Literary Life*, 2 vols (1836), esp. I, pp.482–56 ('The Spencer Library'); II, pp.557–94 ('Althorp')

Dictionary of National Biography (1885–1986

Dod, Charles Roger, *Dod's Parliamentary Pocket Companion* (1833 ff.)

Dodsley, R. and J., *London and its Environs Described*, 6 vols (1761)

Draper, Marie P. G., 'When Marlborough's Duchess Built', *Country Life* (2 August 1962), pp.248–50

Dunlop, Ian, 'Northumberland House, London', *Country Life* (30 July 1953), pp.346–9

Edwards, Ralph, and L. G. G. Ramsey, *The Regency Period 1810–1830* (1958)

Egerton, Judy (ed.), *George Stubbs, 1724–1806*, exh. cat. Tate Gallery, 1984

Emmerling, Ernst, *Pompeo Batoni* (Darmstadt, 1932)

Eriksen, Svend, and F. J. B. Watson, 'The "Athenienne" and the Revival of the Classical Tripod', *Burlington Magazine* (March 1963), pp.108–112

Exhibition of Gemstones and Jewellery, City of Birmingham Museum and Art Gallery (1960)

Fergusson, Alexander (ed.), *Letters and Journals of Mrs Calderwood of Polton from England, Holland, and the Low Countries in 1756* (Edinburgh, 1884)

Field, Leslie, *Bendor, The Golden Duke of Westminster* (1983)

Finch, Mary E., 'Spencer of Althorp', in *The Wealth of Five Northamptonshire Families 1540–1640* (O.U.P., 1956), chap. III, pp.38–65

Fitz-Gerald, David, *The Norfolk House Music Room* (Victoria and Albert Museum, 1973)

Fitzgerald, Brian (ed.), *The Correspondence of Emily, Duchess of Leinster (1731–1814)*, 3 vols (Dublin, 1949–57)

Flaxman, John, *Compositions from the Tragedies of Aeschylus, Designed by John Flaxman, engraved by Thomas Piroli, The Original Drawings in the Possession of the*

Countess Dowager Spencer (1795)

Fleming, John, *Robert Adam and his Circle in Edinburgh and Rome* (1962)

Forrester, Eric G., *Northamptonshire County Elections and Electioneering 1695–1832* (O.U.P., 1941)

Foster, Vere H. L., *The Two Duchesses; Georgiana, Duchess of Devonshire, Elizabeth, Duchess of Devonshire* (1898)

Fothergill, Brian, *Sir William Hamilton, Envoy Extraordinary* (1969)

Foxcroft, H. C., *The Life and Letters of Sir George Savile, Bart, first Marquis of Halifax*, 2 vols (1898)

Fransolet, Mariette, *François Duquesnoy, Sculpteur d'Urbain VIII 1597–1643* (Brussels, 1942)

Fraser, Flora, *Beloved Emma: The Life of Emma, Lady Hamilton* (1986)

Fréart de Chambray, Roland, *Parallèle de l'Architecture Antique avec la Moderne* (Paris, 1650)

Friedman, Joseph, 'Spencer House', *Apollo* (August 1987), pp.81–99

Further Wellington Gems and Historic Rings, exh. cat., S. J. Phillips, June 1978

Galleria Giustiniana del Marchese Vincenzo Giustiniani, 2 vols (Rome, 1631)

Garlick, Kenneth, 'A Catalogue of Pictures at Althorp', *Walpole Society*, 45 (1974–76)

Garlick, Kenneth, and Angus Macintyre (eds), *The Diary of Joseph Farington* (Paul Mellon Centre for Studies in British Art, 1978 ff.); index by and courtesy of Evelyn Newby

Garrick, David, *The Private Correspondence of David Garrick with the most Celebrated Persons of his Time*, 2 vols (1831–32)

Gaunt, William, *Stubbs* (1977)

Gentleman's Magazine (1731–1868)

Gerard, Frances A., *Angelica Kauffmann, A Biography* (1893)

Gere, Charlotte, *Nineteenth-Century Decoration, The Art of the Interior* (1989)

Gibbs, James, *A Book of Architecture* (1728)

– *Rules for Drawing the Several Parts of Architecture* (1732)

Gilbey, Sir Walter, Bt, *Life of George Stubbs R.A.* (1898)

Girouard, Mark, 'A New Use for Marlborough House', *Country Life* (5 April 1962), pp.760–61

– *Life in the English Country House, A Social and Architectural History* (1978)

Godber, Joyce, 'The Marchioness Grey of Wrest Park', *Bedfordshire Historical Society*, XLVII (1968)

Goddard, Nicholas, *Harvests of Change: The Royal Agricultural Society of England 1838–1938* (1988)

Goodison, Nicholas, 'Mr Stuart's Tripod', *Burlington Magazine* (October 1972), pp.695–705

Goodreau, David, *Nathaniel Dance 1735–1811* (1977)

Gordon, Peter, *The Red Earl: The Papers of the Fifth Earl Spencer 1835–1901*, 2 vols (Northampton, 1981–86)

Gori, Antonio Francesco, *Le Gemme Antiche di Anton-Maria Zanetti di Girolamo* (Venice, 1750)

Gotch, J. Alfred, *Squires' Homes and other Old Buildings of Northamptonshire* (1939)

Gower, Lord Ronald, *My Reminiscences* (1883)

Graham, J. M. (ed.), *Annals of Correspondence of the Viscount and 1st and 2nd Earls of Stair* (Edinburgh, 1875)

Graves, Algernon, *A Dictionary of Artists who have exhibited works in the Principal London Exhibitions from 1760 to 1893* (1895)

– *The Royal Academy of Arts, A Complete Dictionary of Contributors and their Work from its Foundation in 1769 to 1904*, 8 vols (1905–06)

– *The Society of Artists of Great Britain 1760–1791; The Free Society of Artists 1761–1783, A Complete Dictionary of Contributors and their Work* (1907)

Graves, Algernon, and William Vine Cronin, *A History of the Works of Sir Joshua Reynolds P.R.A* (1899)

Gray, John M., *James and William Tassie, A Biographical and Critical Sketch, with a Catalogue of their portrait medallions of modern personages* (Edinburgh, 1894)

Greece, H.R.H. Christopher, Prince of, *Memoirs of H.R.H. Prince Christopher of Greece* (Plymouth, 1938)

Green, David B., *Sarah, Duchess of Marlborough* (1967)

Grimwade, Arthur, 'Silver at Althorp', *The Connoisseur*: I 'The Marlborough Plate' (October 1962); II 'The Candlesticks and Candelabra' (March 1963); III 'The Hugenot Period' (June 1963); IV 'The Rococo and Regency Periods' (December 1963); V 'Silver at Althorp' (March 1964)

Gunnis, Rupert, *Dictionary of British Sculptors 1660–1851* (1951)

Guppy, Henry, *The John Rylands Library, Manchester 1899–1924* (1924)

Gwynn, John, *London and Westminster Improved* (1766)

Halley, J. M. W., 'Lichfield House', *Architectural Review* (May 1910), pp.273–8

Haly, Ann (ed.), *The Complete Servant by Samuel and Sarah Adams* (Southover Press, Lewes, 1989)

Hamilton, Sir William, *A Catalogue of a Well-Known and Approved Collection of Pictures [i.e. of Sir William Hamilton] ... Likewise some Curious Bronzes and Terra Cottas which will be sold by Auction by Messrs Prestage and Hobbs ... on Friday and Saturday the 20th and 21st of February 1761*

Harcourt, Edward William (ed.), *The Harcourt Papers*, 14 vols (Oxford, 1880–1905)

Harcourt Smith, Sir Cecil, *Historical Notices of the Society of Dilettanti* (privately printed, 1855)

– *The Society of Dilettanti, Its Regalia and Pictures* (1932)

Hardwick, James, *The Restoration and Refurbishment of Spencer House* (seminar paper, S. B. Teitz & Partners, 29 May 1991)

Hardy, John, 'The Building and Decoration of Apsley House', *Apollo* (Sept 1973)

Hardy, John, and Helena Hayward, 'Kedleston Hall, Derbyshire', *Country Life* (2 February 1978), pp.262–6

Harris, Eileen, *The Furniture of Robert Adam* (1963)

Harris, Frances, 'Holywell House, St Albans', *Architectural History*, 28 (1985), pp.32–6

– 'Holywell House: A Gothic Villa at St. Albans', *The British Library Journal*, 12, No.2 (Autumn 1986), pp.176–83

– *A Passion for Government: The Life of Sarah, Duchess of Marlborough* (Oxford, 1991)

Harris, John, *Regency Furniture Designs from Contemporary Source Books 1803–26* (1961)

– 'Early Neo-Classical Furniture', *Furniture History: Journal of the Furniture History Society*, 2 (1966), pp.1–6

– *Sir William Chambers, Knight of the Polar Star* (1970)

– *Catalogue of British Drawings for Architecture etc... in American Collections* (New Jersey, 1971)

– 'William Kent's 44 Berkeley Square', *Apollo* (August 1987), pp.100–04

Harris, John, *et al., The King's Arcadia: Inigo Jones and the Stuart Court* (1973)

– *The Destruction of the Country House 1875–1975* (1974)

Harris, John, and Gordon Higgott, *Inigo Jones, Complete Architectural Drawings* (1989)

Hartcup, Adeline, *Angelica: The Portrait of an Eighteenth-Century Artist* (1954)

Hasted, Edward, *History and Topographical Survey of the County of Kent*, IX (1800)

Hayes, John, *Gainsborough: Paintings and Drawings* (1975)

– *Gainsborough* (1980)

Hecht, Joseph Jean, 'Continental and Colonial Servants in Eighteenth-century England', in *Smith College Studies in History*, XL (Northampton, Massachusetts, 1954)

– *The Domestic Servant Class in Eighteenth-century England* (1956)

Herbert, Lord (ed.), *Henry, Elizabeth and George 1734–80, Letters and Diaries of Henry, Tenth Earl of Pembroke and his Circle* (1939)

– *Pembroke Papers (1780–94), Letters and Diaries of Henry, Tenth Earl of Pembroke and His Circle*, (1950)

Higham, C. S. S., *Wimbledon Manor House under the Cecils* (1962)

Hill, George Birbeck (ed.), *Letters of Samuel Johnson*, 2 vols (Oxford, 1892)

Hilles, Frederick W. (ed.), *Letters of Sir Joshua Reynolds* (1929)

Hilles, Frederick W., and Philip B. Daghlian (eds), *Anecdotes of Painting in England; [1760–1795] with some Account of the principal Artists; and incidental Notes on other Arts; collected by Horace Walpole* (O.U.P., 1937)

Hobhouse, Hermione, *Lost London, A Century of Demolition and Decay* (London 1971)

Home, J. A. (ed.), *The Letters and Journals of Lady Mary Coke*, 4 vols (Edinburgh, 1889–96)

Honour, Hugh, 'Adaptations from Athens', *Country Life* (22 May 1958), pp.1120–21

Hopkinson, Martin, 'Note on a portrait by James Stuart', *Burlington Magazine* (November 1990), pp.794–5

Horwood, Alfred J., 'The Manuscripts of the Right Honourable Earl Spencer at Spencer House, St. James's', in *Second Report of the Royal Commission on Historical Manuscripts* (1871), pp.177–89

Howard, Seymour, 'Boy on a Dolphin: Nollekens and Cavaceppi', *The Art Bulletin* (June 1964), pp.12–20

Howgego, James, *Printed Maps of London, circa 1553–1850*, 2nd edn (Folkstone, 1978)

Hughes, Edward (ed.), *Letters of Spencer Cowper, Dean of Durham, 1746–74* (1956)

Hughes, G. Bernard, 'A Drawing Room in Glass', *Country Life* (24 May 1956), p.1128

Hussey, Christopher, 'Burlington House, Piccadilly', *Country Life* (3 May 1924), pp.694 702

– 'Dorchester House, London', *Country Life* (5–12 May 1928), pp.646–52, 684–90

– 'Panshanger, Hertfordshire', *Country Life* (11–18 January 1936), pp.38–40, 64–9

– *Clarence House* (1949)

– *The Story of Ely House* (1953)

– 'Shugborough, Staffordshire', *Country Life* (25 February, 4–11 March, 15–22 April 1954), pp.510–13, 590–93, 676–9, 1126–9, 1220–23

– *English Country Houses*, 3 vols (1955)

– 'Althorp, Northamptonshire, The Seat of Earl Spencer', *Country Life* (19–26 May 1960), pp.1122–5, 1186–9

Hussey, Christopher and Arthur Oswald, *Home House, No 20 Portman Square, An Architectural and Historical Description* (1934)

Ilchester, Lady & Lord Stavordale, (eds), *The Life and Letters of Lady Sarah Lennox 1745–1825*, 2 vols (1901)

The Illustrated London News (30 January 1875)

Ince, William & John Mayhew, *The Universal System of Household Furniture* (1762)

Irwin, David, 'Gavin Hamilton: Archaeologist, Painter, and Dealer', *Art Bulletin*, XLIV (June 1962), pp.87–102

– *English Neoclassical Art* (1966)

– 'Jacob More, Neo-Classical Landscape Painter', *Burlington Magazine*, CXIV, No. 836 (November 1972), pp.775–9

– *John Flaxman 1755–1826, Sculptor, Illustrator, Designer* (1979)

Jackson, Stanley, *The Great Barnato* (1970)

Jackson-Stops, Gervase, 'Spencer House, London', *Country Life* (29 November 1990), pp.42–7

Jameson, Mrs, 'Althorp. A Fragment', in *Visits and Sketches at Home and Abroad*, 2 (1834), pp.201–30

Jekyll, Joseph, *Personal Remembrance among the Joys of the Other World Set Forth in A Discourse Occasioned by the Death of the Honourable Richard Spencer, Youngest Son of the Earl and Countess Spencer* (1791)

Jenkins, Elizabeth, *Lady Caroline Lamb* (1973)

Jervis, Simon, and Maurice Tomlin, *Apsley House, Wellington Museum* (1984)

Jones, A. E., *Old English Gold Plate* (1907)

Jones, Anna Maria, *The Works of Sir William Jones*, 6 vols (1799)

Jones, Sir William, *The Muse Recalled: an Ode on the Nuptials of Lord Viscount Althorpe and Lavinia Bingham* (Paris, 1782)

Jones, Stephen, 'Roman Taste and Greek Gusto: The Society of Dilettanti and the building of Spencer House, London', *Antiques* (June 1992), pp.968–77

Jourdain, Margaret, *Decoration in England from 1660 to 1770*, (1914)

– *Furniture in England from 1660 to 1760*, (1914)

– *English Decoration and Furniture of the later XVIIIth Century, 1760–1820*, (1923)

– *Decoration in England from 1640 to 1760*, 2nd edn revised (1927)

– 'Furniture Designed by James Stuart at Althorp' *Country Life* (24 August 1935), pp.204–05

– *Georgian Cabinet-Makers*, (1944)

– *English Interior Decoration 1500–1830*, (1950)

– *English Furniture, The Georgian Period (1750–1830)*, (1953)

– *Regency Furniture 1795–1820*, revised edn by Ralph Fastnedge (1965)

Jourdain, Margaret, and C. R. Edwards, *Georgian Cabinet-Makers c1700–1800*, (1955)

Jourdan, Mary, *The Althorp Picture Gallery and other Poetical Sketches* (Edinburgh, 1836)

Joy, Edward T., *English Furniture 1800–1851* (1977)

Kendall, Alan, *David Garrick: A Biography*

(1985)

Kent, William, *The Designs of Inigo Jones*, 2 Vols (1727)

Kenworthy-Browne, John, 'Joseph Nollekens: The Years in Rome', *Country Life*: I 'Establishing a Reputation'; II 'Genius Recognized' (7–14 June 1979), pp.1844–8, 1930–31

Kenyon, J. P., *Robert Spencer, Earl of Sunderland 1641–1702* (1958)

Kielmansegge, Count Friedrich von, *Diary of a Journey to England 1761–62* (1902)

Kip, J., *Britannia Illustrata; or View of several of the Royal Palaces as also of the principal seats of the Nobility and Gentry of Great Britain*, 2 vols (1720)

Koch, Guntram, and Hellmut Sichtermann, *Römische Sarkophage* (Munich, 1982)

La Chausse, Michelange de, *Le Gemme Antiche Figurate* (Rome, 1700)

– *Romanum Museum, sive Thesaurus eruditae antiquitatis etc*, 2 vols (Rome, 1746)

Lambert, Elizabeth, 'The Rebirth of Spencer House', *Architectural Digest* (February 1991), pp.134–43

Landy, J., 'Stuart and Revett: Pioneer Archaeologists', *Archaeology*, IX (December 1956), pp.252–9

Lavin, Marilyn Aronberg, *Seventeenth-century Barberini Documents and Inventories of Art* (New York, 1985)

Lawrence [Lewis], Lesley, 'Stuart and Revett: their Literary and Architectural Careers', *Journal of the Warburg Institute*, II (1938–39), pp.128–46

– 'The Architects of the Chapel at Greenwich Hospital', *Art Bulletin*, XXIX (1947), pp.260–67

– 'Greece and Rome at Greenwich', *Architectural Review*, CIX (January, 1951), pp.16–24

– *Connoisseurs and Secret Agents in Eighteenth-century Rome* (1961)

– 'Elizabeth, Countess of Home, and her house in Portman Square', *Burlington Magazine*, CIX (1967), pp.443–53

Le Marchant, Sir Denis, *Memoir of John Charles Viscount Althorp Third Earl Spencer* (1876)

Le Roy, J. D., *Les Ruines des Plus Beaux Monuments de la Grèce* (Paris, 1758)

Leconfield, Lady Maud and John Gore (eds), *Three Howard Sisters, Selections from the Writings of Caroline Lascelles, Lady Dover, and Countess Gower 1825 to 1833* (1955)

Ledoux-Lebard, Denise, *Les Ebénistes du XIXe Siècle 1795–1889: leurs Oeuvres et leurs Marques* (Paris, 1984)

Lees-Milne, James, 'Shugborough', *Connoisseur* (April–May 1967), pp.4–11, 211–15

– *Ancestral Voices* (1975)

– *Prophesying Peace* (1977)

Lever, Jill, *Architect's Designs for Furniture* (1982)

Leveson Gower, Iris I., *The Face without a Frown, Georgiana, Duchess of Devonshire* (1944)

Leveson Gower, Sir George and Iris Palmer (eds), *Hary-O, The Letters of Lady Harriet Cavendish 1796–1809* (1940)

Lewinsohn, Richard, *Barney Barnato: From Whitechapel Clown to Diamond King* (1937)

Lewis, Lady Theresa (ed.), *Extracts of the Journals and Correspondence of Miss Berry from the Year 1783 to 1852*, 3 vols (1865)

Lewis, W. S. (ed.), *The Yale Edition of Horace Walpole's Correspondence*, 48 vols (O.U.P., 1895–1979)

Little, David Mason (ed.), *Pineapples of Finest Flavour, or a Selection of Sundry Unpublished Letters of the English Roscius, David Garrick* (Harvard University Press, 1930)

Llanover, Lady (ed.), *The Autobiography and Correspondence of Mary Granville, Mrs Delaney*, 6 vols (1861–62)

Loftie, W. J., 'The Old War Office', *The Architectural Review* (1907), pp.89–94; (1909), pp.286–94

Londonderry, Lady, *Retrospect* (1938)

Longstaffe-Gowan, Todd, *Historical Report of the Garden at Spencer House* [unpublished] (June 1989)

Lugt, Frits, *Repertoire des Catalogues de Ventes Publiques* (The Hague, 1938)

Macdonald, John, *Memoirs of an Eighteenth-Century Footman*, first published as *Travels in Various Parts of Europe, Asia and Africa* (1790), reissued under the editorship of Peter Quennell (1985)

Macky, John, *A Journey Through England*, 2 vols (1714–22)

Maclean, Sir John, *An Historical and Genealogical Memoir of the Family of Poyntz* (Exeter, 1886)

Maffei, Paolo Alessandro, *Raccolta di Statue Antiche e Moderne* (Rome, 1704)

Mahon, Lord (ed.), *The Letters of Philip Stanhope, Earl of Chesterfield*, 5 vols (1845–53)

Major, Thomas, *The Ruins of Paestum* (1768)

Mallalieu, Huon, *The Dictionary of British Water Colour Artists up to 1920*, 3 vols (1976–90)

Malton, Thomas, *A Picturesque Tour through the Cities of London and Westminster* (1800)

Manners, Lady Victoria, and Dr. G. C. Williamson, *John Zoffany, His Life and Works 1735–1810* (1920)

– *Angelica Kauffmann, R.A., Her Life and Work* (1924)

Manning, Owen, and William Bray, *The History and Antiquities of the County of Surrey*, 3 Vols (1814)

Marchant, Nathaniel, *A Catalogue of One Hundred Impressions from Gems* (1792)

Markham, Christopher A., and J. Charles Cox (eds), *Records of the Borough of Northampton*, 2 vols (1948)

Marlborough, John Winston, Duke of, *Catalogue of the Books in the Library at Blenheim Palace collected by Charles, third Earl of Sunderland* (Oxford, 1872)

Marlborough, Sarah, Duchess of, *A True Copy of the Last Will and Testament of Her Grace Sarah late Duchess Dowager of Marlborough with the Codicil Thereto Annexed* (1744)

Marshall, John, *Royal Naval Biography* (1829)

Marshall, Rosalind, *The Days of Duchess Anne, Life in the Household of the Duchess of Hamilton* (1973)

Martyn, Thomas, *The English Connoisseur*, 2 vols (1766)

Masters, Brian, *Georgiana, Duchess of Devonshire* (1981)

Maxwell, Sir Herbert (ed.), *The Creevey Papers*, 2 vols (1904)

Mayne, Ethel Colburne, *A Regency Chapter: Lady Bessborough and her Friendships* (1939)

McCalmont, Rose E., *Memoirs of the Binghams* (1915)

McCarthy, Michael, 'New Light on Thomas Major's "Paestum" and later English Drawings of Paestum', in *Paestum and the Doric Revival 1750–1830* (National Academy of Design, New York, 1986), pp.47–50

Melville, Lewis (ed.), *The Berry Papers, Being*

the Correspondence Hitherto Unpublished of Mary and Agnes Berry (1763–1852) (1914)

Michaelis, Adolf, *Ancient Marbles in Great Britain* (C.U.P., 1882)

Michel, Oliver, 'L'Aprentissage Romain de Francois Joseph Lonsing', in *Mélanges de l'Ecole Française de Rome*, 84 (1972)

Millar, Oliver, *Zoffany and his Tribuna* (1967)

Milward, Richard, *Historic Wimbledon* (1989)

Mingay, G. E., *English Landed Society in the Eighteenth Century* (1963)

Montfaucon, Bernard de, *L'Antiquité Expliquée*, 10 vols (Paris, 1719–24)

Montgomery Hyde, H., *Londonderry House and its Pictures* (1937)

Morrison, Venetia, *The Art of George Stubbs* (1989)

Morton, David, *Catalogue of the Pictures at Althorp House, in the County of Northampton, with Occasional Notices, Biographical or Historical* (privately printed, 1851)

Murphy, Sophia, *The Duchess of Devonshire's Ball* (1984)

Musgrave, Clifford, *Regency Furniture* (1961)

– *Adam and Hepplewhite and other Neo-Classical Furniture* (1966)

Namier, Sir Lewis, and John Brooke, *The History of Parliament: The House of Commons 1754–1790* (1964)

Napier, Priscilla, *A Memoir of the Lady Delia Peel, born Spencer, 1889–1981* (privately printed, Norfolk, 1984)

Nares, G., 'Hagley Hall, Worcestershire', *Country Life* (19 September 1957), pp.546–9

Nash, Ernest, *Pictorial Dictionary of Ancient Rome*, 2 vols, revised edn (1968)

Needham, Raymond, and Alexander Webster, *Somerset House Past and Present* (1905)

Nevill, Ralph (ed.), *Leaves from the Note-Books of Lady Dorothy Nevill* (1907)

Newton, Lady (ed.), *The Lyme Letters 1660–1760* (1925)

Northumberland House: Its Saloon and Picture Gallery, with a Description of its Magnificent Staircase (1851)

Nulty, Matthew, *A Catalogue of a Capital Collection of Antique and Modern Marble Statues, Bustos, Cinerary and Ossuary Urns, Basso Relievos ... the whole collected in Rome by the late Matt. Nulty, Painter and Cicherone [sic], Thirty Years Resident in that City*, sale cat., Christie & Ansell, 27–28 March 1783

O'Byrne, William R., *A Naval Biographical Dictionary*, 2 vols (1849)

Oswald, Arthur, 'Londonderry House, Park Lane', *Country Life* (10 July 1937), pp.38–44

– 'Norfolk House, St. James's Square', *Country Life* (25 December 1937), pp.654–60

Paget, Guy, *History of the Althorp and Pytchley Hunt 1634–1920* (1937)

Palladio, Andrea, *Quattro libri dell' Architettura* (see Isaac Ware, *The Four Books of Andrea Palladio's Architecture*)

Pancrazi, G. M., *Antichità Siciliane spiegate colle notizie generali di questo regno* (Naples, 1751)

Papworth, W., 'William Newton and the Chapel of Greenwich Hospital', RIBA *Journal*, XXVII–XXVIII (1891), pp.417–20

Parker, Constance-Anne, *Mr Stubbs the Horse Painter* (1971)

– *George Stubbs: Art, Animals, and Anatomy* (1984)

Parsons, Catherine, E., 'Horseheath Hall and its Owners', *Proceedings of the Cambridge Antiquarian Society*, XLI (1948)

Pearce, David, *London's Mansions: The Palatial Houses of the Nobility* (1986)

Penny, Nicholas (ed.), *Reynolds*, exh. cat., Royal Academy, 1986

Pepper, Stephen, *Guido Reni, A Complete Catalogue of His Works* (1984)

Perrier, François, *Icones et Segmenta illustrium e marmore tabularum que Romae adhuc exstant* (Rome and Paris, 1645)

Piranesi, Giovanni Battista, *Le Antichità Romane de' Tempi della Republica, e de' Primi Imperatori*, 4 vols (Rome, 1756)

– *Della Magnificenza ed Architettura de' Romani* (Rome, 1761)

– *Antichità d'Albano e di Castel Gandolfo* (Rome, 1764)

– *Diverse Maniere d'adornare i Cammini* (Rome, 1769)

– *Vasi, Candelabri, Cippi, Sarcofagi, Tripodi, Lucerne ed Ornamenti Antichi*, 2 vols (Rome, 1778)

Plowden, Alison, 'The Spencers of Althorp', in *Lords of the Land* (1984)

Ponsonby, Major-General Sir John, *The Ponsonby Family* (1929)

Pope, Willard Bissell (ed.), *The Diary of Benjamin Robert Haydon*, 5 vols (Harvard University Press, 1963)

Price, Cecil, *The Letters of Richard Brinsley Sheridan*, 3 vols (Oxford, 1966)

Quaritch, Bernard, 'George John Earl Spencer 1758–1834', in *A Dictionary of English Book-Collectors*, Part III (Bernard Quaritch, October 1892)

Quennell, Peter (ed.), *The Private Letters of Princess Lieven to Prince Metternich 1820–26* (1937)

Raikes, Thomas, *A Portion of the Journal kep by Thomas Raikes, Esq. from 1831 to 47*, 4 vols (1856–57)

Raspe, R. E., *A Descriptive Catalogue of a General Collection of Ancient and Modern Engraved gems ... by James Tassie, modeller* 2 vols (1791)

Raymond, Harry, *B. I. Barnato: A Memoir* (1897)

Reade, Brian, *Regency Antiques* (London 1953)

Reid, S. J., *John and Sarah, Duke and Duchess of Marlborough* (1914)

Reilly, C. H., 'Old Burlington House, Piccadilly', *Country Life* (13 January 1923), pp.37–40

Reitlinger, Gerald, *The Economics of Taste, The Rise and Fall of Picture Prices 1760–1960*, 3 vols (1961–70)

Reynolds, Donald Martin, *The Architecture of New York City* (New York, 1984)

RIBA, *Catalogue of the Drawings Collection of the Royal Institute of British Architects*, 9 vols (1968–89)

Richardson, A. E., and C. Lovett Gill, *London Houses from 1660 to 1820* (1911)

Richardson, G., *Iconology*, 2 vols (1778–79)

Ridgeway, J. (publ.), *The Trial of the Hon. Richard Bingham for Criminal Conduct wit Lady Elizabeth Howard, Wife of B. E. Howard Esq., Presumptive Heir to the Duke of Norfolk, and Daughter to the Earl of Fauconberg before Lord Kenyon and a Specia Jury, Feb 24th 1794* (1794)

Ridout, Brian, 'Dry Rot and Destruction', *The Architects' Journal (Renovation Supplement)* (18 October 1989), pp.28–33

Riou, Stephen, *The Grecian Orders of Architecture* (1768)

Roberts, William (ed.), *The Memoirs of the Life and Correspondence of Mrs Hannah More*, 2 vols (New York, 1834)

Robinson, John Martin, *The Wyatts: an*

Architectural Dynasty (O.U.P., 1979)

– *Georgian Model Farms* (O.U.P., 1983)

– *Spencer House* [guide book] (1991)

Rollett, Hermann, *Die Drei Meister der Gemmoglyptik, Antonio, Giovanni, und Luigi Pichler* (Vienna, 1874)

Roscoe, Ingrid, 'James "Athenian" Stuart and the Scheemakers Family: A Lucrative Partnership between Architect and Sculptors', *Apollo* (September 1987), pp.178–84

Roth, Cecil, and Geoffrey Wigoder (eds), *The New Standard Jewish Encyclopaedia* (1970)

Rowe, R., *Adam Silver* (1965)

Royalton-Kisch, Martin, *Adriaen van de Venne's Album in the Department of Prints and Drawings in the British Museum* (1980)

Russell, Jack, *Nelson and the Hamiltons* (1969)

Russell, Lord John (ed.), *The Memoirs, Journal and Correspondence of Thomas Moore*, 8 vols (1853–56)

Sadie, Stanley (ed.), *The New Grove Dictionary of Music and Musicians*, 20 vols (1980)

Scarisbrick, Diana, 'A. M. Zanetti and the Althorp Leopard', *Apollo*, cx, No. 213 (November 1979), pp.425–7

– *Ancestral Jewels* (1989)

Schallman, Lázaro, *Baron Mauricio de Hirsch* (Buenos Aires, 1969)

Scharlieb, Mary, *Reminiscences* (1924)

Schaub, Hon. Sir Luke, *A Catalogue of the Grand and Capital Collection of Italian, Flemish and Dutch Paintings of the Hon. Sir Luke Schaub, lately deceased*, sale cat., Langford, 26–28 April 1758

Schroder, Timothy B., *The Gilbert Collection of Gold and Silver*, exh. cat., Los Angeles County Museum of Art, 1988

Seidman, Gertrud, *An English Gem-engraver's Life: Nathaniel Marchant* (1739–1816)

Seymour, Lady Helen, 'Old Grosvenor House', *Blackwood's Magazine* (June 1961)

Sheraton, Thomas, *The Cabinet-Maker and Upholsterer's Drawing Book*, 2 vols (1793–94)

Sheridan, Richard Brinsley, *Verses to the Memory of Garrick. Spoken as a Monody at the Theatre Royal in Drury Lane* (1779)

Shore, John, Lord Teignmouth, *Memoirs of the Life, Writings, and Correspondence of Sir William Jones* (1804)

Shute, Nerina, *The Royal Family and the Spencers: Two Hundred Years of Friendship* (1986)

Sichel, Walter, *Sheridan, from new and original material; including a manuscript diary by Georgiana, Duchess of Devonshire*, 2 vols (1909)

– *Sterne: A Study, to which is added The Journal to Eliza* (1910)

Simpkinson, Nassau, *Righteousness and Mercy: A Sermon preached in the Parish Church of Brington on Sunday, January 3, 1858, on occasion of the Funeral of Frederick, Earl Spencer, K.G.* (Northampton, 1858)

Smith, J. T., *Nollekens and his Times* (1828)

Smith, John Edward, *Parliamentary Representation of Surrey from 1290 to 1924* (1927)

The Social Register (Social Register Association of New York)

Early History of the Spencer Family, n.a. (*c*1931)

Spencer, Albert Edward John, 7th Earl, 'Althorp, Northamptonshire, A Seat of the Earl Spencer', *Country Life* (11, 18, 25 June, 2 July 1921), pp.714–21, 764–71, 792–7; 14–20

– 'Furniture at Althorp', *Country Life* (11–18 June 1921), pp.721–3, 771–3

– 'Spencer House', *Country Life* (30 October and 6 November 1926), pp.660–67, 698–704

– 'Furniture at Spencer House', *Country Life* (13 November 1926), pp.757–9

– 'John Charles, Viscount Althorp, Third Earl Spencer', *The Quarterly Review*, No.566 (October 1945), pp.468–80

– *A Short History of Althorp and the Spencer Family* (Northampton, 1949)

– 'Spencer MSS. The Archives of the Spencer Family belonging to Albert Edward John, 7th Earl Spencer', *Bulletin of the National Register of Archives* (Historical Manuscripts Commission, No. 13, 1964), pp.21–6

Spencer, Albert Edward John, 7th Earl, and Christopher Dobson (eds), *Letters of David Garrick and Georgiana, Countess Spencer, 1759–1779* (Cambridge, 1960)

Spencer, Albert Edward John, 7th Earl, and Henry S. Eeles, *Brooks's 1764–1964* (1964)

Spencer, Charlotte, Countess, *Charlotte, Countess Spencer: A Memoir* (privately printed, Northampton, 1907)

Spencer, Charlotte, Countess (ed.), *East and West* (1871)

Spencer, George John, 2nd Earl, *A Catalogue of the Rich and Elegant Household Furniture ... and other Valuable Effects of Earl Spencer, brought from His Lordship's Villa at Wimbledon Park, Surry*, sale cat., Christie's, 14–16 June 1785

– *Catalogue of A Superb Cabinet of Drawings; The Entire Collection of a Nobleman*, sale cat., Thomas Philipe, 10–18 June 1811

– *Catalogue of the Pictures at Althorp, the Seat of the Right Honourable the Earl Spencer K.G.*, n.a. (Northampton, 1823)

– *Catalogue of the Pictures at Althorp House in the County of Northampton*, n.a. (privately printed, 1831)

Spencer, John Charles, 3rd Earl, *Letters of Lord Althorp* (1793–1833) (privately printed, *c*1879)

Spencer, John Poyntz, 5th Earl, *An Imperfect Narrative of the Gay Doings and Marvellous Festivities Holden at Althorp in the County of Northants on the Occasion of my Lord John Poyntz, Viscount Althorp, completing his twenty-first year on the 27th Day of October in the Year of Grace 1856*, n.a. (privately printed, 1857)

– *Catalogue of an Art Exhibition at Spencer House by the Kind Permission of Earl Spencer K.G. in aid of the East London Branch of the Girls' Friendly Society... 16th–22nd March 1887*, exh. cat. (William Clowes, 1887)

Spencer, Lady Sarah Isabella, *Catalogue of the China at Althorp House in the County of Northampton* (privately printed, 1857)

The Spencer Library, *Lord Spencer's Library: A Sketch of a Visit to Althorp* (1870)

Steegman, John, 'Some English Portraits by Pompeo Batoni', *Burlington Magazine* LXXVIII, No. 516 (March 1946), pp.54–63

Steinman, G., *Althorp Memoirs* (privately printed, 1869)

Stenton, Michael, and Stephen Lees (ed.), *Who's Who of British Members of Parliament*, 4 vols (Harvester Press, Sussex, 1976–81)

Stern, Robert, *et al*, *New York 1900: Metropolitan Architecture and Urbanism 1890–1915* (New York, 1983)

– *New York 1930, Architecture and Urbanism between the Two World Wars* (1987)

Sterne, Laurence, *The Life and Opinions of*

Tristram Shandy Gentleman, Books V & VI (1762)

Stewart, Lawrence D., *John Scott of Amwell* (University of California Press, 1956)

Stewart, Robert G., *Robert Edge Pine: A British Portrait Painter in America 1784–1788* (1979)

Stillman, Damie, *The Decorative Work of Robert Adam* (1966)

– *English Neo-Classical Architecture*, 2 vols (1988)

Stirling, A. M. W. (ed.), *The Letter-Bag of Lady Elizabeth Spencer-Stanhope*, 2 vols (1913)

Stokes, Hugh, *The Devonshire House Circle* (1917)

Stone, Lawrence, 'Cole Green Park, Herts', in *The Country Seat: Studies in the History of the British Country House*, Howard Colvin and John Harris (eds) (1970), pp.75–80

Stone, George Winchester Jr., and George M. Kahrl, *David Garrick, A Critical Biography* (1979)

Stroud, Dorothy, *Capability Brown*, 2nd edn (1957)

– *Henry Holland, His Life and Architecture* (1966)

– 'Amid Stately Woods and Groves: Althorp, Northampton, in its Setting', *Country Life* (30 July 1981), pp.375–8

Stuart, James, *A Discourse delivered to the Students of the Royal Academy, on the distribution of Prizes, 10 December 1771*

Stuart, James, and A. M. Bandini, *De Obelisco Caesaris Augusti e Campi Martii ruideribus nuper eruto* (Rome, 1750)

Stuart, James, and Nicholas Revett, *Antiquities of Athens*, 4 Vols (1762–1816)

[Stuart, James], *Critical Observations on the Buildings and Improvements of London* (1771)

Stuart Jones, H., *A Catalogue of the Ancient Sculptures Preserved in the Municipal Collections of Rome: The Sculpture of the Museo Capitolino* (Oxford, 1912)

Summerson, Sir John, 'The Society's House: An Architectural Study', *Journal of the Royal Society of Arts* (15 October 1954), pp.920–33

– *Architecture in Britain 1530–1830*, 7th edn (1983)

– *Georgian London*, 3rd edn (1988)

Survey of London, esp. vols 29–32, 'The Parish of St James's, Westminster' (1960–63)

Swift, Jonathan, *Directions to Servants* (1745)

Sykes, Christopher Simon, *Private Palaces: Life in the Great London Houses* (1985)

Tait, A. A., 'Home House', *Apollo* (August 1987), pp.75–80

Tait, Hugh (ed.), *The Art of the Jeweller: A Catalogue of the Hull Grundy Gift to the British Museum: Jewellery, Engraved Gems and Goldsmiths' Work*, 2 vols (1984)

Tate Gallery, *Illustrated Catalogue of Acquisitions 1982–84* (1984)

Tauranac, John, *Elegant New York: The Builders and the Buildings 1885–1915* (New York, 1985)

Taylor, Basil, *Stubbs*, 2nd edn (1975)

Temple, J. A., *Temple Memoirs* (1925)

Thieme, Ulrich, and Felix Becker, *Allgemeines Lexikon der Bildenden Kunstler etc*, 37 vols (Leipzig, 1978)

Thompson, F. M. L., *English Landed Society in the Nineteenth Century* (1963)

Thompson, Nicholas, *et al*, *A House in Town: 22 Arlington Street, Its Owners and Builders* (1984)

Thomson Scott, Gladys, *Life in a Noble Household 1641–1700* (1937)

– *The Russells in Bloomsbury 1669–1771* (Bedford House, 1940)

Thomson Scott, Gladys (ed.), *Letters of a Grandmother 1732–1735, Being the Correspondence of Sarah, Duchess of Marlborough with her granddaughter Diana, Duchess of Bedford* (1943)

Thorne, R. G., *The House of Commons 1790–1820*, 5 vols (1986)

Thornton, Peter, *Authentic Decor, The Domestic Interior 1620–1820* (1984)

Thornton, Peter, and John Hardy, 'The Spencer Furniture at Althorp', *Apollo*: 'Section I: Baroque and Palladian Furniture and John Vardy's Work for Spencer House' (March 1968), pp.179–89; 'Section II: James Stuart's Neo-Classical Furniture from Spencer House and the Work of Gordon the Chair-maker' (June 1968), pp.440–51; 'Section III: Lady Spencer's Furniture from Spencer House and Furnishings Provided for Althorp by Henry Holland' (October 1968), pp.266–77

Timmins, Samuel, *Lord Spencer's Library: A Sketch of a Visit to Althorp* (1870)

Tipping, H. Avray, *English Homes*, 9 vols (1920–37)

– 'Furniture at Althorp', *Country Life* (18 June 1921), pp.771–3

– 'Wentworth Woodhouse, Yorkshire', *Country Life* (4 October 1924), pp.512–19

Tomlin, Maurice, *Catalogue of Adam Period Furniture* (Victoria and Albert Museum, 1982)

Toynbee, Mrs Paget (ed.), *Lettres de Madam du Deffand à Horace Walpole 1766–80*, 3 vols (1912)

'Horace Walpole's Journals of Visits to Country Seats & c', *Walpole Society*, XVI (1927–28)

Toynbee, Paget, and Leonard Whibley (eds), *Correspondence of Thomas Gray*, 3 vols (O.U.P., 1935)

Travlos, John, *Pictorial Dictionary of Ancient Athens* (1971)

Treasures for the Nation, exh. cat., National Heritage Memorial Fund, British Museum, 1988

Treasures from Althorp, exh. cat., Victoria and Albert Museum, 1970

Turnbull, George, *A Treatise on Ancient Painting* (1740)

– *A Curious Collection of Antique Paintings* (1741)

Udy, David, 'The Furniture of James Stuart and Robert Adam', *Discovering Antiques*, No.42 (1971)

– 'The Classical Sources of English Neo-Classical Furniture', *Arte Illustrata*, No. 52 (February 1973)

– 'New Light on the Sources of English Neo-Classical Design', *Apollo* (March 1976), pp. 202–07

Vanderbilt Balsan, Consuelo, *The Glitter and the Gold* (1953)

Vardy, John, *Some Designs of Mr Inigo Jones and Mr William Kent* (1744)

Vasi, Giuseppe, *Delle Magnificenze di Roma Antica e Moderna* (Rome, 1747–61)

Venuti, Rodolfo, *Collectanea Antiquitatum Romanarum* (Rome, 1736)

Verney, Lady, *Verney Letters of the 18th Century*, 2 vols (1930)

Visconti, Ennio Quirino, *Museo Pio Clementino*, 7 vols (1782)

Waagen, Dr., *Treasures of Art*, 3 vols (1854)

Walford, Edward, *Londoniana*, 2 vols (1879)

– *Old and New London*, 8 vols (1897–98)

Ward, A., *et al*, *The Ring from Antiquity to the Twentieth Century* (1981)

Ward-Jackson, Peter, *English Furniture Designs of the Eighteenth Century* (1984)

Ware, Isaac, *The Four Books of Andrea Palladio's Architecture*, Book IV (1738)

– *A Complete Body of Architecture* (1756)

Warwick, Frances, Countess of, *Afterthoughts* (1931)

Wasson, Ellis Archer, 'The Third Earl Spencer and Agriculture 1818–1845', *Agricultural History Review*, 26 (1978), pp.89–99

– *Whig Renaissance, Lord Althorp and the Whig Party 1782–1845* (1987)

Waterhouse, Sir Ellis Kirkham, *Reynolds* (1941)

– 'The British Contribution to the Neo-Classical Style in Painting', *Proceedings of the British Academy*, XL (Rome, 1954), pp.57–74

– *Gainsborough* (1958)

– *Dictionary of Eighteenth-Century British Painters in Oil and Crayons* (1983)

Watkin, David, *Athenian Stuart: Pioneer of the Greek Revival* (1982)

Watkin, David (ed.), *Sale Catalogues of Libraries of Eminent Persons*, 4, 'Architects' (1972)

Watson, F. B., *Louis XVI Furniture* (1960)

– 'Holland and Daguerre: French Undercurrents in English Neo-Classic Furniture Design', *Apollo*, XCVI, No.128 (October 1972), pp.282–7

Webb, Margaret, 'Chimney pieces by Scheemakers', *Country Life* (14 March 1957), pp.193–5

Webster, Mary, *Johan Zoffany 1733–1810* (1976)

Wharncliffe, Lord (ed.), *The Letters and Works of Lady Mary Wortley Montagu*, 3 vols (1837)

Wheatley, Henry B., *Round About Piccadilly and Pall Mall* (1870)

– *London Past and Present*, 3 vols (1891)

Wheatley, Henry B. (ed.), *The Historical and the Posthumous Memoirs of Sir Nathaniel William Wraxall, 1772–1784*, 5 vols (1884)

Whiffen, Marcus, 'Bridgewater House, St. James's', *Country Life* (13 May 1949), pp.1118–21

Whinney, Margaret, *Sculpture in Britain 1530–1830* (1964)

– *Home House* (1969)

White, Roger, 'John Vardy, 1718–1765: Palladian into Rococo', in *The Architectural Outsiders*, Roderick Brown (ed.) (1965), pp.63–81, 212–13

Whitfield, Clovis, *England and the Seicento*, exh. cat., Agnew's, 1973

Whitley, William T., *Thomas Gainsborough* (1915)

Wiebenson, Dora, *Sources of Greek Revival Architecture* (1969)

Williams, Basil, *Carteret and Newcastle, A Contrast in Contemporaries* (C.U.P., 1943)

Williams, Moelyn I., *A Directory of Rare Book and Special Collections in the United Kingdom and the Republic of Ireland* (1985)

Willis, Peter, *Charles Bridgeman and the English Landscape Garden* (1977)

Wilson, Michael I., *William Kent, Architect, Designer, Painter, Gardener, 1685–1748* (1984)

Wilson, Philip Whitwell (ed.), *The Greville Diary*, 2 vols (1927)

Wilton Ely, John, *A Tercentenary Tribute to William Kent*, exh. cat., Ferens Art Gallery, Kingston-upon-Hull, 1985

– 'Pompeian and Etruscan Tastes in the Neo-Classical Country House Interior', in *The Fashioning and Functioning of the British Country House*, Gervase Jackson-Stops (ed.) (National Gallery of Art, Washington, D.C, 1989)

Wood, Robert, *The Ruins of Palmyra* (1753)

– *The Ruins of Balbec* (1757)

Woolfe, John, and James Gandon, *Vitruvius Britannicus*, IV (1767); V (1771)

Worsley, Giles, 'Out from Adam's Shadow', *Country Life* (14 May 1992), pp. 100–03

– 'Spencer House, London', *Country Life* (24–31 December 1992), pp.38–41

Yorke, P. C., *The Life and Correspondence of Philip Yorke, Earl of Hardwicke*, 3 vols (Cambridge, 1913)

Yorke, Philip, 'The Travel Journal of Philip Yorke 1744–63', *Bedfordshire Historical Record Society*, XLVII (1968), pp.125–63

Yung, Nicholas K. K. (ed.), *National Portrait Gallery Complete Illustrated Catalogue 1856–1979* (1981)

PHOTOGRAPHIC ACKNOWLEDGEMENTS

Grateful acknowledgement is due to the following for supplying photographic material and for permission to reproduce it. Arabic numerals indicate monochrome illustrations, Roman numerals colour plates.

Arnold Wiggins & Sons Ltd 281

Ashmolean Museum, Oxford 169, 200

Author's Collection 179

B. T. Batsford Limited 5

Ronald G. Bell 282

British Architectural Library, RIBA, London 31, 32, 33, 37, 67, 88, 90, 101, 138, 205, III, IV

British Library (by permission of the British Library) 3, 16, 20, 38, 39, 52, 84, 85, 156, 164, 168, 204, 232, 233

British Museum (by courtesy of the Trustees of the British Museum) 60, 61, 76, 78, VII

Capitoline Museum 173

Christie's Archives (© Christie's) 253

Clerical Medical and General 190

The Connoisseur Magazine 69

Cooper-Hewitt Museum (Cooper-Hewitt National Museum of Design, Smithsonian Institution. Photo: Ken Pelka) 50

Corporation of London, Greater London Record Office, *endpapers*; 17, 28, 34, 40, 191, 192, 209, 210, 219 (photos: Godfrey New); 243, 248, V, VIII

Country Life 53, 70, 74, 80, 83, 86, 108, 112, 113, 124, 126, 130, 142, 170, 172, 177, 183, 184, 187, 230, 236, 237, 238, 239, 240, 241, 242, 244

Courtauld Institute (private collection) 19; (Althorp) 26; (The Society of Dilettanti) 27, 100; (Conway Library) 62, 182; (Trustees of the Chatsworth Settlement) 91, 228, 229

'L'Erma' di Bretschneider (Accademia Italiana) 79

Mark Fiennes *frontispiece, part-title illustration (Foreword)* 30, 44, 48, 54, 58, 71, 73, 81, 93, 105, 106, 114, 117, 119, 122, 123, 127, 132, 140, 141, 143, 144, 145, 146, 147, 148, 149, 151, 152, 188, 189, 262, 268, 269, 270, 271, 272, 277, 279, 280, 283, *jacket illustrations*, XI, XII, XIII, XIV, XV, XVI, XVII, XVIII, XIX, XX, XXI, XXII, XXIII, XXIV, XXV, XXVI, XXVII, XXVIII, XXXIV, XXXV, XXXVI, XXXVII, XXXVIII, XXXIX

Gabinetto Fotografica Nazionale, Rome (Istituto Centrale per il Catalogo e la Documentazione) 63, 181

Dennis Gilbert 257, 258, 260, 263, 264, 266, 267, 273, 274, 275, 276, XXXI, XXXII, XXXIII

Guildhall Library, Corporation of London 10, 21, 22, 23, 208, 215

Hertfordshire Record Office 198

Hulton Deutsch Company Limited 1, 2, 7, 220, 231, 247

Lucinda Lambton IX, XXX

Duke of Marlborough (reproduced by kind permission of His Grace the Duke of Marlborough) 11 (photo: Chris Andrews); 12 (photo: Jeremy Whitaker)

Paul Mellon Centre for Studies in British Art (Waterhouse Archive) 15

Museum of Fine Arts, Boston (Gift of Mr and Mrs Robert S. Pirie) 87

Museum of London 211

The National Gallery (by courtesy of the Trustees, The National Gallery, London) 65

National Portrait Gallery, London 9, 98, 195, 213, 222, 224

Public Record Office 193

Renovation, supplement to *The Architects Journal* 259a, 259b, 261a, 261b, 261c, 261d

Lord Rothschild (reproduced by kind permission of Lord Rothschild) 196

Royal Collection (Royal Collection, St James's Palace. © Her Majesty Queen Elizabeth II) 202

The Royal College of Music 194

Royal Commission on the Historical Monuments of England (National Monuments Record) 4, 6, 8, 45, 59, 64, 66, 96, 116, 121, 137, 218, 223, 225, 226, 227, 245, 246

Royal Library (Royal Library, Windsor Castle. © Her Majesty Queen Elizabeth II) 18, 125

Scottish National Portrait Gallery 136

Sir John Soane's Museum (by courtesy of the Trustees of Sir John Soane's Museum) 35, 36, 41, 43, 46, 47, 56, 57, 68, 72, 75, 82, 92, 94, 99, 103, 107, 109, 111, 115, 118, 120, 128, 129, 131, 133, 134, 135, 150, 153, 154, 155, 160, 178 (photos: Godfrey New); 157, 162, 163, 171, 174, 176, 206, VI

Collection Earl Spencer (reproduced by kind permission of Earl Spencer) 13, 14, 24, 25, 51, 89, 102, 110, 139, 185, 186, 197, 199, 201, 203, 207, 212, 214, 216, 217, 221, 234, 235, I, II, X

Syborn Atkinson & Colborn Architects 249, 250, 251, 252, 254, 255, 256

Peter Thuring 278, XXIX

Victoria and Albert Museum (by courtesy of the Board of Trustees of the Victoria and Albert Museum, London) 29, 42, 55, 77, 95, 97

The Warburg Institute 49, 104, 158, 159, 161, 165, 166, 167, 175, 180

Charlotte Wood 265

INDEX

Front to the Street of

Elevation vers la Rueë de la Mais

J. Vardy Arch.t